Yijing

Wisdom of 4 Sages

A complete translation and appreciation of *Yijing (易經)*

Jingwei (景維)

jjingwei11@gmail.com

Singapore
March 2019

Publication Data

Disclaimer:
Every precaution has been taken in the preparation of this monograph.
The publisher and author apologise for any errors or omissions that may remain.
The publisher and author assume no liability whatsoever, for damages suffer from its usage.

Self-Published by Jingwei (景維)
Email: jjingwei11@gmail.com
Title Availability (to be set-up):
Worldwide (order online)
Print-on-demand (POD) by Lightning Source, UK
Distribution through Ingram International
The Book Depository.co.uk (with free delivery worldwide)
Espresso Book Machine
Amazon.com
List price: SGD$30.00

National Library Board, Singapore Cataloguing-in-publication Data
Name(s): Jingwei, 1945-
Title: Yijing : wisdom of 4 sages : a translation and appreciation of the Yijing /
    Jingwei.
Description: Singapore : Jingwei, 2019. | Includes bibliographical references.
Identifier(s): OCN 1081299469 | ISBN 978-981-14-0204-3 (paperback)
Subject(s): LCSH: Yijing--Commentaries. | Divination -- China. | Philosophy,
    Chinese--To 221 B.C.
Classification: DDC 299.51282--dc23

Cover design: fury of the Yellow River
First Print: 10 copies, February 2019. Ultra Supplies. Singapore
Second Print: 50 copies, February 2019. Xorex Press. Singapore
Print on demand by Lightning Source UK, March 2019

Book type: B & W 6x9 in or 156x234 mm (Royal 8vo) Perfect Bound on White w/Gross Lam.
Page Count: 312
Weight: 450g (approx.)

Dedication to all Humankind
Paradise on Earth
A Description in the *Rites of Zhou* (周礼 .礼運)

大道之行也	Great Dao in Action that's
天下為公	Heaven Beneath its All about Fairness
選賢與能	Selection of the Virtuous and Talented
講信修睦	Talk of Trust Cultivation of Harmony
故人不獨親其親	Hence People Not Only Love Their Beloved
子其子	Sons And Sons (of others)
使老有所終	Enabling the Old to Have Provision for Closure
壯有所用	the Strong Have Provision for Employment
幼有所長	the Youngs have Provision for Growth
矜寡孤獨廢疾者	Weak,Widowed,Single,Lonely,Abandoned,Sick
皆有所養	All Have Provision for Care
男有分	Man Has Separate (family)
女有歸	Woman Has Home (to return)
貨	Commodities
惡其棄於地也	Hate They be Abandoned On Floor that's
不必藏於己	No Need to Store With Self
力	Efforts
惡其不出於身也	Hate They Not of Self-contribution that's
不必為己	No Need Working for Self (only)
是謀閉而不興	Thus Scheming Close-door-policy Is Not Popular
盜竊亂賊而不作	Bandits Thieves Rioters Robbers Are Not Active
故外户而不閉	Hence Outer Doors Are Not Lock
是謂大同	This is Called the Great Common

Portraits of the 4 Sages

Fuxi (c.3000)

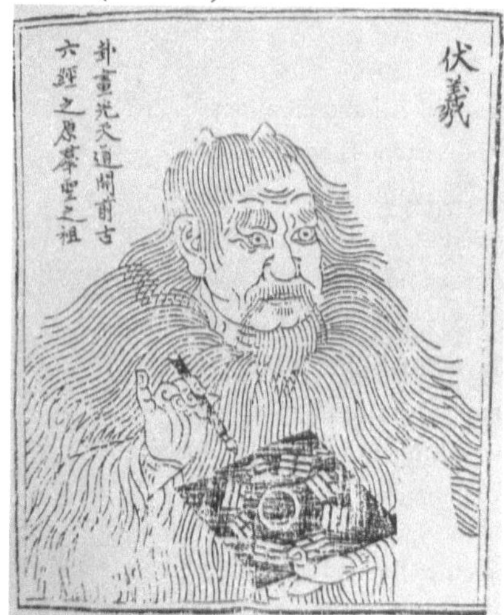

King Wen (c.1066BC)

Duke of Zhou (c.1046BC)

Kongzi (551-479BC)

(source: Mao and Li, 1989 Edit.)
(Of History, Mountains and Rivers : Chinese History in Pictures)

Burial pit containing more than 10 thousands pieces of oracle shells and bones. From the 1993 archaeological excavation site at the Ruins of Shang Dynasty (殷墟, c.1600-1066 BC).

SYNOPSIS

The *Yijing* (易經) or *Book of Changes* is the best known Chinese book in the West.
There are translations and much academic interests in its teaching and philosophy.
However there is no comprehensive popular version in the shop for the general public.
This title, *"Yijing: Wisdom of 4 Sages"*, presents the ancient book in its entirety.
It includes King Wen's 64 Hexagrams that developed from Fuxi's 8 Trigrams;
King Wen's Hexagram assessments; Zhougong's 384 Liner descriptions and advice;
Together with all '10 Wings' of Kongzi's comprehensive explanations, commentaries.
Both ancient texts and English translation are arranged side by side for easy reference.
And author's analysis and comments placed on the same page for immediate reading.

The *Yijing* Hexagrams depict 64 images of life, each with 6 Liners for societal strata.
A total of 384 human situations are covered with predictions and advice for actions.
Life is never static, *Yijing* basic tenet are Changes with inter-conversion of Hexagrams.
A total of 64x64 or 4096 combinations, covering any imaginable situation variations.
Hence the *Yijing* has been popular for oracular consultation down the centuries.

Herein are topical discussions of what can be learned from the *Yijing* in its entirety.
Examples of consultation are also documented to illustrate enjoyment of using *Jijing*.
For teaching morals and counselling, the *Yijing's* full potential has yet to be realised.
Kongzi says reading the *Yijing* is like getting council from our parents (如臨父母).
Towards this end, the general public and scholar may find this self-help manual useful.

PREFACE

I am a research-biochemist retired since 2007 and first self-published in October, 2012.
Laozi: Quest for the Ultimate Reality (ISBN 978-981-07-3758-0), 206 pp, nonfiction.
It offers a new translation and analysis of the ancient Chinese text, the *Daodejing*.
It is listed among the "Indie Books Worth Discovering", 15 May 2017, *Kirkus Reviews*.
Available Print-on-demand (POD) by Lightning Source Inc, Amazon.com, other online stores.
More than 300 complimentary copies had been given to individuals and Institutions.
They include tourists, local & overseas Public Libraries, Schools and University Libraries.
More than 100 National Libraries and University Libraries worldwide, accepted donations.
I have done enough promotion and firmly believe its inherent merits will carry it forward.
Now I concentrate on Book 2, a new complete translation and analysis of the *Yijing* (易 经).

The *Yijing* has been acknowledged as 'First' among the 5 ancient Chinese Classics.
It is thoroughly studied by scholars who took the imperial exams to enter officialdom.
Purportedly, 4 ancient Sages are credited for collective creation of its different parts.
1.   Fuxi (~3000 BC) for drawing the 8 Trigrams.
2.   King Wen (~1066 BCE) for the development of 64 Hexagrams and Hexagram-Texts.
3.   Duke Zhougong (~1066 BC) for the 6 Liner-Texts of each Hexagram, in total 384.
4.   Kongzi (551-479 BC) for the '10 Wings' (Texts) of annotations and commentaries.

The *Yijing* is a well known Chinese text in the world for the West to understand the far East.
Also a divination manual, the 10 Commentaries of Kongzi has enriched its philosophical value.
For 2500 years since, countless more commentaries and interpretations have been written.
Often, the *Yijing* has not been presented in an easy, popular form for the general public.
Hence only a dedicated few can enjoy the *Yijing*, even among the Chinese.
English translations are often half-hearted without the full '10 Wings' Texts of Kongzi.

The *Yijing* has often been dismissed as a text, only fit for divination and such practices.
Really the *Yijing* has much more to offer, with situation analysis and advice for action.
Kongzi even suggests that reading *Yijing* is like consulting one's parents or wise seniors.
The ancient *Yijing* is certainly hard to read and comprehend without clear guidance.
The challenge here is to create a *Yijing* in a presentation that people can read and enjoy.
To create a guidebook for understanding the *Yijing*, a handbook for practical consultation.

The title chosen for this work is:
Yijing: **The Wisdom of 4 Sages** (a complete translation and appreciation)

<u>Contents</u>

Natural Imageries reflective of the 8 Trigrams of Fuxi

Heaven
(strength)

Earth
(support)

Fire
(shine)

Water
(danger)

Mountain
(blocking)

Wetland
(happy)

Wind
(conforming)

Thunder
(action)

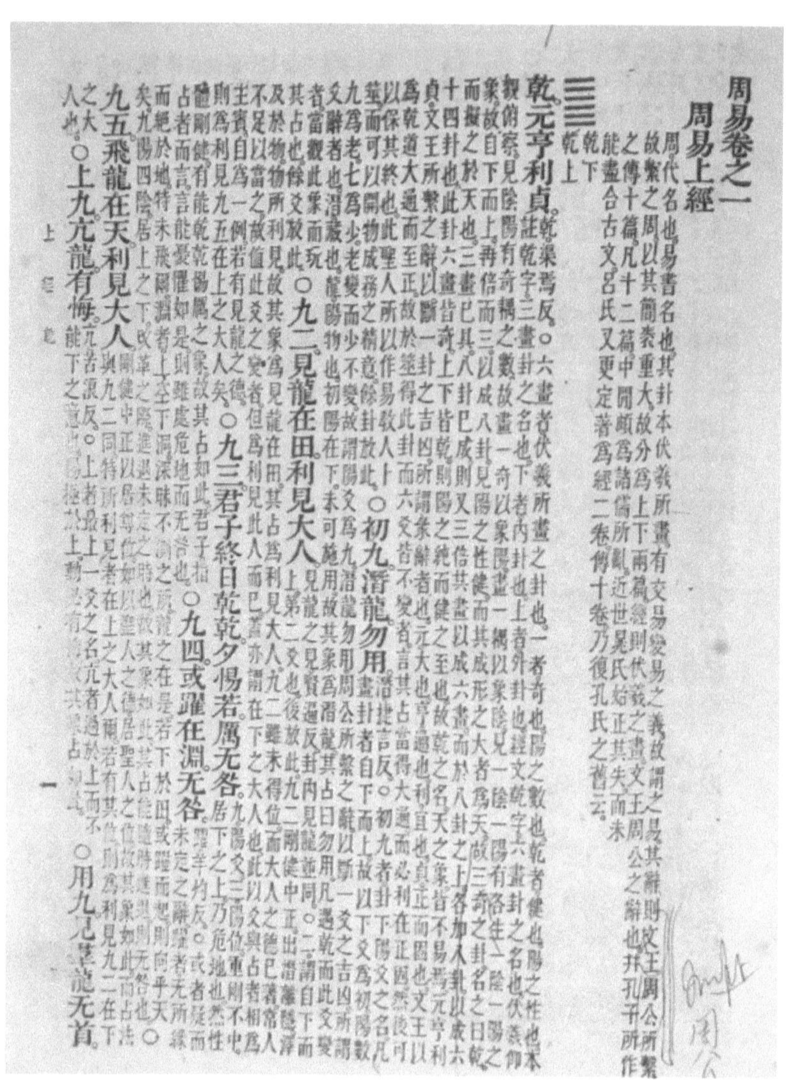

周易卷之一
周易上經

乾

乾元亨利貞。

初九潛龍勿用。

九二見龍在田利見大人。

九三君子終日乾乾夕惕若厲无咎。

九四或躍在淵无咎。

九五飛龍在天利見大人。

上九亢龍有悔。

用九見羣龍无首。

Original Chinese Text of *Yijing* (Zhu Xi, Song. c.1130–1200CE)

Introduction

Yijing is 'Top' of the 5 Classics that scholars studied for the imperial exams in ancient China.
It has been listed among the 100 most influential books ever written (Seymour-Smith 1998).
There is great interest in its study by Western scholars for understanding Eastern Thoughts.
There are translations and commentaries by academics, scholarships that few can appreciate.
However few popular translations exist that allow the general public easy access to its Wisdom.
With success of a popular version of Laozi's *Daodejing*, I aspire to make a contribution here.

Xia Dynasty has its *Yijing* named *Lianshan* (連山), Shang Dynasty has its *Guicang* (歸藏).
These older versions have been mentioned in the *Liji* (礼記) but have never been seen.

Fortunately for us, the Zhou Dynasty's version *Zhouyi* (周易), has largely survived to this day.
Just a manual for Divination, it was spared the 'burning of books' by the first Emperor of China.

The complete *Yijing* that we see today is formed of 3 sections:
1. Fuxi's imagery of Yin and Yang Liners that form 8 Trigrams, that form 64 Hexagrams.
2. King Wen and Zhougong, their attached Hexagram Texts and Liner Texts.
3. Kongzi's 10 'Wings' or commentaries which are invaluable in explaining the Texts.

(__ __) 2-shorts Liner symbol of Yin (陰), for Darkness, Earth, female, negatives,…

(______) 1-long Liner symbol of Yang (陽), stands for Light, Heaven, male, positives,.
Yin-liners (call Sixers) and Yang-liners (call Niners) are stacked up to 6 levels for a Hexagram.
The 6 Liners are labeled as Sixer or Niner with a number reflective of positional level.

Heaven (Hex.1) of 6 Yang-liners is illustrated here with Divination Liner Texts (by Zhougong):

TopNiner	______	Stubborn Dragon Has Regrets
Niner5	______	Flying Dragon in Heaven, Favors Seeing GreatOne (emerge)
Niner4	______	Or Leaping Dragon On Ocean-depth, No Fault
Niner3	______	Junzi Whole Day Highly Active, Night-time Alert, Grave
Niner2	______	Visible Dragon On Field, Favors Seeing GreatOne (Niner5)
FirstNiner	______	Submerged Dragon, Don't Act

Imagery of 6 dragons initially submerge, then emerge and rise into Heaven from Ocean-depth.
Reflective of the emergence, struggle, rise and decline of an individual in various stages of life.
The 64 Hexagrams depict situations that are familiar in human life, Encounters, Ostracism, ...
And the 6 liners of each Hexagram situation give rise to a total of 384 conditional variations.
In raising a Hexagram for consultation, conversion to another Hexagram may also be indicated.
Giving 64x64 or 4096 possible combinations, covering an immense area of human experience.

The *Yijing* is a manual for divination in ancient China, very popular in the Shang Dynasty.
Script on oracle-bones reveal Shang king's repeated divinations, for the trivial to making wars.
And I do find the *Yijing* useful and productive for consultation on any particular situation.
With a Hexagram that seems unfavorable, we may take notice of the warnings to improve.
With a Hexagram that seems favorable, we take notice of the positives to reinforce for success.
As Kongzi says, "In need of guidance, consult the *Yijing* as you would of your parents."

The 4 Sages

Fuxi (伏羲)
c.3000 BC (lengendary sovereign of ancient China, credited for drawing the Trigrams)
In *Yijing* itself, Kongzi has described how Fuxi has gone about creating the 8 Trigrams.
However Fuxi is only the name of a legendary figure who is said to have existed prehistorically!
Sima Qian's (c.145-87BCE) *Historic Records* starts with 5 Emperors before Xia (五帝本紀).
And no words on early tribal leaders, like Suiren Fuxi and Shennong (燧人, 伏羲, 神農).
Fuxi has been depicted as having the head of a man and the body of a snake (Yu et.al. 2011).
Excavating Ruins of Shang Dynasty (殷虛) recovers thousands of oracle shells, bones.
Oracles are probably read from the run-patterns of line-cracks in numbers, length and direction.
From these line-cracks pattern, it is not too hard to imagine the emergence of 3-Liners Trigrams!

King Wen (文王)
c.1096 BC (Zhou. father of founder-King Wu, co-author of *Zhouyi*)
Before overthrowing the Shang Dynasty, King Wen was Duke of West under the evil King Zhou.
He was confined for 7 years at Youli, where unfazed, he has pondered and developed the *Zhouyi*.
His ministers secured his release with gift-offers of precious stones, beauties and fine horses.
His benevolent Rule lay a strong foundation for his son to overthrow the Shang Dynasty later.
All scholars who came after, have accepted his important contribution in the creation of *Yijing*.

Duke of Zhou (周公, Zhougong)
c.1046 BC (Zhou. brother of founder-King Wu, co-author of *Zhouyi*)
The 4th son of King Wen, had helped brother King Wu in establishing the Zhou Dynasty.
On Wu's death, held the Kingdom 7 years for his young nephew to grow up and be King.
Creator of etiquettes characteristic of the Zhou Dynasty (周礼), his virtures are legendary.
Thus he is highly capable of expressing the great sensitivities that exist in the 384 liner-texts.
We admire Zhougong, for he has done what he preached by returning kingship to his nephew!

Kongzi (孔子)
551 - 479 BC (Zhou. Spring Autumn period. Chinese philosopher, author of *Yijing's* 10 'Wings')
Kongzi was born of a poor scholar family in decline, in the State of Lu (魯國).
As a child he was keen to learn and displayed early, a love for knowledge, etiquette and order.
By this twenties he lost both parents, and already gained reputation as a good teacher.
In his thirties, he had come of age and been much sort after for consultation by head of states.
At forties, state affairs were bad, so he focused on writing, teaching students from far and wide.
At fifties, Lu had a good leader and he served in senior positions doing the state of Lu proud.
Jealous and fear of his successes, foes from within and without sabotaged, and Kongzi left Lu.
For 14 years he visited many other states with his disciples, living some dangerous encounters.
Aged 68 he returned to Lu to concentrate on writing and the study of *Yijing*, and died at age 73.
Teaching without bias (有教无類) Kongzi had 3 thousands students, and 72 Multi-talented.
He has been credited with writing and restoring the 5 Classics of China (五經).

Style of Presenting the 64 Hexagrams (Hex.)

Hexagrams are presented with Kongzi's commentaries embedded in the style of Zhu Xi (Song).
And author's comments are inserted at each juncture to assist appreciation of the ancient texts.
Conveniently, this may serve as a handbook for divination in tradition of the *Yijing or Zhouyi*.

Hexagram Imagery

Drawn on top of the page is a stack of 6 Liners (Sixer for Yin and Niner for Yang).
Each Liner is labeled with type (Sixer or Niner), level-number and Fuxi's Trigrams identify.
Yin-Liners or Yang-liners, or a variable-mix of both; Adorning (Hex.22) is illustrated here:

TopNiner	________)	
Sixer5	__ __)	**Gen (艮) Mountain, Trigram above**
Sixer4	__ __)	
Niner3	________)	
Sixer2	__ __)	**Li (離) Fire, Trigram below**
FirstNiner	________)	

Hexagram Text (卦辭)

King Wen's original Chinese text and English translation.

Tuan Says (彖曰)

Kongzi's original Chinese text (explains Wen's Hexagram Text) and English translation.
(Extraction from Kongzi's commentaries in 1st /2nd 'Wings' embedded in the style of Zhu Xi.)
Comments: author's appreciation of King Wen's Hexagram Text and Kongzi's Tuan Says.

HexagramSign Says (大象曰)

Kongzi's Chinese text (his explanation of the Hexagram as a whole) and English translation.
(Extraction from Kongzi's commentaries in the 3rd 'Wings', embedded in the style of Zhu Xi.)
Comments: author's appreciation of Kongzi's commentary.

Liner Text (爻辭)

Zhougong's original Chinese Text and English translation for each of the 6 Liners.

LinerSign Says (小象曰)

Kongzi's original Chinese text (his explanation of each Liner) and English translation.
(Extraction from Kongzi's commentaries in the 4th 'Wings' embedded in the style of Zhu Xi.)
Comments: author's appreciation of Zhougong's Liner Text and Kongzi's commentary.

Conclusions

A condensation on all that have been said by King Wen, Zhougong and Kongzi for better focus.
Appreciation of each Hexagram scenario and situation analysis from different levels of society.
Fore-knowledge prepares us to handle real-life situations, to avoid pit-falls and to succeed.

Lessons Learned

Core lessons learned from study of each Hexagram with the help of wisdom from the 4 Sages.

N.B. *The ancient dictionary of Xu Shen (Han c.220BC) Words Explain was much consulted.*
The dictionary findings are documented close-by with page numbers like, [Xu: 坤286地也].

Design of this study
This is a translation and analysis of the *Yijing*.
The monograph is designed and presented as follow:

Introduction: *Yijing, the 4 Sages, Design of this study, Writing style and Tutorial.*

Presentation of the *Yijing*:
    Translation of 64 Hexagrams complete with embedded commentaries from Kongzi.
    Translation of Kongzi's commentaries (5th, 6th, 8th, 9th and 10th 'Wings').

Summary: *teachings of the 64 Hexagrams, development sequence, the 8 facets of human life.*

Discussion: *8 controversies surrounding the Yijing and its usage.*

Conclusions:
    Divination: interpretations, raising a Hexagram, examples of Consultation with the Yijing
    Wisdom of 4 Sages
    Looking forward
    After Thoughts

Bibliographies

Appendices:
    Acknowledgement
    Imagery Chart of the 64 Hexagrams for easy reference
    Listing of 64 Hexagrams in sequence for easy reference
    List of important dates
    Glossary

Writing style
The *Yijing* is composed with a minimum of Chinese characters, their meaning not easy to grasp.
Hence the importance of Kongzi's commentaries (10 'Wings') for insights and clarification.
A near verbatim translation of original Chinese characters is done to better present the *Yijing*.
Chinese style construct of sentences is adopted, short phrases separated with commas for clarity.
Main English words for verbatim translation begin with a Capital letter, not article words ...
And English words needed to clarify implied meaning, to assist comprehension are bracketed.
Translation done over 2 years, different words of close meaning are used in different sections.
No attempt is made for uniformity as together the differences may give a broader perspective.
Shorter and simpler English words are favored when meaning and spirit are not compromised.
All sentence are constructed so as to confine to a single line for easy reading.

Hope to achieve
A popular version in English so that the general public can gain easy access to the *Yijing*.
A fun version that the general public can use DIY style, for divination and for consultation.
A window to Eastern wisdom of Junzi in self-cultivation, in harmony with self and the world.

Yijing

The 64 Hexagrams Chart

Upper Trigram > / Lower Trigram v	乾 Qian2 Heaven	坤 Kun1 Earth	震 Zhen4 Thunder	坎 Kan3 Water	艮 Gen4 Mountain	巽 Xun4 Wind	離 Li2 Fire	兌 Dui4 Wetland
乾 Qian2 Heaven	1 乾 Heaven-lead	11 泰 Interaction	34 大壯 Great Excess	5 需 Supplies	26 大畜 Great Constraint	9 小畜 Small Constraint	14 大有 Abundance	43 夬 Ostracism
坤 Kun1 Earth	12 否 Isolation	2 坤 Earth-support	16 豫 Happiness	8 比 Neighbors	23 剝 Stripping	20 觀 Observing	35 晉 Advance	45 萃 Gathering
震 Zhen4 Thunder	25 无忘 No Delusion	24 復 Return	51 震 Thunder- action	3 屯 Sprouting	27 頤 Nurturing	42 益 Benefits	21 噬嗑 Biting-Close	17 隨 Following
坎 Kan3 Water	6 訟 Litigation	7 師 Army	40 解 Resolving	29 坎 Water-pit danger	4 蒙 Ignorance	59 渙 Dispersion	64 末济 Prior Completion	47 困 Trapped
艮 Gen4 Mountain	33 遯 Retreat	15 謙 Humility	62 小过 Small Excess	39 蹇 Limp	52 艮 Moutain-block	53 漸 Progress	56 旅 Traveling	31 咸 Empathy
巽 Xun4 Wind	44 姤 Encounters	46 升 Rising	32 恆 Everlasting	48 井 water-Well	18 蠱 Belly-worms	57 巽 wind-conform	50 鼎 Tripod	28 大過 Great Excess
離 Li2 Fire	13 同人 Comrades	36 明夷 Enlighten Hurt	55 豐 Expansion	63 既濟 Completion	22 賁 Adoming	37 家人 Family People	30 離 Fire-shine	49 革 Changes
兌 Dui4 Wetland	10 履 Treading	19 臨 Overseeing	54 歸妹 Married Maid	60 節 Thrift	41 損 Reduction	61 中孚 Core Thrust	38 睽 Visions	58 兌 Wetland-Joy

Tutorial before reading the 64 Hexagrams

Legendary Fuxi (c.30th century BCE) has been credited for drawing the 8 Trigrams.
He looks up to Heaven to observe and bends down to Earth to examine all matters.
He discovers that all things has Singles and Doubles and draws 2 Sign-representations.
Yangs are represented with Single long lines, and thus all Odd numbers are Yang numbers.
Yins are represented with Double short lines, and thus all Even numbers are Yin numbers.
A hand has 5 fingers numbered 1, 2, 3, 4, 5 which consist of 3 Odd and 2 Even numbers.
1 plus 3 plus 5 equal 9 (all Odd numbers), Yang numbers, hence Yang-liners are called Niners.
2 plus 4 equal 6 (all Even numbers), Yin numbers, hence Yin-liners are called Sixers.

Yin and Yang

Yin-liner (陰爻)   ___ ___   2 short lines call Sixer (Even number 2)

Yang-liner (陽爻)   _______   1 long line call Niner (Odd number 1)

8 Trigrams

Putting 3 Liners together (representing Heaven, Human and Earth) Fuxi drew the first Trigram.
And all possible combinations of 3-Liners (Yin and Yang) give rise to the 8 Trigrams (八卦).
Yang Trigrams' focus is the single Yang-liner and Yin Trigrams's focus is the single Yin-liner.

The 8 Trigrams are drawn and named:

Qian乾	Kun坤	Zhen震	Xun巽	Kan坎	Li離	Gen艮	Dui澤
Heaven (Yang)	Earth (Yin)	Thunder (Yang)	Wind (Yin)	Water (Yang)	Fire (Yin)	Mountain (Yang)	Wetland (Yin)

64 Hexagrams

King Wen next created 64 (8x8) Hexagrams (6-Liners) by stacking two Trigrams (3-Liners),
Yin-liners call Sixers and Yang-liners call Niners, are stacked and numbered from bottom up.
Ex: Interation (Hexagram 11) is formed of Earth (Trigram above), Heaven (Trigram below).
Earth Trigram is formed of 3 Yin-Sixers and Heaven Trigram is formed of 3 Yang-Niners.
Thus Interaction (Hex.11) composes of FirstNiner, Niner2, Niner3, Sixer4, Sixer5 and TopSixer:

(第十一卦) 泰   **Interaction (Hexagram 11)**

    (上六   ___ ___   **TopSixer**)

地，上卦 (六五   ___ ___   **Sixer5**)   **Earth, Trigram above**

    (六四   ___ ___   **Sixer4**)

    (九三   _______   **Niner3**)

天，下卦 (九二   _______   **Niner2**)   **Heaven, Trigram below**

    (初九   _______   **FirstNiner**)

Reading of Hexagrams
Interpretation of the 6-liners Hexagrams are only possible when we accept the following:
1. The Yin and Yang liners have different Attributes such as with Gentleness, Strength, ..
2. The 8 Trigrams have different Associations such as with Action, Danger, Joy, ...
3. The relative Properties of 6 hierarchy positions such as lowly, upright, trust, honor, ...

Attributes of Yin-liners and Yang-liners (陰爻陽爻)
Yang (陽爻): The solid Niners are for Heaven, creative, male, strength, Sun, all things positive.

Yin (陰爻): The split Sixers are for Earth, female, gentleness, Moon, and all things negative.

A Word of Caution:

Yin: may not be read for female only, as also can be read for a weak male.

Yang: similarly may not be read for male only, as also can be read for a strong female.

Associations of the 8 Trigrams (八卦)
Associations with Activities, Elements of Nature, Family members, Body-parts, Animals, others.
Associations extend coverage, meanings, connotations that enliven the Trigrams for Divination.

Heaven Trigram (Qian 乾): Strength, Control, Head, Father, Horse, King, jade, ...

Earth Trigram (Kun 坤): Support, Compliant, Stomach, Mother, Cow, Cloth, ...

Thunder Trigram (Zhen 震): Action, Warning, Elder-son, Legs, Dragon, Reeds, Health, ...

Wind Trigram (Xun 巽): Following, Pervasive, Elder-daughter, Buttock, Chicken, Wood, ...

Water Trigram (Kan 坎): Trap, Danger, Middle-son, Ears, Pig, Moon, Red, Bandit, ...

Fire Trigram (Li 離): Brightness, Enlighten, Middle-daughter, Eyes, Pheasant, Sun, ...

MountainTrigram (Gen 艮): Stillness, Blocking, Young-son, Hands, Dog, Trail, ...

Wetland Trigram (Dui 兌): Joy, Attraction, Young-daughter, Mouth, Goat, Concubine, ...

Properties of the 6 Liners Hierarchy-positions
The hierarchical status of the 6 Liners increasing from bottom up, Lowly to Honored positions.
Liners of Trigram above are seniors authority, liners of Trigram below are juniors subordinates.
Positions from bottom up are Commoners, Scholars, Generals, Lords, Kings and past Kings.
The timing factor, Beginning with FirstLiner, progressing upward to Ending with TopLiner.
Note: FirstLine/Liner3/Liner5 are 3 Yang-positions, Liner2/Liner4/TopLiner are 3 Yins-position.
Yang in Yang positions like FirstNiner, Niner3, Niner5, are in correct positions and are stronger.
Yang in Yin positions like Niner2, Niner4, TopNiner, are incorrect in position and are weaken.
Yin in Yin positions like Sixer2, Sixer4, TopSixer, all in correct positions, has better outcome.
Yin in Yang positions like FirstSixer, Sixer3, Sixer5, wrong positions, less favorable outcome.
Corresponding Liners of external and internal Trigrams are considered for special partnerships.
FirstLiner and Liner4 are bottoms, Liner2 and Liner5 are centres, Liner3 and TopLiner are tops.
The centres are covet positions, denoting uprightness, unbiased, commanding and honored.
The bottoms are lowly and weak positions whereas the tops are most active for strong actions.
When corresponding Liners are mixed in kind (Yin-Yang), could be a husband-wife partnership.
When corresponding Liners are of similar kind (Yins or Yangs), it is comradeship or antagonists.
Yang Niners are favored for strength, authority, superiority and all things positive.
Yin Sixers are favored for gentleness docility, but handicap for weakness and all things negative.
Liner above is commanding over liner below, whereas liner below is supportive of liner above.
Thus Yang Niner above a Yin Sixer is favored whereas Yin Sixer over a Yang Niner is stressed.

Liners: Yin Yang Sign and Positional Characteristics
FirstLiner: Yang position, Lower Trigram Bottom, responder is Liner4, the Beginning, is Lowly.
Liner2: Yin position, Lower Trigram Centre, has Trust, Upright, responder is Liner5, has Talents.
Liner3: Yang position, Lower Trigram Top, responder is TopLiner, Emerging out, has Danger.
Liner4: Yin position, Upper Trigram Bottom, next to authority Liner5, suffer Suspicion Doubts.
Liner5: Yang position, Upper Trigram Centre, has Trust, Upright, the Honored spot, Auspicious.
TopLiner: Yin position, Upper Trigram Top, the upper limit of matters, the Ending, has Regrets.

Liners as foci of Trigrams, of Hexagrams
Focus of Trigram: the minority liner i.e. bottom Yang-liner of Thunder, top Yin-liner of Wetland.
Hexagram has 1 or 2 foci for obvious reasons; FirstSixer the lone Yin, focus of Return (Hex.24).
Sixer3 and Sixer4 are foci of Core Trust (Hex.61); TopSixer and Niner3 of Empathy (Hex.31).
Foci liners are significant in their added importance for the interpretation of a Hexagram.

Hexagram Images and Naming
The 2 Trigrams conjure up images and symbolics in combination specific for each Hexagram.
Their interactions or non-interaction reflect a unique situation for Naming of a Hexagram:
- *Interaction (Hexagram 11):* form with Earth Trigram above and Heaven Trigram below.
Image: Earth (heavy) settles down, Heaven (light) rises up thus crossing paths, *Interaction*.
- *Isolation (Hexagram 12):* form with Heaven Trigram above and Earth Trigram below.
Image: Heaven (light) rises up, Earth (heavy) settles down, not crossing paths, *Isolation*.
- *Family People (Hexagram 37):* form with Wind Trigram above and Fire Trigram below.
Image: cooking Fire burning-up, Wind above moving smoke out of chimney, *Family People*.

Hexagrams derivation and interconversion
There are important interpretation for divination in how the Hexagrams inter-relate.
With Return (Hex.24), the lone Yang moves up to form 5 more unique Hexagrams.
With Encounter (Hex.44), the lone Yin moves up to form 5 more unique Hexagrams.
With Overseeing (Hex.19), the 2 Yangs moves up to form 14 more unique Hexagrams.
With Retreat (Hex.33), the 2 Yins moves up to form 14 more unique Hexagrams.
With Interaction (Hex.11), the 3 Yangs moves up to form 19 more unique Hexagrams.
But with Isolation (Hex.12), the 3 Yins moves up to form the same 19 unique Hexagrams.
Thus together with Heaven and Earth, there is a total of 64 unique Hexagrams.
And moving liners become foci liners with special significance in the Hexagrams thus formed.

After the 4 Sages
In the centuries that follow, the *Yijing* has associations with many other mystic traditions.
The interpretation of a Hexagram then becomes very involved and difficult to understand.
However these new developments are redundant as the original texts of the *Yijing* are adequate.
The *Yijing* itself is sufficient enough for meaningful consultation and for us to enjoy divination.
Diviners who came after saw additional Hexagrams (互卦) and such, embedded in Hexagrams.
There is no end to 'innovative' introduction, hence best we keep to wisdom of the 4 Sages here.

N.B.
The Yijing is so archaic that one must read through this monograph as least once before any appreciation is possible. Just skimming the book will put one off initially.

Divination Mentality

By chance, raising a Hexagram for divination cannot logically give definitive prediction.
This is reflected in the counselling of King Wu (c.1046BC. Zhou) by Jizi (c.1100BC.Shang sage).

時人作卜筮	Then, Person Requests Turtle-divination Straw-divination
三人卜	3 Persons Divining
則從二人之占	Then Adopting from 2 Persons Their divination (take majority)
汝則有大疑	If You Have Big Indecision
謀及乃心	Consult With Own Heart (of integrity)
謀及卿士	Consult With Ministers Scholars
謀及庶人	Consult With Common People
謀及卜筮	Consult With Turtle-Divination Straw-divination
汝則從	You Then Comply
是之謂大同	This Is Called the Great Common
(書經。洪範)	(Book of History. Grand Governance)

Furthermore the same Hexagram raised can be differently interpreted by different persons.
As Kongzi explains, people see things from their different background and inclination.

仁者見之謂之仁	Benevolent Person Sees It Call It Benevolence
知者見之謂之知	Knowledgeable Person Sees It Call It Knowledge
(繫辭上傳。第五章)	(Attached Text Upper Commentary. 5th 'Wing' para.5)

Nevertheless the wisdom therein the *Yijing* is good and safe.
And as Kongzi puts it, consulting it is like consulting our own father and mother.

又明于憂患與故	Also for Enlightenment On Worries And Sadness
无有師保	Not Having Teacher's Guidance
如臨父母	Like Coming-upon Father Mother
(繫辭下傳。第八章)	(Attached Text Lower Commentary. 6th Wing para.8)

The *Yijing* does not give direct predictive answer of "Yes" or "No".
It just analyzes a situation and gives reasons for an unfavorable or favorable outcome.
And *Yijing* stresses that if you are not a Junzi (Gentleman), you may not enjoy the good fortune.
When an unfavorable Hexagram is raised, one noted the reasons and takes remedial actions.
When a favorable Hexagram is raised, one also noted the reasons and works harder for success.
Thus from the consultation, one may promote success and avoid failure (催吉避凶).

Yijing is a wisdom book, and a great fun to raise a Hexagram for consultation on any matter.

23   *Yijing (易經)*

N.B.

The Yijing is so archaic, one must read through this monograph as least once before any appreciation is possible.
Just skimming the book will likely put us off, initially!

（第一卦）　乾　　　　　**Heaven (Hexagram 1)**

外	上九	＿＿＿＿）	**TopNiner**	**external**
乾（天，上卦）	九五	＿＿＿＿）	**Niner5**	**Qian (Heaven, Trigram above)**
	九四	＿＿＿＿）	**Niner4**	
內	九三	＿＿＿＿）	**Niner3**	
乾（天，下卦）	九二	＿＿＿＿）	**Niner2**	**Qian (Heaven, Trigram below)**
	初九	＿＿＿＿）	**FirstNiner**	**internal**

卦辭《文王》：　　　　　　　　***Hexagram Text (King Wen):***
乾: 元, 亨, 利貞　　　　　　　　Heaven (Qian) : Primal, Prosperity, favors Integrity

爻辭《周公》：　　　　　　　　***Liner Text (Zhougong):***
初九：潛龍勿用　　　　　　　　FirstNiner: Submerged Dragon, Don't Act
九二：見龍在田　　　　　　　　Niner2: Visible Dragon On Field
　　　利見大人　　　　　　　　　　Favors Seeing GreatOne (Niner5)
九三：君子终日乾乾　　　　　　Niner3: CulturedOne Whole Day Highly Active
　　　夕惕若，屬　　　　　　　　　Nightly Alert-like, Grave (situation)
九四：或躍在淵, 无咎　　　　　Niner4: Or Leaping (Dragon) On Ocean-depth, No Fault
九五：飛龍在天　　　　　　　　Niner5: Flying Dragon In Heaven,
　　　利見大人　　　　　　　　　　Favors Seeing GreatOne (created)
上九：亢龍有悔　　　　　　　　TopNiner: Stubborn Dragon Has Regrets
用九：見羣龍无首，吉　　　　ExtNiner: Visible Crowd of Dragons (but) no Leader, Auspicious
象曰《孔子》：　　　　　　　　***Tuan Says (Kongzi Explain):***
大哉乾元　　　　　　　　　　　Great Indeed Qian (Heaven) Primal
萬物資始，乃統天　　　　　　All Matters' Initial Substantiation, In Totality of Heaven.
雲行雨施，品物流形　　　　　Clouds Move Rain Bestow, Kinds and Matters Flowing Forms.
大明終始，六位時成　　　　　Great Clarity of Starts Ends, Six Positions Timely Formed
時乘六龍以御天　　　　　　　In Time Riding the 6 Dragons To Travel Heaven
乾道變化，各正性命　　　　　Qian's Way, Change Transform, Each Accord with Nature Destiny.
保合太和，乃利貞　　　　　　Keep Unity with Primal Harmony, Thus Favors having Integrity.
首出庶物，萬國咸寧　　　　　First Producing All Matters, Many Kingdoms All Peaceful.
Comments:
Like tusked boar (象 *Tuan*) rooting for its food, Kongzi seeks wisdom from the Hexagram Text.
Qian (乾) Primal (元) initiates, Wind and Rain, Freely (亨) all matters in Heaven's Order.

In time the Hierarchy of 6 was established with Integrity (貞), achieving peace among all nation.
Kongzi describes the natural creation of all matters, and Hierarchy of 6 levels of human society.
His great poetic eloquence (appreciated by reading the Chinese text) defies perfect translation!
[Xu: 亢人頸也 ；象197豕也 ；豬196豕而三毛叢居者]

象曰 (孔子) :	**HexagramSign Says (Kongzi):**
天行健	Heaven Moving Strong (sun, moon, stars, ceaseless cycles)
君子以自强不息	CulturedOne likewise By Self-Improvement that Never Cease

Comments:
Heaven (Hex. 1) with 6 Niners (Yangs) do give image of strength and perpetuity in motion.
Hence Kongzi advises that we do likewise and learn to never cease in our self-improvement.

象曰 (孔子) :	**LinerSign Says (Kongzi):**
潛龍勿用，陽在下也	Submerged Dragon, Don't Act, Yang Position Lowly that's
見龍在田，德施普也	Visible Dragon On Field, Virtuous Practices Pervasive that's
終日乾乾，反復道也	Whole Day Alert Alert, Revert Back to The-Way that's
或躍在淵，進无咎也	Or Leap Onto Ocean-depth, Advancement No Fault that's
飛龍在天，大人造也	Flying Dragon in Heaven, GreatOne Created that's
亢龍有悔，盈不可久也	Stubborn Dragon Has Regret, Fullness Can-Not Last that's.
用九，天德不可爲首也	ExtNiner, Heavenly Virtue Can-Not Be Head that's (Extension)

Comments:
Each liner is sensitive to its Yin/Yang (Sixer/Niner) nature, hierarchy and relative relationships...
FirstNiner is Submerged Dragon, lowly and weak as a bottom Liner, hence advise not to act.
Niner2 is Visible Dragon, active making pervasive virtuous contribution in the world.
Niner3, active whole day, strays and needs to revert back and forth to The-Way.
Niner4, entering top Trigram is a leap into uncertainty, but taking chance to advance, no fault.
Niner5 is Flying Dragon with top Authority, be a GreatOne for contributions to the world.
TopNiner, Stiff-neck Dragon, a leader over the top, and full authority cannot last long.
ExtNiner, Heaven's Way for peace, not allowing Headship, hence no contest, no bloodshed.

文言曰(孔子,七翼第一章):	**Text Talk Says (Kongzi, 7th Wing para.1)**
元者，善之長也	Yuan (元) Is, Best Of Kindness that's
亨者，嘉之會也	Heng (亨) Is, Meeting Of the Beautiful that's
利者，義之和也	Li (利) Is, Harmony Of Uprightness that's
貞者，事之幹也	Zhen (貞) Is, Finisher Of Tasks that's
君子體仁足以長人	Junzi Embodiment of Benevolence Enough To Enhancing Others
嘉會足以合禮	Beautiful matters Meeting Enough To Accord with Etiquette
利物足以和義	Benefiting of Matters Enough To Harmonize Uprightness
貞足以幹事	Integrity Enough To Execute Tasks
君子行此四德者	Junzi Practices These 4 virtues that's
故曰乾元亨利貞	Hence Says Qian(乾),Yuan(元),Heng(亨),Li (利),Zhen(貞)

Comments:
Kongzi expanding on King Wen's Hexagram Text, Yuan(元), Heng(亨), Li(利), Zhen(貞).
Upgrading them to 4 specific virtues of Benevolence, Etiquette, Uprightness, Integrity.

文言曰(孔子,七翼 第二章):	*Text Talk Says (Kongzi, 7th Wing para.2)*
初九曰：	**FirstNiner Says (Kongzi)**
潛龍勿用	Submerged Dragon Don't Act
何謂也？	Why Say this? (disciples ask)
子曰：	*Teacher Says:*
龍德而隱者也	Dragon Virtue Like Hermit person that's
不易乎世，不成乎名	Not Changing For World, Not Succeeding for Recognition
遯世无悶	Retired from World, Not Feel Bored
不見是而无悶	Not Seen as Correct And Not Unhappy
樂則行之，憂則違之	Happy Then Do It, Worrying Then Oppose It
確乎其不可拔，潛龍也	Certain That It Not Be Uprooted, Submerged Dragon that's

Comments:
Person of Submerged Dragon wishes anonymity, unaffected by worldly wealth and fame.
Person not bored but happy with self at all time, whether at work or in retirement.

九二曰：	**Niner2 Says:**
見龍在田，利見大人	Visible Dragon On Field, Favors Seeing Great Person
何謂也？	Why Say this? (disciples ask)
子曰：	*Teacher Says:*
龍德而正中者也	Dragon Virtue Of Upright Centrist Person that's
庸言之信，庸行之謹	Common Speech Has Trust, Common Conduct Has Control
閑邪存其誠	Block Evil Retain Its Sincerity
善世而不伐	Benefit World But Not Boasting,
德博而化	Virtue Broad And Influential
易曰：	Yi says:
見龍在田	See Dragon On Field
利見大人，君德也	Favors Seeing Great Person, Kingly Virtue that's

Comments:
Person of Visible Dragon virtue is righteous and centrist, trustworthy and careful in conduct.
And with many talents and capabilities, benefitting the world and not boasting about it.

九三曰：	**Niner3 Says:**
君子終日乾乾	Junzi (Gentleman) Whole Day Working Hard
夕惕若，屬无咎	Evening Alert Like, Serious but No Fault
何謂也？	Why Say this? (disciples ask)
子曰：	*Teacher Says:*
君子進德脩業	Junzi (Gentleman) Take-in Virtues Built Achievements
忠信，所以進德也	Loyalty Trust, Therefore Can Intake Virtues that's
脩辭立其誠	Cultivates Speech, Establishes Its Sincerity
所以居業也	Therefore Can Claim Achievements that's
知至，至之	Knows Limits, Reaches limits

可與幾也	Can Together Discuss that's
知終，終之	Knows Ending, Ends It
可與存義也	Can Together Keep Uprightness that's
是故，居上位而不驕	Therefore, Holding High Position But Not Arrogant
在下位而不憂	On Lowly Position But Not Worry
故，乾乾因其時而惕	Hence, Keep Busy and Because Of the Time Be Alert
雖危无咎矣	Although Dangerous but No Fault Indeed

Comments:
Junzi with hard work, achieve top position in the lower Trigram, like a provincial governor.
Not arrogant to subordinates, not worry with higher authority, though in danger suffers no fault.

九四曰：	**Niner4 Says:**
或躍在淵，无咎	Or Leap Onto Ocean-depth, No Fault
何謂也？	Why Say this? (disciples ask)
子曰：	***Teacher Says:***
上下无常	Up or Down, No Certainty
非爲邪也	Not Doing Evil that's
進退无恒	Advance or Retreat, Not Permanent
非離羣也	Not Leaving Group that's
君子進德脩業	Junzi Imbibes Virtues Building Achievements
欲及時也	Wishes Right Timing that's
故无咎	Hence No Fault

Comments:
Career advancement to Niner4 position next to Authority is a leap into great uncertainty.
Junzi is not leaving colleagues behind, only wishes progress with time, hence no fault.

九五曰：	**Niner5 says:**
飛龍在天，利見大人	Flying Dragon In Heaven, Favors Seeing Great Person
何謂也？	Why Say this? (disciples ask)
子曰：	***Teacher Says:***
同聲相應	Same Sound (language) Mutually Resonate
同氣相求	Same Breath (aspiration) Mutually Request
水流濕，火就燥	Water Flow to Wetland, Fire Incline to Parch-land
雲從龍，風從虎	Clouds Follow the Dragon, Winds Follow the Tiger
聖人作而萬物覩	The Sage Acts And All Things Beautify
本乎天者親上	Originate Of Heaven Affiliates with Above
本乎下者親下	Originate Of Below Affiliates with Below
則各從其類也	Then Each Follows It Kind, that's

Comments:
Flying Dragon, is in position of Authority to be the GreatOne, works to benefit all subjects.
All matters are free to associate with own kinds, follow own nature for best life experience.

上九曰：	**TopNiner Says:**
亢龍有悔	Stubborn Dragon Has Regrets
何謂也？	Why Says this? (disciples ask)
子曰：	*Teacher Says:*
貴而无位， 高而无民	Noble Yet No Position, High Has No Citizens
賢人在下位而无輔	Virtuous Person On Lowly Position Has No Assistance
是以動而有悔也	Therefore Act And Has Regrets, that's

Comments:

Stubborn Dragon in top position but has no authority and no subjects, hence has regrets.
Likewise, virtuous person in lowly position with no support has regrets, ineffective in action.

文言曰(孔子,七翼第三章)：	*Text Talk Says (Kongzi, 7th Wing para.3)*
潛龍勿用，下也	Submerged Dragon Don't Act, Lowly that's
見龍在田，時舍也	Visible Dragon On Field, Time Abiding that's
終日乾乾，行事也	Whole Day Working Hard, Running Tasks that's
或躍在淵，自試也	Or Leap Onto Ocean-depth, Self Trying that's
飛龍在天，上治也	Flying Dragon In Heaven, Top Governing that's
亢龍有悔，窮之災也	Stubborn Dragon Has Regrets, End-stage's Disaster that's
乾元用九，天下治也	Qian Primal Extend-Niner, The World Well-managed that's

Comments:

Kongzi explaining reasons for different actions taken at different levels of human hierarchy.

文言曰(孔子,七翼第四章)：	*Text Talk Says (Kongzi, 7th Wing para.4)*
潛龍勿用，陽氣潛藏	Submerged Dragon Don't Act, Yang Energy Submerged Stored
見龍在田，天下文明	Visible Dragon On Field, The World Civilised and Cultured
終日乾乾，與時偕行	Whole Day Working Hard, With Time Together Advancing
或躍在淵，乾道乃革	Or Leap Onto Ocean-depth, Heaven's Way For Changes
飛龍在天，乃位乎天德	Flying Dragon In Heaven, Like Positions In Heaven's Virtue
亢龍有悔，與時偕極	Stubborn Dragon Has Regrets, With Time All at End-limit
乾元用九，乃見天則	Qian Primal Extend-Niner, Thereupon See Heaven's Rules

Comments:

Kongzi highlights different results from the actions taken at each level of human hierarchy.

文言曰(孔子,七翼第五章)：	*Text Talk Says (Kongzi, 7th Wing para.5)*
乾元者，始而亨者也	Qian (乾) Primal (元) Are, Initials For Prosperity (亨) that's
利貞者，性情也	Li (利) Zhen (貞) are, Nature and Desires that's (of human)
乾始能以美利，利天下	Qian Initials Able By Beautiful Gain, Benefits The World
不言所利，大矣哉！	Not Boasting What has Benefited, Greatness Indeed!
大哉乾乎	Great Indeed Qian (Heaven) Is!
剛健中正，純粹精也	Tough Strong Centrist Righteous, Pure Fine Essence that's
六爻發揮，旁通情也	Six Liners Extent Expression, Laterally Connecting Desires that's

時乘六龍以御天也	Timely Riding 6 Dragons To Travel Heaven that's
雲行雨施，天下平也	Cloud Moves Rain Delivers, The World Peaceful that's

Comments:
Kongzi lauds Heaven (乾), with Primal (元), freedom (亨), integrity (貞), benefit (利) the World.
Junzi rides the 6 dragons, accords with Heaven, brings beauty prosperity and peace to the World.

文言曰(孔子,七翼第六章):	***Text Talk Says (Kongzi, 7th Wing para.6)***
君子以成德爲行	Junzi (Gentleman) With Formed Virtues For Conduct
日可見之行也	Daily Can See His Conduct that's
潛之爲言也	Submerged This As Talking-point that's
隱而未見，行而未成	Concealed And Not yet Seen, Act And Not yet Complete
是以君子弗用也	Therefore Junzi Not Acting that's
君子學以聚之	Junzi Learns To Accumulate Them (knowledge)
問以辨之	Asks To Differential Them
寬以居之	Accommodation To Possess Them
仁以行之	Benevolence To Implement Them

Comments:
Kongzi elaborates on 'Submerged' FirstNiner, not to be seen and premature for action.
Like Junzi needs more knowledge and ability to work with accommodation and compassion.

易曰：	*Yi Says:*
見龍在田	Visible Dragon On Field
利見大人，君德也	Favors Seeing GreatOne, Kingly virtue that's

Comments:
Kongzi elaborates on 'Visible' Niner2, ready as GreatOne can perform with Kingly virtue.

九三，重剛而不中	Niner3, Double Strength But Not Centre
上不在天，下不在田	Above Not In Heaven, Below Not On Field
故乾乾因其時而惕	Hence Busy Working, Because Time situation Be Alert
雖危无咎矣	Although Dangerous No Fault that's

Comments:
Kongzi explains that Niner3 is Yang in Yang position 3, hence double strength but not centre.
Position not rooted on field or in Heaven, needs to work hard and be alert to avoid danger.

九四，剛而不中	Niner4, Strong But Not Centre
上不在天，下不在田	Not in Heaven above, not on field below
中不在人，故或之	Centre not on people, hence doubt it
或之者，疑之也，故无咎	Doubting It that's, Suspicious of It that's, Hence No Fault

Comments:
Kongzi explains that Niner4 is Yang has strength but not central in upper Trigram.
In Yin position 4, not on field not in Heaven, hence has uncertainty and doubt but no faults.

夫大人者	O' GreatOne that's (Niner5)
與天地合其德	With Heaven Earth Accord with Their Virtue
與日月合其明	With Sun Moon Accord with Their Brightness
與四時合序	With 4 Seasons Accord with Sequence
與鬼神合其吉凶	With Devils God-spirits Accord with Their Fortune Misfortune
先天而天弗違	Ahead of Heaven And Heaven Not Oppose
後天而奉天時	After Heaven With Support of Heaven's Timing
天且弗違	Heaven Even Not Opposing
而況於人乎！	Then How Can Humans that's !
況於鬼神乎！	How Can Devils and God-spirits that's !

Comments:
Kongzi explains, Niner5 is in tune with Heaven and Earth, illuminates like the Sun and Moon.
Flowing with the 4 seasons, in harmony with the devils, god-spirits and all nature.

亢之爲言也	Stubborn This As Description that's
知進而不知退	Knows Advancement But Not Knows Retreat
知存而不知亡	Knows Survival But Not Knows Death
知得而不知喪	Knows Gain But Not Knows Loss
其唯聖人乎	That Only Sage Person Can !
知進退存亡	Knows Advance/Retreat Survival/Death
而不失其正者	And Not Lost It Uprightness.
其唯聖人乎	That Only Sage Person Can !

Comments:
Kongzi explains 'Stubborn' Dragon, incorrigibly one-sided, knows not when to compromise.
The Sage ever righteous, knows the need to balance advance/retreat, survival/death, loss/gain.

文言曰 (孔子, 七翼) :   *Text Talk Says (Kongzi, 7th Wing)*

The *Text Talk Says*, purportedly by Kongzi, is only written for 2 Hexagrams, Heaven and Earth.
This writing helps to show the way to interpret each Liner in all other Hexagrams (total 6x64).
That is, the 6 Liners represent the 6 levels of Hierarchy positions as seen in human society.
The *status* of authority increasing from First Liner to Liners 2, 3, 4, 5, through to Top Liner.
The *interrelationship* between Liners of bottom Trigram and Liners of authority in top Trigram.
These concepts of attributes, inter-relationships, .. are important for interpreting the Hexagrams.
Today, without Kongzi's careful explanation, we may not appreciate the *Yijing* many teachings.
Starting from Heaven (Hexagram 01) through to Hexagram 64, is a treasure trove of wisdom.
I may not have captured the poetry and eloquence of expression of Kongzi's words here.

Hopefully enough ideas are captured to guide us in life, to avoid danger and survive (催吉避凶).

Conclusions:

Heaven (Hexagram 01): Heaven Trigram below and Heaven Trigram above.
Image: all 6 Niners (Yangs) give image of strength and perpetuity in motion.
Symbolic: of 6 dragons traversing the Heaven, showing the working of Heaven's Way.

King Wen:

Heaven (乾) is Primal (元) Prosperity (亨), Favors (利) having Integrity (貞).

Zhougong:

FirstNiner: Submerged Dragon, Don't Act (潛龍勿用)
Niner2: Visible Dragon On Field Favors Seeing GreatOne (見龍在田，利見大人)
Niner3: Junzi Whole Day Highly ActiveNightly Alert-like, Grave (君子终日乾乾, 夕惕若, 厲)
Niner4: Or Leaping Dragon On Ocean-depth, No Fault (或躍在淵, 无咎)
Niner5: Flying Dragon In Heaven, Favors Seeing GreatOne (created) (飛龍在天, 利見大人)
TopNiner: Stubborn Dragon Has Regrets (亢龍有悔)
ExtNiner: Visible Crowd of Dragons (but) no Leader, Auspicious (見羣龍无首, 吉)

Kongzi:

Clouds and Rain assisting, all kinds of things flowing into forms, and Hierarchy of 6 established.
Favoring (利) Integrity (貞) and such conditions to bring harmony and peace among nations.
(乾：剛，雜卦傳) (Heaven : strength - Misc.10th Wing)
Selection of Heaven Hexagram for more attribute highlights - 6th Wing para.12.
夫乾：天下之中健也，德行恆易，以知險 - 繫辭下傳，第12章
O'Heaven: the World's most Strong that's, Virtuous Conduct ever Easy, to know Danger

Image: Heaven Trigram below and Heaven Trigram above, it's all Heaven the Initiator!
Symbolic: Dragons' strength, of perpetual continuity like the Sun, the Moon, the 4 Seasons.
FirstNiner, Submerged Dragon, immature, learning stage, Not be Seen.
Niner2, Visible Dragon, displaying talents working virtuously, the making of Great Person.
Niner3, Junzi alert day and night, back and forth working the Virtuous-Way, Grave.
Niner4, Leaping Dragon, taking the leap into big-time big affairs of the kingom, has Doubts.
Niner5, Flying Dragon, high-flying, has authority, peaking in status, Auspicious.
TopNiner, Stubborn Dragon, retired, reviewing life-performance, has Regrets.
ExtNiner, extending beyond hierarchies, no leaders, no contests no bloodshed, Auspicous.
Heaven: all liners Yang, strength, showing the way for all other Hexagrams!

Lessons (Heaven Hex. 01):

Heaven revolving eternally, likewise we may never stop self-improvement (自强不息).

Heaven's way not to contest for Headship, to achieve harmony among nations (天德不可為首).

（第二卦）坤　　　　　　　　　**Earth (Hexagram 02)**

<table>
<tr><td>外</td><td>上六</td><td>__ __)</td><td>**TopSixer**</td><td>**eternal**</td></tr>
<tr><td>坤（地，上卦）</td><td>六五</td><td>__ __)</td><td>**Sixer5**</td><td>**Kun (Earth, Trigram above)**</td></tr>
<tr><td></td><td>六四</td><td>__ __)</td><td>**Sixer4**</td><td></td></tr>
<tr><td></td><td>六三</td><td>__ __)</td><td>**Sixer3**</td><td></td></tr>
<tr><td>坤（地，下卦）</td><td>六二</td><td>__ __)</td><td>**Sixer2**</td><td>**Kun (Earth, Trigram below)**</td></tr>
<tr><td>內</td><td>初六</td><td>__ __)</td><td>**FirstSixer**</td><td>**internal**</td></tr>
</table>

卦辭 *(文王)*：	*Hexagram Text (King Wen) :*
坤, 元亨, 利牝馬之貞	Earth, Primal Freedom, Favours Female Horse's Reliability,
君子有攸往	Junzi Has Leisurely Advance
先迷後得主	Initially Confuse Later Gain Master
利西南得朋, 東北喪朋	Favors West South Gain Friends, East North Lose Friends
安貞吉	Quietly with Integrity Auspicious

象曰 *(孔子)*：	*Tuan Says (Kongzi explains) :*
至哉坤元	Supreme Indeed Earth Primal
萬物資生, 乃順承天	All Matters Materially Created, In Accord Supportive of Heaven
坤厚載物, 德合无疆	Earth Thick Support Matters, Virtues Combine No Borders
含弘光大, 品物咸亨	Possess Sound Light Hugely, Matters Kinds All in Harmony
牝馬地類, 行地无疆	Female Horse Land Kind, Traveling Earth with No Boundaries
柔順利貞, 君子攸往	Gentle Obedient Favors Integrity, Junzi Leisurely Proceeding
先迷失道, 後順得常	Initially Confuse Lost Way, Later Compliant Gain Normalcy
西南得朋, 乃與類行	West South Gain Friends, Still Traveling With (own) Kind
東北喪朋, 乃終有慶	East North Lost Friends, Still Finally Has Celebration
安貞之吉, 應地无疆	Quiet Integrity Its Auspicious, Responsive Earth with No Borders

Comments:
Earth Hexagram signifies Primal Freedom, with Integrity typical of the gentle, obedient mare.
Junzi may leisurely go forward to explore the great landscape, North South East & West.
Acts in accords of Heaven like mare's compliant with its master, else lose its way.
Acts with Earth's Quietude Auspicious, better than running confused, gaining and losing friends.
[Xu: 坤286地也 ；君32尊也 ；攸68水行也 ；安150静也; 至247鳥飛下至地也; 含170嗛也; 嗛
31口有所銜; 弘170弓聲也; 應217當也; 當291田相值也; 值167措也; 措252置也; 置158赦也]

象曰 *(孔子)*：	*HexgramSign Says (Kongzi) :*
地勢坤	Earth's Landscape, Kun (Earth)
君子以厚德載物	Junzi With Thick Virtues Support Matters

Comments:
Kongzi urges that highly virtuous Junzi to emulate Earth in Support of all matters.

爻辭 *(周公) :*	*Liner Text (Zhougong) :*
初六 ：	**FirstSixer:**
履霜	Treading on Snow
堅冰至	Hard Ice Coming (to expect)
象曰 *(孔子) :*	*LinerSign Says (Kongzi) :*
履霜堅冰，陰始凝也	Treading Snow Solid Ice, Yin (Cold) Starts to Solidfy that's
馴致其道，至堅冰也	Teaches Limit of This Path, Leads to Hard Ice that's

Comments:
Treading on snow, one knows Cold is setting in, will lead to extreme weather with ice formation.

六二 ：	**Sixer2:**
直方大	Honest, Righteous, Big (inclusive)
不習无不利	Not Pracice None Not Favorable
象曰 *(孔子) :*	*LinerSign Says (Kongzi) :*
六二之動	Sixer2 Its Action
直以方也	Honest By Uprightness that's
不習无不利	Not (seen) Practice None Not Favorable
地道光也	Earth's Way Luminous that's

Comments:
Sixer2 is honest and righteous at home and abroad, practicing the Luminous Way of Earth.
Not seen practiced in any new places, not being disadvantaged as the Reputation is Good.
[Xu: 方176併船也象兩舟省(糹怱)頭形；習74數飛也；

六三 ：	**Sixer3:**
含章可貞	Possessing Talents Be Trustworthy
或從王事	Or Running King's affairs
无成有终	No Success (claiming for self) but Has Completion
象曰 *(孔子) :*	*LinerSign Says (Kongzi) :*
含章可貞	Possessing Talents Be Trustworthy
以時發也	By Timely Showing-off that's
或從王事	Or Running King's Affairs
知光大也	Knows it's for Greater Glory (of the Kingdom) that's

Comments:
Has talents, performs for the Great Glory of the Kingdom and claiming no personal credit.
[Xu: 章58樂竟爲一章从音从十十數之盡也；竟58樂曲盡爲竟

六四 ：	**Sixer4:**
括囊	Tighten (string) of Sack
无咎无譽	No Fault No Honor
象曰 *(孔子) :*	*LinerSign Says (Kongzi) :*
括囊无咎，慎不害也	Close Bag, No Fault, Being Careful No Harm that's

Comments:
Guarding purse-string of the Kingdom no fault; being careful and thrifty no harm.
[Xu: 括255絜也]

六五：	**Sixer5:**
黄裳	Yellow Frock
元吉	Primally Auspicious
象曰 *(孔子)：*	***LinerSign Says (Kongzi) :***
黄裳元吉	Yellow Frock (lower garment) Primaly Auspicious
文在中也	Civility At Centre that's

Comments:
At Sixer5 governing position, and mention of Yellow Frock signifys humility and gentleness.
This augurs well as there is civility at centre of authority, Primaly Auspicious.

上六：	**TopSixer:**
龍戰于野	Dragons Waring In the Wilderness
其血玄黄	Their Blood are Black and Yellow
象曰 *(孔子)：*	***LinerSign Says (Kongzi) :***
龍戰于野	Dragons Fighting In the Wilderness
其道窮也	Their Path is Terminal that's

Comments:
TopSixer is extreme development (6 Yins in row), when gentleness has morphed into violence.
This is a good illustration of *Yijing*'s concept that changes will occur at the extremes of matters.

用六：	**ExtSixer:**
利永貞	Favours Everlasting Integrity
象曰 *(孔子)：*	***LinerSign Says (Kongzi) :***
用六利永貞	ExtSixer Favours Everlasting Integrity
以大终也	As the Great Ultimate that's.

Comments:
ExtSixer cautions, Everlasting Integrity is needed to prevent the bloodshed seen in TopSixer.
Meaning bloodshed is not inevitable if only Integrity is everlastingly honored and never lost.

文言曰 *(孔子, 七翼)：*	***Text Talk Says (Kongzi, 7th Wing)***
坤至柔, 而動也剛	Earth Extremely Gentle, But in Action Also Tough
至静而德方	Extreme Quietude With Righteous Virtue
後得主而有常	Later Gain Master Then Has Normalcy
含萬物而化光	Inclusion of All Matters In Glorious Transformation
坤道其順乎	Earth's Way, It's Conformity that's
承天而時行	Supportive of Heaven With Timely Actions

Comments:
Conforming to Heaven with timely actions, Earth with quietude transform of all matters.
The concept of the lowly status of Earth as compare to Heaven is eloquently expounded here.

積善之家	Families That Accumulate Goodness
必有餘慶	Certainly Have Excess Fortune
積不善之家	Families That Accumulate Evil
必有餘殃	Certainly Have Excess Misfortune
臣弒其君，子弒其父	Minister Killing The King, Son Killing The Father
非一朝一夕之故	Not Matters of A Day or A Night
其所由來者，漸矣	The Reasons Concerned A-coming That's, Gradual indeed
由辯之不早辯也	Reasons to Discuss It, yet No Early Discussion that's

Comments:
Kongzi notes that extremism has gradual incubation period before explosive manifestation.
He warns of evil deeds accumulation and suggests that early awareness is critical to pre-empt.

易曰:	*Yijing Says:*
履霜堅冰至	Treading Snow Hard Ice is here
蓋言順也	All Said Sequential that's

Comments:
FirstSixer treading on snow can expect arrival of hard ice, a natural sequence of events.

直其正也，方其義也	Straighten The Uprightness that's, Squaring The Justice that's
君子敬以直內，義以方外	Junzi Respect With Honesty Inside, Justice By Squaring Outside
敬義立而德不孤	Respect Justice Setup And Virtues Not Lonely
直方大，不習无不利	Honest Justice Big, Not Practise None Not Favorable
則不疑其所行也	Then No Suspicion of Its Implemented Actions that's

Comments:
Sixer2 shows respect inside and uprightness outside, hence never been doubted in conduct.

陰雖有美，含之	Yin Though Has Beauty (talents), Conceal Them
以從王事，弗敢成也	For Work on King's Affairs, Not Dare Succeed (claim credit)
地道也，妻道也，臣道也	Earth's Way that's, Wife's Way that's, Minister's Way that's
地道无成，而代有终也	Earth's Way No Credit claim, But Changes Has Completion that's
天地變化，草木蕃	Heaven Earth Changes Transform, Grass Woods Luxuriant
天地閉，賢人隱	Heaven Earth Close, Virtuous Person Retires

Comments:
Sixer3 has talents but keeps low profile, and never take credit for successes in service.
[Xu: 代165更也 ; 更68改也 ; 蕃27艸茂 ; 茂22艸豐盛也]

易曰:	*Yijing Says:*
括囊无咎无譽	Tighten (string) of Sack, No Fault No Honor
蓋言謹也	All Said, being Careful that's

Comments:
Sixer4 lowest position in the upper Trigram of authority, needs be guarded in all actions.

君子黃中通理	Junzi, a Yellow (mild) Centrist, Understands Reasons
正位居體, 美在其中	Right Position All Embodied, Beauty (virtues) In Its Midst
暢於四支	Relaxes Through 4 Appendages (arms and legs)
發於事業, 美之至也	Manifest In Career Achievement, Beauty Is Achieved that's

Comments:

Sixer5 shows humility, 'Beauty' at heart reflecting beautiful achievements in Kingship.

陰疑於陽必戰	Yins Suspicious of Yangs, Certain to Fight
爲其嫌於无陽也	Because They are Unhappy Having No Yangs that's
故稱龍焉	Hence Address as Dragons that's
猶未離其類也，故稱血焉	Still has Not Leave Their Kind that's, Hence Mention Blood that's
夫玄黃者, 天地之雜也	O'Dark Yellow That's, Heaven Earth Their Mixing that's
天玄而地黃	Heaven is Dark And Earth is Yellow

Comments:
TopSixer at extreme of Yin forces (6 in a row) is unhappy in the absence of Yang forces.
No interaction resulted in suspicion and clashes, spilling dark yellow blood of Heaven Earth.
Kongzi notes, interaction is needed to avoid suspicion and clashes, even among same kind.
[Xu: 嫌263不平於心也一曰疑也；疑310惑也；惑221亂也]

Conclusions:
Earth (Hexagram 02): formed of Earth Trigram above and Earth Trigram below.

Image: formed with a Earth Trigram above and a Earth Trigram below, all 6 Yins, no Yangs.
Symbolic: 6 Yin liners, signifying gentleness, humility, low-profile, naturally cautious.

King Wen:
Earth Hexagram signifies Primal Freedom, with Integrity typical of the gentle, obedient mare.
Earth is liken to mare, running confused and lost, then finds its master and returns to normalcy.

Zhougong:
FirstSixer: treading snow, one knows coming of extreme weather with ice formation.
Sixer2: is Centre Righteous practicing the luminous Way of Earth, Reputation Good.
Sixer3: has Talents for the Greater Glory of the Kingdom and claims No Credit.
Sixer4: guarding Purse-string of the Kingdom, being careful and thrifty No Fault.
Sixer5: Yellow Frock signifies humility and civility at centre of authority, Primally Auspicious.
TopSixer: 6 Yins in row when extreme gentleness has morphed into Violence with suspicions.
ExtSixer: everlasting Integrity is needed to Prevent Bloodshed finally.

Kongzi:
Concept of Earth, low status, with Quietude support all matters in accord with Heaven above.
Kongzi urges that highly virtuous Junzi to emulate Earth in Support of all matters
(坤：柔，雜卦傳) (Earth : gentle - Misc.10th Wing)

Lessons (Earth Hexagram 02):
Earth: basic concept of Yijing (Book of Changes) illustrated, extremes will lead to changes.
Emulating Earth, Junzi supports all matters with Quietude with Everlasting Integrity.
Kongzi notes that extremism has gradual incubation period before explosive manifestation.

（第三卦） 屯　　　　　　　　　**Sprouting (Hexagram 03)**

外　　　　上六　＿＿ ＿＿)　**TopSixer**　　　　external

坎（水,上卦）　九五　＿＿＿＿＿)　**Niner5　Kan　(Water, Trigram above)**

六四　＿＿ ＿＿)　**Sixer4**

六三　＿＿ ＿＿)　**Sixer3**

震（雷,下卦）　六二　＿＿ ＿＿)　**Sixer2　Zhen　(Thunder, Trigram below)**

內　　　　初九　＿＿＿＿＿)　**FirstNiner**　　　　internal

卦辭 *(文王)* :	*Hexagram Text (King Wen)* :
屯 :	Sprouting :
元亨利貞	Primal Prosperity Favors having Integrity
勿用有攸往	Don't Act, Has Gentle Venture
利建侯	Favors Making of Lords

彖曰 *(孔子)* :	*Tuan says (Kongzi explains)* :
屯 :	Sprouting (difficulty) :
剛柔始交而難生	Yangs Yins Start Interaction And Difficulties Arise
動乎險中	Actions In Danger Centres
大亨貞	Great Prosperity, has Integrity
雷雨之動滿盈	Thunder Rain, Their Actions Filling Brimful
天造草昧	Heaven Creating Grass-chaotic in the Dim-of-dawn
宜建侯而不寧	Suitable for Creation of Lords In None Peaceful (conditions)

Comments:
Image: Thunder action below, Water danger above, Sprouting difficulty (seeds germination).
Symbolic: Focus FirstNiner action starts beneath 2 Yins, Niner5 in danger between 2 Yins.
Wen: Reflective in confinement, Integrity, slow venture, favors creation of Lords (became King).
Kongzi: Thunder Rain in actions, Heaven's creation chaotic, time for the rise of great Lords.
[Xu: 屯15難也,象艸木之初生屯然而難；昧137爽旦明也,一曰闇也]

象曰 *(孔子)* :	*HexagramSign says (Kongzi)* :
雲雷，屯	Clouds Thunder, Sprouting (difficulty before rain)
君子以經綸	Junzi By Thread-Loom (talent, handling chaotic threads)

Comments:
Clouds Thunder before Rain, Sprouting difficulty of seeds pushing above ground to meet Sun.
Like difficulty with chaotic threads at loom, Junzi has talent to tame chaos, be king like Wen.
[Xu: 經271織也，綸274青絲綬；綬274載維；維276車蓋維也]

爻辭 *(周公)* ：	*Liner Text (Zhougong)* ：
初九：	**FirstNiner:**
磐桓	Rocks Trees
利居貞，利建侯	Favors Staying Truthful, Favors Creation of Lords
象曰 *(孔子)* ：	*LinerSign says (Kongzi)* ：
雖磐桓	Big Rocks Trees (blocking difficulties)
志行正也	Wills Actions Correct that's
以貴下賤	As Nobility, be Lowly and Humble
大得民也	Greatly Winning-over Citizens that's (gain support)

Comments:

FirstNiner, lowly, meet blocking difficulties, staying truthful, situation favors creation of Lords.
Like Wen, been confined, nobility suffered, won citizen support, overthrew evil, finally be king.

六二：	**Sixer2:**
屯如邅如	Sprouting Like Wavering Like (not going forth)
乘馬班如	Riding Horses Splitting Like (disorderly)
匪寇婚媾	Unlawful Bandits, Marriage-Union
女子貞不字	Young Girl Purity No Salutation (not married)
十年乃字	10 Years Then Titled (married)
象曰 *(孔子)* ：	*LinerSign says (Kongzi)* ：
六二之難，乘剛也	Sixer2's Difficulties, Riding Yang that's (atop FirstNiner)
十年乃字，反常也	10 Years Then Titled, Return to Normalcy that's

Comments:

Sixer2 weak, atop and troubled by FirstNiner's proposal, hesitant of going to partner Niner5.
Sixer2, right position, centre, resisted Difficulty, 10 years later married Niner5, Norms returned.

[Xu: 亶111多穀 ；班14分瑞玉 ；匪268器似竹筐 ；寇68暴 ；婚259婦家娶以昏時; 媾259重婚]

六三：	**Sixer3:**
即鹿无虞，惟入于林中	Wild Deer Not Tame, Thinking of Entering Into Forest Inside
君子幾不如舍，往吝	Junzi Alerted, No Better, Abandon, Venture be Grief
象曰 *(孔子)* ：	*LinerSign says (Kongzi)* ：
即鹿无虞，以從禽也	Wild Deer Not Tame, Has Joined other Beasts
君子舍之，往吝窮也	Junzi Abandoned It, Venture be Shamed, Nothing-to-gain

Comments:

Sixer3, weak, chases wild deer in forest, alert to danger, better abandon, else comes to grief.

六四：	**Sixer4:**
乘馬班如	Riding Horses Splitting Like (disorderly forward)
求婚媾，往吉	Request Marriage Union, Venture Auspicious
无不利	None Not Favorable
象曰 *(孔子)* ：	*LinerSign says (Kongzi)* ：
求而往，明也	Request And Venture, Enlightened

Comments:

Sixer4, riding horses disorderly forward, as cannot forward to union with Premier Niner5.
Enlightened, then humbly descend to marry rightful partner FirstNiner below, Auspicious.

九五：	**Niner5:**
屯其膏	Sprouting Its Meat
小貞吉，大貞凶	Small Truth Auspicious, Big Truth Ominous
象曰 *(孔子)*：	*LinerSign says (Kongzi) :*
屯其膏	Sprouting Its Meat (wealth)
施未光也	Bestowing Not Shining that's (not sharing with Citizens)

Comments:
Niner5 has meat, shares Small with cronies Auspicious, not share Big with citizens, Ominous.
Alluding to evil King Zhou's "wine pool, meat forest" with cronies, lost Citizens lost Kingdom.
[Xu: 膏67肥也；肥90多肉]

上六：	**TopSixer:**
乘馬班如	Riding Horses, Half-hearted Like
泣血漣如	Sobbing Blood, Waves Like
象曰 *(孔子)*：	*LinerSign says (Kongzi) :*
泣血漣如	Sobbing Blood in Waves
何可長也	How Can Long-lasting, that's

Comments:
TopSixer, weak, no partner, already top, above venture to nowhere, only has worries and fear.
End of Sprouting Difficulty, sobbing blood, this situation cannot last long, that's.
[Xu: 漣230大波爲瀾或从連]

Conclusions:
Sprouting (Hexagram 03), Thunder Trigram below and Water Trigram above.
Image: Thunder Action beneath Water Danger, Sprouting beans' difficulty breaking surface.
Symbolic: Yang Yin interactions, FirstNiner stirring beneath 2 Yins, Niner5 trapped by 2 Yins.

King Wen:
Reflective, confinement difficulty, stays Quiet, be Truthful, slow Venture, finally emerges King.

Zhougong:
FirstNiner, like Wen, noble in lowly position, stays Truthful, Citizens' support, emerges Lord.
Sixer2, split between FirstNiner and partner, 10 years later married Niner5, back to Normalcy.
Sixer3, misplaced, weak, no partner, chasing deers, danger alert, to abandon No Grief.
Sixer4, difficulty with Niner5, humbly venture to partner FirstNiner, enlightened Auspicious.
Niner5, like evil Zhou, cronyism with "wine pool, meat forest", lost Citizens, Ominous.
TopSixer, weak, no partner, atop nowhere to venture, only worries and fear, not lasting.
Sprouting: FirstNiner and Niner5, reflective of King Wen's and evil King Zhou's lives.

Kongzi:
Sprouting Difficulty before Rain, time Junzi (Gentleman) exercise talents, put Chaos to Order.
(屯：見而不失其居，雜卦) (Sprouting: Visible Not Lost Its Position - Misc. 10th Wing)

Lessons learned (Sprouting Hex. 03):
Highlighting individuals to expect and to surmount difficulties at initial stage for any endeavour.
Chaotic time is also time for Great Talents to emerge to achieve Greatness, establishing Orders.

（第四卦）　蒙　　　　　　　　Ignorance (Hexagram 04)

外		上九	_______)	**TopNiner**	**external**
艮　（山，上卦）		六五	__ __)	**Sixer5**	**Gen　(Mountain, Trigram above)**
		六四	__ __)	**Sixer4**	
		六三	__ __)	**Sixer3**	
坎　（水，下卦）		九二	_______)	**Niner2**	**Kan　(Water, Trigram below)**
內		初六	__ __)	**FirstSixer**	**internal**

卦辭 *(文王)：*	***Hexagram Text (King Wen) :***
蒙：	Ignorance :
亨	Prosperity
匪我求童蒙	Not I who Request of Child Ignorance
童蒙求我	Child Ignorance Requests of Me
初筮告，再三瀆	First Divination Inform, Again Thrice Ditch
瀆則不告，利貞	Ditch Then Not Inform, Favors Truthfulness

象曰 *(孔子)：*	***Tuan says (Kongzi explains) :***
蒙，山下有險	Ignorance, Mountain Below Has Danger
險而止，蒙	Danger Then Stop, Ignorance
蒙亨，以亨行時中也	Ignorance Prosperity, With Prosperity Action Time Centre
匪我求童蒙	Not I who Request of Child Ignorance
童蒙求我，志應也	Child Ignorance Requests of Me, Wills Responding that's
初筮告，以剛中也	First Divination Inform, With Yang Centre (ref. Niner2)
再三瀆	Thrice Again, then Ditch
瀆則不告，瀆蒙也	Ditch Then Not Inform, Ditch Ignorance that's
蒙以養正，聖功也	Ignorance To Nurture with Correctness, Sage-hood that's

Comments:
Image: Area of Ignorance, trap between Water (Danger) below and Mountain (Blocking) above.
Symbolic: Focus Niner2, Yang teacher among the Ignorance of Yins and partner Sixer5.
Wen: Child Ignorance requests, first inform, no after thrice requests, favors Truthfulness.
Kongzi: Nurturing Correctness in the Ignorance, this is achievement of Sage-hood.

[Xu: 蒙26王女也；筮96易卦用蓍；蓍20蒿屬生十歲百莖易以爲數；瀆232溝,水瀆廣四尺深四尺]

象曰 *(孔子)：*	***HexagramSign says (Kongzi) :***
山下出泉，蒙	Mountain Below Emerges Water-spring, Ignorance
君子以果行育德	Junzi With Productive Action, Nurturing Virtues.

Comments:
Mountain below emerges spring-clear Water, Ignorance (or Innocence).
Junzi with productive action, nurturing virtues (starting with Child Innocence).

爻辭 (周公)：	**Liner Text (Zhougong) :**
初六：	**FirstSixer:**
發蒙	Dispel Ignorance
利用刑人	Favors Using Criminal People
用説桎梏	Using Relief of Leg-shackle Hand-shackle (Ignorance-freed)
以往吝	And Going-forward with Shame (and be criminal no more)
象曰 *(孔子)* ：	*LinerSign says (Kongzi) :*
利用刑人，以正法也	Favors Using Criminal People, By Justice of the Laws that's

Comments:
Dispel Ignorance at low level, use Punishment deterrence on criminals, by Justice of the Laws.
After released of shackles, lessons learned, going-forth knows shame, and be criminal no more.
[Xu: 發270躲也； 桎125足械；梏125手械；刑92到也]

九二：	**Niner2:**
包蒙，吉	Accommodating Ignorance, Auspicious
納婦，吉	Marry Woman, Auspicious (ref. Sixer5)
子克家	Son Supporting Family (ref. Niner2)
象曰 *(孔子)* ：	*LinerSign says (Kongzi) :*
子克家，剛柔接也	Son Supporting Family, Yang Yin Connecting that's

Comments:
Niner2 centre, the wisdom below accommodating Ignorance among the Yins, Auspicious.
Marry partner Sixer5 above, the son below, support family, dispel Ignorance, twice Auspicious.
[Xu: 納271絲溼納納也； 克143肩也象屋下刻木之形, 與人肩膊之義, 通能勝此物]

六三：	Sixer3:
勿用取女	Don't Act to Take Girl
見金夫	See Golden Person (wealthy)
不有躬	Not Has Body (lose chastity)
无攸利	No Easy Gain
象曰 *(孔子)* ：	*LinerSign says (Kongzi) :*
勿用取女	Don't take Action to Marry this Girl
行不順也	Conduct Not Proper that's

Comments:
Sixer3, Yin misplaced, not centre, Ignorant, met wealthy man, lost chastity.
Conduct not proper, don't marry her, this is no easy gain of a good wife.

六四：	**Sixer4:**
困蒙，吝	Trapped Ignorance, Shame
象曰 *(孔子)* ：	*LinerSign says (Kongzi) :*
困蒙之吝	Trapped Ignorance, Its Shame
獨遠實也	Uniquely Faraway from Solid that's (ref. Yang Niner2)

Comments:
Sixer4, Yin between 2 Yins, isolated from Yang Niner2, is Trapped Ignorance, what a Shame.
Solids are Yang liners, here in Ignorance are teachers for dispelling Ignorance.

六五：	**Sixer5:**
童蒙，吉	Child Ignorance, Auspicious
象曰 *(孔子)* ：	*LinerSign says (Kongzi) :*
童蒙之吉	Child Ignorance, Its Auspicious
順以巽也	Docile With Xun (Wind) that's (learning like a breeze)

Comments:
Sixer5, premier position, is Child Ignorance, is Child Innocence, open to be taught, Auspicious.
Also Sixer5 is partner of Niner2 and neighbor of TopNiner, 2 Yangs for dispelling Ignorance.

上九：	**TopNiner:**
擊蒙	Hitting Ignorance
不利爲寇	Not Favor Being Bandits
利禦寇	Favors Fending-off Bandits
象曰 *(孔子)* ：	*LinerSign says (Kongzi) :*
利用禦寇，上下順也	Favors Actions Fending-off Bandits, Above Below in Accord that's

Comments:
TopNiner, top Yang, too strong in management action with bandit-like tactics Hitting Ignorance.
Better TopNiner be gentle, like fending-off bandits, then accord achieved with above and below.
[Xu: 擊257支也 ； 支67小擊也 ； 禦9祀也 ； 祀8祭無已也]

Conclusions:
Ignorance (Hexagram 04) Water Trigram below and Mountain Trigram above.
Image: Water (danger) below, Mountain (blocking) above, in-between area of Ignorance.
Symbolic: Focus Niner2 and TopNiner, 2 Yangs task with dispelling Ignorance of the Yins.

King Wen:
Maybe not welcome so don't go to teach, but let Child Ignorance come with request, then help.
After thrice requesting means not productive then don't no help; be Truthful gets Prosperity.

Zhougong:
FirstSixer, lowly, to dispel Ignorance to mete out Punishment, uphold Justice of the Laws.
Niner2, accommodating Ignorance, teaching the Yins with compassionate education.
Sixer3, misplaced Ignorance, lost chastity to the wealthy, case of education failure.
Sixer4, trapped Ignorance between 2 Yins, isolated from Yang teachers, missed education.
Sixer5, important to start young with Child Innocence, to receive redouble education.
TopNiner, fierce teacher hitting Ignorance hard like a bandit, wrong tactic for education.
Ignorance: at various levels, to dispel with various tactics in educational provisions.

Kongzi:
Dispelling Ignorance with cultivation of Correctness, is an achievement of Sage-hood.
Face with Ignorance, Junzi (Gentleman) cultivates virtues with productive actions.
(蒙：雜而著，雜卦傳)　　　(Ignorance : confuse and suffering - Miscellaneous 10th Wing)

Lessons (Ignorance Hex.04) :
Don't go around teaching others, rather let those who wish to learn, come and ask.
Education, important with Child Innocence, starting young with redoubling efforts.
Education should not be with force tactics, best with compassionate methods.

(第五卦) 需　　　　　　　　**Supplies (Hexagram 05)**

<pre>
外　　　　上六　__ __)　TopSixer　　　　external
坎 (水, 上卦)　九五　_____)　Niner5　　Kan (Water, Trigram above)
　　　　　　六四　__ __)　Sixer4

　　　　　　九三　_____)　Niner3
乾 (天, 下卦)　九二　_____)　Niner2　　Qian (Heaven, Trigram below)
　　　　　　初九　_____)　FirstNiner　　internal
</pre>

卦辭 *(文王)* ：	***Hexagram Text (King Wen)* :**
需：	Supplies :
有孚，光亨	Has Trust, Bright Prosperity
貞吉，利涉大川	Integrity Auspicious, Favors Venturing Big Rivers

象曰 *(孔子)* ：	***Tuan says (Kongzi explains)* :**
需，須也	Supplies, Needs that's
險在前也	Danger In Front that's
剛健而不陷	Yang Strength Hence Not Trapped
其義不困窮矣	Its Justice, Not Trapped in Poverty that's
需，有孚	Supplies, Has Trust
光亨，貞吉	Bright Prosperity, Integrity Auspicious
位乎天位	Positioned In Heaven's Position
以正中也	With Correctness Uprightness that's
利涉大川	Favors Venturing Big Rivers
往有功也	Going-forth Has Achievement, that's

Comments:
Image: Water above Heaven, Supplies of Rain for Harvests.
Wen: Supplies has Trust, Transparency, Prosperity, Integrity, Auspiciousness.
Kongzi: Supplies are Needs, Danger in Front, with Shining Trust, not trapped in Corruption.
[Xu: 需242須也,遇雨不進止須也；須184面毛也,....借爲所須之須]

象曰 *(孔子)* ：	***HexagramSign says (Kongzi)* :**
雲上於天，需	Clouds Rise To Heaven, Supplies
君子以飲食宴樂	Junzi With Drink and Food, makes Feast and Merriment

Comments:
Clouds rising up Heaven, Supplies of Rain-clouds for a good Harvest.
Junzi with Food and Drink for Body, makes Merriment Feast for Spiritual Well-being.

爻辭 *(周公)* ：	*Liner Text (Zhougong) :*
初九：	**FirstNiner:**
需于郊	Supplies At Countryside
利用恆，无咎	Favors Using Perseverance, No Faults
象曰 *(孔子)* ：	*LinerSign says (Kongzi) :*
需于郊	Supplies At Countryside
不犯難行也	Not Disturbed by Difficult Transportation, that's
利用恆无咎，不失常也	Favors Using Perseverance No Faults, Not Losing Norms, that's

Comments:

FirstNiner, early stage, Supplies in Countryside.
Not disturbed by Difficult Transport on land, may resolve using boats, No Faults.
[Xu: 恆286常也,从心从舟在二之閒上下心以舟施,恆也]

九二：	**Niner2:**
需于沙	Supplies On Sand
小有言，終吉	Small Has Words, Ending Auspicious
象曰 *(孔子)* ：	*LinerSign says (Kongzi) :*
需于沙，衍在中也	Supplies On Sand, Canals In Centre that's
雖小有言	Although Small (people) Has Words (complaints)
以吉終也	With Auspicious Ending, that's

Comments:

Niner2 transporting Supplies across Sand, and Small people have complaints.
There are canals through the desert land, and the Ending is Auspicious.
[Xu: 衍232溝水行也；溝232水瀆廣四尺深四尺]

九三：	**Niner3:**
需于泥，致寇至	Supplies In Mud, Causing Bandits A-coming
象曰 *(孔子)* ：	*LinerSign says (Kongzi) :*
需于泥，災在外也	Supplies In Mud (mired), Disaster Is Outside, that's
自我致寇	From Myself Causing Bandits (appearance)
敬慎不敗也	Respect Caution then Not Defeated, that's

Comments

Niner3, Yang, rash action causing Supplies to mire in Mud and appearance of Bandits.
Admitting own mistakes, has Respects and take precautions, finally No Failure, that's.

六四：	**Sixer4:**
需于血	Supplies In Blood
出自穴	Emerging from Own Cave (store)
象曰 *(孔子)* ：	*LinerSign says (Kongzi) :*
需于血	Supplies In Blood (under attack)
順以聽也	Docile And Listening, that's

Comments:

Sixer4, weak Yin, guarding Supplies Store, under Bloody attack.
Sixer4 correct position, docile, willing to listen to advice for defence, finally save the day.

九五：	Niner5:
需于酒食，貞吉	Supplies In Wining Dining, Integrity Auspicious
象曰 (孔子)：	*LinerSign says (Kongzi) :*
酒食貞吉	Wining Dining with Integrity, Auspicious
以中正也	With Centre (Upright) Correct (conduct), that's

Comments:
Niner5 King, Upright, Correct conduct, sharing Wine and Food with Citizens, Auspicious.

上六：	TopSixer:
入于穴	Enter Into Cave (store)
有不速之客	Has Un-invited Such Guests
三人來	3 Persons Came
敬之終吉	Respect Them, Ending Auspicious
象曰 (孔子)：	*LinerSign says (Kongzi) :*
不速之客來	Not Invited These Guests Came
敬之終吉	Respect Them Ending Auspicious
雖不當位，未大失也	Although Not Correct Position, No Big Loss, that's

Comments:
TopSixer, weak Yin, at top level of Supplies, but unlike King, not in position of power.
In Store, found 3 Un-invited Guests, treated them with Respect, thus preventing Big Loss.
[Xu: 速40疾也]

Conclusions:
Supplies (Hexagram 05): Heaven Trigram below and Water Trigram above.
Image: Water (Clouds) rising above Heaven, producing rain for crops, Supplies.
Symbolic: 3 Yangs (Heaven) transporting Supplies, meeting Danger (Water) all the way.

King Wen:
Supplies, has Trust Transparency with Integrity Auspicious, hence Favoring Big Ventures

Zhougong:
FirstNiner: Supplies at Countryside, favors using lowly slow boats for transport, No Faults.
Niner2: Supplies on Sand, transport on canals, Small people complain, Ending Auspicious.
Niner3: Supplies mired in mud, rash action invites bandits, respectfully cautious, Ends Well.
Sixer4: Supplies in Blood, Yin positioned, docile, listening, quell Rebellion, emerged a Survivor.
Niner5: Supplies for Wining and Dining, King Upright shares with citizens, Truly Auspicious.
TopSixer: 3 Un-invited Guests in Supplies store, respect them, no big loss, Ending Auspicious.
Supplies: Transport from countryside to King's store, Supplies need be guarded all the way.

Kongzi:
Strength (Heaven), meeting Danger (Water), Yangs have Trust, be Upright, not be trapped.
Junzi, has Wine and Food for nourishing the body, Merry Feasting for spiritual Well-being.
(需：不進也，雜卦傳)　　(Supplies : not advancing that's - Miscellaneous 10th Wing)

Lessons (Supplies Hex.05):
Wine and Dine, nourishment of body, merry feasting for spiritual Well-being, No Faults.
Supplies are always in danger, hence best be shared with Respect, Trust and Transparency.

(第六卦) 訟　　　　　　　　**Litigation (Hexagram 06)**

外	上九	＿＿＿)	**TopNiner**		external
乾（天，上卦）	九五	＿＿＿)	**Niner5**	**Qian（Heaven, Trigram above）**	
	九四	＿＿＿)	**Niner4**		
	六三	＿＿ ＿＿)	**Sixer3**		
坎（水，下卦）	九二	＿＿＿)	**Niner2**	**Kan（Water, Trigram below）**	
内	初六	＿＿ ＿＿)	**FirstSixer**		internal

卦辭 *(文王)*：	***Hexagram Text (King Wen) :***
訟：	Litigation :
有孚窒	Has Trust Blockade
惕中吉，終凶	Respect Upright Auspicious, Finally Ominous
利見大人	Favors Seeing Great Person
不利涉大川	Not Favor Venturing Big River
彖曰 *(孔子)*：	***Tuan says (Kongzi explains) :***
訟，上剛下險	Litigation, Above Strength (Heaven), Below Danger (Water)
險而健，訟	Danger To Strength, Litigation
訟有孚窒	Litigation Has Trust Blockade
惕中吉	Respect Upright Auspicious
剛來而得中也	Yang Cometh And Get Centre, that's (ref. Niner2)
終凶	Ending Ominous
訟不可成也	Litigation Not Allow to Form, that's
利見大人	Favors Seeing Great Person
尚中正也	Aspire to be Upright and Correct that's
不利涉大川	Not Favor Venturing Big River
入于淵也	Enter Into Ocean-depth, that's

Comments:
Image: Water flows down, Heaven rises up, no interaction, Litigation; only Niner5 right position.
Wen: Litigation, has Trust Blockade, with Respect Upright Auspicious, but in Finality Ominous.
Kongzi: Above Strength pressure subordinates, below Danger of insubordination, Litigation.
[Xu: 訟56爭也,日謂訟 ；窒153塞也 ；惕223敬也]

象曰 *(孔子)*：	***HexagramSign says (Kongzi) :***
天與水違行，訟	Heaven And Water Opposing Flow, Litigation
君子以作事謀始	Junzi, Working With Task, first Plan Beginning

Comments:
In Heaven Sun, Moon, Stars go West, Water below Rivers go East, opposite flows, Litigation.
Junzi on task, first plan beginning, alert to clash of interests, nipping Litigation in the bud.

爻辭 (周公)：	*Liner Text (Zhougong)* :
初六：	**FirstSixer**
不永所事	Not Prolonging Whatever Affair
小有言，終吉	Small Has Words, Ending Auspicious
象曰 (孔子)：	*LinerSign says (Kongzi)* :
不永所事，訟不可長也	Not Prolong Whatever Affair, Litigation Not Allow to Grow, that's
雖小有言，其辯明也	Though Small Has Words, The Argument Clear, that's

Comments:

FirstSixer weak Small, though has good arguments not prolonging Litigation, ending Auspicious.

[Xu: 永240長也象水至理之長；至239水脈也；辯309治也]

九二：	**Niner2:**
不克訟，歸而逋	Not Winning Litigation, Homing And Lost (disappear)
其邑人三百户，无眚	The Town People, 300 Households, No Calamity
象曰 (孔子)：	*LinerSign says (Kongzi)* :
不克訟	Not Winning Litigation
歸逋竄也	Return-home Lost and Fallen that's (drop into oblivion)
自下訟上，患至掇也	From Below Litigate against Above, Troubles Come Self-pickup

Comments:

Niner2, Yin placed, subordinate started Litigation with counterpart Niner5, the strong authority.
Lost, returned and fell into oblivion personally, but home-Town of 300 households no calamity.

[Xu: 逋41亾也；眚73目病生翳也；竄153墜也；掇255拾取也]

六三：	**Sixer3:**
食舊德，貞，屬終吉	Consume Old Virtues, Integrity, Grave but Ending Auspicious
或從王事，无成	Or be Follower of King's Affairs, No Achievement
象曰 (孔子)：	*LinerSign says (Kongzi)* :
食舊德	Consume Old Virtues (inherited credits)
從上吉也	Following Above Auspicious, that's

Comments

Sixer3, Yang placed, weak between 2 Yangs, living on old inherited credits, situation Grave.
With Integrity be Follower of King, no achievement No Litigation, but finally Auspicious.

九四：	**Niner4:**
不克訟	Not Winning Litigation
復即命，渝	Turn-back to Accord with Destiny, Changes
安貞，吉	Quietly Truthfully, Auspicious
象曰 (孔子)：	*LinerSign says (Kongzi)* :
復即命	Turn-back to Accord with Reasons
渝安貞，不失也	Changes Quietly Sincerely, Not Lost that's

Comments:

Niner4, Yang not centre contentious, Yin positioned weak cannot win Litigation.
Changes, to Turn-back to accord with Right-values, so not lost, quietly sincerely Auspicious.

[Xu: 渝237變汙也；汙237人液也]

九五：	**Niner5:**
訟	Litigation
元吉	Primally Auspicious
象曰 *(孔子)：*	***LinerSign says (Kongzi) :***
訟元吉	Litigation Primally Auspicious
以中正也	With Centre (Upright), Correctness, that's

Comments:
Niner5 is the Great Person to see, the Justice in Litigation, Primally Auspicious.
Premier, Yang in Yang, only one in correct position, centre Upright, strong to administer justice.

上九：	**TopNiner:**
或錫之鞶帶	Or be Awarded With Broad Belt
終朝三褫之	End of Day, 3 times Stripped of It
象曰 *(孔子)：*	***LinerSign says (Kongzi) :***
以訟受服	With Litigation Awarded Decoration
亦不足敬也	But Not Worthy of Respect, that's

Comments:
TopNiner Yang, very contentious at upper limit of Litigation, awarded with Broad Belt.
At end of the day, 3 times stripped of Decor, hence winning by Litigation is not respectable,
[Xu: 錫293銀鉛之間；賜130予，鞶60大帶也，朝……，褫172奪衣，奪77手持隹失之]

Conclusions:
Litigation (Hexagram 06): of Water Trigram below and Heaven Trigram above.
Image: Water flow East, Heaven revolve West, only Niner5 right position, contentious.
Symbolic: self Danger (Water) below, opposing Strength (Heaven) above, contentious sign.

King Wen:
Litigation has Trust and Blockade, see Great Person, resolves with Respect Justice, Auspicious.
Else Endings always Ominous, and Litigation time is missing time for great ventures.

Zhougong:
FirstSixer: small Yin, not to Prolong Litigation, but has Clear Arguments, Ending Auspicious.
Niner2: lost Litigation to Niner5, self-pick Oblivion, but Town of 300 household No Calamity.
Sixer3: wrong placed, lives on past Credits, King's Follower no Litigation, Ending Auspicious.
Niner4: contentious Yang, Yin position cannot win Litigation, turn-back quietly, Auspicious.
Niner5: Yang Premier, Centre position Upright, Great Litigation Judge, Primally Auspicious.
TopNiner: Yang at Litigation peak, Decorated 3 times then stripped, Winnings not Respectable.
Litigation: Describes endings of Litigation at different levels of society for different reasons.

Kongzi:
Litigation, Top pressurise subordinates, and subjects serve with dangerous insubordination.
Junzi plans well at start of task, to mitigate all conflict of interests, to avoid Litigation later.
(訟：不親也，雜卦傳)　　　(Litigation : not loving that's - Miscellaneous 10th Wing)

Lessons learned (Litigation Hex.06):
Junzi, alert to clash of interest, nip litigation in the bud at start of planning a task.
If unavoidable in defence, opt for early settlement, as in its finality Litigation is Ominous.

（第七卦）師　　　　　　　　**Army (Hexagram 07)**

<pre>
外   上六   __ __) TopSixer   external
坤 (地，上卦) 六五   __ __) Sixer5   Kun (Earth, Trigram above)
          六四   __ __) Sixer4

          六三   __ __) Sixer3
坎 (水，下卦) 九二   _____) Niner2   Kan (Water, Trigram below)
          內   初六   __ __) FirstSixer   internal
</pre>

卦辭 *(文王)*：	*Hexagram Text (King Wen) :*
師：	Army:
貞	Trusted
丈人，吉	Elder Person, Auspicious
无咎	No Faults

彖曰 *(孔子) :*	*Tuan says (Kongzi explains) :*
師	Army
衆也	People that's
貞，正也	Trusted, Upright that's
能以衆正	Can Make the People Upright
可以王矣	Can Be King indeed
剛中而應	Strong (Niner2) Centre Has Responder (Sixer5)
行險而順	Treading Danger with Ease
以此毒天下而民從之	By This Poison The World And Citizens Follow King
吉又何咎	Auspicious, But What Faults?

Comments:
Image: Army of 5 Yins subject to the Command of Niner2, the only Yang.
Wen: Army ought be leaded by an Elder who is Upright and Trusted, Auspicious.
Kongzi: Army is Poison, but King needs an Upright Citizen Army for defence, No Faults.
[Xu: 師127二千五百人爲師]

象曰 *(孔子) :*	*HexagramSign says (Kongzi) :*
地中有水，師	Earth Inside Has Water, Army
君子以容民畜衆	Junzi by accommodating Citizens, Caring for the Masses

Comments:
Water (Danger) inside Earth (Support), embedded Army of Citizens in mother Earth.
Junzi builds a citizen Army by being Compassionate and Caring for the Masses.

爻辭 *(周公)* :	*Liner Text (Zhougong) :*
初六 :	**FirstSixer:**
師出以律	Army Deploy With Discipline
否臧凶	Not Virtuous Ominous
象曰 *(孔子)* :	*LinerSign says (Kongzi) :*
出師以律	Deploying Army With Discipline
失律凶也	Lost Discipline, Danger that's

Comments:
Indeed an Army of non-Virtuous people and without Discipline is Dangerous.

九二 :	**Niner2:**
在師中，吉	In Army Upright, Auspicious
无咎	No Faults
王三錫命	King Thrice Bestowed Appointments
象曰 *(孔子)* :	*LinerSign says (Kongzi) :*
在師中吉	In Army Upright Auspicious
承天寵也	Receives Heaven's Favor that's
王三錫命	King Thrice Bestowed Commandership
懷萬邦也	Caring of All States that's

Comments:
Niner2 Upright in the Army Auspicious and King Thrice made Commander-in-chief.
Receiving Favors of Heaven and King, Niner2 feels responsible for well-being of all states.

六三 :	**Sixer3:**
師或輿尸	Army, Or Carting Corpses
凶	Ominous
象曰 *(孔子)* :	*LinerSign says (Kongzi) :*
師或輿尸	Army, Or Cartloads of Corpses
大无功也	High (position), No Achievements that's

Comments
Sixer3, weak in Yang position (wrong placing), not centre (not Upright), Ominous.
High position in Army but no success on battlefields, bring back corpses by the cartloads,

六四 :	**Sixer4:**
師左次	Army, Supporting Auxiliary
无咎	No Faults
象曰 *(孔子)* :	*LinerSign says (Kongzi) :*
左次无咎	Supporting Auxiliary, No Faults
未失常也	Not Lost Norms (orderly retreat) that's

Comments:
Sixer4 weak, right-placed in supporting Army, retreats orderly as situation demand, no Faults.

六五：	**Sixer5:**
田有禽	Fields Have Flying-birds
利執言，无咎	Favors Seizing (rights of) Speech, no Faults
長子帥師	Elder Son, Army Commander-in-chief
弟子輿尸，貞凶	Brother Carting Corpses, Truly Ominous
象曰 (孔子)：	*LinerSign says (Kongzi) :*
長子帥師	Elder Son (Niner2) Commander-in-chief of Army
以中行也	With Upright Conduct that's
弟子輿尸，使不當也	Brother (Sixer3) Carting Corpses, Deployment Not Right that's

Comments:
'Fields have Flying-birds' symbolic of prosperity, coming of invaders to steal crops of labor.
Sixer5 Upright, not war starter, has Rights of Speech to say "No" to invaders of his fields.
Deployment of Upright Elder son Niner2 as Commander of Army, no Faults.
Sixer3, not Upright, high placement in Army, Ominous causing cartloads of casualties.

上六：	**TopSixer:**
大君有命，開國承家	Great King Has Orders, Founding States Building Families
小人勿用	Small People Not Use (not deploy)
象曰 (孔子)：	*LinerSign says (Kongzi) :*
大君有命，以正功也	Great King Has Orders, With Fairness (establish) Credits
小人勿用，必亂邦也	Small People Not Use, Certain (to cause) Chaotic States

Comments:
End of Army campaign, Great King issues orders, determining Credits, awarding Lands, Titles.
Small People are to be excluded from power-sharing, as certain to cause chaos in States.

Conclusions:
Army (Hexagram 07): is formed of Water Trigram below and Earth Trigram above.
Image: Army of 5 Yins in support of the only Yang, Niner2 as Commander.
Symbolic: Inside Earth (Support) is Water (Danger), embedded Army.

King Wen:
Army best be led by an Elder with Integrity, then Auspicious, no Faults.

Zhougong:
FirstSixer: Army not of virtuous people, without Discipline, Ominous.
Niner2: centre position, Upright in Army, Thrice conferred Commandership, Auspicious
Sixer3: not Upright, in Yang position restive, suffering cartloads of Casualties Ominous.
Sixer4: gentle, right placing in Support Army, as situation demands retreat Orderly, no Faults.
Sixer5: deploys Defence Army, Upright Niner2 in Command, Sixer3 wrong placing, Ominous.
TopSixer: end of Army campaign, award lands/titles on merits, not for chaotic Small people.
Army : describes the important of leadership qualities and their consequences on the battlefields.

Kongzi:
Army is Poison, but we need an upright citizen Army for defence.

(師：憂，雜卦傳)	(Army : worrying - Miscellaneous 10th Wing)

Lessons learned (Army Hex. 07):
Army is poison, to be deployed only in defence.
With Care and Compassion, to build a Virtuous Citizen Army for Defence.

（第八卦）　比　　　　　　　　　**Neighbors (Hexagram 08)**

外	上六	__ __)	**TopSixer**		**external**
坎（水，上卦）	九五	______)	**Niner5**	**Kan**	**(Water, Trigram above)**
	六四	__ __)	**Sixer4**		
	六三	__ __)	**Sixer3**		
坤（地，下卦）	六二	__ __)	**Sixer2**	**Kun**	**(Earth, Trigram below)**
内	初六	__ __)	**FirstSixer**		**internal**

卦辭 *(文王)* ：	***Hexagram Text (King Wen) :***
比：	Neighbors :
吉，原筮元永貞	Auspicious, First Divination Primal Everlasting Truth
无咎	No Faults
不寧方來	Not Peaceful Quarters A-coming
後夫凶	Last Person, Ominous

象曰 *(孔子)：*	***Tuan says (Kongzi explains) :***
比，吉也	Neighbors, Auspicious that's
比輔也	Neighbors Support that's
下順從也	Subordinates, Docile Obedient that's
原筮元永貞无咎	Original Divination Primal Everlasting Truth, No Faults
以剛中也	With Strong Centre that's (ref. Niner5 Yang Upright)
不寧方來	Not Peaceful Quarters A-coming
上下應也	Above Below Responding that's (ref. the 5 Yins)
後夫凶	Last Person Ominous (ref. TopSixer)
其道窮也	Its Way Terminal that's (conduct not virtuous)

Comments:
Image: Water on Earth, closely connected, Neighbors; below and above Yins support Niner5.
Wen: trusted Auspicious, welcomes troubled Neighbors, warns that last to come Ominous.
Kongzi: Neighbors supportive with docility lasting Truth, but if person lost virtue, Ominous.

[Xu: 比169密也二人爲,從反,從爲 ；輔303人頰車也 ；頰182面旁 ；寧150安也]

象曰 *(孔子)：*	***HexagramSign says (Kongzi) :***
地上有水，比	Earth Above Has Water, Neighborhood
先王以建萬國親諸侯	Past Kings To Build Many Kingdoms, Befriend Feudal Lords

Comments:
Earth above has Water, Neighbors with close connectivity.
Likewise past Kings created kingdoms by befriending the feudal lords to gain support.

爻辭 (周公) :	**Liner Text (Zhougong) :**
初六 :	**FirstSixer:**
有孚比之	Has Trust Neighboring It (be neighborly)
无咎	No Faults
有孚盈缶	Has Trust Filling Earthen-ware
終來有他，吉	Finally A-coming Has Him, Auspicious (ref. above Sixer2)
象曰 (孔子) :	**LinerSign says (Kongzi) :**
比之初長	Neighborliness Its Early Growth
有他吉也	Has Trust Auspicious that's

Comments:
FirstSixer, lowly Yin has good start in neighborliness with Sixer2, No Fault.
As Sixer2, right position, centre Full of Trust, coming from above, Auspicious.
[Xu: 缶109瓦器所以盛酒漿]

六二 :	**Sixer2:**
比之自內	Neighborly with It From Within
貞吉	Truly Auspicious
象曰 (孔子) :	**LinerSign says (Kongzi) :**
比之自內	Neighborly with It From Within (ref. partner Niner5)
不自失也	Not Self Lost that's (ref. Sixer2)

Comments:
Sixer2 only Yin with partner, that's Niner5 like a Neighbor from within, Truly Auspicious.
Sixer2, right position, centre upright, will not lose own virtuosity in the shadow of Niner5.

六三 :	**Sixer3:**
比之匪人	Neighborly With Bad People
象曰 (孔子) :	**LinerSign says (Kongzi) :**
比之匪人	Neighborly with Bad People
不亦傷乎	Not Also Hurting that's!

Comments:
Sixer3 weak Yin, misplaced not centre, Neighbors above and below all Yins, negative influences.
TopSixer co-partner also a Yin, so be warned, such situation is certainly harmful.

六四 :	**Sixer4:**
外比之	Outward Neighboring It (ref. Niner5 above)
貞吉	Truly Auspicious
象曰 (孔子) :	**LinerSign says (Kongzi) :**
外比於賢	Outward Neighboring With the Virtuous
以從上也	Be Follower of Above that's (ref. Niner5)

Comments:
Niner5 is Yang Neighbor above, Premier position, centre, a truly virtuous person.
Sixer4 correct position, a weak Yin Follower of Niner5, Truly Auspicious.

九五：	**Niner5:**
顯比	Luminary Neighbor (king neighbor)
王用三驅	King Uses 3-directional Herding (in hunting)
失前禽	Lost Front Animals
邑人不誡，吉	Country Men Not Faze, Auspicious
象曰 *(孔子)：*	*LinerSign says (Kongzi) :*
顯比之吉	Luminous Neighbor, Its Auspiciousness
位正中也	Position Correct Centre that's
舍逆取順	Let-go the On-coming, Take the Orderly
失前禽也	Lost Front Animals that's
邑人不誡，上使中也	Country Men Not Face, Above Deployment Upright that's

Comments:
In hunt, 3-sided herding, open-front to allow escape, so that no desperate animals charge back.
Niner5 King, neighbor with safe hunting deployment, hence country men not faze, Auspicious.
[Xu: 顯184頭明飾也；驅201馬馳也；馳201大驅也；逆40迎也；順182理也；誡52敕也]

上六：	**TopSixer:**
比之无首，凶	Neighboring It No Beginning, Ominous
象曰 *(孔子)：*	*LinerSign says (Kongzi) :*
比之无首，无所終也	Neighboring It No Beginning, then None For Ending that's

Comments:
TopSixer weak Yin at top, no more Neighbor above, hence no Beginning no Ending, Ominous.

Conclusions:
Neighbors (Hexagram 08): Earth Trigram below and Water Trigram above.
Image: Earth below and Water above flowing down, in close association as Neighbors.
Symbolic: Focus of Hexagram Niner5 lone Yang, with support of Yins from above and below.

King Wen:
The benevolent king, to whom people from all troubled Neighborhoods A-coming for support.
Auspicious, Primal Everlasting Truth, no Faults, but faraway stragglers who are late, Ominous.
Zhougong:
FirstSixer: Early trusting Neighbor No Fault, as having trustworthy Sixer2 Auspicious.
Sixer2: Right position, Upright, partner-Neighbor of Niner5 above, Auspicious.
Sixer3: Misplaced, not centre, all Yins above and below, a Neighborhood that is Harmful.
Sixer4: Right position, Neighboring virtuous Niner5 above, as Follower Truly Auspicious.
Niner5: Safe hunts with 3-sided herding allowing escapes, hence Citizens unfazed, Auspicious.
TopSixer: Weak, no Neighbors above, no beginning hence no ending, in isolation Ominous.
Neighbors: are generally good, 4 Auspiciousness versus 2 bad Neighborhoods.

Kongzi:
Neighbors, supportive with docility everlasting Truth, but when person lost virtues, Ominous.
Past Kings created kingdoms by going-out, befriending feudal lords to gain support.

(比：樂，雜卦傳)	(Neighbors : Joyous - Miscellaneous 10th Wing)

Lessons learned (Neighbors Hex.08) :
Neighborliness is generally Auspicious, giving support or befriending to gain support.
Between happy Neighbors, Trust and Truthfulness are of utmost importance.

（第九卦）小畜　　　　　　　　**Small Constraint (Hexagram 09)**

<pre>
外   上九   ________)   TopNiner   external
巽（風,上卦）   九五   ________)   Niner5   Xun （Wind, Trigram above）
               六四   __ __)   Sixer4

               九三   ________)   Niner3
乾（天,下卦）   九二   ________)   Niner2   Qian （Heaven, Trigram below）
內   初九   ________)   FirstNiner   internal
</pre>

卦辭 *(文王)* ：	***Hexagram Text (King Wen) :***
小畜：亨	Small Constraint: Prosperity
密雲不雨	Thick Clouds No Rain
自我西郊	From My Western Countryside

象曰 *(孔子)* ：	***Tuan says (Kongzi explains) :***
小畜	Small Constraint
柔得位也而上下應之	Gentle (Yin) Gets Position And Above Below Respond to It
曰小畜	Call-it Small Constraint
健而巽	Strength (Heaven) Then Xun (Wind)
剛中而志行乃亨	Strong (Yang) Centre And Wills Done Hence Prosperity
密雲不雨	Thick Clouds No Rain
尚往也	Aspires Going-forth that's
自我西郊	From My Western Countryside
施未行也	Preparation Before Action that's

Comments:
Image: Wind above Heaven, lone Yin influencing the 5 Yangs, Small Constraint that's.
Wen: Small Constraint, Prosperity, refers to self a Small Force in the West prior to kingship.
Kongzi: Sixer4 in position, all Yangs respond, Niner2 & Niner5 Centres Wills get done.
[Xu: 畜291田畜也,...茲益也]

象曰 *(孔子)* ：	***HexagramSign says (Kongzi) :***
風行天上，小畜	Wind Moving in Heaven Above, Small Constraint
君子以懿文德	Junzi With Beautiful Civility and Virtues

Comments:
Wind moving above Heaven, Image of Wind being a Weak Constraint of Heaven below.
Junzi uses time in Small Constraint for Self-Cultivation and virtuous employment.
(King Wen developed the *Yijing* at Youli while confined for 7 years on orders of evil King Zhou)
[Xu: 懿214專久而美也]

爻辭 *(周公)* ：	*Liner Text (Zhougong) :*

初九： **FirstNiner:**

復自道	Return to Own Way
何其咎，吉	Can This be Faulted! Auspicious
象曰 *(孔子)* ：	*LinerSign says (Kongzi) :*
復自道	Return to Self's Way
其義吉也	This Means Auspiciousness that's

Comments:
FirstNiner, at bottom farthest away, suffer Small Constraint from partner Sixer4.
Yang in Yang position Strong, can Return to Own Virtuous Way hence Auspicious.
[Xu: 復43往來也；義267己之威儀]

九二： **Niner2:**

牽復，吉	Led Return, Auspicious
象曰 *(孔子)* ：	*LinerSign says (Kongzi) :*
牽復在中	Led Return On Centre
亦不自失也	Also No Self Lost, that's

Comments:
Taking the lead of FirstNiner, Niner2 Return to Own Virtuous Way, Auspicious.
Niner2, centre and capable, not losing Self, can avoid Small Constraint from Sixer4.
[Xu: 牽29引前也]

九三： **Niner3:**

輿說輻	Carriage Lost Wheel-spokes (actions restricted)
夫妻反目	Husband Wife Opposing in Views
象曰 *(孔子)* ：	*LinerSign says (Kongzi) :*
夫妻反目	Husband Wife Opposing Views
不能正室也	Not Able be Correct at Home, that's

Comments:
Niner3, neighbor suffers direct Small Constraint by Sixer4, quarrel with differing views
Not rightful partner, Niner3 not able to maintain a proper Family with Sixer4.
[Xu: 輿301車輿也；輻302輪轑也；室150實也, 至所止也]

六四： **Sixer4:**

有孚	Has Trust
血去惕出	Blood Discarded Respect Out
无咎	No Faults
象曰 *(孔子)* ：	*LinerSign says (Kongzi) :*
有孚惕出	Has Trust Respect Display
上合志也	Above has Union of Wills, that's

Comments:
Sixer4, lone Yin in correct position, virtuous has Trust, discarded bad-Blood conduct.
Displays Respect for King Niner5, working with same Wills, No Faults.
[Xu: 惕223敬也；合108合口也]

九五：	**Niner5:**
有孚攣如	Has Trust, Bundle Like
富以其鄰	Wealthy With The Neighbors
象曰 *(孔子)：*	*LinerSign says (Kongzi) :*
有孚攣如，不獨富也	Has Trust, Bundle Like, Not Alone be Wealthy that's

Comments:
Niner5, strong King, bound together with all other Yangs, neighbors far and wide.
Has Trust, sharing wealth with all the rest, as not wishing to be Wealthy Alone.
[Xu: 攣255係也；係167繫束也；繫277麻一耑也]

上九：	**TopNiner:**
既雨既處	Already Rain Already in Position
尚德載，婦貞厲	Aspiring Virtues Cart-loaded, Woman's Purity Grave
月幾望，君子征凶	Moon Nearing Full, Junzi (Gentleman) Campaign, Danger
象曰 *(孔子)：*	*LinerSign says (Kongzi) :*
既雨既處	Already Rain Already Settled
德積載也	Virtues Accumulated, Cart-loads that's
君子征凶，有所疑也	Junzi Campaign Danger, Has Some Suspicions that's

Comments:
Already Rain, Small Constraint settled, Yin and Yangs, all aspiring to accumulating virtues.
Now Moon Full, next waning, woman Gravely warn of Integrity, Junzi to campaign Ominous.
[Xu: 載302乘也；幾84微也，殆也；殆85危也；望267出亡在外望其還也]

Conclusions:
Small Constraint (Hexagram 09): Heaven Trigram below and Wind Trigram above.
Image: Wind moving above Heaven, Small Constraint of Heaven below.
Symbolic: Sixer4 Small lone Yin in position, affecting actions of all 5 Yangs, Small Constraint.

King Wen:
Small Constraint, alluding to Self gathering of Force in the West prior to campaign, Prosperity.

Zhougong:
FirstNiner: return to Self Virtuous-Way, as partner Sixer4 Constraint faraway, Auspicious.
Niner2: following Led Return of FirstNiner, centre Upright, own virtues not lost Auspicious.
Niner3: lost Wheel-spoke, not rightful partner of Sixer4, opposing views, not a Proper Home.
Sixer4: right position has Trust, throw-out bad-Blood, Respect Niner5 of same Wills No Faults.
Niner5: strong King has Trust, Bundling all Yangs in the creation and sharing of Wealth.
TopNiner: rain settled, Full Moon waning, woman chastity Grave, Junzi campaign Ominous.
Small Constraint: Describes the varying effects of loner Sixer4's Small Constraint of 5 Yangs.

Kongzi:
Small Constraint is, Yin in position with responses from above and below, creating Prosperity.
Small Constraint is time for Junzi to self-improve, building up beautiful Character.

(小畜：寡，雜卦傳)　　　　(Small Constraint : Lonely - Miscellaneous 10th Wing)

Lessons learned (Small Constraint Hex.09):
Evil King Zhou confined King Wen for 7 years at Youli where the latter developed the Yijing.
History has many great characters who manage Small Constraint with self-improvement.

（第十卦）履　　　　　　　　**Treading (Hexagram 10)**

外	上九	________)	**TopNiner**		**external**
乾（天，上卦）	九五	________)	**Niner5**	**Qian**	**(Heaven, Trigram above)**
	九四	________)	**Niner4**		
	六三	__ __)	**Sixer3**		
兌（澤，下卦）	九二	________)	**Niner2**	**Dui**	**(Valley, Trigram below)**
內	初九	________)	**FirstNiner**		**internal**

卦辭（文王）：　　　　　　　***Hexagram Text (King Wen) :***
履虎尾　　　　　　　　　　Treading Tiger-Tail
不咥人，亨　　　　　　　　Not Hurting People, Prosperity

象曰（孔子）：　　　　　　***Tuan says (Kongzi explains) :***
履：　　　　　　　　　　　Treading :
柔履剛也　　　　　　　　　Yin Treading Yangs that's (Sixer3 atop FirstNiner, Niner2),
說而應乎乾　　　　　　　　Joy In Response To Heaven (3 Yangs above)
是以履虎尾　　　　　　　　This is Treading Tiger-Tail
不咥人，亨　　　　　　　　Not Hurting People, Prosperity
剛中正　　　　　　　　　　Yang, Upright, Legal
履帝位而不疚　　　　　　　Treading Emperor Position And No Sickness (selfishness)
光明也　　　　　　　　　　Shining Enlightenment, that's

Comments:
Image: Wetland, above Heaven, Sixer3, alone Treading life-path on Wetland beneath Heaven.
Symbolic: Sixer3 Treading Tiger-Tail of 2 Yangs below, meeting Tiger-Head of 3 Yangs above.
Wen: Treading Tiger Tail, Yang Centres (Niner2,-5), benevolent not hurting people, Prosperity.
Kongzi: Yang Centres Upright, Treading Emperor Position Not Selfish, Shining Enlightenment.
[Xu: 履175足所依也；咥32大笑也]

象曰（孔子）：　　　　　　***HexagramSign says (Kongzi) :***
上天下澤，履　　　　　　　Above Heaven, Below Wetland, Treading
君子以辯上下　　　　　　　Junzi For Administration of Above and Below
定民志　　　　　　　　　　Established Citizens's Wills.

Comments:
Above Heaven, below Wetland, Treading (life-path of each individual).
Junzi with discerning observation of Society (above and below), establishes Citizens' Wishes.
[Xu: 辯309治也；治227水出東萊曲城...陽丘山南入海]

爻辭 *(周公) :*   *Liner Text (Zhougong) :*

初九：   FirstNiner:

素履，往无咎   White Treading, Going-forth No Faults

象曰 *(孔子) :*   *LinerSign says (Kongzi) :*

素履之往   White Treading Its Going-forth

獨行願也   Alone Walking, Own Wish that's

Comments:

Start of Treading no partner, not prejudiced on life-path, walks alone own choice, no Fault.

[Xu: 素278白緻繒；繒273帛也]

九二：   **Niner2:**

履道坦坦   Treading Path Quietly Openly

幽人貞吉   Reclusive Person Truly Auspicious

象曰 *(孔子) :*   *LinerSign says (Kongzi) :*

幽人貞吉   Reclusive Person Truly Auspicious

中不自亂也   Upright, Not Self-Confused, that's

Comments:

Niner2, Yang in Yin position of quietude nature, chooses to Treading life-path quietly.
Upright he persists truthfully and not be self-confused with neighbor Sixer3, then Auspicious.

[Xu: 坦287安也；安150靜也]

六三：   **Sixer3:**

眇能視，跛能履   One-eye Can See, Lame Can Walk

履虎尾，咥人凶   Treading Tiger-Tail, Hurting Person Ominous

武人爲于大君   Militant Person Works For Great Lord

象曰 *(孔子) :*   *LinerSign says (Kongzi) :*

眇能視，不足以明也   One-eye Can See, Not Enough For Clarity, that's

跛能履，不足以與行也   Lame Can Tread, Not Enough To Accompany Walking

咥人之凶，位不當也   Hurting Person Its Danger, Position Not Appropriate that's

武人爲于大君，志剛也   Militant Person Works For Great Lord, Wills Strong that's

Comments:

Sixer3, One-eye as incorrect Yang position, and Lame as not Centre, doubly improper.
Sixer3 weak Yin, militant atop of 2 Yangs, Treading improperly for Great Lord, Ominous.

[Xu: 眇73一目小也；跛47行不正也]

九四：   **Niner4:**

履虎尾   Treading Tiger-Tail

愬愬終吉   Mindfully, Mindfully, Finally Auspicious

象曰 *(孔子) :*   *LinerSign says (Kongzi) :*

愬愬終吉   Mindfully, Mindfully Finally Auspicious

志行也   Willing Action, that's

Comments:

Niner4 mindfully supporting Niner5 the superior above is like Treading Tiger-Tail.
Gentle in Yin position, it is also the Wills of Niner4 to give support, hence finally Auspicious.

[Xu: 愬.....；朔141月一日始蘇也；𧼒50不順也]

九五：	**Niner5:**
夬履	Decisive Treading
貞厲	Integrity Grave
象曰 *(孔子)：*	***LinerSign says (Kongzi) :***
夬履，貞厲	Decisive Treading, Integrity yet Grave
位正當也	Position Upright Appropriate, that's

Comments:
Niner5 strong King, Yang in Yang placing, Upright, has Centre position of Authority.
Has Integrity, but Decisive Treading among 4 other Yangs, consequences may be Grave.
[Xu: 夬64分決也]

上九：	**TopNiner:**
視履考祥	Observe Treading, Examine if Fortunate
其旋元吉	The Evolution, Primal Auspiciousness
象曰 *(孔子)：*	***LinerSign says (Kongzi) :***
元吉在上	Primal Auspiciousness On Top
大有慶也	Greatly Has Celebration that's

Comments:
TopNiner at the end, observes the Treading evolution of own life-path to see if Beneficial.
There is big celebration in evolution of his Treading on life-path, Greatly Auspicious.
[Xu: 考173老也；旋140周旋旌旗之指麾也，曰人足随旌旗以周旋，祥7福也]

Conclusions:
Treading (Hexagram 10), of Valley Trigram below and Heaven Trigram above.
Image: Wetland, above Heaven, Sixer3 alone Treading life-path on Wetland beneath Heaven.
Symbolic: Sixer3 atop 2 Yangs (like Treading Tiger-Tail), meets 3 Yangs (Tiger-Head) above.

King Wen:
Life-path is like Treading Tiger-Tail, but with Enlighten leaders, no harm only Prosperity.

Zhougong:
First Niner, starting life-path, no partner, no prejudices, choose to Tread alone, No Fault.
Niner 2, Tread life-path quietly with Integrity, not confused by Sixer3, Auspicious.
Sixer 3, militant like Treading Tiger-Tail of 2 Yangs, facing Tiger-Head of 3 Yangs, Ominous.
Niner 4, like Treading Tiger-Tail next to Niner5, Yin-placed mindful, finally Auspicious.
Niner 5, King Treading Decisive with Integrity among 4 Yangs, but consequences still Grave.
Top Niner, end of Life-path Treading, review history, findings Celebratory.
Treading: description of 6 individuals in society, like Treading Tiger-Tail in their life-paths.

Kongzi:
Strong Upright Proper Leaders Treading Emperor Position, ought not be sick with Selfishness.
Junzi with discerning study of society (above and below), to establish Citizens' Wishes.
（履：不處也，雜卦傳）   (Treading : not staying - Miscellaneous 10th Wing)

Lessons learned (Treading Hex.10):
Treading on life-path hazardous, individuals are warned not to step on Tiger-Tails.
Leaders ought not to have the Selfish sickness when Treading in the Emperor's position.

(第十一卦) 泰　　　　　　　Interaction (Hexagram 11)

上卦	上六	▬▬　▬▬	TopSixer	external
坤　(地,外卦)	六五	▬▬　▬▬	Sixer5	Kun (Earth, Trigram above)
	六四	▬▬　▬▬	Sixer4	
	九三	▬▬▬▬	Niner3	
乾　(天,内卦)	九二	▬▬▬▬	Niner2	Qian (Heaven, Trigram below)
下卦	初九	▬▬▬▬	FirstNiner	internal

卦辭 *(文王)* ：	***Hexagram Text (King Wen) :***
泰：	Interaction:
小往大來	Small (Yins) Gone (above), Great (Yangs) Came (below)
吉，亨	Auspicious, Prosperity

彖曰 *(孔子)* ：	***Tuan Says (Kongzi explains) :***
泰：	Interaction:
小往大來	Small (Yins) Gone (above), Great (Yangs) Came (below)
吉亨	Auspicious, Prosperity
則是天地交而萬物通也	This is Heaven Earth Interaction And All Matters Prosper, that's
上下交而其志同也	Above Below Interact And Their Wills Common, that's
内陽而外陰	Internal Yangs (Heaven) And External Yins (Earth)
内健而外順	Internal Strength (Heaven) And External Docile (Earth)
内君子而外小人	Internal Junzi (Gentleman) And External Small people
君子道長	Junzi's Way Growing
小人道消也	Small People's Way Diminishing

Comments:
Image: Below 3 Yangs of Heaven rise, and from above 3 Yins of Earth descend, Interaction.
Wen: Auspicious Prosperity as the Yins had gone external and Yangs had came internal.
Kongzi: Interaction, Yin Yangs cross-paths producing prosperity with common wills.
[Xu: 泰237滑也]

象曰 *(孔子)* ：	***HexagramSign Says (Kongzi) :***
天地交，泰	Heaven Earth Cross-paths, Interaction
后以裁成天地之道	Thereafter With Creation of The Way of Heaven and Earth
輔相天地之宜	Supplement by Compatibility of Heaven and Earth
以左右民	To Help and Assist Citizens

Comments:
Small and Great people Interaction, supplementing the Way of Heaven Earth, helping citizens.
[Xu: 交214交脛 ；后186發號者君后 ；裁170制衣 ；輔303人頰車也 ；頰182面旁; 宜151所安]

爻辭 *(周公)* :	*Liner Text (Zhougong)* :
初九：	**FirstNiner:**
拔茅茹以其彙	Pull-up Reeds Horse-grass By Its Stolon (horizontal stems)
征吉	Expedition, Auspicious
象曰 *(孔子)* :	*LinerSign Says (Kongzi):*
拔茅征吉	Pull-up Reeds, Expedition Auspicious
志在外也	Ambitions On Outside (territories), that's

Comments:

FirstNiner has ambition to campaign for external expansion.
Interaction ability to unite and pull-along all fellow Yangs for this expedition, Auspicious.

九二：	**Niner2:**
包荒	Embracing Wilderness
以馮河，不遐遺	With Swift Actions, Not Losing Far-off-interests
朋亡，得尚于中行	Friends Lost, Gain Favored By Centrism Practices
象曰 *(孔子)* :	*LinerSign Says (Kongzi) :*
包荒	Embracing wilderness (most accommodating)
得尚于中行	Gain Favored By Centrism Practices
以光大	By Illustrious Expansion that's

Comments:

Niner2, in Yin position, gentle and most accommodating in all Interactions.
Brave in actions, no favouritism, far reaching, to achieve illustrious expansion with Centrism.

九三：	**Niner3:**
无平不陂	No Flatness Not Ruggedness (expect difficulties)
无往不復，難貞无咎	No Forward Not Return, Difficult Integrity No Faults
勿恤其孚	Don't Worry of Its Trustworthiness
于食有福	Regarding Sustenance Has Good-fortune
象曰 *(孔子)* :	*LinerSign Says (Kongzi) :*
无往不復	No Forward Not Return
天地際也	Heaven Earth Meeting-place that's

Comments:

Niner3, in Yang position, strongly expands to end of the World where Heaven and Earth meet.
Has difficulties, but Interacting with Trust and Integrity, will achieve Good-Life, Good-Fortune.

六四：	**Sixer4:**
翩翩不富	Fluttering Fluttering, Not Wealthy
以其鄰，不戒以孚	Because Of Neighbors, Not Guarded, Having Trust
象曰 *(孔子)* :	*LinerSign Say (Kongzi) :*
翩翩不富	Fluttering About (all actions), Not Wealthy
皆失實也	All Lost Reality that's (no substance)
不戒以孚，中心願也	Not On-guard Have Trust, Centre of Heart Wishes, that's

Comments:

Sixer4, in Yin position, trusts other Yin neighbors and wish to work together with them.
But Yins are not effective together and all their actions not productive, hence remain poor.

六五：	**Sixer5:**
帝乙歸妹	Emperor Yi Marry-off Sister
以祉元吉	With Good-fortune, Primally Auspicious
象曰 *(孔子)* :	***LinerSign Says (Kongzi) :***
以祉元吉	With Good-fortune, Primally Auspicious
中以行願也	Upright With Implementing own Wish that's

Comments:
Sixer5, Upright Emperor, wishes and did marry sister to subject Niner2, greatly Auspicious.
[Xu: 祉7福也，中14內也,上下通也，內109入也,自外而入也]

上六：	**TopSixer:**
城復于隍	Walled-city Reverted To Dry-moat
勿用師	Don't Deploy Army
自邑告命	Own State, Orders Notices
貞吝	Truly Regrets
象曰 *(孔子)* :	***LinerSign Says (Kongzi) :***
城復于隍	Walled-city Reverted To Dry-moat (disrepair)
其命亂也	Its Orders Confused that's

Comments:
TopSixer not effective in administration, orders all mix-up, walled-city in ruin with dry moat.
Yin in Yin position, very weak, not deploying army, failed Interaction, hence has regrets.
[Xu: 城288以盛民，盛104黍稷在器中以祀者，隍306城池,有水日池無水日隍，邑131國]

Conclusions:
Interaction (Hexagram 11: Heaven Trigram below and Earth Trigram above.
Image: Heaven (light) rises and Earth (heavy) settles down crossing paths, Interaction.

King Wen:
Sees Yins (Small people) gone-out and Yangs (Great people) came-in as Auspicious.

Zhougong:
FirstNiner: Active, able to unit other Yangs for outward expansion expedition, Auspicious.
Niner2: Gentle, all accommodating, capable no favouritism, achieved expansion, Illustrious.
Niner3: Active, has Trust, leads difficult expansion to the limits, gain Good-life No Faults.
Sixer4: Much activities, not wealthy as working among Yins, non-productive Small people.
Sixer5: Weak, Upright King, willing to marry sister to subject Niner2, Primally Auspicious
TopSixer: Interaction failed, orders confused, city in disrepair, not deploying army, has Regrets.

Kongzi:
Interaction of Yins and Yangs crossing paths, with common wills bring help to all citizens.
(泰：反其類，雜卦傳)   (Interaction : Opposing its kind - Miscellaneous 10th Wing)

Lessons learned (Interaction Hex.11):
Interaction just like present day Globalisation, Auspicious, brings peace and prosperity to all.

（第十二卦）否　　　　　　　Isolation (Hexagram 12)

上卦	上九	________	**TopNiner**	external
乾　(天, 外卦)	九五	________	**Niner5**	**Qian (Heaven, Trigram above)**
	九四	________	**Niner4**	
	六三	__ __	**Sixer3**	
坤　(地, 内卦)	六二	__ __	**Sixer2**	**Kun (Earth, Trigram below)**
下卦	初六	__ __	**FirstSixer**	internal

卦辭 *(文王)* :	***Hexagram Text (King Wen) :***
否：	Isolation :
之匪人	Its Thievish People
不利君子貞	Not Favorable to Junzi's Truthfulness
大往小來	Great (Yangs) Gone (above), Small (Yins) Came (below)
象曰 *(孔子)* :	***Tuan Says (Kongzi explains) :***
否：	Isolation :
之匪人不利	Its Thievish People, Not Favor
君子貞	Junzi (Gentleman) Upright
大往小來	Great (Yangs) Gone (above), Small (Yins) Came (below)
則是天地不交而萬物不通	Heaven Earth Not Interacting, All Matters Not Connecting
上下不交而天下无邦也	Above Below Not Interacting And The World has No States
内陰而外陽	Internal Yins (Earth) And External Yangs (Heaven)
内小人而外君子	Internal Small People And External Junzi (Gentleman)
小人道長	Small People's Way desires-Growing
君子道消也	Junzi's Way desires-Diminishing that's

Comments:
Image: Below heavy Earth descends, above light Heaven rises, going different ways, Isolation.
Wen: Isolation, Great (Yangs) gone Small (Yins) came, Small People Thievish, Junzi Truthful.
Kongzi: Small People's Desires grow, Junzi's Desires diminish in Isolation.
[Xu: 否34不也从口从不，匪268器似竹筐]

象曰 *(孔子)* :	***HexagramSign Says (Kongzi) :***
天地不交，否	Heaven Earth Not Interacting, Isolation
君子以儉德辟難	Junzi (Gentleman) With Low-profile Avoid Problems
不可榮以祿	Can Not Prosper Through Official-status

Comments:
In time of Isolation, Junzi (Gentleman) is to keep low-profile to avoid difficulties.
And not to profit through position of Official-status, that's corruption not allow.
[Xu: 儉165約也，榮117桐木，一曰屋相兩頭起者，祿7福也]

爻辭 (周公)：	**Liner Text (Zhougong) :**

初六： — **FirstSixer:**

拔茅茹以其彙 — Pull-out Grass Shrubs By Their Stolons (joined horizontal stems)

貞吉亨 — Truly Auspicious, Prosperity

象曰 (孔子)： — **LinerSign Says (Kongzi) :**

拔茅貞吉 — Pull-out Grass, Truly Auspicious

志在君也 — Aspiration On being Junzi (Gentleman) that's

Comments:

FirstSixer, least negative of 3 Yins realises that together they are not productive, not so good.
FirstSixer aspires to be the Junzi, uprooted fellow Yins to follow, hence all Auspicious.

[Xu: 拔255擢也，擢255引也，茅17营也，茹25飢馬，飢107糧也

六二： — **Sixer2:**

包承 — Embodied Servitude

小人吉 — Small People Auspicious

大人否，亨 — Great People Oppose, Prosperity

象曰 (孔子)： — **LinerSign Says (Kongzi) :**

大人否，亨 — Great People Oppose (Servitude), Prosperity

不亂羣也 — Not Mix-up the Crowds that's

Comments:

Sixer2, weak Yin, small people, embodied Servitude to survive, Auspicious.
Great people oppose Servitude, not mix-in with the crowd of Small people, hence Prosperity.

[Xu: 包188人裹妊巳在中象子未成形也，承253奉也受也，受84相付也，付164與也]

六三： — **Sixer3:**

包羞 — Embodied Offering-gifts

象曰 (孔子)： — **LinerSign Says (Kongzi) :**

包羞 — Embodied Offering-gifts (Bribery)

位不當也 — Position not proper that's

Comments:

Sixer3, weak in Yang position, no power against the 3 Yangs above, hence offer bribes.

[Xu: 羞310進獻也从羊羊所進也，獻205犬肥者以獻之]

九四： — **Niner4:**

有命，无咎 — Has Destiny, No Faults

疇離祉 — Crop-fields Good-harvest Good-fortune

象曰 (孔子)： — **LinerSign Says (Kongzi) :**

有命无咎 — Has Destiny, No Faults

志行也 — Mission Accomplished that's

Comments:

Niner4 in Yin position is gentle, crop-fields accomplished good-harvest, Good-fortune.
Yang, capable of fulfilling life-Mission in Isolation, No Faults.

[Xu: 疇290耕治之田也 ；離76黃倉庚也鳴則蠶生 ；祉7福也]

九五．：	**Niner5:**
休否	Stop Isolation
大人吉	Great people Auspicious
其亡其亡	Its Death, Its Death
繫于苞桑	Tethered To Luxuriant Mulberry-tree
象曰 *(孔子)：*	*LinerSign Says (Kongzi) :*
大人之吉	Great People, This Auspicious
位正當也	Position Right and Legal that's

Comments:
Niner5, the authority in position to stops Isolation crisis, bringing prosperity.
Stay alert to Death lurking, as peace is precarious like silkworms pupa tethered to the Mulberry.
[Xu: 休125息止也，亡267逃也，苞19艸也，桑127蠶所食葉木，值167措也，措252置也]

上九 ：	**TopNiner:**
傾否	Tipping-over Isolation
先否後喜	Initial Isolation, Afterwards Joy
象曰 *(孔子)：*	*LinerSign Says (Kongzi) :*
否終則傾	Isolation Terminal Hence Discarded
何可長也	How Can It Last that's ?

Comments:
TopNiner, Isolation crisis reaching its end as cannot long-lasting, and be discarded.
Thereafter enjoy peace and harmony.
[Xu: 傾164仄也，仄194側傾也，側164匑也，匑7旁溥也，溥229大也]

Conclusions:
Isolation (Hexagram 12) forms of Heaven Trigram above and Earth Trigram below.
Image: 3 Yangs go up to Heaven, 3 Yins settle on Earth, 2 groups remain in Isolation.

King Wen:
Sees formation of Isolation group favors Great people, not Small people.
Says thievish people not productive, not survive together as nothing to steal from each other!

Zhougong:
FirstSixer: Aspires to become Junzi, uprooting all 3 Yins to come along, Auspicious.
Sixer2: Servitude good for Small people, not joining them Great people oppose Servitude.
Sixer3: Offering-gifts when not in position of strength; Great people also oppose Bribery.
Niner4: Gentle in Yin position, has no problem in Isolation as destined life-mission Achieved.
Niner5: Upright and legal, stops Isolation and in peacetime remains alert to lurking Danger.
TopNiner: Isolation at terminal end, to be discarded and thereafter enjoy peace and harmony.
Isolation: produces hidden conflicts and lurking danger between opposing groups..

Kongzi
In time of Isolation, CulturedOne is to keep low-profile to avoid difficulties.
And in Isolation not to profit through position of official status, that is no corruption.
(否：反其類，雜卦傳)   (Isolation : Opposing its kind - Miscellaneous 10th 'Wing')

Lessons learned (Isolation Hex.12):
Junzi (Gentleman) low-profile, no bribery, and in peacetime stays alert to lurking Danger.

(第十三卦) 同人　　　　　**Comrades (Hexagram 13)**

外卦	上九	————	**TopNiner**		external
乾 (天,上卦)	九五	————	**Niner5**	**Qian (Heaven, Trigram above)**	
	九四	————	**Niner4**		
	九三	————	**Niner3**		
離 (火,下卦)	六二	—— ——	**Sixer2**	**Li (Fire, Trigram below)**	
內卦	初九	————	**FirstNiner**		internal

卦辭 *(文王)* :	*Hexagram Text (King Wen) :*
同人：	Comrades :
于野，亨	At Wilderness, Prosperity
利涉大川	Favors Venturing Big River
利君子貞	Favors Junzi (Gentleman) having Integrity

彖曰 *(孔子)* :	*Tuan says (Kongzi explains) :*
同人	Comrades
柔得位得中	Yin Gain Position Gain Centre (ref.Sixer2)
而應乎乾	And Respond To Qian (Heaven, ref.Niner5))
曰同人	Call-it Comrades
同人曰	Comrades Says
同人于野亨	Comrades At Wilderness, Prosperity
利涉大川，乾行也	Favors Venturing Great River, Qian (Heaven) Action, that's
文明以健	Civilisation build With Strength
中正而應，君子正也	Centre Correctness In Response, Junzi Upright that's
唯君子爲能	Only Junzi has Action Capability
通天下之志	Connecting The World, His Will

Comments:
Image: Fire burn rising upward to join Heaven above, Comrades of same up-lifting spirit.
Symbolic: Sixer2, lone Yin partner Niner5, both right position centre, Comrades of all Yangs.
Wen: Comrades in Wilderness, all the World is One, Prosperity, favors Ventures with Integrity.
Kongzi: Upright, in Response to Heaven, only Junzi has Will to unify World in Comradeship.
[Xu: 同156合會也；人161天地之性最貴者也；野290郊外也从里；唯32諾也；諾52䏮也]

象曰 *(孔子)* :	*HexagramSign says (Kongzi) :*
天與火，同人	Heaven With Fire, Comrades
君子以類族辨物	Junzi By Kinds and Clans Differentiates all Matters.

Comments:
Fire and Heaven are Comrades of the same kind, in spirit up-lifting.
Junzi likewise classifies all Matters by Kinds and Clans (relationships).

爻辭 (周公)：	*Liner Text (Zhougong)：*

初九：	**FirstNiner:**
同人于門	Comrades At Door
无咎	No Faults
象曰 (孔子)：	*LinerSign says (Kongzi)：*
出門同人	Step-out Door, Comrades
又誰咎也	Else Who is Faulting that's

Comments:
FirstNiner young, early Comradeship extending to the Door only, No Faults.
Naturally needs time to develop Comradeship worldwide, so nobody is Faulting him!

六二：	**Sixer2:**
同人于宗，吝	Comrades By Clans, Pitiful
象曰 (孔子)：	*LinerSign says (Kongzi)：*
同人于宗	Comrades Within Clans
吝道也	Pitiful Way that's

Comments:
Sixer2 has Comrades only in own clan, what a pity!
Clannish close-up activity in one village, one kingdom, not interacting Worldwide, not the Way.
[Xu: 宗151尊祖廟也；吝34恨惜；恨221怨也；惜223痛也]

九三：	**Niner3:**
伏戎于莽	Hiding Army In Bushes
升其高陵	Mounting Its High Ground (Look-out)
三歲不興	3 Years No Action
象曰 (孔子)：	*LinerSign says (Kongzi)：*
伏戎于莽，敵剛也	Hiding Army In Ambush, Enemy Strong, that's
三歲不興，安行也	3 Years Not Attacking, Peaceful Conduct, that's

Comments:
Niner3, not centre not partner, in contest for Sixer2 Comradeship, hides army in ambush.
Opposition too strong, not attacking in 3 years, can only accept peaceful conduct that's.
[Xu: 伏167司也；戎266兵也；莽27南昌謂犬善逐菟艸中爲莽；陵304大阜；阜304大陸山]

九四：	**Niner4:**
乘其墉	Sit-on The City-walls
弗克攻，吉	Not Winning Attacking, Auspicious
象曰 (孔子)：	*LinerSign says (Kongzi)：*
乘其墉	Sit-on The City-walls
義弗克也	Upright, Not Attacking that's
其吉，則困而反則也	Its Auspiciousness, As Trapped Then Back to Reasons, that's

Comments:
Niner4 wishing for closer Comradeship of Sixer2, mounts City-wall of Niner3 to attack.
Realised that self not being the rightful partner, rationally breaks away, Auspicious.
[Xu: 墉288城垣也；克143肩也...能勝此物謂之克；攻69擊；則91等畫物；困129故廬也]

九五：	**Niner5:**
同人先號咷	Comrades First Howling Wailing
而後笑	Then Later Laugh
大師克相遇	Great Army Wins, Mutual Meeting
象曰 *(孔子)* ：	***LinerSign says (Kongzi) :***
同人之先	Comrades At First
以中直也	With Centre Uprightness, that's
大師相遇	Great Army, Mutual Meeting
言相克也	Says Mutual Opposition, that's

Comments:
Partner Comrades Niner5 and Sixer2, both centres and correct positions, have strength.
First wailing then uses Great army against Niner3 and Niner4, won and met laughing.
[Xu: 號101呼也 ；呼31外息 ；息217喘 ；喘31疾息也 ；号101痛聲也 ；咷31謂兒泣不止]

上九：	**TopNiner:**
同人于郊，无悔	Comrades At Countryside, No Regrets
象曰 *(孔子)* ：	***LinerSign says (Kongzi) :***
同人于郊	Comrades At Countryside
志未得也	Ambition Not Fulfilled, that's

Comments:
TopNiner has Comrades at Countryside with few people, now not capable of great projects.
Meeting at end of road with Ambition unfulfilled, but as having tried before, so No Regrets.
[Xu: 郊132距國百里爲郊]

Conclusions:
Comrades (Hexagram 13), of Fire Trigram below and Heaven Trigram above.
Image: Below Fire burn uplifting to join Heaven above, Comrades in nature.
Symbolic: Comrades of 5 Yangs, loner Sixer2 and Niner5 are both right positions and centres.

King Wen:
Comrades in Wilderness, Prosperity, favors Venture big rivers, favors Junzi with Integrity.

Zhougong:
FirstNiner: Comrades at Door, no partner above, lowly Yang, actions limited, No Faults.
Sixer2: Comrades in Clan with partner Niner5, not open Comradeship, Pitiful Way of life.
Niner3: not Centre, rash, lying in ambush for 3 years, but Niner 5 too strong, No Fight.
Niner4: mount City-wall of Niner3, gentle in Yin position, rationally back-down, Auspicious.
Niner5: Comrades of Sixer2, both Upright Centre, First Cried, army won, had Last Laugh.
TopNiner: Comrades at Countryside, on top with no partner, Ambition unfulfilled, No Regret.
Comrades: comradeship if Clannish is pitiful, National is contesting, Worldwide is prosperity.

Kongzi:
Enlightened with strength, only righteous Junzi has Will of unifying the world in Comradeship.
Through kinds and clan relationships, Junzi (Gentleman) differentiates all matters.

(同人：親也，雜卦傳)　　(Comrades : Intimacy that's - Miscellaneous 10th Wing)

Lessons learned (Comrades Hex.13):
Comrades are reflective of relationships among Nations today, all Contesting for Self-interests!

（第十四卦）大有　　　　　　　**Abundance (Hexagram 14)**

外	上九	――――――	**TopNiner**　external
離（火，上卦）	六五	――　――	**Sixer5**　Li (Fire, Trigram above)
	九四	――――――	**Niner4**
	九三	――――――	**Niner3**
乾（天，下卦）	九二	――――――	**Niner2**　Qian (Heaven, Trigram below)
内	初九	――――――	**FirstNiner**　internal

卦辭 *(文王)* ：　　　　　　　　***Hexagram Text (King Wen) :***
大有：　　　　　　　　　　　　Abundance :
元亨　　　　　　　　　　　　　Primal Prosperity

象曰 *(孔子)* ：　　　　　　　　***Tuan Says (Kongzi explains) :***
大有：　　　　　　　　　　　　Abundance :
柔得尊位大中　　　　　　　　　Yin Gets Esteemed Position, Great and Upright (ref.Sixer5)
　而上下應之　　　　　　　　　　Accord with Those Above and Below
　日大有　　　　　　　　　　　　　Call-it Abundance
其德剛健而文明　　　　　　　　Its Virtue Strong Competence, Has Civility and Cultured
應乎天而時行　　　　　　　　　Accord With Heaven And Moving with Time
是以元亨　　　　　　　　　　　This Is Primal Prosperity

Comments:
Image: Fire (Sun) in Heaven above, Abundance; 5 Yangs support only Yin Sixer5, Abundance.
Wen: Lone Yin, Upright, in command with support of the Yangs, Abundance, Primal Prosperity.
Kongzi: Heaven's strength meets Fire's shine, action timely in accord with Heaven, Abundance.
[Xu: 大213天大地大人亦大故大象人；有141不宜有也春秋傳曰日月有食之从月又聲]

象曰 *(孔子)* ：　　　　　　　　***HexagramSign Says (Kongzi) :***
火在天上，大有　　　　　　　　Fire in Heaven above, Abundance
君子以遏惡揚善　　　　　　　　Junzi By Stopping Evil, Promoting Goodness
順天休命　　　　　　　　　　　Accords with Heaven and Rest in Destiny

Comments:
Fire in Heaven above, like Sun giving warm and light for all things, creating Abundance.
Junzi (Gentleman) in accord with Heaven's Will, blocks the Evil and promotes the Good.
[Xu: 遏41微止也；揚254飛舉也]

爻辭 *(周公) :*　　　*Liner Text (Zhougong) :*

初九 :　　　**FirstNiner:**

无交害,匪咎　　　No Dealing no Harm, No Faults

艱則无咎　　　Difficulty aware Then No Faults

象曰 *(孔子) :*　　　*LinerSign Says (Kongzi) :*

大有初九　　　Abundance FirstNiner

无交害也　　　No Dealing no Harm that's

Comments:
FirstNiner at bottom, above no partner, initial stage of Abundance, no harm done No Faults.
Knows the difficulty, deal with the difficulty, hence No Faults.

九二 :　　　**Niner2:**

大車以載　　　Big Carts To Carry

有攸往, 无咎　　　Has Leisure Going-forth, No Faults.

象曰 *(孔子) :*　　　*LinerSign Says (Kongzi) :*

大車以載　　　Big Carts To Carry

積中不敗也　　　Accumulate at Centre, Never Fail that's

Comments:
Yang active at centre below, partner Sixer5 above, produce cartloads of Abundance.
Going-forth enriching the central coffer without fail, hence No Faults.

九三 :　　　**Niner3:**

公用亨于天子　　　Lord Makes Gifts to Heaven's Son (King).

小人弗克　　　Small People Not bearing Burden.

象曰 *(孔子) :*　　　*LinerSign Says (Kongzi) :*

公用亨于天子　　　Lord Makes Gifts To Heaven's Son (King).

小人害也　　　Small People Harming that's

Comments:
Niner3, Yang position and top of lower Trigram, a good Lord gives Abundance to his King.
Small People lacking strength fail to bear the burden in contribution thus harming the King.

九四 :　　　**Niner4:**

匪其彭　　　Not beating Own Drum

无咎　　　No Faults

象曰 *(孔子) :*　　　*LinerSign Says (Kongzi) :*

匪其彭, 无咎　　　Not beating Own Drum, No Faults

明辨皙也　　　Clearly Discerning and Understanding that's

Comments:
Niner4 has Abundance, but position not safe next to King Sixer5 and atop Niner3.
Fully aware of situation, not beating own drum, wisely choose to keep a low profile.
[Xu彭102鼓聲也 ; 皙 ….]

六五：	**Sixer5:**
厥孚交如，	Sling-stone Trust Interaction-Like
威如，吉	Stature Like, Auspicious
象曰 *(孔子)：*	*LinerSign Says (Kongzi) :*
厥孚交如	Sling-stone Trust in Interaction-Like
信以發志也	Trustworthy (image) in Declaration of Aspiration that's

Comments:
Sixer5, only gentle Yin in premier position has sling-stone Trust relating to all subjects.
But also need to present image of Authority in declaration of Aspiration and Will.
[Xu: 厥193發石也；發170躲發也；交214脛也；腳88脛也)

上九：	**TopNiner:**
自天祐之	Emanates from Heaven, It's Protection
吉无不利	Auspicious, None Not Beneficial
象曰 *(孔子)：*	*LinerSign Says (Kongzi) :*
大有上吉	Abundance, TopNiner Auspicious
自天祐也	From Heaven's Protection that's

Comments:
In Abundance TopNiner enjoys protection from Heaven, hence Auspicious and all favorable.

Conclusion:
Abundance (Hexagram 14), of Heaven Trigram below and Fire Trigram above.
Image: below Heaven, above Fire, Sun shining for crops in Abundance;
Symbolic: only Yin Sixer5 in king position, with support from 5 Yangs, Abundance.

King Wen:
Lone Yin, Upright in command with support of the 5 Yangs, Abundance, Primal Prosperity.

Zhougong:
FirstNiner, has initial difficulty even in time of Abundance, No Faults.
Niner2, able and upright, produces Abundance, needs big carts to hold, No Faults.
Niner3, in position has Abundance for King; Small People not sending Causes Harm.
Niner4, in precarious position next to King, wise to hide his Abundance, No Faults.
Sixer 5, King has Heaven's strength and Fire's enlightenment in Abundance, Auspicious.
TopNiner, too old to work still needs help in time of Abundance from Heaven, Auspicious.
Abundance: Such time also has its fair share of difficulty, caution and people needing help.

Kongzi:
Abundance, in harmony with Heaven's purpose and timing, hence Primal Prosperity.
(大有：衆，雜卦傳)　　　　　(Abundance : Populace - Misc. Commentary 10th 'Wing')

Lessons learned (Abundance Hex.14):
Abundance, Junzi to stop Evil promote harmony with Heaven's way to protect everybody.

(第十五卦) 謙　　Humility (Hexagram 15)

	外卦	上六	__ __	TopSixer		external
坤 (地, 上卦)		六五	__ __	Sixer5	Kun (Earth, Trigram above)	
		六四	__ __	Sixer4		
		九三	______	Niner3		
艮 (山, 下卦)		六二	__ __	Sixer2	Gen (Mountain, Trigram below)	
	內卦	初六	__ __	FirstSixer		internal

卦辭 *(文王)* ：	*Hexagram Text (King Wen) :*
謙：	Humility:
亨	Prosperity
君子有終	Junzi Has Closure

象曰 *(孔子)* ：	*Tuan says (Kongzi explains) :*
謙亨	Humility, Prosperity
天道下濟而光明	Heaven's Way Lowly Aided, Hence Light Illuminating
地道卑而上行	Earth's Way Humble, Hence Upward Moving
天道虧盈而益謙	Heaven's Way, Deficits Brimful But Benefits Humility
地道變盈而流謙	Earth's Way, Changing Brimful But Flowing Humility
鬼神害盈而福謙	Souls and Spirits, Harming Brimful But Blessing Humility
人道惡盈而好謙	Human's Way, Hating Brimful But Loving Humility
謙尊而光	Humility, Dignify And Enlightened
卑而不可踰	Humble And Not Be Over-taken
君子之終也	Junzi Own Closure, that's

Comments:
Image: High Mountain lying beneath lowly Earth, symbolic of Humility.
Wen: Humility brings Prosperity, Junzi may suffer initially but will end well.
Kongzi: Heaven, Earth, Spirits, Human, all dislike Excessive, but all love Humility.
Humility has Dignity and Enlightenment, and Humbleness may not be cowed.

(Xu: 謙53敬也；濟228水出常山 ...；踰46越也)

象曰 *(孔子)* ：	*HexagramSign says (Kongzi) :*
地中有山，謙	Earth Inside Has Mountain, Humility
君子以裒多益寡	Junzi By Reducing the Rich to Benefit the Poor
稱物平施	Assessing Matters, Levelling Implemented

Comments:
High Mountain lying below Earth level, Image of Humility.
Junzi (Gentleman) taxing the Rich to supplement the Poor, helping to reduce the poverty gap.

| 爻辭 *(周公)：* | *Liner Text (Zhougong) :* |

初六： **FirstSixer:**
謙謙君子 — Humble with Humility, Junzi
用涉大川，吉 — Uses (humility) Crossing Great River, Auspicious
象曰 *(孔子)：* — *LinerSign says (Kongzi) :*
謙謙君子 — Humble with Humility, Junzi (Gentleman)
卑以自牧也 — Humbleness For Self Cultivation, that's
Comments:
Humble Junzi (Gentleman) has been self-disciplined and self-cultivating with Humility.
Humbly and with Humility, Junzi (Gentleman) may attempt any great tasks, Auspicious.

六二： **Sixer2:**
鳴謙 — Well-known Humility
貞吉 — Integrity, Auspicious
象曰 *(孔子)：* — *LinerSign says (Kongzi) :*
鳴謙貞吉 — Well-known Humility, Integrity, Auspicious
中心得也 — Centre (upright) Heart (feeling) Possessed, that's
Comments:
Sixer2, a Yin in Yin position is doubly humble, also upright in central position of Trigram.
Sixer2 is widely known for Humility, having Integrity, Auspicious.

九三： **Niner3:**
勞謙君子 — Accomplished Humility, Junzi
有終吉 — Has Final Auspiciousness
象曰 *(孔子)：* — *LinerSign says (Kongzi) :*
勞謙君子 — Accomplished Humility, Junzi (Gentleman)
萬民服也 — All Citizens Won-over, that's
Comments:
Niner3, the only Yang at top position of Mountain Trigram is much accomplished.
A Junzi (Gentleman) with Humility, won the respect of all citizens, Auspicious.

六四： **Sixer4:**
无不利 — None Not Favorable
撝謙 — Exemplary Humility
象曰 *(孔子)：* — *LinerSign says (Kongzi) :*
无不利撝謙 — None Not Favorable, Exemplary Humility
不違則也 — Not Contradicting Regulations, that's
Comments:
Sixer4, gentle in Yin position, doubly humble, also sitting above Yang, Niner3.
Important to show Exemplary Humility to the Yang with lawful actions, All Favorable.

(Xu: 撝256裂也，一曰手指也；揮255奮也)

六五：	**Sixer5:**
不富以其鄰	Not Wealthy Like Own Neighbors
利用侵伐	Favorable Using Gradual Conquest
无不利	None Not Favorable
象曰 *(孔子)* ：	***LinerSign says (Kongzi)* :**
利用侵伐	Favorable Using Gradual Conquest
征不服也	Conquer the Non-Submissive, that's

Comments:
Sixer5, King with great humility, not wealthier than the citizen neighbors.
Hence those still not submissive, be Conquered with gradual Conquest, All Favorable.
(Xu: 侵165漸也；伐167擊也)

上六：	**TopSixer:**
鳴謙	Well-known Humility
利用行師	Favorable Using Marching Army
征邑國	Conquer Region of State
象曰 *(孔子)* ：	***LinerSign says (Kongzi)* :**
鳴謙，志未得也	Well-known Humility, Ambition Not Fulfilled, that's
可用行師，征邑國也	Can Use Marching Army, Conquer Regions in State, that's

Comments:
TopSixer, Yin in Yin position, extreme in Humility, but no authority, and ambition not fulfilled
But to put-down rebellious regions in own state using Marching Army, Favorable.
(Xu: 邑131國也；國129邦也；邦131國也)

Conclusion:
Humility (Hexagram 15) forms of Earth Trigram above and Mountain Trigram below.
Image: High Mountain comes below Lowly Earth, symbolic of Humility.

King Wen:
Humility augurs Prosperity, and with Integrity Auspicious.

Zhougong:
FirstSixer: Really Humble, been self-cultivating Humility, can take-on any tasks, Auspicious.
Sixer2: Yin, Centre position, Upright and Kind, well-known Humility, has Integrity, Auspicious.
Niner3: Only Yang, strong in Yang position, very Accomplished with Humility, Auspicious.
Sixer4: Yin atop of Yang, needs to show Exemplary Humility, actions legal, all Favorable.
Sixer5: Premier, great Humility, not wealthy like citizens, Fight none-Submissive, all Favorable.
TopSixer: Extreme Humility weak, wills unfulfilled, fighting own rebels, Favorable.
Humility: all Actions are Auspicious and Favorable, even fighting and use of army in defence.

Kongzi:
Heaven, Earth, Spirits, Human, all hate Brimful, but love Humility.
Reducing the Rich to Supplement the Poor, Levelling the Playing field for Future Generations.
(謙：輕，雜卦傳)   (Humility : Light-weight - Miscellaneous 10th 'Wing')

***Lessons learned (Humility Hex.15)* :**
Taxing the Rich to Supplement the Poor, Bridging the Poverty Gap for Stability, Peace on Earth.

（第十六卦）　豫　　　　　　　　　**Happiness (Hexagram 16)**

<table>
<tr><td>　</td><td>外</td><td>上六</td><td>__ __</td><td>**TopSixer**</td><td>**external**</td></tr>
<tr><td>震 (雷，上卦)</td><td></td><td>六五</td><td>__ __</td><td>**Sixer5**</td><td>**Zhen (Thunder, Trigram above)**</td></tr>
<tr><td></td><td></td><td>九四</td><td>______</td><td>**Niner4**</td><td></td></tr>
<tr><td></td><td></td><td>六三</td><td>__ __</td><td>**Sixer3**</td><td></td></tr>
<tr><td>坤 (地，下卦)</td><td></td><td>六二</td><td>__ __</td><td>**Sixer2**</td><td>**Kun (Earth, Trigram below)**</td></tr>
<tr><td></td><td>内</td><td>初六</td><td>__ __</td><td>**noFirstSixer**</td><td>**internal**</td></tr>
</table>

卦辭 *(文王)* ：	***Hexagram Text (King Wen)** :*
豫	Happiness
利建侯，行師	Favors Creation of Lords, Marching Armies

象曰 *(孔子)* ：	***Tuan says (Kongzi explains)** :*
豫	Happiness
剛應而志行	Yang has Responses And Wills Implemented (ref. Niner4)
順以動，豫	Support For Action, Happiness
豫順以動	Happiness, Support For Action
故天地如之	Hence Heaven Earth Like This
而況建侯行師乎	So Also Creation of Lords and Marching of Armies
天地以順動	Heaven Earth With Support Action
故日月不過	Hence Sun Moon Not Over-taking (each other)
而四時不忒	And 4 Seasons Not Changing-over (in sequence)
聖人以順動	Sage Person With Support Action
則刑罰清而民服	Thus Criminal Punishment Clear And Citizens Submissive
豫之時義大矣哉	Happiness Its Timing Justice Great Indeed that's

Comments:
Image: Earth (Support), above Thunder (Action), Happiness; Niner4 lone Yang, focus of 5 Yins.
Wen: Happiness, favors Creation of Lords and Marching of Armies.
Kongzi: Nature has orders, Sage metes out criminal punishment fairly, and citizens respect.
[Xu: 豫198象之大者不害於物；忒220更也；變68更也]

象曰 *(孔子)* ：	***HexagramSign says (Kongzi)** :*
雷出地奮，豫	Thunder Emerges from Earth A-stirring, Happiness
先王以作樂崇德	Past Kings With Making Music Honoring Virtues
殷薦之上帝	Eager Offering Them to Emperor-above
以配祖考	In Accord With Ancestors of Old

Comments:
In Spring, Thunder emerges from Earth, all matters A-stirring, Happiness.
Past Kings honor Virtues, making music offering to Emperor-above, as their ancestors did.
[Xu: 崇191嵬高也；殷 … ；薦 … ；配312酒色也]

爻辭 *(周公)* ：	*Liner Text (Zhougong)* ：
初六 ：	**FirstSixer:**
鳴豫，凶	Extolling Happiness, Ominous
象曰 *(孔子)* ：	*LinerSign says (Kongzi)* ：
初六鳴豫	FirstSixer Extolling Happiness
志窮凶也	Wills Lost, Ominous that's

Comments:
FirstSixer weak, only Yin with partner Niner4, is over-joy extolling Happiness, Ominous.
Wills for achievement lost, whole time submerged in making merriment.

[Xu: 鳴82鳥聲也]

六二 ：	**Sixer2:**
介于石	Set In Rock (determine to resist merriment)
不終日	Not Whole Day (in merry making)
貞吉	Truly Auspicious
象曰 *(孔子)* ：	*LinerSign says (Kongzi)* ：
不終日貞吉	Not Whole Day, Truly Auspicious
以中正也	Being Centre (upright) and Correct that's (virtuous)

Comments:
Sixer2, staunch as rock resists making merry whole day long, Truly Auspicious.
Correct in Yin position and centre, Sixer2 is virtuous that's. (Kongzi elaborates, 6thWing para5)

[Xu: 介28畫也；畫65界也,象田四界聿所以畫之；界291境也]

六三 ：	**Sixer3:**
盱豫悔	Look-up Happiness, Regrets
遲有悔	Late Has Regrets
象曰 *(孔子)* ：	*LinerSign says (Kongzi)* ：
盱豫有悔	Look-up Happiness Has Regrets
位不當也	Position Not Proper that's

Comments:
Sixer3 not centre, Yang position incorrect, Look-up to neighbor Niner4 for Happiness.
Not corresponding partner hence has regrets, and better regret soon, else too late to regret.

[Xu: 盱71目多白也,一曰張目]

九四 ：	**Niner4:**
由豫	Source of Happiness (only Yang among 5 Yins)
大有得，勿疑	Greatly Has Gain, Don't Suspect
朋盍簪	Friends Gathered in Hair-pin (liken)
象曰 *(孔子)* ：	*LinerSign says (Kongzi)* ：
由豫大有得	Source of Happiness Greatly Has Gain
志大行也	Wills Greatly Move (accepted) that's

Comments:
Niner4, source of Happiness, not suspected, friends gathered like hair-pin gathering hairs.
The only Yang, the focus of 5 Yins, greatly has gain, Wills get accepted and fulfilled.

[Xu: 由 … ；盍 ….]

六五：	**Sixer5:**
貞疾	Persistence Sickness
恒不死	Everlasting Not Dying
象曰 (孔子)：	*LinerSign says (Kongzi) :*
貞疾	Persistence Sickness
乘剛也	Sit-on Yang (Niner4) that's
恒不死，中未亡也	Everlasting Not Dying, Centre Not Lost that's

Comments:
Sixer5 sitting atop of Niner4, persistently submerged in merry-making sickness.
King position, centre upright virtue not lost, will survive and not going to die.

上六：	**TopSixer:**
冥豫	Waning Happiness
成有渝	Set (in merriment) Has Changes
无咎	No Faults
象曰 (孔子)：	*LinerSign says (Kongzi) :*
冥豫在上	Sunset Happiness On Top
何可長也	How Can Long (lasting) that's

Comments:
TopSixer on top, Yin in extreme Waning Happiness, cannot long last.
However, TopSixer atop of Thunder (action), able to make changes, finally No Faults.
[Xu: 冥141幽也 ；幽84隱也..十六日日而月始虧幽也 ；隱305蔽也 ；渝237變汗; 汗237人液]

Conclusions:
Happiness (Hexagram 16) forms of Earth Trigram below and Thunder Trigram above.
Image: Earth beneath Thunder, Support below for Action above, Happiness.
Symbolic: Niner4, the only Yang with the focus and support of 5 Yins, Happiness.

King Wen:
Happiness, Support for Action, for new lords, marching armies to overthrow evil King Zhou.

Zhougong:
FirstSixer: Lowly weak, Tolling Happiness, overjoy with support of partner Niner4, Ominous.
Sixer2: Correct position, centre, staunch as rock against whole day merriment, Auspicious.
Sixer3: Look-up to Niner4 for Happiness, not rightful partner, soon has Regrets, Not Too Late.
Niner4: Only Yang, Happiness source, Yins' support, like Hair-pin gathered friends, Wills Done.
Sixer5: Sitting atop Yang, persistent sickness of making merry, but King centre, Will Survive.
TopSixer: Weak, extreme of Waning Happiness, atop of Thunder action, can change, No Faults.
Happiness: Warns against extolling of overjoy, decadent whole day merry-making.

Kongzi:
Heaven Earth, orderly action, Sun and Moon not overtaking each other, Seasons in sequence.
Happiness, Citizen accept Sage's fair judgement, making music honoring gods and ancestors.

(豫：怠也，雜卦傳)	(Happiness : Lethargy that's - Miscellaneous 10th 'Wing')

Lessons learned (Happiness Hex.16) :
Happiness is having Support for Action, time for great ventures, achievement of Wills.
However drowning in merry-making is an ever present danger for the weak in Character

(第十七卦) 隨　　　　　　　　**Following (Hexagram 17)**

<table>
<tr><td>　</td><td>外</td><td>上六</td><td>__ __</td><td>**TopSixer**</td><td>**external**</td></tr>
<tr><td>兌 (澤, 上卦)</td><td></td><td>九五</td><td>______</td><td>**Niner5**</td><td>**Dui (Wetland, Trigram above)**</td></tr>
<tr><td></td><td></td><td>九四</td><td>______</td><td>**Niner4**</td><td></td></tr>
<tr><td></td><td></td><td>六三</td><td>__ __</td><td>**Sixer3**</td><td></td></tr>
<tr><td>震 (雷, 下卦)</td><td></td><td>六二</td><td>__ __</td><td>**Sixer2**</td><td>**Zhen (Thunder, Trigram below)**</td></tr>
<tr><td></td><td>內</td><td>初九</td><td>______</td><td>**FirstNiner**</td><td>**internal**</td></tr>
</table>

卦辭 *(文王)* :	***Hexagram Text (King Wen) :***
隨 :	Following:
元亨	Primal Prosperity
利貞，无咎	Favors Integrity, No Faults

象曰 *(孔子)* :	***Tuan says (Kongzi explains) :***
隨 :	Following:
剛來而下柔	Strong (Yangs) Come To Below Gentle (Yins)
動而説，隨	Action (Thunder) Then Joy (Wetland), Following
大亨貞无咎	Great Prosperity, has Integrity No Faults
而天下隨時	In The World, Time of Following
隨之時，義大矣哉	Time Of Following, Justice Important Indeed, that's

Comments:
Image: all Yangs come below the YIns, that's all actions are Following behind the Yins.
Wen: Following means no arguments, augurs Great Prosperity, has Integrity then no Fault.
Kongzi: Action of Thunder Follow by Joy of Wetland, in Time of Following Justice is important.
(Xu: 隨39从也)

象曰 *(孔子)* :	***HexagramSign says (Kongzi) :***
澤中有雷，隨	Wetland Inside Has Thunder, Following
君子以嚮晦宴息	Junzi (Gentleman) To Follow Nightfall with Quiet Rest

Comments:
Ancient belief, that in winter Thunder go underground to rest, re-emerging the Following spring.
Junzi (Gentleman) to Follow Nature, have a quiet rest when night falls.
(Xu: 晦138月盡也；宴150安息；安150靜也；息217喘也；喘31疾息；疾154病也)

爻辭 *(周公)* ：	*Liner Text (Zhougong) :*
初九：	**FirstNiner:**
官有渝，貞吉	Official Has Changed, Integrity Auspicious
出門交有功.	Out-door, Interaction Has Success
象曰 *(孔子)* ：	*LinerSign says (Kongzi) :*
官有渝	Official Has Changed (role to being follower)
從正吉也	Following the Upright (Sixer2) Auspicious that's
出門交有功，不失也	Out-door Interaction Has Success, No Loss that's

Comments:
FirstNiner, lowly Yang official, role changed to Following Sixer2, a higher Yin official.
With Integrity, has success and no loss in dealing with upright Sixer2, Auspicious.
(Xu: 渝237變汙也；汙235一曰小池爲汙)

六二 ：	**Sixer2:**
係小子	Tie-up with Small Person (FirstNiner)
失丈夫	Lost Husband (Niner5)
象曰 *(孔子)* ：	*LinerSign says (Kongzi) :*
係小子	Tie-up with Small Person (FirstNiner)
弗兼與也	No Double Relationships, that's

Comments:
Sixer2 may choose to Following neighbor FirstNiner, a Small Person below.
Or chooses above partner Niner5 as husband, cannot have both relationship at the same time.
(Xu: 弗265撟也；撟254舉手也,一曰撟擅也；擅254專也；兼146幷也,兼持二禾)

六三 ：	**Sixer3:**
係丈夫，失小子	Tie-up with Husband (Niner4), Lost Small Person (FirstNiner)
随有求得，利居貞	Following Has Request Gains, Favors Staying with Integrity
象曰 *(孔子)* ：	*LinerSign says (Kongzi) :*
係丈夫	Tie-up with Husband
志舍下也	Wishes to Abandon the Lowly (FirstNiner), that's

Comments:
 Wishing to abandon FirstNiner below, Sixer3 takes Niner4 above as husband,
As Niner4 not a co-partner, Sixer3 requests of him should be proper with Integrity.

九四 ：	**Niner4:**
随有獲，貞凶	Following Has Gain, with Integrity but Ominous
有孚在道以明，何咎	Has Trust on Principles with Transparency, What Fault ?
象曰 *(孔子)* ：	*LinerSign says (Kongzi) :*
随有獲，其義凶也	Following Has Gain, Its Meaning Ominous, that's
有孚在道，明功也	Has Trust on Principles, Open with Success, that's

Comments:
Niner4 has success Following King, but also in danger of the latter's suspicions.
Display Trust openly, be transparent in success leaving no doubts, No Faults.
(Xu: 獲205獵所獲也)

九五：	Niner5:
孚于嘉，吉	Trust And Caring, Auspicious
象曰 *(孔子)*：	*LinerSign says (Kongzi) :*
孚于嘉吉	Trust And Caring, Auspicious
位正中也	Positions Right and Centre, that's

Comments:
Both Niner5 King and Following Minister Sixer2 are positioned right and centre.
This partnership of Trust and Caring creates a good administration, Auspicious.
(Xu: 嘉102美也；美78甘也,美與善同意)

上六：	TopSixer:
拘係之	Locked, Tie-up with It (Heaven)
乃從維之	By Following Exclusively with It (Heaven)
王用亨于西山	King Makes Offerings at Mount West
象曰 *(孔子)*：	*LinerSign says (Kongzi) :*
拘係之，上窮也	Locked and Tie-up with It (Heaven), Upper Limit that's

Comments:
King makes Offerings to Heaven on Mount West.
This is the Upper limit of Following (Heaven), Locked Tie-up and Exclusive.
(Xu: 係167絜也；絜277麻一耑；維276車蓋也)

Conclusions:
Following (Hex. 17) is formed of Wetland Trigram above and Thunder Trigram below.
Symbolic: All 3 Yangs come down below the 3 Yins, their actions are Following.

King Wen:
Following then no contest, augurs Great Prosperity, have sustained Integrity no Fault.

Zhougong:
FirstNiner: Yang Following Yin Sixer2, has Integrity and interaction successes, Auspicious.
Sixer2: Following neighbor FirstNiner, loses husband partner Niner5, cannot have both.
Sixer3: Following neighbor Niner4, best have Integrity when requesting favors as not a partner.
Niner4: Has success Following King, suspicions endanger, have Integrity on display, no Fault.
Niner5: Trusted King, upright partner Sixer2 Following, achieve Beautiful Administration.
TopSixer: King, staunch Follower of Heaven's Way, makes Offerings on Mount West.
Following: Often a matter of inclination and convenience of choice with consequences.

Kongzi:
Action of Thunder Follow by Joy of Wetland, in Time of Following Justice is important.
Junzi (Gentleman) to Follow Nature, go-in for quiet rest when night falls.
(隨：无故，雜卦傳)　　　　(Following : no old-friends - Miscellaneous 10th 'Wing')

Lessons learned (Following Hex. 17):
Following is Peaceful and Beautiful with Trust, an open display of staunch Devotion.
Following has limitations, like follow A lose B cannot have both, also may arouse suspicions.
It is good advice for us to Follow the natural cycle and have a quiet rest when night falls.

（第十八卦）蠱　　　　　　　　　　　**Belly-worms (Hexagram 18)**

<pre>
        外   上九   ________   TopNiner   external
艮（山，上卦） 六五   __ __   Sixer5 Gen (Mountain, Trigram above)
        六四   __ __   Sixer4

        九三   ________   Niner3
巽（風，下卦） 九二   ________   Niner2   Xun (Wind, Trigram below)
        初六   __ __   FirstSixer   internal
</pre>

卦辭 *(文王)*：	***Hexagram Text (King Wen) :***
蠱	Belly-worms
元亨	Primal Prosperity
利涉大川	Favors Venturing Big River
先甲三日	Before First-Date, 3 Days
後甲三日	After First-date, 3 Days

彖曰 *(孔子)：*	***Tuan Says (Kongzi explains) :***
蠱	Belly-worms
剛上而柔下	Yang (TopNiner) Above And Yin (FirstSixer) Below
巽而止，蠱	Xun (Wind) And Stop (Mountain), Belly-worms
蠱元亨	Belly-worms, Primal Prosperity
而天下治也	And Heaven-Below (world) is Managed that's
利涉大川	Favors Venturing Big River
往有事也	Going-forth Has Tasks that's
先甲三日	3 Days Before First-date (to investigate)
後甲三日	3 Days After First-date (to investigate)
終則有始，天行也	Ending Certain to Have Beginning, Heaven Way that's

Comments:
Image: Mountain (TopNiner), Wind (FirstSixer), Yang Yin no interactions, Belly-worms.
Wen: Belly-worms, to know cause and effect, 3 days before and after, Greatly Auspicious.
Kongzi: Ending has a Beginning, Heaven's way, hence knowing this, the World is managed.
(Xu: 蠱284腹中蟲也，皿蟲爲蠱，嗨淫之所生也)

象曰 *(孔子)：*	***HexagramSign Says (Kongzi) :***
山下有風，蠱	Mountain, Below Has Wind, Belly-worms
君子以振民育德	Junzi (Gentleman) To Invigorate Citizen, Cultivate Virtues

Comments:
Mountain, below Wind blocked, go whirling around, image of swirling Belly-worms in poo.
Managing society, Junzi (Gentleman) to invigorate Citizens cultivate Virtues.

爻辭 (周公) :	*Liner Text (Zhougong) :*

初六： — **FirstSixer:**

幹父之蠱	Cleaning Father's Belly-worms
有子考，无咎	Has Son Filial, No Faults
厲，終吉	Grave, Ending Auspicious
象曰 (孔子) :	*LinerSign Says (Kongzi) :*
幹父之蠱	Cleaning Father's Belly-worms (mess)
意承考也	Wills to Support the Old that's

Comments:
Has filial son to clean up Father's mess, though serious problem, finally Auspicious.
[Xu: 考173老也]

九二： — **Niner2:**

幹母之蠱	Cleaning Mother's Belly-worms
不可貞	Not Able be Chaste (pure)
象曰 (孔子) :	*LinerSign Says (Kongzi) :*
幹母之蠱	Cleaning Mother's Belly-worms (mess)
得中道也	Achieve Centre Way, that's

Comments:
Cleaning up mess of Mother (Sixer5) in premier position.
Niner2, strong Yang in Yin position, as filial son in support of Mother, needs to exercise caution.

九三： — **Niner3:**

幹父之蠱	Cleaning Father's Belly-worms
小有悔也	Small-way Has Regrets, that's
无大咎	No Big Faults
象曰 (孔子) :	*LinerSign Says (Kongzi) :*
幹父之蠱	Cleaning Father's Belly-worms (mess)
終无咎也	Ending No Faults, that's

Comments:
Niner3, Yang in Yang positions, very strong, may make small mistakes in action.
As filial son, cleaning up Father's mess, finally no Big Faults.

六四： — **Sixer4:**

裕父之蠱	Forgiving Father's Belly-worms
往見吝	Going-forward See Pain
象曰 (孔子) :	*LinerSign Says (Kongzi) :*
裕父之蠱	Forgiving Father's Belly-worms (mess)
往來未得也	Forward Backward, Not Achieving, that's

Comments:
Sixer4 weak, Forgiving towards Father's mess, problems not getting resolve.
Going forward and backward, meeting with more problems and Pain.

[Xu: 裕172衣物饒也，饒108飽也，吝34恨惜也，惜222痛也]

六五：	**Sixer5:**
幹父之蠱	Cleaning Father's Belly-worms
用譽	Uses the Reputable.
象曰子）：	***LinerSign Says (Kongzi) :***
幹父用譽	Cleaning Father's, Uses the Reputable
承以德也	Support With Virtues, that's

Comments:
Sixer5, weak Yin in Yang role, but upright in premier position to clean up Father's mess.
Uses support of Niner2, a partner who is strong and able, with a Reputation of Respect.
[Xu: 譽53(言再)]

上九：	**TopNiner:**
不事王侯	Not Serving Kings, Lords
高尚其事	Highly Respected Own Affairs
象曰 (孔子)：	***LinerSign Says (Kongzi) :***
不事王侯	Not Servicing Kings, Lords
志可則也	Wills Are Obvious, that's

Comments:
TopNiner above, Strong, not be involved with cleaning the messes of Kings and Lords.
Wishes only to manage own affairs that are more respectable, and of high values.

Conclusions:
Belly-worms (Hexagram 18), of Wind Trigram below and Mountain Trigram above.
Image: Wind blocked, whirling at foot of Mountain, like swirling mess of Belly-worms in poo.
Symbolic: Foci, TopNiner (Yang rises) and FirstSixer (Yin settles), no interaction spells trouble.

King Wen:
Belly-worms, study the cause for 3 days before and the effect for 3 days after event First-date.
Past problems needs study before and after events, then go forward to resolve, Great Prosperity.

Zhougong:
FirstSixer: cleaning Father's mess, has Filial son doing it, no Faults, Grave, ends Auspiciously.
Niner2: cleaning Mother's Mess (premier Sixer5), Filial son not to push too hard for Chastity.
Niner3: cleaning Father's Mess, Strong Yang position, small mistakes and Regrets, No Faults.
Sixer4: cleaning Father's Mess, Forgiving, back and forth not resolving, consequences Painful.
Sixer5: Premier, cleaning Father's Mess, Uses help of Niner2 who has reputation of Respect.
TopNiner: Strength above, not servicing Kings Lords, wishes to do Own Things of Great Values.
Belly-worms: about juniors fixing past messes of seniors, with compassion, but not with laxity.

Kongzi:
Ending has a Beginning, Heaven's way, hence knows this and the World is managed.
Belly-worms: resolving past messes, Junzi invigorates citizenry by cultivating Virtues.
(蠱：則飭，雜卦傳)   (Belly-worms : is correction - Miscellaneous 10th 'Wing')

Lessons learned (Belly-worms Hex.18):
Causes and Effects, hence first study events before and after First-date prior to fixing troubles.
Juniors fixing the messes of seniors need to have compassion but no laxity.

(第十九卦) 臨　　　　　　　　**Overseeing (Hexagram 19)**

<table>
<tr><td>外</td><td>上六</td><td>__ __</td><td>**TopSixer**</td><td>**external**</td></tr>
<tr><td>坤　(地，上卦)</td><td>六五</td><td>__ __</td><td>**Sixer5**</td><td>**Kun (Earth, Trigram above)**</td></tr>
<tr><td></td><td>六四</td><td>__ __</td><td>**Sixer4**</td><td></td></tr>
<tr><td></td><td>六三</td><td>__ __</td><td>**Sixer3**</td><td></td></tr>
<tr><td>兌　(澤，下卦)</td><td>九二</td><td>______</td><td>**Niner2**</td><td>**Dui (Wetland, Trigram below)**</td></tr>
<tr><td>内</td><td>初九</td><td>______</td><td>**FirstNiner**</td><td>**internal**</td></tr>
</table>

卦辭 *(文王)* ：	*Hexagram Text (King Wen) :*
臨：	Overseeing:
元亨利貞	Primal Prosperity, Favor Having Integrity
至于八月有凶	Un-till 8 Months, Has Danger

象曰 *(孔子) ：*	*Tuan Says (Kongzi explains) :*
臨:	Overseeing:
剛浸而長	Yangs (FirstNiner, Niner2) Stealthy In Growth
說而順	Joy (Wetland) Then Supportive (Earth)
剛中而應	Yang (Niner2) Centre And Partner (Sixer5)
大亨以正	Great Prosperity by Being Correct
天之道也	Heaven's Way that's
至于八月有凶	Un-till 8 Months Has Danger
消不久也	Oblivion Not Long (soon), that's

Comments:
Image: stealthy growth of 2 Yangs below, Overseeing the 4 Yins above.
Wen: Overseeing, favors practice of Integrity, bringing Primal Prosperity.
Kongzi: warns of Oblivion in 8 months on a flip to being Observed (8-steps to Hexagram 20).

[Xu: 臨170監臨也，浸…，消225盡也]

象曰 *(孔子) ：*	*HexagramSign Says (Kongzi) :*
澤上有地，臨	Wetland, Above Has Earth, Overseeing
君子以教	Junzi (Gentleman) With Teaching
思无窮	Thinking No End (ceaselessly)
容保民无疆	Accommodating, Protecting Citizens with No Boundaries

Comments:
Earth upon Wetland, Image of Overseeing, Junzi inspired to teach and think ceaselessly.
Like Earth accommodating, Wetland nurturing, to boundlessly protect citizens.

[Xu: 澤331光潤也，疆291界也]

爻辭 (周公) :	*Liner Text (Zhougong) :*
初九 :	FirstNiner:
咸臨	Inclusive Overseeing
貞吉	Integrity, Auspicious
象曰 (孔子) :	*LinerSign Says (Kongzi) :*
咸臨貞吉	Inclusive Overseeing, with Integrity Auspicious
志行正也	Ambition Fulfilled, Upright that's

Comments:
FirstNiner, Yang and correct position for Inclusive Overseeing the 4 Yins above, Auspicious.
With Integrity and Upright conduct achieved Ambition that's.
[Xu: 咸32皆也悉也，皆74俱詞也，悉28詳盡也]

九二 :	**Niner2:**
咸臨 :	Inclusive Overseeing:
吉，无不利	Auspicious, None Not Favorable
象曰 (孔子) :	*LinerSign Says (Kongzi) :*
咸臨吉无不利	Inclusive Overseeing, Auspicious None Not Favorable
未順命也	Not Obeying Orders, that's

Comments:
Niner2, Yang and centre position for Inclusive Overseeing the 4 Yins above, Auspicious.
All Favorable and actions are not obeying orders of above counterpart, King Sixer5.
[Xu: 未311昧也, 六月滋味, 五行木老於未象木重枝葉也]

六三 :	**Sixer3:**
甘臨	Sweet Overseeing
无攸利	No Soft Gain
既憂之，无咎	Since Worrying it, No Faults
象曰 (孔子) :	*LinerSign Says (Kongzi) :*
甘臨	Sweet Overseeing
位不當也	Position Not Correct that's
既憂之	Since Worrying it
咎不長也	Faults Not Growing that's

Comments:
Sixer3 weak not centre, atop 2 Yangs, resorts to Sweet Overseeing (frivolous tactics).
But does know that this is wrong and worry about it, hence Faults will not increase.

六四 :	**Sixer4:**
至臨，无咎	Down-to-earth Overseeing, No Faults
象曰 (孔子) :	*LinerSign Says (Kongzi) :*
至臨无咎	Down-to-earth Overseeing, no Faults
位當也	Position Correct, that's

Comments:
Sixer4, Yin in Yin position, and having co-partner FirstNiner to help,
Has strength for Down-to-Earth Overseeing the 2 Yangs below, hence No Faults.
[Xu: 至247鳥飛從高下至地也, 不上出而至下來也]

六五：	**Sixer5:**
知臨	Knowledge Overseeing
大君之宜，吉	Great King's Appropriateness, Auspicious
象曰 *(孔子)：*	***LinerSign Says (Kongzi) :***
大君之宜	Great Premier"s Appropriateness
行中之謂也	This's Called Centrism in Action, that's

Comments:
Sixer5, Great King is appropriate with Knowledge Overseeing the whole kingdom.
Has co-partner Niner2 to assist, Auspicious.
[Xu: 宜151所安也]

上六：	**TopSixer:**
敦臨	Honest Overseeing
吉，无咎	Auspicious, No Faults
象曰 *(孔子)：*	***LinerSign Says (Kongzi) :***
敦臨之吉	Honest Overseeing
志在内也	Focus On Internal, that's

Comments:
TopSixer on top, has vast experience can provide kingdom with Honest Overseeing.
With Will to focus Internally on all subjects, hence No Faults and Auspicious.
[Xu: 敦68怒也, 詆也, 誰何也]

Conclusions:
Overseeing (Hexagram 19) formed of Earth Trigram above and Wetland Trigram below.
Image: Earth upon Wetland, of 2 Yangs' Inclusive Overseeing of the 4 Yins above.

King Wen:
The 2 Yangs Overseeing the 4 Yins above, bringing Primal Prosperity upon Integrity.
He also warns of Danger when in 8 step-changes, Overseeing becomes being Observed!

Zhougong:
FirstNiner: Yang position, Inclusive Overseeing of Yins above base on Integrity is Auspicious.
Niner2: Inclusive Overseeing of Yins above, not obeying partner King, favorable, Auspicious.
Sixer3: weak Sweet Overseeing with frivolity of Yangs below, worries, Faults not increased.
Sixer4: Down-to-Earth Overseeing, in position with strength over 2 Yangs below, no Faults.
Sixer5: King's appropriate Knowledge Overseeing, with counterpart and Centrism, Auspicious.
TopSixer: Honest Overseeing, Wills to focus internally on subjects, no Faults Auspicious.
Overseeing: different levels of society with different tactics, but Integrity Knowledge important.

Kongzi:
Image of Wetland upon Earth, Overseeing, Junzi (Gentleman) is inspired to think ceaselessly.
Like accommodating Earth, nurturing Wetland, giving boundless protection to all citizens.
(臨觀之義：或與或求，雜卦傳)　　(Overseeing Observing meanings: Or Bestow Or Request
- Miscellaneous 10th Wing)

Lessons learned (Overseeing Hex.19)
Be warned, Overseeing and being Observed are two sides of a coin, thus Centrism important.

(第二十卦) 觀   **Observing (Hexagram 20)**

外	上九	________	**TopNiner**	external
巽 (風,上卦)	九五	________	**Niner5**	**Xun (Wind, Trigram above)**
	六四	__ __	**Sixer4**	
	六三	__ __	**Sixer3**	
坤 (地,下卦)	六二	__ __	**Sixer2**	**Kun (Earth, Trigram below)**
內	初六	__ __	**FirstSixer**	internal

卦辭 *(文王)* ：   ***Hexagram Text (King Wen) :***
觀：   Observing :
盥而不薦   Hand-washing (rites) And No Commendation (self-praising)
有孚顒若   Has trust, Head-raise-admiring Like

象曰 *(孔子):*   ***Tuan Says (Kongzi explains) :***
大觀在上   Great Observing On High
順而巽   Docile (Earth) And Xun (Wind)
中正以觀天下   Centrism Uprightness For Observing The World
觀盥而不薦   Observing Hand-washing-rites And Not Self-praising
有孚顒若   Has Trust, Head-raise-admiring Like
下觀而化也   Subordinates Observing And be Influenced that's
觀天之神道   Observing Heaven The God-like Way
而四時不忒   And in the 4 Seasons has No Excessive (desires)
聖人以神道設教   The Sage With God-like Way Establishes Teachings
而天下服矣   And The World in Submission indeed

Comments:
Image: 4 Yins below, looking-up on the 2 Yangs above, Observing.
Wen: Observing rites giving thanks to Heaven, without self-praising conduct.
Kongzi: thus creating trust in citizens below who raise their heads to Observing admiringly.
Observing Heaven's Way, the Sage established teachings, the world accepted in submission.
[Xu: 觀177諦視也，盥177諦觀也，諦52審也，薦…，顒182大頭也，若24擇菜也，忒22也，
更68改也]

象曰 *(孔子):*   ***HexagramSign Says (Kongzi) :***
風行地上，觀   Wind Traveling On Earth, Observing
先王以省方   Past Kings By Touring Places (the states)
觀民設教   Observing Citizens' livelihood, Established Teachings.

Comments:
Wind traveling on Earth surface, accessing all places and Observing everything.
Past kings traveled the kingdoms Observing citizens livelihood, established teachings.
[Xu: 省74視也，方176併船也，併164並也]

爻辭 (周公) :	*Liner Text (Zhougong) :*
初六 :	**FirstSixer:**
童觀	Child Observing
小人无咎	Small People, No Faults
君子吝	Junzi (Gentleman) Regrettable
象曰 (孔子) :	*LinerSign Says (Kongzi) :*
初六童觀	FirstSixer, Child Observation
小人道也	Way of Small People that's

Comments:
FirstSixer at bottom is like a Child Observing, superficial understanding at best, No Fault.
Childish Observation is alright for Small People but regrettable for Junzi (Gentleman).

六二 :	**Sixer2:**
闚觀	Peeping Observation
利女貞	Favors Woman's Chastity
象曰 (孔子) :	*LinerSign Says (Kongzi) :*
闚觀女貞	Peeping Observation, Woman's Chastity
亦可醜也	Also Can-be Ugly that's

Comments:
Sixer2, Yin and centre, Observing behind doors is alright to protect woman's chastity.
However such behaviour can be Ugly practice for a Junzi (Gentleman).

六三 :	**Sixer3:**
觀我生	Observing My Life
進退	Advance Retreat
象曰 (孔子) :	*LinerSign Says (Kongzi) :*
觀我生進退	Observing My Life, to Advance to Retreat
未失道也	Not Losing Way (have Principles) that's

Comments:
Sixer3 top of lower Trigram facing top Trigram, is at crossroad of life, to Advance or Not.
Observing own life and ability so far, to decide to advance or remain a big fish in a small pond!

六四 :	**Sixer4:**
觀國之光	Observing State's Luminaries
利用賓于王	Favored Guests for Service of the king.
象曰 (孔子) :	*LinerSign Says (Kongzi) :*
觀國之光	Observing State's Luminaries
尚賓也	Admiring Guests that's

Comments:
Sixer4 next to the throne in service of the king is working with State's Luminaries
A Yin at close quarters is able to learn by Observing and admiring these illustrious people.

九五：	**Niner5:**
觀我生	Observing My Life
君子无咎	Junzi (Gentleman) no Faults
象曰 *(孔子)：*	***LinerSign Says (Kongzi) :***
觀我生	Observing My Life (leadership)
觀民也	Observing Citizens that's (reflective of leadership)

Comments:
Niner5, Junzi (Gentleman) Observing own life conduct in leadership finds No Faults.
Good or bad leadership is also reflected by Observing the livelihood of citizens.

上九：	**TopNiner:**
觀其生	Observing Own Life
君子无咎	Junzi (Gentleman) No Faults
象曰 *(孔子)：*	***LinerSign Says (Kongzi) :***
觀其生	Observing Own Life
志未平也	Ambitions Not Fulfilled that's

Comments:
TopNiner, as a Junzi (Gentleman) in Observing own life so far finds No Faults.
However atop of Observing and past prime now, has no power to fulfil unfinished dreams.

Conclusions:
Observing (Hexagram 20) formed of Wing Trigram above and Earth Trigram below.
Image: Wind moving across Earth, accessing all places, visiting and Observing.
Symbolic: 4 Yins below looking-up to the 2 Yangs above, Observing, assessing their conduct.

King Wen:
Leaders on high are Observing rites to Heaven with no self-praising conduct.
Citizens below are also Observing the leaders, feeling Trust and Admiration for them.

Zhougong:
FirstSixer: like Child Observing from below, Small People no faults, but regrettable for Junzi.
Sixer2: Observing behind doors, alright for woman's chastity, but Ugly for Junzi (Gentleman).
Sixer3: Observing own life and ability for forward planning, without losing upright Principles.
Sixer4: Observing luminaries in king's court, appreciates those in illustrious service of the king.
Niner5: Observing self-conduct in leadership which is reflected by citizens' livelihood.
TopNiner: Observing own past, Junzi No Faults, but also no power now for unfulfilled dreams.
Observing: from far below, behind doors, close-quarters and self-reviewing at the top.

Kongzi:
Observing Heaven's Way, the Sage established teachings, and world accepted in submission.
Past kings traveled the kingdoms Observing citizens livelihood, established teachings.
(臨觀之義：或與或求，雜卦傳)   (Overseeing Observing meanings: Or Bestow Or Request
                          - Miscellaneous 10th Wing)

Lessons learned (Observing Hex.20)
Besides self-Observing, to observe people's livelihood which is reflective of leadership.

(第二十一卦)　噬嗑　　　　　　　　**Biting-Close (Hexagram 21)**

外	上九	———	**TopNiner**	external
離（火，上卦）	六五	—— ——	**Sixer5**	Li (Fire, Trigram above)
	九四	———	**Niner4**	
	六三	—— ——	**Sixer3**	
震（雷，下卦）	六二	—— ——	**Sixer2**	Zhen (Thunder, Trigram below)
內	初九	———	**FirstNiner**	internal

卦辭 *(文王)* ：　　　　　　　　　　***Hexagram Text (King Wen)* :**

噬嗑　　　　　　　　　　　　　　　Biting-Close

亨，利用獄　　　　　　　　　　　　Prosperity, Favors Using Punishment

彖曰 *(孔子)* ：　　　　　　　　　　***Tuan Says (Kongzi explains)* :**

頤中有物　　　　　　　　　　　　　Mouth Inside Has Substance

曰噬嗑　　　　　　　　　　　　　　Says Biting-Close (judgement)

噬嗑而亨　　　　　　　　　　　　　Biting-Close For Prosperity (deterrent of wrong-doings)

剛柔分，動而明　　　　　　　　　　Yangs (3) Yins (3) Balanced, Action With Enlightenment

雷電合而章　　　　　　　　　　　　Thunder Lightning Combined To Shine (for justice)

柔得中而上行　　　　　　　　　　　Yin (Sixer5) Gain Centre With Upward Move (from Hex.12)

雖不當位　　　　　　　　　　　　　Though Not Proper Position (Sixer5)

利用獄也　　　　　　　　　　　　　Favors Using Punishment that's

Comments:

Image: Thunder, Lightning above, 3 Yins 3 Yangs, Niner4 is meat in mouth Biting-to-Close.

Symbolic: Focus Sixer5, Yin's action with enlightenment for fair-Trial, Justice, and Deterrent.

Wen: Biting-Close, favors using punishment to deter evil-doings, results in ultimate Prosperity.

Kongzi: Thunder stern action with Lightning visible fairness to shine in punitive Judgement.

[Xu: 噬31咬也噥也；咬31食也；嗑33多言；獄206确也二犬所以守；頤183舉目視人皃]

象曰 *(孔子)* ：　　　　　　　　　　***HexagramSign Says (Kongzi)* :**

雷電，噬嗑　　　　　　　　　　　　Thunder Lightning, Biting-Close

先王以明罰勅法　　　　　　　　　　Past Kings With Enlightened Punishment, Strong Laws

Comments:

Thunder Lightning, Biting-Close, deterrent of crimes with enlightened trials thunderous penalty.

Past Kings with enlightened judgement, set strong laws to fight wrong-doings keep peace,

[Xu: 勅292勞也；勞292劇也]

爻辭 *(周公)* ：	*Liner Text (Zhougong) :*
初九：	**FirstNiner:**
履校滅趾	Foot Shackles Destroy Toes
无咎	No Faults
象曰 *(孔子)* ：	*LinerSign Says (Kongzi) :*
履校滅趾	Foot Shackles Destroy Toes
不行也	No Action that's (criminal action deterrent)

Comments:
FirstNiner small wrongdoing, Foot Shackled at toes, lesson learned no more wrong-doing.
Stop crime at the early stage with punishment, no Faults. (Kongzi elaborates, 6th Wing para.5)
[Xu: 履175履也；履175足所依也；校124木囚也；滅237盡也]

六二：	**Sixer2:**
噬膚滅鼻	Biting Skin Destroy Nose
无咎.	No Faults
象曰 *(孔子)* ：	*LinerSign Says (Kongzi) :*
噬膚滅鼻.	Biting Skin Destroy Nose
乘剛也.	Riding-on Yang (FirstNiner) that's

Comments:
Sixer2 Biting Skin, administering the softest of punishment on strong FirstNiner.
Weak Yin, make mistake hurt nose in the process, but Sixer2 centre upright, No Fault.

六三：	**Sixer3:**
噬腊肉	Biting Preserved Meat
遇毒，小吝	Encounter Poison, Small Pain
无咎	No Fault
象曰 *(孔子)* ：	*LinerSign Says (Kongzi) :*
遇毒	Encounter Poison
位不當	Position Not Proper that's

Comments:
Sixer3 Biting on tough Preserved Meat, encountered poison, Small Pain.
Sixer3 weak misplaced not-centre, meeting Resistance administering Justice, No Fault.

九四：	**Niner4:**
噬乾胏	Biting Dried Meat-on-bone
得金矢	Gain Golden Arrow
利艱貞，吉	Favors Difficult Perseverance, Auspicious
象曰 *(孔子)* ：	*LinerSign Says (Kongzi) :*
利艱貞吉	Favors having Difficult Perseverance, Auspicious
未光也	Prior Shining that's

Comments:
Niner4 Biting Meat-on-bone, hard contesting in court, won Golden Arrow, Auspicious.
Not centre, misplaced, not yet a Shining star, with difficult perseverance upholding Justice.
[Xu: 乾308上出也,从乙乙物之達也]
[<<周礼.秋官.大司寇>>以兩造禁民訟,....獄訟入鈞金束矢而後聽之...]

六五：	**Sixer5:**
噬乾肉	Biting Dry Meat
得黃金	Gain Yellow (soft color) Gold
貞厲，无咎	Perseverance Serious, No Faults
象曰 *(孔子)* ：	***LinerSign Says (Kongzi) :***
貞厲无咎	Perseverance Serious No Faults
得當也	Has Correctness that's (Premier position)

Comments:
Sixer5 Biting Dry Meat, administering Justice in court, gain compassionate Gold, No Faults.
Gentle Yin, King in-charge, with serious perseverance in building peace and order.

上九：	**TopNiner:**
何校滅耳	Carrying Shackles Destroying Ears
凶	Ominous
象曰 *(孔子)* ：	***LinerSign Says (Kongzi) :***
何校滅耳	Carrying Shackles Destroying Ears
聰不明也.	Hearing Not Understanding that's

Comments:
TopNiner, Yang at extreme of Biting-Close, Carrying Shackles Hurting Ears, Ominous.
Has Ears not listen well to virtuous advice early in life, committing evil, now pay-back time.
(Kongzi further elaborates when question by disciples, 6th 'Wing' para.5)
[Xu: 何163儋也即負何；聰250察也]

Conclusions:
Biting-Close (Hexagram 21) with Thunder Hexagram below and Fire Hexagram above.
Image: Niner4, like a piece of meat in mouth with TopNiner upper and FirstNiner as lower Jaws.
Symbolic: Thunderous Action with Fire Enlightenment to Shine in the Deterrent of Evil-doings.

King Wen:
Favors using Punitive as deterrent against evils to build a peaceful orderly Prosperity.

Zhougong:
FirstNiner small crimes, shackled toes, early lesson deters further wrong-doings, No Faults.
Sixer2 metes punitive on strong FirstNiner, has mistake, but as centre upright, No Faults.
Sixer3 metes punitive on others, weak not centre meets with resistance, has Pains No Faults.
Niner4 Minister metes punitive with perseverance, gain Gold arrow in court, Auspicious.
Sixer5 King metes punitive with Integrity, gain Yellow Gold subjects acceptance, No Faults.
TopNiner extreme evil not listen to good advice, now Neck-Shackled in retribution, Ominous.
Biting-close: stresses importance of early deterrence, open and fair administration of justice.
Kongzi:
Thunder and Lightning combine to shine, stern punitive combine with enlightened trials.
Past Kings with enlightened punishment and strong laws keep peace and order.
(噬嗑：食也，雜卦傅)   (Biting-Closed : is Food - Miscellaneous 10th 'Wing')

Lessons (Biting-Close Hex. 21):
Warning that not listening to good advice early and do evils, will suffer severe retribution.
Favors Enlightened Judgement in court and Stern Punitive as deterrent against criminals.

(第二十二卦) 賁　　　　　　　　Adorning (Hexagram 22)

外	上九	———	TopNiner	external
艮　(山，上卦)	六五	—— ——	Sixer5	Gen (Mountain, Trigram above)
	六四	—— ——	Sixer4	
	九三	———	Niner3	
離　(火，下卦)	六二	—— ——	Sixer2	Li　(Fire, Trigram below)
內	初九	———	FirstNiner	internal

卦辭 *(文王)*：	***Hexagram Text (King Wen) :***
賁：	Adorning:
亨	Prosperity
小利有攸往	Small Advantage, Has Gentle Progress

象曰 *(孔子)*：	***Tuan Says (Kongzi explains) :***
賁，亨	Adorning, Prosperity
柔來而文剛，故亨	Yin (TopSixer, Hex.11) Comes To Adorn Yangs, Hence Prosperity
分剛上而文柔	Parting Yang (Niner2, Hex.11) Rises To Adorn the Yins
故小利有攸往	Hence Small Advantage, Has Gentle Progress
天文也	Heaven Adorning that's
文明以止	Civility With Restrictives
人文也	Human Adorning that's
觀乎天文以察時變	Observation Of Heaven Adorning To Study Time Changes
觀乎人文以化成天下	Observation Of Human Adorning To Transform The World

Comments:
Image: Conversion of Hex.11 in which, TopSixer comes down to be Sixer2 to Adorn the Yangs.
Niner2 parted and rises to be TopNiner to Adorn the Yins, thus forming Adorning Hexagram.
Wen: Adorning, a small advantage to have, gentle progress bringing Prosperity.
Kongzi: Observe Heaven Adorning to study Nature, observe Human Adorning to know Society.
[Xu: 賁130飾也；文185錯畫也,象交文]

象曰 *(孔子)*：	***HexagramSign Says (Kongzi) :***
山下有火，賁	Mountain Below Has Fire, Adorning
君子以明庶政	Junzi by-which to Enlighten All Governance
无敢折獄	Not Dare Dismantle Dungeons

Comments:
Mountain, below has Fire, Adorning the whole landscape.
Junzi with Adorning brighten all governance, but not dare dismantle dungeons deterrent.
[Xu: 庶193屋下眾；析125破木也, 一曰折；獄206确也；确194石堅也]

爻辭 *(周公)* :   *Liner Text (Zhougong)* :

初九：   **FirstNiner:**

賁其趾   Adorning The Toes

舍車而徒   Abandon Carriage To Walk

象曰 *(孔子)* :   *LinerSign Says (Kongzi)* :

舍車而徒   Abandon Carriage To Walk

義弗乘也   Rightly Not Riding that's

Comments:
FirstNiner at Adorning Toes, too lowly status to ride carriage.
Hence rightfully has abandoned carriage and chooses to walk.

六二：   **Sixer2:**

賁其須   Adorning The Beard

象曰 *(孔子)* :   *LinerSign Says (Kongzi)* :

賁其須   Adorning The Beard

與上興也   Befriend Above (Niner3) to Prosper that's

Comments:
Sixer2, right position and centre, but no partner has Adorning the Beard.
This gives some advantage to engage with neighbor Niner3 above and to prosper.

九三：   **Niner3:**

賁如濡如   Adorning Like, Well-being Like

永貞，吉   Everlasting Integrity, Auspicious

象曰 *(孔子)* :   *LinerSign Says (Kongzi)* :

永貞之吉   Everlasting Integrity, Its Auspicious

終莫之陵也   Finally Nobody's Victim, that's

Comments:
Niner3, strong Yang positions between 2 Yins, may suffer excessive Adorning.
Cautioned to maintain lasting Integrity, then Auspicious.

[Xu: 濡228水出涿郡.. ；陵304大陸山無石者]

六四：   **Sixer4:**

賁如皤如   Adorning like, White Like

白馬翰如   White Horse Flying Like

匪寇婚媾   Not Bandits, Marriage Party

象曰 *(孔子)* :   *LinerSign Says (Kongzi)* :

六四   Sixer4

當位疑也   In Position of Suspicion that's (with Niner3)

匪寇婚媾，終无尤也   Not Bandits, Marriage Party, Ending No Worries, that's

Comments:
Partner FirstNiner coming fast on White horse in a marriage party of Adorning White.
Sixer4 is suspicious of Bandits as Niner3 is in-between, then finally No Worries.

[Xu: 皤160老人白也 ；翰75天雞赤羽 ；婚259婦家也, 禮娶婦以昏時 ；媾259重婚也]

六五：	**Sixer5:**
賁于丘園	Adorning At Hill Garden
束帛戔戔	Bundle Silks In Tatters
吝，終吉	Painful, Ending Auspicious
象曰 *(孔子)：*	***LinerSign Says (Kongzi) :***
六五之吉	Sixer5 Its Auspiciousness
有喜也	Has Joy that's

Comments:
Sixer5 Adorning at Hill Garden in Tatters, Thrifty, no needs to build grand palaces.
Painful to Premier, but to Citizens this is Joyous situation, hence Ending Auspicious.
[Xu: 丘169土之高也；束128縛也；帛160繪也；戔266賊也；賊166敗也；吝34恨惜也；惜222痛也；恨221怨也]

上九：	**TopNiner:**
白賁，无咎	White Adorning, No Faults
象曰 *(孔子)：*	***LinerSign Says (Kongzi) :***
白賁无咎	White Adorning No Faults
上得志也	On-High Attained Wills (success) that's

Comments:
TopNiner White Adorning has no need for colourful decor, No Faults.
TopNiner having attained life ambitions is at peace with self and with the world.

Conclusions:
Adorning (Hexagram 22) of Fire Trigram below and Mountain Trigram above.
Image: Fire at foot of Mountain, brightening the Mountain, Adorning.
Symbolic: Adorning from transformed Hexagram 11, Top Sixer and Niner 2 changing positions.

King Wen:
Adorning, small add-on advantage, has gentle progress to Prosperity.

Zhougong:
FirstNiner: Adorning Toe, low status, no rights for riding carriage, rightfully to Walk.
Sixer2: Adorning Beard, weak, no right partner, needs to depend on Niner3 to Prosper.
Niner3: strong, Adorning between 2 Yins, caution to have lasting Integrity, Auspicious.
Sixer4: partner comes Adorning on white horse, has doubts with Niner3, finally No Worries.
Sixer5: Adorning at Hill Garden in tatters, Thrifty King needs no grand Palaces, Citizens' Joy.
TopNiner: White Adorning, no needs for colors, ambitions fulfilled No Faults.
Adorning: appropriate, excessive or none, individuals of different status make their own choices.

Kongzi:
Adorning, observe Heaven to study Nature, observe Human to know Civilisation..
Junzi with Enlightenment establishes governance, but not dared abandon dungeon-deterrent.
(賁：无色，雜卦傳)   (Adorning : no colour - Miscellaneous 10th 'Wing')

Lessons (Adorning Hex. 22):
Adorning has small add-on advantage, not of core importance, diminishing with rising status.

(第二十三卦) 剝   **Stripping (Hexagram 23)**

<table>
<tr><td>　</td><td>外</td><td>上九</td><td>_______</td><td>**TopNiner**</td><td>**external**</td></tr>
<tr><td>艮</td><td>(山,上卦)</td><td>六五</td><td>__ __</td><td>**Sixer5**</td><td>**Xun (Mountain, Trigram above)**</td></tr>
<tr><td>　</td><td>　</td><td>六四</td><td>__ __</td><td>**Sixer4**</td><td>　</td></tr>
<tr><td>　</td><td>　</td><td>六三</td><td>__ __</td><td>**Sixer3**</td><td>　</td></tr>
<tr><td>坤</td><td>(地,下卦)</td><td>六二</td><td>__ __</td><td>**Sixer2**</td><td>**Kun (Earth, Trigram below)**</td></tr>
<tr><td>　</td><td>内</td><td>初六</td><td>__ __</td><td>**FirstSixer**</td><td>**internal**</td></tr>
</table>

卦辭 *(文王)* ：	***Hexagram Text (King Wen)*** ：
剝 ：	Stripping ：
不利有攸往	Not Favor Going-Forth Slowly

象曰 *(孔子)* ：	***Tuan says (Kongzi explains)*** ：
剝 ：	Stripping:
剝也	Stripping that's
柔變剛也	Gentle (Yins) Turn Strong that's (5 in numbers)
不利有攸往	Not Favor Going-Forth Slowly
小人長也	Small People Grown that's (in numbers)
順而止之	Obedient (Earth below) Then Stop (Mountain above)that's
觀象也	Observed Image that's (of Stripping Hexagram)
君尚消息盈虛	Junzi Respects Death/Life, Fullness/Emptiness (changes)
天行也	Heaven's Way that's

Comments:
Image: Earth below, Mountain above; 5 Yins turn strong against lone Yang above, Stripping.
Wen: Stripping, 5 Yins, small people all over the place, not safe so Not Going-forth.
Kongzi: Junzi respects life/death, fullness/emptiness changes, that's the Way of Heaven.

[Xu: 剝92裂也 ；消235盡也 ；息217喘也 ；喘31疾息也]

象曰 *(孔子)* ：	***HexagramSign says (Kongzi)*** ：
山附于地，剝	Mountain Leaning-on To Earth, Stripping
上以厚下安宅	Top (leaders) By Well-treating Subjects, Peaceful Homeland

Comments"
Not rising high above, Mountain lean-on to Earth, image of having suffered Stripping.
Junzi (Gentleman) well-treats subjects below to earn their support bringing peace to homeland.

[Xu: 附305附婁小土山也]

爻辭 (周公) :	*Liner Text (Zhougong) :*

初六 :	**FirstSixer:**
剝牀以足	Stripping Stool At Legs
蔑貞凶	Disdain of Integrity, Ominous
象曰 (孔子) :	*LinerSign says (Kongzi) :*
剝牀以足	Stripping Stool At Legs
以滅下也	To Destroy from Ground-level that's

Comments:
Stripping Stool at Legs signifies disdain of Integrity, Ominous.
FirstSixer weak Yin, the first to suffer Stripping that starts from bottom up that's.
[Xu: 牀121安身之坐者]

六二 :	**Sixer2:**
剝牀以辨	Stripping Stool At Frame (halved)
蔑貞凶	Disdain of Integrity, Ominous
象曰 (孔子) :	*LinerSign says (Kongzi) :*
剝牀以辨	Stripping Stool At Frame (halved)
未有與也	Before Having Partner that's

Comments:
Stripping Stool at Frame, again meaning disdain of Integrity, Ominous.
Sixer2 with no partner from above to help, suffers Stripping that has progress upward.
[Xu: 辨91判也]

六三 :	**Sixer3:**
剝之无咎	Stripping That's No Faults
象曰 (孔子) :	*LinerSign says (Kongzi) :*
剝之无咎	Stripping That's No Faults
失上下也	Loss Top and Bottom that's

Comments:
Sixer3 follows partner TopNiner and does not join the other Yins in Stripping, hence No Faults.
However in do so, loss connections with the 2 Yins above and the 2 Yins below.

六四 :	**Sixer4:**
剝牀以膚	Stripping Stool At Skin
凶	Ominous
象曰 (孔子) :	*LinerSign says (Kongzi) :*
剝牀以膚	Stripping Stool At Skin
切近災	Close Up Disaster that's

Comments:
Stripping Stool at Skin, Ominous.
For Sixer4, danger already coming upon the person, disastrous.

六五：	**Sixer5:**
貫魚以宮人寵	String-line of Fishes, With Palace Beauties Doting
无不利	None Not Favorable
象曰 *(孔子)：*	***LinerSign says (Kongzi) :***
以宮人寵	With Palace Beauties Doting (serving TopNiner)
終无尤也	Finally No Worries that's

Comments:
Line-up like fishes, the court beauties dote on the only Yang TopNiner above, Favorable.
Sixer5 in command of the Yins and having served Yang TopNiner well, finally has No Worries
[Xu: 貫 ….]

上九：	**TopNiner:**
碩果不食	Big Fruit Not Eaten
君子得輿	Junzi (Gentleman) Gains Carriage
小人剝廬	Small Person Stripping of Abode
象曰 *(孔子)：*	***LinerSign says (Kongzi) :***
君子得輿，民所載也	Junzi (Gentleman) Gains Carriage, Citizens' Support that's
小人剝廬，終不可用也	Small Person Stripped of Abode, Finally Can Not be Used that's

Comments:
If TopNiner is a Junzi (Gentleman), will gain carriage from citizens' support, Auspicious.
If TopNiner is a Small Person petty and selfish, will get stripped of abode, Ominous.
[Xu: 碩182頭大也；廬192寄也秋冬去春夏居]

Conclusions:
Stripping (Hexagram 23) of Mountain Trigram above and Earth Trigram below.
Image: Yins 5 in a row, growing strong and disrespectful, advance to stripping the Top Yang.

King Wen:
Recognises danger in the large accumulation of Yins, 5 in a row gaining strength.
He cautions the lone Yang on top not to go forward, tempering with the Yins, and gets stripped.

Zhougong:
First Sixer: Stripping, disdain for Integrity, starting at the bottom, Ominous.
Sixer 2 : Stripping, disrespecting Integrity progressing to higher level, Ominous.
Sixer 3 : has partner, not joining the other 4 Yins in Stripping activities, No faults.
Sixer 4 : Stripping at Skin is immediate danger upon the person, Ominous.
Sixer 5 : remains Loyal, leading Palace beauties in-line to service TopNiner, No Worries.
Top Niner : surviving as Junzi gains Carriage, as Small Person gets Stripped of abode.
Stripping: disrespectful of Integrity, such acts always Ominous, to survive be Junzi always.

Kongzi:
Junzi respects changes of life/death and fullness/emptiness, for that's the Way of Heaven.
Junzi (Gentleman) needs to treat subjects well to get their support and have peace at home.
(剝：爛也，雜卦傳)   (Stripping : Refining that's - Miscellaneous 10th 'Wing')

Lessons (Stripping Hex. 23) :
Mountain needs Earth's support; leaders also need support, so must treat citizens well.
Stripping time, Junzi survives winning fortune, whereas petty person suffers with losses.

(第二十四卦) 復　　　　　　　　**Return (Hexagram 24)**

	上六	＿＿　＿＿	**TopSixer**	external
坤 (地，上卦)	六五	＿＿　＿＿	**Sixer5**	**Kun (Earth, Trigram above)**
	六四	＿＿　＿＿	**Sixer4**	
	六三	＿＿　＿＿	**Sixer3**	
震 (雷，下卦)	六二	＿＿　＿＿	**Sixer2**	**Zhen (Thunder, Trigram below)**
	初九	＿＿＿＿＿	**Firs Niner**	internal

卦辭 *(文王)：*　　　　　　*Hexagram Text (King Wen) :*

復：	Return:
亨	Prosperity
出入无疾	In Out, No Hurry
朋來无咎	Friends Come No Faults
反復其道	Back Forth, Its Principles
七日來復	7 Days Come Return
利有攸往	Favors For Slow Advance

象曰 *(孔子)：*　　　　　　*Tuan says (Kongzi explains) :*

復亨	Return Prosperity
剛反	Yang Return
動而以順行	Actions (Thunder) And By Obedient Implementation (Earth)
是以出入无疾	Therefore Out In No Hurry
朋來无咎	Friends Come No Faults
反復其道	Back Forth Its Principles
七日來復，天行也	7 Days Come Return, Heaven's Way that's
利有攸往，剛長也	Favors To Slowly Forward, Yangs Growing that's
復其見天地之心	Return, That's Sees Heaven Earth Their Heart

Comments:

Image: Return, of single Yang FirstNiner after cycle of 7 steps (rising 5 steps, out, then back).
Wen: Return, In/Out no hurry, rejoice in the coming of friends, Life is free and prosperous.
Kongzi: Return, we see the 'heart' of Heaven and Earth, the recycling changes of fortune!

[Xu: 復43往來也]

象曰 *(孔子)：*　　　　　　*HexagramSign says (Kongzi) :*

雷在地中，復	Thunder Inside of Earth, Return
先王以至日閉關	Past Kings on Ji Day (winter-arrive), Closed Pass (city-gate)
商旅不行	Traders and Travelers No Movement
后不省方	Empress Not Visiting Places

Comments:

In Winter not heard, Thunder perceived resting inside Earth, signifying Return of the Yangs.

City-gate closed on Winter-arrive (冬至) Day for all to rest, to celebrate Return, a rebirth.

爻辭 *(周公) :*　　　　*Liner Text (Zhougong) :*

初九 :　　　　**First Niner:**
不遠復　　　　Not Far Return
无祇悔　　　　No Goodness, to Regret
元吉　　　　Primal Auspicious
象曰 *(孔子) :*　　　　*LinerSign says (Kongzi) :*
不遠之復　　　　Not-Far This Return
以脩身也　　　　For Cultivating Self that's
Comments:
FirstNiner straying not far, Return to self-cultivation of virtues, No Regrets, Primally Auspicious.
(Kongzi elaborates when ask by disciples, in: Attached Text Lower Commentary para.5)

六二 :　　　　**Sixer2:**
休復　　　　Retired Return
吉　　　　Auspicious
象曰 *(孔子) :*　　　　*LinerSign says (Kongzi) :*
休復之吉　　　　Retired Return Its Auspiciousness
以下仁也　　　　With Subordinate, Benevolent that's
Comments:
Sixer2, gentle upright, a Retired Return to marry subordinate neighbor FirstNiner, Auspicious.
[Xu:休125息止也从人依木]

六三 :　　　　**Sixer3:**
頻復　　　　Frequent Return
属无咎　　　　Serious, No Fault
象曰 *(孔子) :*　　　　*LinerSign says (Kongzi) :*
頻復之属　　　　Frequent Return Its Seriousness
義无咎也　　　　Uprightness, No Faults that's
Comments:
Sixer3 in Yang position, often stray but makes Frequent Return to right path, No Faults.

六四 :　　　　**Sixer4:**
中行　　　　Centre in Line-up
獨復　　　　Lone Return
象曰 *(孔子) :*　　　　*LinerSign says (Kongzi) :*
中行獨復　　　　Centre in Line-up (among 5 Yins), Alone Return
以從道也　　　　To Follow Path that's
Comments:
Sixer4 centre in the line-up of 5 Yins in a row and a counterpart of FirstNiner.
Hence alone is influenced to Return to the right Path.

六五：	**Sixer5:**
敦復	Honest Return
无悔	No Regrets
象曰 *(孔子)：*	***LinerSign says (Kongzi) :***
敦復无悔	Honest Return, No Regrets
中以自考也	Centre With Self Awareness that's

Comments:
Sixer5 in Premier position, personifies Honest Return with No Regrets.
As a centred and an Upright person, always mindful and self-aware of own conduct.

上六：	**TopSixer:**
迷復，凶	Lost Return, Ominous
有災眚	Has Disastrous Cataract
用行師	Deploy Marching Army
終有大敗	Finally Has Big Defeat
以其國君凶	For The State's King, Ominous
至于十年不克征	Up to 10 Years, Not Winning Campaign
象曰 *(孔子)：*	***LinerSign says (Kongzi) :***
迷復之凶，反君道也	Lost Return Its Ominousness, Opposing Junzi's Path that's

Comments:
TopSixer on high, does not practice with Junzi's virtues, hence Lost Return to virtuous Path.
Like a 'blind' person leading the army to big defeat and putting the king in danger, Ominous.

Conclusions:
Return (Hexagram 24) of Earth Trigram above and Thunder Trigram below.
Symbolic: FirstNiner initiates Return of the Yangs, starting new cycle of growth and prosperity.

King Wen:
Sees Return of Yangs, a 7-steps-cycle changes, rising 5 steps, out and then back to Return.
Return cycling, Heaven's Way, no hurry, rejoice friends' coming, Life is Freedom, Prosperity.

Zhougong:
FirstNiner: urges the straying youngsters to promptly Return to the virtuous Path, Auspicious.
Sixer2: urges Return to the practice of benevolence among neighbors, Auspicious.
Sixer3: urges the actives who stray often, to frequent Return to virtuous Path, No Faults.
Sixer4: urges that the Virtuous be influential so that strays be Return to the virtuous Path.
Sixer5: urges leaders be mindful of honesty and Return to the virtuous Path, No Regrets.
TopSixer: urges past leaders not be lost and Return to the virtuous Path, else Ominous
Return: urges individuals and leaders alike to Return to the virtuous Path at all time.

Kongzi:
Reads in Return, Yang's cycle (of actions, rest, rebirth), Way of Heaven /Earth reflected.
Ancient kings closed Pass to rest traders and travellers, a pause in life to think is important.

Lessons (Return Hex.24):
Endless cycles of life (action, rest, return), Return to the virtuous Path and have no Danger.

				No Delusion (Hexagram 25)	

(第二十五卦) 无妄 — **No Delusion (Hexagram 25)**

外	上九	________	**TopNiner**	**external**
乾 (天，上卦)	九五	________	**Niner5**	**Qian** (Heaven, Trigram above)
	九四	________	**Niner4**	
	六三	__ __	**Sixer3**	
震 (雷，下卦)	六二	__ __	**Sixer2**	**Zhen** (Thunder, Trigram below)
內	初九	________	**FirstNiner**	**internal**

卦辭 *(文王)* ：	***Hexagram Text (King Wen) :***
无妄：	No Delusion :
元亨利貞	Primal Prosperity, Favors Truthfulness
其匪正有眚	If Not Upright Has Eye-disease
不利有攸往	Not Favor Having Gentle Venture

彖曰 *(孔子)* ：	***Tuan Says (Kongzi explains) :***
无妄	No Delusion
剛自外來	Yang From Outside Cometh (Niner2 of Litigation Hex.05)
而爲主於內	And Be Master On Inside (FirstNiner of this Hex.25)
動而健	Actions (Thunder) With Strength (Heaven)
剛中而應	Yang (Niner5) Centre And Partner (Sixer2)
大亨以正，天之命也	Great Prosperity With Justice, Heaven's Order, that's
其匪正有眚	If Not Upright Has Eye-sickness
不利有攸往	Not Favor Having Gentle Venture
无妄之往，何之矣	No Delusion Its Venture, Any Venture that's (alright)
天命不祐，行矣哉	Heaven's Order Not Protecting, Action that's Alas!

Comments:
Image: Beneath Heaven, Thunder Rolling, awakening all Matters alike with No Delusion.
Symbolic: Niner2 of Litigation Hex. came here be FirstNiner, the master liner of No Delusion.
Wen: No Delusion, Primal Prosperity favors Truth; not upright is blindness, don't Venture.
Kongzi: Great Prosperity, be Upright, No Delusion, Heaven protects, then any Venture alright.
[Xu:無267亡也,无奇字通於元者王育說天屈西北爲无;亡267逃也;妄263亂也;眚73目病生翳]

象曰 *(孔子)* ：	***HexagramSign Says (Kongzi) :***
天下雷行	Heaven Beneath Thunder Rolling
物與无妄	Matters With No Delusion
先王以茂對時育萬物	Past Kings With Luxuriant Correct Timing Nurture All Matters

Comments:
Thunder rolling beneath Heaven, Awakening all Matters alike with No Delusion.
Likewise, past Kings following the natural luxuriance and timing of nature, nurtured all matters.
[Xu: 茂22艸豐盛也]

爻辭 *(周公)* :	*Liner Text (Zhougong) :*
初九 :	**FirstNiner:**
无妄，往吉	No Delusion, Venture Auspicious
象曰 *(孔子)* :	*LinerSign says (Kongzi) :*
无妄之往	No Delusion Its Venture
得志也	Achieve Ambition that's

Comments:
FirstNiner, master liner of this Hexagram, also master liner of lower Trigram Thunder for action.
At start, no partner, no prejudices, No Delusion venturing out, achieving ambition, Auspicious.

六二 :	**Sixer2:**
不耕穫	Not Ploughing Not Harvesting
不菑畬	No 1year-farmland, 3year-farmland
則利有攸往	Hence Favors Having Gentle Venture.
象曰 *(孔子)* :	*LinerSign says (Kongzi) :*
不耕穫，未富也	Not Ploughing Harvesting, Not Wealthy that's

Comments:
Sixer2, right positioned, gentle, has Niner5 partner, wishing to venture above to join him.
Hence not ploughing, not harvesting and has No Delusion of getting Wealthy either.
[Xu: 耕93犂也；穫145刈穀也；菑24不耕田也；畬290三歲治田

六三 :	**Sixer3:**
无妄之災	No Delusion Its Calamity
或繫之牛	Or Tethered The Oxen
行人之得	Passerby Person, His Gain
邑人之災	Local People, Their Calamity (loss)
象曰 *(孔子)* :	*LinerSign says (Kongzi) :*
行人得牛	Passerby Person Gain Oxen
邑人災也	Country People, Calamity that's

Comments:
Sixer3, weak, not centre, wrong position, stands accused when Passerby took tethered Oxen.
However, this unexpected calamity, Local People has No Delusion that Sixer3 is innocence.
[Xu: 災209天火；邑131國也]

九四 :	**Niner4:**
可貞，无咎	Able be Truthful, No Faults
象曰 *(孔子)* :	*LinerSign says (Kongzi) :*
可貞无咎	Able be Truthful, No Faults.
固有之也	Long-time Has It, that's

Comments:
Niner4, strong but wrong position, no partner below, Truthful, No Faults.
Suitable for maintaining existing conditions, and has No Delusion for changes.

九五：	**Niner5:**
无妄之疾	No Delusion Its sickness
勿藥有喜	Don't take-Medicine, Has Joy
象曰 *(孔子)* ：	***LinerSign says (Kongzi) :***
无妄之藥	No Delusion Its Medicine (untried)
不可試也	Not Allow Trying, that's

Comments:
Niner5, right, centre and Premier position, partner below, best of health, peak of No Delusion.
Suffers sudden unexpected sickness, don't try untried medicine, will self-resolved, has Joy.

上九：	**TopNiner:**
无妄	No Delusion
行有眚	Ventures Have Eye-sickness
无攸利	No Easy Gain
象曰 *(孔子)* ：	***LinerSign says (Kongzi) :***
无妄之行	No Delusion Its Venture
窮之災也	End-of-road Its Calamity, that's

Comments:
TopNiner, Yang strong, has No Delusion, just End-of-road life situation, Calamity.
In advance age, best take a rest, any action is like blind venture, and success not easy.

Conclusions:
No Delusion (Hexagram 25) of Thunder Trigram below and Heaven Trigram above.
Image: Beneath Heaven, Thunder rolling, awakening all matters alike with No Delusion.
Symbolic: Actions with Strength, that's FirstNiner with Niner5 and partner, Primally Auspicious.

King Wen:
No Delusion is Primal Prosperity favors Truth; not Upright is blindness not favoring Ventures.

Zhougong:
FirstNiner: urges the young to venture with No Delusion, to achieve ambition, Auspicious
Sixer2: urges that not planting not harvesting, to have No Delusion of being Wealthy.
Sixer3: urges that unexpected lost can happen, to have No Delusion of accused, Calamity.
Niner4, urges that maintaining status quo, No Delusion for ventures, No Faults.
Niner5, urges not to try Delusional Medicine, sickness will self-resolved, has Celebration.
TopNiner, urges to have No Delusion about end of life calamity.
No Delusion: people ought to have No Delusion at all time, but the Unexpected can happen.

Kongzi:
Below Heaven Thunder rolling, No Delusion, Heaven protects, then any Venture alright.
Action with Strength, like past Kings, nurture all matters with No Delusion, by observing nature.
(无妄：災也，雜卦傳)   (No Delusion : disastrous that's - Miscellaneous 10th 'Wing')

Lessons learned (No Delusion Hex.25)
Action meet Strength, nurture all matters with No Delusion, observe Nature's way and timing.
Likewise in society it seems Delusional to declare "Me First" and expect all others to agree!

(第二十六卦) 大畜　　　　　　　　　　**Great Constraint (Hexagram 26)**

外		上九	________	**TopNiner**		**external**
艮	(山，上卦)	六五	__ __	**Sixer5**	**Gen**	**(Mountain, Trigram above)**
		六四	__ __	**Sixer4**		
		九三	________	**Niner3**		
乾	(天，下卦)	九二	________	**Niner2**	**Qian**	**(Heaven, Trigram below)**
	內	初九	________	**FirstNiner**		**internal**

卦辭 *(文王)*：	***Hexagram Text (King Wen) :***
大畜：	Great Constraint:
利貞	Favors Integrity
不家食，吉	Not Family Feed, Auspicious (official employment)
利涉大川	Favors Venturing Big River

象曰 *(孔子)：*	***Tuan says (Kongzi explains) :***
大畜：	Great Constraint :
剛健篤實輝光	Yangs Strength Earnest Solid Shining Bright
日新其德	Daily Renew Its Virtues
剛上而尚賢	Strong Above (Mountain) Has Respect for Virtuous-Talents
能止健，大正也	Able Halting Strength (Heaven), Greatly Upright that's
不家食吉	Reject Family Feeds (earning official pay) Auspicious
養賢也	Nuture Virtuous-Talents that's
利涉大川	Favors Venturing Big River
應乎天也	Accord With Heaven that's

Comments:
Image: Mountain above, blocking strength of Heaven's 3 Yangs below, Great Constraint.
Wen: Reject Family Feed, to earn official pay, favors venturing out, with Integrity, Auspicious.
Kongzi: Pool of Yangs' strength below, daily renewal, nurturing talents, in accord with Heaven.
[Xu: 畜(chu4)291田畜从田从茲, 茲益也；篤200馬行頓遲；遲40徐行也；徐43安行也]

象曰 *(孔子)：*	*HexagramSign says (Kongzi) :*
天在山中，大畜	Heaven In Mountain Within, Big Containment
君子以多識前言往行	Junzi With More Knowledge of Ancients' Sayings and Actions
以畜其德	To Store-up Own Virtues

Comments:
Heaven beneath Mountain, Image of Great Constraint.
Junzi seeks more knowledge of Ancient's sayings and actions, to enrich own store of Virtues.

爻辭 *(周公)* :   *Liner Text (Zhougong) :*

初九 :   **FirstNiner:**
有厲   Has Gravity
利巳   Favors Ceased
象曰 *(孔子)* :   *LinerSign says (Kongzi) :*
有厲利巳   Has Seriousness, Advantages Ceased
不犯災也   Not Committing Disaster, that's

Comments:
In Great Constraint, Yin and Yang, partner's favoring each other ceased.
Contained by Sixer4 above, FirstNiner is not venturing to court disaster, as situation Grave.
[Xu: 巳311巳藏萬物見成文章故巳爲蛇象]

九二 :   **Niner2:**
輿說輹   Carriage Dislodged Axle
象曰 *(孔子)* :   *LinerSign says (Kongzi) :*
輿說輹   Carriage Dislodged Axle
中无尤也   Centre, No Worries that's

Comments:
In Great Constraint, between Yin Yang partnership favors ceased, Nine2 constraint by Sixer5.
Niner2, Yin position, Axle broken like self-Constraint, not going forward, No Worries.
[Xu: 輿301車輿也；輹301車軸縛也]

九三 :   **Niner3:**
良馬逐   Fine Horses Chasing (playing)
利艱貞   Favors Difficult Integrity
日閑輿衞   Daily Practice Charioteering, Defences
利有攸往   Favors Having Gentle Progress
象曰 *(孔子)* :   *LinerSign says (Kongzi) :*
利有攸往   Favors Having Gentle Progress
上合志也   Above (TopNiner) Accord of Wishes that's

Comments:
In Great Constraint, Yang and Yang partnership, not opposing but having Accord of Wills.
Niner3 and TopNiner like fine horses frolicking together, favors gentle progress.

六四 :   **Sixer4:**
童牛之牿   Young Ox, Its Horn-guard
元吉   Primally Auspicious
象曰 *(孔子)* :   *LinerSign says (Kongzi) :*
六四元吉   Sixer4, Primally Auspicious
有喜也   Has Joy, that's

Comments:
In Great Constraint, Sixer4 taming of FirstNiner is like a Young Ox with Horn-guard.
Starting Constraint early is important, easy to succeed, Primally Auspicious.
[Xu: 牿29牛馬牢；告30牛觸人角,箸橫木所以告人]

六五：	**Sixer5:**
豶豕之牙	Castrated Boar, Its Tasks
吉	Auspicious
象曰 *(孔子)：*	***LinerSign says (Kongzi) :***
六五之吉	Sixer5 Own Auspiciousness
有慶也	Has Celebration, that's

Comments:
Wild Boar Constraint by castration, then its Tasks become fearsome no more.
Symbolic of Sixer5, Premier achieving Great Constraint of the Yangs below, Auspicious.
[Xu: {豕賁}197{羊夷}也......；豕196彘也竭其尾故謂之豕]

上九：	**TopNiner:**
何天之衢	O'What Heavenly Thorough-fares!
亨	Auspicious
象曰 *(孔子)：*	***LinerSign says (Kongzi) :***
何天之衢	O'What Heavenly Thorough-fare!
道大行也	The-Way Great Adoption, that's

Comments:
TopNiner, break-out of Great Constraint by Mountain, enjoys Freedom Heavenly Thorough-fare.
Great Adoption of The-Way, cultivating talents of good governance for the world, Prosperity.
[Xu: 衢44四達謂之衢]

Conclusions:
Great Constraint (Hexagram 26) of Heaven Trigram below and Mountain Trigram above.
Image: Great Constraint of Heaven beneath, with Mountain blocking above.
Symbolic: store of Heaven's strength 3 Yangs below, Mountain above Great Constraint above.

King Wen:
Great Constraint, no Home Feed, favors venturing for Official service, with Integrity Auspicious.

Zhougong:
In Great Constraint, Yang-Yang opposition, Yin-Yang partnership advantages no longer apply.
Bottom 3 Liners, weaknesses reflect varied responses to Great Constraint by Authority above.
Top 3 Liners reflect varied ways applied in Great Constraint on those beneath.
Great Constraint break-out, to Heaven'ly Freedom, World Adoption of The-Way to Prosperity.
Great Constraint: means constraint for the strong Yangs and all partnership favors ceased.

Kongzi:
Daily Renewal of Virtues, nurturing talents, with World Adoption of the-Way, Prosperity.
Great Store of Virtues in the sayings and actions of the ancients for nurturing talents.
(大畜：時也，雜卦傅)　　　 (Great Constraint : Timing that's - Miscellaneous 10th Wing)

Lessons learned (Great Constraint Hex.26) :
Junzi, learns more from the sayings and actions of the Ancients, to enrich store of Virtues.

(第二十七卦) 頤　　　　　　　　　　　**Nurturing (Hexagram 27)**

<pre>
　　　　外　　　上九　________　TopNiner　　　　　　external
艮 (山, 上卦)　六五　__ __　Sixer5　　Gen (Mountain, Trigram above)
　　　　　　　六四　__ __　Sixer4

　　　　　　　六三　__ __　Sixer3
震 (雷, 下卦)　六二　__ __　Sixer2　　Zhen (Thunder, Trigram below)
　　　　內　　　初九　________　FirstNiner　　　　　internal
</pre>

卦辭 *(文王)* ：	***Hexagram Text (King Wen)*** :
頤 ：	Nurturing:
貞吉	Integrity Auspicious
觀頤	Watch Nurturing
自求口實	Self Seeking Mouth Solid (food)

象曰 *(孔子)* ：	***Tuan says (Kongzi explains)*** :
頤，貞吉	Nurturing, has Integrity Auspicious
養正則吉也	Nurturing Right Then Auspicious that's
觀頤	Watch Nurturing
觀其所養也	Watch It How Being Nurtured
自求口實	Self Seeking Mouth Solid (food)
觀其自養也	Watch The Self Feeding that's
天地養萬物	Heaven Earth Nurturing All Matters
聖人養賢以及萬民	The Sage Nurturing Virtuous-Talents, Including All Citizens
頤之時大矣哉	Time of Nurturing, Great Indeed that's

Comments:
Image: FirstNiner (lower jaw), TopNiner (upper jaw), 4 Yins (cavity), mouth for Nurturing.
King Wen: encourage nurturing Integrity Auspicious, self seeking sustenance be independent.
Kongz: Heaven and Earth nourish all matters, the Sage nurtures Talents to help all people.

(Xu: 頤183舉目視)

象曰 *(孔子)* ：	***HexagramSign says (Kongzi)*** :
山下有雷，頤	Mountain below has Thunder, Nurturing
君子以慎言語	CulturedOne be Careful with Speech
節飲食	Thrifty with Food and Drink

Comments:
Maxim: Illness enter through mouth, Misfortune exit through mouth.
Kongzi warns, Junzi (Gentleman) be careful with speech and be thrifty in wining and dining.

爻辭 *(周公)* :	*Liner Text (Zhougong) :*
初九 :	**FirstNiner:**
舍爾靈龜	Give-up Bright Spiritual Turtle
觀我朵頤，凶	Watch Me Drop-Jaw, Ominous
象曰 *(孔子)* :	*LinerSign says (Kongzi) :*
觀我朵頤	Watch Me Drop-Jaw (with desires)
亦不足貴也	Also Not Worthy be Valued, that's

Comments:
FirstNiner foresaking the innocence of Spiritual Turtle that does not feed.
Watching partner Sixer4 drop-jaw with desires, should not be encouraged, Ominous.
[Xu: 舍108市居曰舍；爾70麗與爽同意；爽70明也；朵119樹木垂朵朵]

六二 :	**Sixer2:**
顛頤拂經	Upset Nurturing, Brush-off the Norms
于丘頤，征凶	For High Nurturing, Expedition Ominous
象曰 *(孔子)* :	*LinerSign says (Kongzi) :*
六二征凶	Sixer2 Expedition Ominous (to Top Niner)
行失類也	Action Lost Kind that's (not same kind)

Comments:
Upsetting the norms, Sixer2 does not seek Nurturing from near neighbor FirstNiner below.
Instead going to TopNiner above, and also Yangs are of a different kind from Yins, Ominous.
[Xu: 顛181頂也；經271織也；織271作帛之總名也；丘169土之高也非人所爲]

六三 :	**Sixer3:**
拂頤，貞凶	Brush-off Nurturing, with Integrity still Ominous
十年勿用，无攸利	Ten Years Not be Used, No Easy Gain
象曰 *(孔子)* :	*LinerSign says (Kongzi) :*
十年勿用	Ten Years Not be Used
道大悖也	Way, Great Confusion that's

Comments:
Sixer3, Yang position, not upright, also at top of action Thunder, rash in actions, Ominous.
Brush-off Nurturing, Sixer3's action is Confusion with the virtuous Way, not be allowed.
[Xu: 拂257過擊也；悖54亂也]

六四 :	**Sixer4:**
顛頤，吉	Reverse Nurturing, Auspicious
虎視眈眈	Tiger look, Gaze Intensive
其欲逐逐，无咎	Its Desires Chasing Chasing, No Faults
象曰 *(孔子)* :	*LinerSign says (Kongzi) :*
顛頤之吉	Revers Nurturing, its Auspiciousness
上施光	Above Bestowing Sunshine, that's

Comments:
Sixer4, a Yin in correct senior position above, and is the right partner of FirstNiner below.
Reverse Nurturing disbursing from above, Sixer4 tiger-gazing of First Niner, Auspicious.
[Xu: 眈71視近而志遠；逐41追也]

六五：	**Sixer5:**
拂經，居貞吉	Brush-off the Norms, Stay with Integrity Auspicious
不可涉大川	Not Allow Treading Great River
象曰 *(孔子)*：	***LinerSign says (Kongzi) :***
居貞之吉	Stay with Integrity, its Auspiciousness
順以從上也	Docile And Obey Above (TopNiner), that's

Comments:
Sixer5, weak as King, and against the norms not able to provide sustenance for the people.
But has Integrity, is docile and obey TopNiner the source of Nurturing, Auspicious.
(Xu: 拂257過擊也; 經271織也)

上九：	**TopNiner:**
由頤，屬吉	Source of Nurturing, Gravely Auspicious
利涉大川	Favors to Tread Great River
象曰 *(孔子)*：	***LinerSign says (Kongzi) :***
由頤屬吉	Source of Nurturing, Grave responsibility Auspicious
大有慶也	Great Having Celebrations, that's

Comments:
TopNiner, Yang on high position, able to Tread Great River, means able to handle Great Task.
With King approval, Grave responsibility provides Nurturing services for all people, Auspicious.

Conclusions:
Nourishment (Hexagram 27): Mountain Trigram above and Thunder Trigram below.
Image: non-moving Mountain Jaw above and moving Thunder Jaw below, forming the Mouth.
Symbolic: Mouth of nourishment for body, and of speech for communication, feelings.

King Wen:
Observes our Nurturing of Virtues, especially of our Integrity, Auspicious,
Encourages self-seeking Sustenance, better be independent than relying on others to feed us.

Zhougong:
FirstNiner: Abandon Chastity, observing Sixer4, drop-jaw with desires, Ominous
Sixer2: Upset Nurturing norms, seeking from TopNiner Yang of different kind, Ominous.
Sixer3: Brush-off Nurturing, top of Thunder, rash not Virtuous, 10 years cut-off, Ominous.
Sixer4: Reverse Nurturing, Tiger-gazing lowly FirstNiner, sustenance from high, Auspicious.
Sixer5: weak, Brush-off Nurturing, trusts Top Niner to provide, has Integrity Auspicious
TopNiner: Nurturing source in high position, Grave responsibility for all people, Auspicious.
Nurturing: Danger for people of the 3 lower-levels, but Auspicious for 3 above-levels.

Kongzi:
Heaven and Earth Nurturing all matters, the Sage nurtures Talents to help all people.
Junzi Nurturing self with Care in Speech and Thrift in Food and Drink.
(頤：養正也，雜卦傳)   (Nurturing : Nourishing Correct that's- Miscellaneous 10th Wing)

Lessons (Nurturing Hex.27):
One has to be Careful in Speech and Communication and be thrifty in Wining and Dining.
Nurturing Hexagram truly reflects real life, with people below struggle daily to make ends meet.

(第卦二十八)　大過　　　　　　　　**Great Excess (Hexagram 28)**

<table>
<tr><td></td><td>外</td><td>上六</td><td>__ __</td><td>**TopSixer**</td><td>external</td></tr>
<tr><td>兌 （澤，上卦）</td><td></td><td>九五</td><td>_______</td><td>**Niner5**</td><td>**Dui (Wetland, Trigram above)**</td></tr>
<tr><td></td><td></td><td>九四</td><td>_______</td><td>**Niner4**</td><td></td></tr>
<tr><td></td><td></td><td>九三</td><td>_______</td><td>**Niner3**</td><td></td></tr>
<tr><td>巽 （風，下卦）</td><td></td><td>九二</td><td>_______</td><td>**Niner2**</td><td>**Xun (Wind, Trigram below)**</td></tr>
<tr><td></td><td>內</td><td>初六</td><td>__ __</td><td>**FirstSixer**</td><td>internal</td></tr>
</table>

卦辭 *(文王)* ：	***Hexagram Text (King Wen)* :**
大過：	Great Excess:
棟橈	Highest-beam Bend
利有攸往	Favor Having Slow Progress
亨	Prosperity

彖曰 *(孔子)* ：	***Tuan says (Kongzi explains)* :**
大過	Great Excess
大者過也	Great (Yangs) They're in Excess that's
棟橈	Highest-beam Bend
本末弱也	Origin (FirstSixer) End (TopSixer) weak (Yins), that's
剛過而中	Strong (Yangs) in Excess and Central
巽而說，行	Xun (Wind) And Joy (Wetland), Actions
利有攸往	Favor Having Slow Progress
乃亨	Hence Prosperity
大過之時大矣哉	Time of Great Excess, Great Indeed, that's

Comments:
Image: Wind below Wetland, centrally 4 Yangs, Great Excess of Yangs, weak Yins at the ends
Wen: Image of Highest-beam Sagging from Excess Yangs, augurs progress, prosperity.
Kongzi: Wind (Conform) in actions with Wetland (Joy), Great Excess, Time of Greatness.

[Xu: 過39度也；度65法制也；棟120極也；橈119曲木也；曲268象器受物之形；矣110語已詞；哉32言之閒]

象曰 *(孔子)* ：	***HexagramSign says (Kongzi)* :**
澤滅木，大過	Wetland Destroys Wood (Xun, Wind), Great Excess
君子以獨立不懼	Junzi In Standing Alone, Not Fearful
遯世无悶	Retreats from Society, Not Unhappy

Comments:
Wetland kills Wood below, Image of Great Excess of Water destroying Wood.
Junzi stands steadfast, alone, Fearless, not Unhappy even when Ostracised, Greatness.

[Xu: 滅237盡也；懼218恐也]

爻辭 *(周公)* :	*Liner Text (Zhougong)* :

初六： — **FirstSixer:**

藉用白茅，无咎 — Rituals Use White Thatch, No Faults

象曰 *(孔子)* : — *LinerSign says (Kongzi)* :

藉用白茅 — Rituals Use White Thatch

柔在下也 — Softness (FirstSixer) At Bottom, that's

Comments:
For Rituals and ceremonies, using white (for purity) Thatch grass as flooring, No Faults.
White Thatch symbolises lowly FirstSixer's humble Purity in servitude.
(Kongzi elaborates when asked by disciples, 5th Wing para.8)
[Xu: 藉24祭藉，一日艸不編也 ；　茅17菅也从艸]

九二： — **Niner2:**

枯陽生梯 — Withering Poplar (tree) Growing Roots

老夫得其女妻，无不利 — Old Man Gets His Girl Wife, None Not Favorable

象曰 *(孔子)* : — *LinerSign says (Kongzi)* :

老夫得其女妻 — Old Man Gets His Girl Wife

過以相與也 — Excess By Mutual Engagement, that's

Comments:
Niner2, in Yin position, gentle, taking young neighbour FirstSixer as wife, not Unfavorable.
In Great Excess of Yangs, this happening with mutual willingness, may be expected.
[Xu: 枯119槀也 ；梯123木階 ；階306陛也 ；陛306升高階也]

九三： — **Niner3:**

棟橈，凶 — Highest-beam Sagging, Ominous

象曰 *(孔子)* : — *LinerSign says (Kongzi)* :

棟橈之凶 — Highest-beam Sagging, This Ominousness

不可以有輔也 — Not Possible Having Assistance, that's

Comments:
Niner3, Yang in Yang position, is strongest in Great Excess, that no one can assist, Ominous.
Like Highest-beam once Sagging, cannot be helped with pillars, only be replaced.
[Xu: 輔303人頰車也 ；頰182面旁]

九四： — **Niner4:**

棟隆，吉 — Highest-beam Robust, Auspicious

有它吝 — Having Another, Painful

象曰 *(孔子)* : — *LinerSign says (Kongzi)* :

棟隆之吉 — Highest-beam, Its Auspiciousness

不橈乎下也 — Not Bending Towards Below, that's

Comments:
Niner4, Robust in Yin position, hence tempered in actions, Auspicious.
If inclined towards partner FirstSixer below, further tempered in actions, Painful experience.
[Xu: 隆127豐大也从生 ；乎101語之餘也，象聲上越揚之形也]

九五：	**Niner5:**
枯陽生華	Withering Poplar Growing Flowers
老婦得其士夫	Old Woman Gets Her Scholar Husband
无咎无譽	No Faults, No Honors
象曰 *(孔子)：*	*LinerSign says (Kongzi) :*
枯陽生華	Withering Poplar Growing Flowers
何可久也	How Can Be Lasting, that's
老婦士夫	Old Woman, Scholar Husband
亦可醜也	Also Can be Ashamed, that's

Comments:
Niner5, Premier of the Yangs, marrying old neighbor TopSixer, no Faults.
No Honors for the old woman, young man may be ashamed, as this is not the expected norms.

上六：	**TopSixer:**
過涉滅頂，凶	Excess Immersion Loses Head, Ominous
无咎	No Faults
象曰 *(孔子)：*	*LinerSign says (Kongzi) :*
過涉之凶	Excess Immersion, Its Ominous
不可咎也	Not Allow be Faulted, that's

Comments:
In the upper limits of Excessive involvement in affairs, TopSixer risks losing Head, Ominous.
However the Greatness of risking one's life for a good cause may not be Faulted.
[Xu: 潛233涉水也, 一曰藏也]

Conclusions:
Great Excess (Hexagram 28): Wetland Trigram above and Wind Trigram below.
Image: Yins are Small, Yangs are Great, 4 Yangs in-a-row Excess, hence Great Excess.

King Wen:
Image of Highest-beam with concentration of Great Yangs (Strength), augurs prosperity.

Zhougong:
FirstSixer: lowly, cheap White Thatch symbolises purity in servitude, No Faults.
Niner2: First of Excess Yangs, taking neighbor as young wife, Not Unfavourable.
Niner3: Strongest of Excess Yangs, cannot be assisted like Sagging Highest-beam, Ominous.
Niner4: Gentle in Yin position, Auspicious; incline to flirting with married First Sixer, has Pain.
Sixer5: Marrying old neighbor, for woman No Honor, for man be Ashamed as Not Norms.
TopSixer: Excessive involvement, risking life for a good cause, such Greatness No Faults.
Great Excess: is time for the Revelation of Greatness, and what are Not The Norms.

Kongzi:
Wetland kills Trees, time of Excess water, time of Danger, also time for Revelation of Greatness.
CulturedOne, be steadfast standing alone, Fearless, and not Unhappy even when ostracised.
(大過：顛也，雜卦傳)   (Great Excess : Upsetting that's - Miscellaneous 10th Wing)

Lessons (Great Excess Hex.28) :
Time for Junzi (Gentleman) to be Fearless when Alone, and not Unhappy when Ostracized.

(第二十九卦) 坎   **Water-Pit (Hexagram 29)**

	上六	— —	**TopSixer**		external
坎 (水, 上卦)	九五	———	**Niner5**	Kan	(Water, Trigram above)
	六四	— —	**Sixer4**		
	六三	— —	**Sixer3**		
坎 (水, 下卦)	九二	———	**Niner2**	Kan	(Water, Trigram below)
	初六	— —	**FirstSixer**		internal

卦辭 *(文王)* :	*Hexagram Text (King Wen)* :
習坎 :	Water-Pit :
有孚，維心亨	Has Trust, Exclusively Heart's Freedom
行有尚	Action Has Aspiration

彖曰 *(孔子)* :	*Tuan says (Kongzi explains)* :
習坎	Water-Pit (danger)
重險也	Double Danger that's
水流而不盈	Water Flowing And Not Full
行險而不失其信	Treading Danger And Not Lost Its Trust
維心亨	Exclusively Heart's Freedom
乃以剛中也	Thus With Strong (Yang) Centres that's
行有尚，往有功也	Action Has Aspiration, Venture Has Achievement that's
天險不可升也	Heaven's Danger Not Possible Rising-above that's
地險山川丘陵也	Earth's Danger Mountains, Rivers, Hills, Mound that's
王公設險以守其國	Kings Lords Setup Danger-barriers For Guarding Their Kingdoms
險之時用大矣哉	Danger, Its Timing and Usage Great Indeed, that's

Comments:
Image: Water (Danger), above Water (Danger), Double Danger; Yangs Centres between 2 Yins.
Wen: Double Danger, Yangs Centres have Trust, Hearts' Free Actions have Aspirations.
Kongzi: Treading Danger not lost Trust, setup Danger-barriers in defence, Great Deployment.
[Xu: 坎288陷也，陷305高下也，習74數飛也]

象曰 *(孔子)* :	*HexagramSign says (Kongzi)* :
水洊至，習坎	Water Flowing Arrive, Water-Pit
君子以常德行	Junzi With Ever Virtuous Actions
習教事	Repeated Teaching Missions

Comments:
Water flowing continuously, Water-Pit; non-stop supply of Nourishment.
Likewise Junzi non-stop self-cultivation and non-stop teaching others ever virtuous conduct.
[Xu: 洊 ....]

爻辭 (周公) :	*Liner Text (Zhougong) :*

初六 :	**FirstSixer:**
習坎	Water-Pit
入于坎窞，凶	Enter Into Pit's Small-Pit, Ominous
象曰 (孔子) :	*LinerSign says (Kongzi) :*
習坎入坎，失道凶也	Water-Pit Enter Small-Pit, Lost Way Ominous that's

Comments:
FirstSixer, weak in Yang position lost Way, falling into Double Danger, hence Ominous.
[Xu: 窞152坎中小坎也]

九二 :	**Niner2:**
坎有險	Pit Has Danger
求小得	Request, Small Gain
象曰 (孔子) :	*LinerSign says (Kongzi) :*
求小得	Request, Small Gain
未出中也	Not Out of Centre that's (stay upright)

Comments:
Niner2, a Yang in Yin position, benevolent in Double Danger.
As stays Centre and Upright has Trust, may request and have Small Gain.

六三 :	**Sixer3:**
來之坎坎	Coming, Its Pit on Pit
險且枕	Danger Also Head-rest (on Danger)
入于坎窞，勿用	Enter Into Pit and Pit-in-Pit, Don't Do-it
象曰 (孔子) :	*LinerSign says (Kongzi) :*
來之坎坎	Coming, The Pit on Pit (Danger upon Danger)
終无功也	Finally No Achievement that's

Comments:
Sixer3, weak, misplaced, not centre, treads in Danger (Water), faces coming Danger (Water).
In Double Danger, not a time for action and cannot expect success in the end.
[Xu: 且299薦也 ；枕121臥所薦首者]

六四 :	**Sixer4:**
樽酒簋貳	Bottle of Wine, Two Lacquer-trays (of food)
用缶	Using Earthen-ware (for simple rites)
納約自牖	Reception of Agreement Through Window (facing Heaven)
終无咎	Finally No Faults
象曰 (孔子) :	*LinerSign says (Kongzi) :*
樽酒簋貳	Bottle of Wine, Two Lacquer-trays
剛柔際	Yang Yin Meeting (alliance) that's (Sixer4 and Niner5)

Comments:
Sixer4, right position, not centre, next to Premier, weak, enters into alliance in time of Danger.
Simple Rites avowing alliance, through window in open scrutiny of Heaven, finally no Faults.
[Xu: 樽 .. ；簋97黍稷方器 ；貳130副益 ；副91判 ；牖143穿壁以木爲交蔥 ；際300壁會也]

九五：	Niner5:
坎不盈	Pit Not Full
祗既平，无咎	Land Harvest Levelled, No Faults (fairly shared)
象曰 *(孔子)*：	*LinerSign says (Kongzi)*：
坎不盈	Pit Not Full
中未大也	Centre Not Big that's

Comments:
Niner5 Premier, being Centre and Upright, Not just filling own coffer and Not acting Big.
In Double Danger, with land and harvest sharing fairly with citizens, No Faults.
[Xu: 祗8地祗提出萬物者也；既106小吃也]

上六：	TopSixer:
係用徽纆	Tie-up Using Tight Rope
寘于叢棘	Place In Bush of Thorns
三歲不得，凶	3 Years No Gain, Ominous (not release)
象曰 *(孔子)*：	*LinerSign says (Kongzi)*：
上六失道	TopSixer Lost the Way
凶三歲也	Danger for 3 Years, that's

Comments:
TopSixer at Extreme of Danger, weak, no responder below, lost virtuous Way that's.
Liken to being tied up and confined in the thorny bush for 3 years with no hope of relief.
[Xu: 係167緊束也；徽 … ；纆272繞也；寘152置也；棘143小棗叢]

Conclusions:
Water-Pit (Hexagram 29): Water Trigram above and Water Trigram below.
Image: Water below and above, Double Danger; 2 Yang Centres, trapped between Yins.
Symbolic: Both Yangs trapped between 2 Yins, Yangs at centres have Trust, No Partnerships.

King Wen:
In double Danger, has Trust, keeps Freedom of Heart and Venture with Aspirations.

Zhougong:
FirstSixer: In Double Danger, misplaced, not centre, lost Way (virtues), no responder, Ominous.
Niner2: In Pit, has Danger, Yin position Gentle and Centre Upright, may Quest for Small Gain.
Sixer3: Misplaced in Yang, Water (Danger), Facing more Water, Don't Act, finally No Success.
Sixer4: In Danger avow allegiance with Niner5, Heaven witnesses simple rites, finally NoFaults.
Niner5: King, Upright, not self-centred, shares land and harvest fairly with citizens, No Faults.
TopSixer: Danger Peak, weak, no responder, tied, confined in thorny bush 3 years, Ominous.
Water-Pit: is Ominous time, needs to keep low-profile, and stay the virtuous Way to survive.

Kongzi:
Water-Pit, Kings and Lords setup Danger-barriers in defence of Kingdom, Great Deployment.
Water flowing continuously, Junzi likewise is non-stop in self-cultivation and teaching others.
(坎：下也，雜卦傳)   (Water-Pit : Down-flowing that's - Miscellaneous 10th 'Wing')

Lessons (Water-Pit Hex.29):
Mountains and rivers are barriers and dangers in peace, but are also defences in wars.
In Danger think positive, stays the Way to free hearts and minds, to venture with aspirations.

(第三十卦) 離   **Fire (Hexagram 30)**

	上九	______	**TopNiner**	external
離（火, 上卦）	六五	__ __	**Sixer5**	**Li (Fire, Trigram above)**
	九四	______	**Niner4**	
	九三	______	**Niner3**	
離（火, 下卦）	六二	__ __	**Sixer2**	**Li (Fire, Trigram below)**
	初九	______	**FirstNiner**	internal

卦辭 *(文王) :*   ***Hexagram Text (King Wen) :***

離 :   Fire :

利貞，亨   Favours Integrity, Prosperity

畜牝牛，吉   Keep Female Cow, Auspicious

象曰 *(孔子) :*   ***Tuan Says (Kongzi explains) :***

離 :   Fire :

麗也   Shine that's

日月麗乎天   Sun Moon Shine In Heaven.

百穀草木麗乎上   Hundred (all) Cereals Grasses Woods, Shine-on From Above.

重明以麗乎正   Double Lights To Shine On the Righteous.

乃化成天下   Thus Transforming Successfully The World.

柔麗乎中正，故亨 Yins Shine On Centrist and Righteous, Hence Prosperity.

是以   Therefore

畜化牛，吉也   Keep Female Cows, Auspicious.

Comments:

Image: Fire Trigrams above and below, 2 Yin Centres pressured by Yangs on both sides.

Wen: Integrity then Prosperity, keeps gentleness and docility like female cow, Auspicious.

Kongzi: Fire, shine of sun and moon on crops and fields, also on the Righteous.

[Xu: 離76黃倉庚也鳴則蠶生 ；麗203旅行也鹿之性見食急則必旅行]

象曰 *(孔子) :*   ***HexagramSign Says (Kongzi) :***

明兩作，離   Light Twice Rising, Fire (sun and moon)

大人以繼明   Great Person By Successive Light

照于四方   Light Up Four Directions (the world).

Comments:

Sun and Moon double rising to shine day and night, Fire-shine.

Likewise Great Person endowed with enlightenment ought to help, lighting up the whole world.

[Xu: 繼272續也 ；續272連也]

爻辭 *(周公)*：	*Liner Text (Zhougong)* :
初九：	**FirstNiner :**
履錯然	Steps Unsteady Expected
敬之无咎	Respect This No Faults
象曰 *(孔子)*：	*LinerSign Says (Kongzi)* :
履錯之敬	This Respect of Steps Unsteady
以辟咎也	To Avoid Regrets that's.

Comments:
FirstNiner, at the dawn of Light with gait unsteady is expected.
Respect this fact as normal, take care thus avoiding falls and has No Regrets.
[Xu: 錯295金涂也；涂225水出益州…；然207燒也从火]

六二：	**Sixer2:**
黃離，元吉	Yellow Fire, Primally Auspicious
象曰 *(孔子)*：	*LinerSign Says (Kongzi)* :
黃離元吉	Yellow Fire Primally Auspicious
得中道也	Has Central Way that's

Comments:
Sixer2, a Yin has correct position and centre, is gentle Yellow Fire-shine.
Sixer2 is Upright and living the virtuous Way, hence Primally Auspicious.
[Xu: 黃291地之色也从田]

九三：	**Niner3:**
日昃之離	Day at Dusk This Fire-shine
不鼓缶而歌	Not Drumming Musical-urn And Sing
則大耋之嗟，凶	That's Great Elder's sighing, Ominous
象曰 *(孔子)*：	*LinerSign Says (Kongzi)* :
日昃之離	Day at Dusk This Fire-shine
何可久也	How Can it Last that's

Comments
Niner3 is sunset Fire-shine, the day at dusk.
Niner3 like an Elder, singing (sighing) not beating the musical-urn in the waning Twilight.
[Xu: 昃138日在西方時側也；耋173年八十曰耋；缶109瓦器所以盛酒漿]

九四：	**Niner4:**
突如其來如	Sudden Like That Cometh Like,
焚如,死如,棄如	Burning Like, Dying Like, Abandoning Like.
象曰 *(孔子)*：	*LinerSign Says (Kongzi)* :
突如其來如	Sudden Like That Cometh Like,
无所容也	None That Can Accommodate that's

Comments:
Niner4 makes a Fiery entry at the top Fire Trigram.
Like a rebel Leader bringing Fire destruction, death and desolation, as Not Accommodating.
[Xu: 突153犬从穴中暫出也；如262从隨也从女；容150盛也…盛受也]

六五：	**Sixer5:**
出涕沱若	Exuding Tears Deluge Like
戚嗟若，吉	Huge Sighing Like, Auspicious
象曰 *(孔子)：*	***LinerSign Says (Kongzi) :***
六五之吉	Sixer5 Its Auspiciousness
離王公也	Fire-shine King Lord that's

Comments:
Sixer5, Yin in honored position, misplaced between 2 Yangs, hence bawling in fear.
But as King of Fire, is gentle centre and Upright, has army support Auspicious.
[Xu: 戚267戍也；戍266斧也]

上九：	**TopNiner:**
王用出征	King Deployed Out on Campaign.
有嘉折首	Had Congratulation on Killing Head (rebel)
獲匪其醜，无咎	Capture Rebel Hordes, No Faults.
象曰 *(孔子)：*	***LinerSign Says (Kongzi) :***
王用出征	King Deployed Out on Campaign
以正邦也	To Put-right the States that's

Comments:
TopNiner deployed by King on a campaign to put-right the states.
The celebrated General killed the rebel Head, captured his horde, No Faults.
[Xu: 醜189可惡也；邦131國也从邑]

Conclusions:
Fire (Hexagram 30): Fire Trigram above and Fire Trigram below.
Image: Fire below Fire above, sun and moon shining day and night.
Symbolic: Sixer2 and Sixer5, 2 Yins gain centre positions, the Upright and Righteous shining.

King Wen:
Fire favors Integrity Prosperity, keeps gentleness docility like female cow, Auspicious.

Zhougong:
FirstNiner, Fire-shine at dawn, unsteady steps, respect this reality, and with care No Regrets.
Sixer2, right placed, soft Yellow Fire-shine, centre Upright, hence primally Auspicious.
Niner3, sunset Fire-shine, like an Elder, singing (sighing) without music in the waning Twilight.
Niner4, rebel Head's fiery entry at top Trigram, brings death, desolation, as Not Accommodating.
Sixer5, misplaced bawl in fear between 2 Yangs, Fire-shine King with army support, Auspicious.
TopNiner, General, celebrated, killed rebel Head, captured his horde, restored states. No faults.
Fire-shine: shining on commoners and leaders alike, shining for the Upright.

Kongzi:
Fire, shining of sun and moon on crops and fields, also on the Upright.
Suggests that Great Person endowed with enlightenment, helps to illuminate the world.

(離：上，雜卦傳)	(Fire-shine : Up-rising - Miscellaneous 10th 'Wing')

Lessons (Fire-shine Hex.30):
The Great Person endowed with Fire-shine enlightenment, ought to help illuminate the world.
Likewise Talented leaders ought to come out and serve with enlightenment, not to plunder.

（第三十一卦）咸   **Empathy (Hexagram 31)**

	外	上六	—— ——	**TopSixer**	external
兌（澤，上卦）		九五	————	**Niner5**	**Dui (Wetland, Trigram above)**
		九四	————	**Niner4**	
		九三	————	**Niner3**	
艮（山，下卦）		六二	—— ——	**Sixer2**	**Gen (Mountain, Trigram below)**
	內	初六	—— ——	**FirstSixer**	internal

卦辭 *(文王)* ：	*Hexagram Text (King Wen) :*
咸：	Empathy :
亨，利貞	Prosperity, Favors Integrity
取女吉	Take Girl, Auspicious

象曰 *(孔子)* ：	*Tuan says (Kongzi explains) :*
咸，感也	Empathy, Feeling that's
柔上而剛下	Yin (Sixer3) Rises And Yang (TopNiner) Descends (of Hex.12)
二氣感應	2 Energies (Yin, Yang) Feeling Responding
以相與	By Mutually Engaging
止而說	Stop (Mountain) Then Joy (Wetland)
男下女	Boy (Niner3) Below Girl (TopSixer) (courting)
以亨利貞	For Prosperity Favors having Integrity
取女吉也	Take Girl Auspicious that's
天地感而萬物化生	Heaven's Earth's Feeling And All Matters Transformed Alive
聖人感人心而天下和平	Sage's Feeling touches People's Heart And The World at Peace
觀其所感	Observing All That Feelings
而天地萬物之情可見矣	Then Heaven Earth All Matters, Their Loves Can be Seen

Comments:
Image: Mountain (Stop) below, Wetland (Joy) above, Controlled then Joy, Empathy.
Wen: Empathy, favors having Integrity for Prosperity, take girl in marriage Auspicious.
Kongzi: Heaven Earth Empathy transformed all matters alive; Sage's Empathy brings Peace.
[Xu: 咸33皆也悉也；悉28詳盡也；感222動人心也；取64捕取，獲者取左耳]

象曰 *(孔子)* ：	*HexagramSign says (Kongzi) :*
山上有澤，咸	Mountain, Above Has Wetland, Empathy
君子以虛受人	Junzi With Humility Accept People

Comments:
Mountain (Block) above has Wetland (Joy), Stop then Joy Empathy.
Junzi with Humility accepting all others.

爻辭 *(周公)* :	*Liner Text (Zhougong) :*
初六 :	**FirstSixer:**
咸其拇	Empathy At Big-toe
象曰 *(孔子) :*	*LinerSign Says (Kongzi) :*
咸其拇，志在外也	Empathy At Big-toe, Will On Outside that's

Comments:
FirstSixer, Yin weak, lowly, has shallow Empathy at Big-toe level.
Its Will is naturally to go outside and to meet partner Niner4 at Trigram above.

六二 :	**Sixer2:**
咸其腓，凶	Empathy At Leg-calf, Ominous
居吉	Stay-put Auspicious
象曰 *(孔子) :*	*LinerSign Says (Kongzi) :*
雖凶居吉	Although Danger, Stay-put Auspicious
順不害也	Docile then No Harm, that's

Comments:
Sixer2, Empathy at Leg-calf level, to meet partner Niner5 above, Ominous.
A weak Yin, better stay-put, docile, no harm waiting for Niner5 to come for her, Auspicious.
[Xu: 腓88脛腨也]

九三 :	**Niner3:**
咸其股	Empathy At Thigh
執其隨	Hold-on The Followers (FirstSixer, Sixer2)
往吝	Going-forth Painful (to Niner5)
象曰 *(孔子) :*	*LinerSign Says (Kongzi) :*
咸其股，亦不處也	Empathy At Thigh, Also Not Stay-put that's
志在隨人	Wishes On Follower-People (FirstSixer, Sixer2)
所執下也	That being Held are Below, that's

Comments:
Niner3, block by Niner4, Niner5 on way to partner TopSixer, going-forth Painful.
Hence Empathy at Thigh, Niner3 wishes to Hold-on to Followers FirstSixer and Sixer2.
[Xu: 股88髀也；執214捕罪人也]

九四 :	**Niner4:**
貞吉，悔亡	Integrity Auspicious, Regrets Lost
憧憧往來	Wavering Wavering Back and Forth
朋從爾思	Friends Agreeing to Thy Thinking
象曰 *(孔子) :*	*LinerSign Says (Kongzi) :*
貞吉悔亡，未感害也	Integrity Auspicious Regrets Lost, Not Feeling Harmed that's
憧憧往來，未光大也	Wavering Wavering Back and Forth, Not Shining Big that's

Comments:
Niner4, misplaced Regrets, Empathy at Heart centre of 3 Yangs, gain acceptance, Auspicious.
Wavering Thoughts accepted among friends, but Thoughts not bright, not extending beyond.
(Kongzi further elaborates when questioned by disciples, in: 6th 'Wing' para.5)
[Xu: 憧220意不定也]

九五：	**Niner5:**
咸其脢	Empathy At Back-muscle
无悔	No Regrets
象日 *(孔子)：*	***LinerSign Says (Kongzi) :***
咸其脢	Empathy At Back-muscle
志末也	Wills to all Tip-ends, that's (of tree branches)

Comments:
Niner5, Premier, Empathy at Back-muscle with no bias feelings, No Faults.
As Wills have reached the Farthest Corners in the Kingdom.
[Xu: 脢87背肉也 ；末118木上曰末, 一在其上]

上六：	**TopSixer:**
咸其輔頰舌	Empathy At Jaw Cheek Tongue
象日 *(孔子)：*	***LinerSign Says (Kongzi) :***
咸其輔頰舌	Empathy At Jaw Cheek Tongue
滕口說也	Gushing Mouth Joy, that's

Comments
TopSixer, weak Empathy at Face level with Jaw Cheek and Tongue.
TopSixer past prime, Gushing with talks and Tongue wagging, but no Actions!
[Xu: 輔303人頰車也 ；頰182面(旁)也 ；舌49在口所以言也別味也 ；滕230水超涌]

Conclusions:
Empathy (Hexagram 31): Mountain Hexagram below and Wetland Hexagram above.
Image: Mountain (Blocking), above Wetland (Joy), Controlled feeling meets Joy, Empathy.
Symbolic: Mountain (young son), above Wetland (young daughter), all Liners are Partnered.

King Wen:
Empathy, Integrity for Prosperity, young Boy courting young Girl above, Takes girl, Auspicious.

Zhougong:
FirstSixer: Weak, shallow Empathy at Big-toe level, wishes to join partner Niner4 above.
Sixer2: Empathy at Leg-calf, moving Ominous, Docile stay-put for Niner5 to come, Auspicious.
Niner3: Empathy at Thigh, held-on to Followers below, blocked to TopSixer above Painful.
Niner4: Wavering Empathy, not Luminous, no Harm, Heart of 3 Yangs, no regrets, Auspicious.
Niner5: Empathy at Back-muscle, non-feel non-bias, reaches all corners of State, No Regrets.
TopSixer: Weak, Empathy at Face, Tongue wagging Mouth gushing with Talks, but No Action!
Images of Empathy: feeling at body-parts, from Big-toe, Thigh to Face, Mouth and Tongue!

Kongzi:
Heaven's Earth's Empathy (no heart, non-bias) all embracing, transform all matters, all Lives.
Sage's Empathy moving People's Heart, brings Harmony and Peace.
Empathy, Junzi with Humility accepting all others.
(大過：顛也，雜卦傳)   (Great Excess : Upsetting that's - Miscellaneous 10th 'Wing')

Lessons (Empathy Hex.31) :
Empathy: With Blocking and Joy, confused feeling among Liners, reflective of Society.
Killings, unrests of the World today, show a lack of Empathy among religions and cultures.

（第卦三十二）恆　　　　　　　　　　**Everlasting (Hexagram 32)**

<table>
<tr><td>　</td><td>外</td><td>上六</td><td>__　__</td><td>TopSixer</td><td>external</td></tr>
<tr><td>震（雷，上卦）</td><td></td><td>六五</td><td>__　__</td><td>Sixer5</td><td>Zhen (Thunder, Trigram above)</td></tr>
<tr><td></td><td></td><td>九四</td><td>______</td><td>Niner4</td><td></td></tr>
<tr><td></td><td></td><td>九三</td><td>______</td><td>Niner3</td><td></td></tr>
<tr><td>巽（風，下卦）</td><td></td><td>九二</td><td>______</td><td>Niner2</td><td>Xun (Wind, Trigram below)</td></tr>
<tr><td>　</td><td>內</td><td>初六</td><td>__　__</td><td>FirstSixer</td><td>internal</td></tr>
</table>

卦辭(文王)：	**Hexagram Text (King Wen) :**
恆：	Everlasting:
亨，无咎，利貞	Prosperity, No Faults, Favors Integrity
利有攸往	Suitable having Slow Progress

彖曰(孔子)：	***Tuan says (Kongzi explains) :***
恆：	Everlasting:
久也	Longtime that's
剛上而柔下	Strong (Thunder) Above and Gentle (Wind) Below
雷風相與，巽而動	Thunder Wind Mutually Engaged, Flowing In Motion
剛柔皆應，恆	Yangs Yins All Corresponding, Everlasting (are partnered)
恆，亨，无咎，利貞	Everlasting, Prosperity, No Faults, Favors Integrity
久於其道也	Longtime Embraces The Way that's
天地之道，恆	Heaven Earth Their Way, Everlasting
久而不已也	Longtime And Not Over that's (still existing)
利有攸往，終則有始也	Favorable Having Slow Progress, Ends Thus Have Beginnings
日月得天而能久照	Sun Moon Have Heaven (blessing) Thus Can Longtime Shine
四時變化而能久成	Four Seasons Change Transform Thus Can Longtime Succeed
聖人久於其道	Sage Person Longtime In This Way
而天下化成	Thus The World's Transformation Succeeded
觀其所恆	Observing That Which been Everlasting
而天地萬物之情可見矣	Thus Heaven Earth All Matters, Their Nature Are Seen, indeed

Comments:
Image: Wind above Thunder, flowing in action Everlasting, all Yangs Yins have partners.
Wen: Everlasting brings Prosperity, No Faults, Integrity, suitable for gentle progress.
Kongzi: Everlasting existence of Heaven Earth, endless cycles of Sun, Moon, the 4 Seasons.
[Xu: 恆286常也从心从舟在二之閒上下心以舟施恆也；情217人之陰气有欲者也]

象曰(孔子)：	***HexagramSign says (Kongzi) :***
風雷，恆	Wind Thunder, Everlasting
君子以立不易方	Junzi By Standing on No-Change Side.

Comments:
Wind flowing Thunder action, flowing action, image of Everlasting.
Junzi stands on the un-wavering side of Everlasting Virtues.

爻辭 (周公) :	*Liner Text (Zhougong) :*

初六 :	**FirstSixer:**
浚恆，貞凶	Deep Everlasting, Integrity, Danger
无攸利	No Soft Gain
象曰 (孔子) :	*LinerSign says (Kongzi) :*
浚恆之凶	Deep Everlasting, The Danger
始求深也	Beginner (FirstSixer) Proposal Deep (to Niner4), that's

Comments:
FirstSixer has Integrity, but a premature proposal to Niner4 deep in Everlasting, Ominous.
Highlighting danger in the yearning for in-depth Everlasting relation at the start.
[Xu: 浚227水在臨淮从水]

九二 :	**Niner2:**
悔亡	Regrets Lost
象曰 (孔子) :	*LinerSign says (Kongzi) :*
九二悔亡	Nine2, Regrets Lost
能久中也	Able Longtime Centred, that's

Comments:
Niner2, Yang in Yin position has Regrets.
But also happy maintaining Centre Upright in Everlasting, hence Regrets no more.

九三 :	**Niner3:**
不恆其德	Not Everlasting His Virtues
或承之羞，貞吝	Or Supportive-role His shame, Integrity Painful
象曰 (孔子) :	*LinerSign says (Kongzi) :*
不恆其德	Not Everlasting His Virtues
无所容也	Not Been Accommodated, that's

Comments
Yang in Yang position, restive, has Integrity, but not keeping Everlasting Virtues.
Support role at top of lower Trigram, but not been accommodated in higher position, Painful.

九四 :	**Niner4:**
田无禽	Fields No Flying-birds
象曰 (孔子) :	*LinerSign says (Kongzi) :*
久非其位	Longtime Not In position
安得禽也	How to Have Flying-birds that's

Comments:
Niner4, Yang in Yin position, Longtime not in Rightful place, hence not able to run his life well.
This situation is reflected in his barren fields, no crops, and no Flying-birds come to eat.

六五：	**Sixer5:**
恒其德，貞	Everlasting Its Virtues, Integrity
婦人吉，夫子凶	Woman Auspicious, Gentleman Danger
象曰 *(孔子)：*	***LinerSign says (Kongzi) :***
婦人貞吉，從一而終也	Woman Faithful, Auspicious, Follow One Till End that's
夫子制義，從婦凶也	Gentleman Makes Appearances, Follow Woman Ominous that's.

Comments:
Everlasting Virtues: woman with Integrity marry one man, stays faithful till the End, Auspicious.
For man making appearances outside the house, following woman's docility, Ominous.

上六：	**TopSixer:**
振恆	Shaking Everlasting
凶	Ominous
象曰 *(孔子)：*	***LinerSign says (Kongzi) :***
振恆在上	Shaking Everlasting On High
大无功也	Great, No Achievement that's

Comments:
TopSixer weak Yin at the upper limit of Shaking Everlasting, Ominous.
Very senior with no achievement, hence position insecure.

Conclusions:
Everlasting (Hexagram 32): Wind Trigram below and Thunder Trigram above.
Image: Thunder above Wind, continuous flowing actions; Yins Yangs are paired for creations.
Symbolic: all Yins Yangs are partnered for creation of future generations, Everlasting.

King Wen:
Everlasting, Prosperity, no Faults, favors having Integrity, suitable for gentle progress.

Zhougong:
FirstSixer: Weak, Beginner's proposal to Niner4 in the bottom of Everlasting, Ominous.
Niner2: Yin positioned, but happy it is Centre of Everlasting, hence Regrets no more.
Niner3: of lower Trigram supportive, not been accommodated, Everlasting Virtues Painful.
Niner4: Longtime not in rightful position, now left with barren fields with No Flying-birds.
Sixer5: Everlasting with One man Auspicious for woman; for man woman's way Ominous.
TopSixer: Great on high, but weak with no achievement, in Shaking Everlasting, Ominous.
Everlasting: of Virtues desirable, of bad situations not desirable, of sexual bias unacceptable.

Kongzi:
Wind supporting Thunder, each of 3 Yins has a corresponding Yang, Everlasting procreation.
Advises Junzi (Gentleman) to stand steadfast on the un-wavering side of Everlasting Virtues.
(恆：久也，雜卦傳)   (Everlasting : long-lasting that's - Miscellaneous 10th 'Wing')

Lessons (Everlasting Hex.32)
In midst of Wind and Thunder, Junzi stands steadfast on the side of Everlasting Virtues.

(第三十三卦)　遯　　　　　　　　**Retreat　(Hexagram 33)**

外	上九	______	**TopNiner**	**external**
乾　(天，上卦)	九五	______	**Niner5**	**Qian　(Heaven, Trigram above)**
	九四	______	**Niner4**	
	九三	______	**Niner3**	
艮　(山，下卦)	六二	__　__	**Sixer2**	**Gen　(Mountain, Trigram below)**
內	初六	__　__	**FirstSixer**	**internal**

卦辭 *(文王)*：	***Hexagram Text (King Wen) :***
遯：	Retreat:
亨，小利貞	Prosperity, Small (Yins) Favor having Integrity

彖曰 *(孔子)*：	*Tuan says (Kongzi explains) :*
遯亨	Retreat, Prosperity
遯而亨也	Retreat, Thus Prosperity that's
剛當位而應	Yang (Niner5) in Position And has Partner (Sixer2)
與時行也	With Time Marches that's
小利貞	Small (Yins) Favor having Integrity
浸而長也	Stealthily And Growing that's
遯之時義大矣哉	Time Of Retreat, Uprightness Big Indeed that's

Comments:
Image: Yins growth forcing Yangs' Retreat, but Niner5 still centre and has partner Sixer2.
Wen: Retreat is Prosperity and Yins (Small) need Integrity at time of Retreat.
Kongzi: at time of Retreat, the exercise of uprightness is of utmost importance.
[Xu: 遯41逃也；義267已之威儀也从我羊..曰與善同意故从羊]

象曰 *(孔子)*：	***HexagramSign Says (Kongzi) :***
天下有山，遯	Heaven Beneath Has Mountain, Retreat
君子以遠小人	Junzi (Gentleman) To Distance from Small Person
不惡而嚴	Not Fiercely but Firmly

Comments:
The Mountain rising from below, and limitless Heaven above Retreat to accommodate.
Likewise, not fierce but with firmness Junzi Retreat to be distanced from Small Person.

爻辭 *(周公)* ：	*Liner Text (Zhougong) :*

初六 ： — **FirstSixer:**

遯尾，厲	Retreat Tail-end, Serious
勿用有攸往	Don't Act, Has Slow Progress
象曰 *(孔子)* ：	*LinerSign Says (Kongzi)*
遯尾之厲	Retreat Tail-end, Its Seriousness
不往何災也	Not Going-forth, What Disaster that's ?

Comments:
FirstSixer at Retreat tail-end, hence in grave situation.
Advise not to have action and not to go forward, then what danger can there be?

六二 ： — **Sixer2:**

執之用黃牛之革	Hold It With Yellow Cow's Leather
莫之勝說	None Who Succeed Breaking
象曰 *(孔子)* ：	*LinerSign Says (Kongzi) :*
執用黃牛	Hold With Yellow Cow (leather)
固志也	Strong Wills that's

Comments:
Sixer2 in correct Yin position, holds ideals like tethered with leather that none can break.
Strenghten with Niner5 partnership, Sixer2 is No Retreat from centre Upright position.

九三 ： — **Niner3:**

係遯	Tethered Retreat
有疾，厲	Has Sickness, Grave (situation)
畜臣妾，吉	Keeping Official Concubines, Auspicious
象曰 *(孔子)* ：	*LinerSign Says (Kongzi) :*
係遯之厲	Tethered Retreat, Its Seriousness
有疾憊	Has Sickness, Exhaustion that's
畜臣妾吉	Caring for Official Concubines, Auspicious
不何大事也	Not For Big Affairs that's

Comments:
Niner3 Tethered Retreat with official concubine (neighbor Sixer2) may be Auspicious.
But such emotional Retreat, actions are not suitable for handling big state's affair.

九四 ： — **Niner4:**

好遯	Loves Retreat
君子吉	Junzi (Gentleman) Auspicious
小人否	Small Person Not so
象曰 *(孔子)* ：	*LinerSign Says (Kongzi) :*
君子好遯	Junzi (Gentleman) Love Retreat
小人否也	Small Person Not at all that's

Comments:
Junzi (Gentleman) being courteous loves to Retreat in deference, Auspicious.
Whereas Small Person will not Retreat, thinking that this is a sign of weakness.

九五：	**Niner5:**
嘉遯	Celebrated Retreat
貞吉	Integrity, Auspicious
象曰 *(孔子)：*	*LinerSign Says (Kongzi) :*
嘉遯貞吉	Happy Retreat, Integrity Auspicious
以正志也	With Righteous Wills that's

Comments:
Niner5 the authority has Integrity, exercises Celebrated Retreat Auspicious.
That's Retreat in favour of citizens' wishes, demonstrating Uprightness of Wills.

上九：	**TopNiner:**
肥遯	Fat Retreat
无不利	None Not Favorable
象曰 *(孔子)：*	*LinerSign Says (Kongzi) :*
肥遯无不利	Fat (prosperous) Retreat, None Not Favorable
无所疑也	None Being Doubted that's

Comments:
TopNiner at high-end and having achieved, Retreat in prosperous retirement.
Relaxed and with no more doubts in life, able to practice Fat Retreat favorably.

Conclusions:
Retreat (Hexagram 33): Mountain Trigram below and Heaven Trigram above.
Image: 2 Yins together infiltrate at bottom, forcing the 4 Yangs above to Retreat.
Symbolic: limitless Heaven withdrawing to accommodate small Mountain growing below.

King Wen:
Sees Prosperity with Niner5 in-charge partnering Sixer2, but Small Person needs Integrity.

Zhougong:
FirstSixer: grave situation at Retreat tail-end, advised no action, not going forth No Danger.
Sixer2: centred with partner Niner5, Upright ideals tethered with strong leather, is No Retreat.
Niner3: Tethered Retreat alright with domestic affairs but for state's affairs is Sickness.
Niner4: Junzi Love Retreat promoting harmony; Small Person fears loss does not Love Retreat.
Niner5: with upright ideals, Celebrated Retreat, meets people's wish for good life, Auspicious.
TopNiner: Fat Retreat in affluent retirement, achieved, no more doubts in life, all Favorable.
Retreat: forced or willing, should be practiced with upright integrity, firmly and not in anger.

Kongzi:
At time of Retreat, the exercise of uprightness is of utmost importance.
Not fierce but with firmness Junzi Retreat to be distanced from Small Person.

(遯：則退也，雜卦傳)   (Retreat : is withdrawal that's - Miscellaneous 10th Wing)

Lessons (Retreat Hex.33):
Not fierce but firmly, Junzi steps back to put distance to conflicts, to maintain harmony.
If only leaders can Retreat a step and think of World-interest, not just National-interest.

（第三十四卦）大壯　　　　　　　**Great Strength (Hexagram 34)**

```
外          上六   __  __    TopSixer          external
震 (雷,上卦)  六五   __  __    Sixer5   Zhen (Thunder, Trigram above)
             九四   ______    Niner4
             九三   ______    Niner3
乾 (天,下卦)  九二   ______    Niner2   Qian (Heaven, Trigram below)
    内        初九   ______    FirstNiner        internal
```

卦辭 *(文王)*：	***Hexagram Text (King Wen)*** *:*
大壯：	Great Strength:
利貞	Favors having Integrity

彖曰 *(孔子)*：	***Tuan says (Kongzi explains)*** *:*
大壯：	Great Strength:
大者壯也	Great Stuff (Yangs) are Strength, that's
剛以動，故壯	Yangs (Heaven) For Action (Thunder), Hence Strength
大壯利貞	Great Strength, favors having Integrity
大者正	Great Stuff, Uprightness that's
正大而天地之情可見矣	Upright Great Thus Heaven-Earth's Compassion Be Seen Indeed

Comments:
Image: Heaven (Strength) below Thunder (Action) above, 4 Yangs for action, Great Strength.
Wen: Great Strength to be a positive force, advantageous to having Integrity.
Kongzi: Greatness is Uprightness, revealing the compassion of Heaven and Earth.
[Xu: 壯14大也从士]

象曰 *(孔子)*：	***HexagramSign says (Kongzi)*** *:*
雷在天上，大壯	Thunder In Heaven Above, Great Strength
君子以非禮弗履	Junzi (Gentleman) Where Etiquette-lacking, Not Tread

Comments:
Even in a position of Great Strength, Junzi (Gentleman) do not tread where Etiquette is lacking.
Besides Integrity and Uprightness, Kongzi also stress the importance of Etiquette.

爻辭 *(周公)* :	*Liner Text (Zhougong)* :
初九：	**FirstNiner**
壯于趾	Strength At Toes
征凶	Expedition Ominous
有孚	Has Trust
象曰 *(孔子)* :	*LinerSign Says (Kongzi)*
壯于趾	Strength at Toes (level)
其孚窮也	Its Trust Lacking that's

Comments:
FirstNiner active Yang starting campaign at Toes level, Ominous.
Has Trust but not enough, still lacking at this lowly bottom level.

九二：	**Niner2:**
貞吉	Integrity Auspicious
象曰 *(孔子)* :	*LinerSign Says (Kongzi)* :
九二貞吉	Niner2, Integrity Auspicious
以中也	Being Upright that's

Comments:
Niner2 gentle in Yin position, is centre and Upright.
Still needs to have Integrity to be Auspicious.

九三：	**Niner3:**
小人用壯	Small Person Uses Strength
君子用罔，貞厲	Junzi Uses None, Integrity Grave
羝羊觸藩	Male Goat Butted Fence
羸其角	Entangled its Horns
象曰 *(孔子)* :	*LinerSign Says (Kongzi)* :
小人用壯	Small Person Uses Strength
君子罔也	Junzi (uses) None that's

Comments:
Niner3 at Yang position, restive like male goat butting fence and gotten entangled by the horns.
Hence mindful Junzi will not use Great Strength for own advantage, has Integrity still Grave.

[Xu: 羝78牡羊也；蕃27艸茂也；羸78瘦也从羊]

九四：	**Niner4:**
貞吉，悔亡	Integrity Auspicious, Regrets lost
藩決不羸	Fence Breaks Not Entangling
壯于大輿之輹	Strength Of Big Carriage, Its Axle
象曰 *(孔子)* :	*LinerSign Says (Kongzi)* :
藩決不羸，尚往也	Fence Breaks Not Entangling, Favors Going-forth that's

Comments:
Yang in Yin position, has Integrity, hence Auspicious and no Regrets.
Two weak Yins in front are no barrier fence to its Great Strength carriage going-forth.

[Xu:羸輿301車輿也；輹301軸縛]

六五：	**Sixer5:**
喪羊于易，无悔	Loss Goats at Transactions, No Regrets
象曰 *(孔子)：*	***LinerSign Says (Kongzi) :***
喪羊于易，位不當也	Loss Goats at Transaction, Position Not Correct, that's

Comments:
Sixer5 weak in Yang position, suffers losses in transactions with the Yangs.
However in Premier position, is still in command, hence no Regrets.
[Xu: 喪35凵也从哭从凵]

上六：	**TopSixer:**
羝羊觸藩	Male Goat Butted Fence
不能退，不能遂	Not Able to Retreat, Not Able to Escape
无攸利，艱則吉	No Slow Gaining, Difficulty Then Auspicious
象曰 *(孔子)：*	***LinerSign Says (Kongzi) :***
不能退，不能遂	Not Able to Retreat, Not Able to Escape
不詳也	Not Deciding that's
艱則吉	Difficulty (aware of) Then Auspicious
咎不長也	Faults Not Increase that's

Comments:
At end of Great Strength, like male goat butting fence, gotten trapped, no easy gain.
TopSixer, a gentle Yin realises difficulty, acts with caution, no increase in faults, Auspicious.

Conclusions:
Great Strength (Hexagram 34): Heaven Trigram below and Thunder Trigram above.
Image: Heaven (Strength) below for Thunder (Action) above, 4 Yangs-in-a-row, Great Strength.

King Wen:
Sees Great Strength in 4 Yangs in a row, advancing against 2 Yins above.
But still caution that having Integrity is needed to favor Great Strength in actions.

Zhougong:
FirstNiner: Great Strength at Toe level for expedition, Trust not enough, Ominous.
Niner2: centre Yin position gentle Upright in Great Strength, still needs Integrity, Auspicious.
Niner3: Great Strength like male goat, gets horns entangled, thus Junzi does not force, Grave.
Niner4: gentle, no resistance from Yins above, has Great Strength, to go-forth Favorable.
Sixer5: misplaced suffer losses in transaction, but in Premier position, hence no Regrets.
Sixer6: End of Great Strength, weak, not for actions, aware of difficulties, hence no Faults.
Great Strength: Even in Great Strength, Yangs do not have all things their way.

Kongzi:
Great Strength is great Uprightness, reflecting the compassion of Heaven and Earth.
Junzi does not use Great Strength to force actions, does not tread where Etiquette is lacking.
(大壯：則止，雜卦傳)   (Great Strength : then Desist - Miscellaneous 10th Wing)

Lessons (Great Strength Hex.34):
With Great Strength, Junzi (Gentleman) does not bully, does not tread on immoral grounds.
Likewise, big nations ought not bully small nations, and there will be less misery on Earth.

（第三十五卦）晉　　　　　　　**Advance (Hexagram 35)**

外	上九	————	**TopNiner**	**eternal**
離 （火，上卦）	六五	—— ——	**Sixer5**	**Li (Fire, Trigram above)**
	九四	————	**Niner4**	
	六三	—— ——	**Sixer3**	
坤 （地，下卦）	六二	—— ——	**Sixer2**	**Kun (Earth, Trigram below)**
内	初六	—— ——	**FirstSixer**	**internal**

卦辭 *(文王)* ：　　　　　　　*Hexagram Text (King Wen) :*

晉：　　　　　　　Advance :

康侯用錫馬蕃庶　　　　　　　Lord Kang Receiving Gift Horses Many Times

晝日三接　　　　　　　Whole Day 3 times Received (by King)

象曰 *(孔子)* ：　　　　　　　*Tuan Says (Kongzi explains) :*

晉：　　　　　　　Advance:

進也　　　　　　　Progress that's

明出地上　　　　　　　Light (Sun) Emerges Above Earth

順而麗乎大明　　　　　　　Docile (Earth) And Shine (Fire), That's Great Enlightening

柔進而上行　　　　　　　Yin (of Hex.Observe) Advance And Up Moving (Sixer5)

是以康侯用錫馬蕃庶　　　　　　　This is Lord Kang Receiving Gift Horses Many Times

晝日三接也　　　　　　　Whole Day, 3 times Receiving, that's

Comments:
Image: Sun rises above Earth, Advance; Sixer4 (of Hex.Observing) Yin Advances be Sixer5.
Wen: Advance, illustrated with Lord Kang, Gift Horses aplenty, 3 times received by King!
Kongzi: Advance is Sun rising Above Earth, Great Enlightenment for the whole world.
[Xu:晉138進也日出萬物進；晝65日之出入與夜爲界；蕃27艸茂也；庶193屋下眾也; 眾169
多也]

象曰 *(孔子)* ：　　　　　　　*HexagramSign Says (Kongzi) :*

明出地上，晉　　　　　　　Sun Emerges Above Earth, Advance

君子以自昭明德　　　　　　　Junzi With Self-Brilliance, Teaching Virtues

Comments:
Sun rises above Earth, Advance.
Junzi likewise with self-Brilliance to enlighten (to teach) citizens as to what virtues are.
[Xu: 昭137日明也]

爻辭 *(周公)* :	*Liner Text (Zhougong) :*
初六 :	**FirstSixer:**
晉如摧如	Advance Like Beaten Like
貞吉，罔孚	Integrity Auspicious, No Trust
裕无咎	Affluent No Faults
象曰 *(孔子)* :	*LinerSign Says (Kongzi) :*
晉如摧如	Advance Like Beaten Like
獨行正也	Alone Acting with Uprightness that's
裕无咎	Affluent, No Faults
未受命也	Prior to Receiving Official-Appointment, that's

Comments:

At bottom, prior to receiving official appointment, acting alone with Integrity, Auspicious.
FirstSixer, misplaced, No Trust, Beaten to Advance, Affluent, No Fault.

[Xu:摧257敲擊也；罔157网或从亡；网157庖犧所結繩以渔；裕172衣物饒也；饒108飽也]

六二 :	**Sixer2:**
晉如愁如，貞吉	Advance Like Worrying Like, Truthfully Auspicious
受茲介福	Receiving Much Allocated Good-fortune
于其王母	From The King's Mother
象曰 *(孔子)* :	*LinerSign Says (Kongzi) :*
受茲介福	Receiving Much Allocated Good-fortune
以中正也	With Upright Justice that's

Comments:

Sixer2, has position, centre Upright, but no responding partner, has worry in Advance.
However has Integrity, receives reserved Good-fortune from King's Mother, Sixer5, Auspicious.

[Xu: 受84相付也；付164與也；茲22艸木多益也；介28畫也从八从人；畫65界也象田聿所以畫之]

六三 :	**Sixer3:**
衆允，悔亡	Group Approval, Regrets Lost
象曰 *(孔子)* :	*LinerSign says (Kongzi) :*
衆允之志，上行也	Group Approval Their Wills, Upward Moving that's

Comments:

FirstSixer, Sixer2 and Sixer3 have common Wills to Advance.
Sixer3, misplaced, not centre, has Regrets, now with group approval, Regrets no more.

[Xu: 允176信也]

九四 :	**Niner4:**
晉如鼫鼠，貞厲	Advance Like Marmot Rodent, Truthful yet Grave
象曰 *(孔子)* :	*LinerSign Says (Kongzi) :*
鼫鼠貞厲，位不當也	Marmot Rodent Truthfully Grave, Position Not Proper that's

Comments:

Niner4, misplaced, not centre, weak, afraid of people like Marmot Rodent.
Hungry to Advance to high position next to Premier, even if Truthful, situation Grave.

[Xu: 鼫206五枝鼠,能飛不能過屋,能緣不能窮木,能游不能度谷,能穴不能掩身,行不能先人]

六五：	**Sixer5:**
悔亡	Regrets Lost
失得勿恤	Loss Gain Don't Worry
往吉，无不利	Venture Auspicious, None Not Favorable
象曰 (孔子)：	***LinerSign Says (Kongzi) :***
失得勿恤，往有慶也	Loss Gain Don't Worry, Venture Has Celebration that's

Comments:
Sixer5, Premier, Yin misplaced, has Regrets, but in Advance, Regrets no more.
Above Enlightening (Fire), subjects below docile (Earth), Venture has Celebration, Auspicious.
[Xu: 恤219憂也]

上九：	**TopNiner:**
晉其角，維用伐邑	Advance In Corner, Only Action Attack Kingdoms
屬吉无咎，貞吝	Grave, Auspicious, No Fault, Truthful, Painful
象曰 (孔子)：	***LinerSign Says (Kongzi) :***
雜用伐邑	Mixed Actions of Attacking Kingdoms
道未光也	Path-way Not Enlightening that's

Comments:
TopNiner, Yang at top Corner of Advance, can only attack small rebellious vassal states.
Grave, Auspicious, No Fault, Truthful, Painful, this Path-way not Enlightening.
With better Administration, small vassal states are happy, no need to put down rebellions.
[Xu: 維276車蓋維也 ；伐167擊也 ；邑131國也 ；雜172五彩相會从衣]

Conclusions:
Advance (Hexagram 35): Earth Trigram below and Fire Trigram above.
Image: Fire (Sun) emerges above Earth, Enlightenment shines for Advancement.
Symbolic: gentle Sixer4 of Hex.Observe, Advances to Premier position as Sixer5 here.

King Wen:
Describes the Advance of Lord Kang, bestowed with numerous Gift Horses and such.
And was honored with Receptions with the King, Thrice in a day!

Zhougong:
FirstSixer: bottom, no Trust, given a kick in the ass to Advance, Affluent, Truthful Auspicious.
Sixer2: Advance worries, centre Upright, Goodwills from King Mother, Truthful Auspicious.
Sixer3: misplaced, has Regrets, has approval of Yins below for Advance, no more Regrets.
Niner4: weaken, Advance like Marmot Rodent sneaky, situation Grave, thus be Truthful.
Sixer5: misplaced, Premier position Regrets Lost, no worry of Gain/Lost, Venture, Auspicious.
TopNiner: in top corner, Advance on rebellious states, Gravely Auspicious, Painful, No Shine.
Advance: advise individuals on their different pathways in life, to achieve Advancement.

Kongzi: Advance is the Sun rising above Earth, Great Enlightenment for the whole world.
Junzi likewise with self-Brilliance to enlighten (to teach) citizens as to what virtues are.

(晉：晝也，雜卦傳)　　　　(Advance : daytime that's - Miscellaneous 10th 'Wing')

Lessons (Advance Hex.35):
Advance with Enlightenment Auspicious; Advancement by conquests non-illustrious.
Thus it is never an honorable option to build Advance by taking advantage of the weak.

(第三十六卦) 明夷　　　　　　　　**Enlighten-Hurt (Hexgram 36)**

外	上六	__ __	**Top Sixer**	external
坤 (地，上卦)	六五	__ __	**Sixer 5**	**Kun** (Earth, Trigram above)
	六四	__ __	**Sixer 4**	
	九三	______	**Niner 3**	
離 (火，下卦)	六二	__ __	**Sixer 2**	**Li** (Fire, Trigram below)
內	初九	______	**First Niner**	internal

卦辭 *(文王)* ：　　　　　　　　　*Hexagram Text (King Wen) :*

明夷：　　　　　　　　　　　　　Enlighten-Hurt:

利艱貞　　　　　　　　　　　　　Favors Difficult Integrity (in difficult times)

象曰 *(孔子) :*　　　　　　　　　*Tuan Says (Kongzi explains) :*

明入地中，明夷　　　　　　　　　Light (Fire) Enters Earth Inside, Enlighten-Hurt

明夷　　　　　　　　　　　　　　Enlighten-Hurt

內文明而外柔順　　　　　　　　　Inside Enlighten (Fire) And Outside Gentle Docile (Earth)

以蒙大難　　　　　　　　　　　　To Sustain Great Calamity

文王以之　　　　　　　　　　　　King Wen Like This (imprisoned by King Zhou)

利艱貞　　　　　　　　　　　　　Favors Difficult Integrity

晦其明也　　　　　　　　　　　　Dim The Brilliance that's (show humility)

內難而能正其志　　　　　　　　　Inwardly Difficult Then Can Upright The Aspiration

箕子以之　　　　　　　　　　　　Jizi Like This, that's

Comments:

Image: Fire (enlighten) inside, Earth (docile) outside, Enlighten-Hurt.
Wen: The Enlighten-Hurt in difficult time. ability to sustain Integrity, favorable.
Kongzi: gives example of King Wen showing docility outwardly even when imprisoned.
Also Jizi, faking madness to avoid persecution and death from nephew tyrant, King Zhou.

(Xu: 郎141明也；夷213平也，一曰東方之人也；蒙26王女也)

象曰 *(孔子) :*　　　　　　　　　*HexagramSign Says (Kongzi) :*

明入地中，明夷　　　　　　　　　Light (Fire) Enters Inside Earth, Enlighten-Hurt

君子以莅衆　　　　　　　　　　　Junzi (Gentleman) When Facing People (citizens)

用晦而明　　　　　　　　　　　　Uses Dullness (outward humility) and Enlightenment (inwardly)

Comments:

Fire beneath Earth, symbolic of Enlightenment got hurt and goes under-cover of docility.
Junzi with Enlightenment inside, be humble outwardly, with humility to gain Trust of people.

爻辭 *(周公)* ：	*Liner Text (Zhougong)* :
初九：	**FirstNiner:**
明夷于飛，垂其翼	Enlighten-Hurt In Flight, Drooping Its Wings
君子于行，三日不食	CulturedOne On the Move, 3 Days Not Eating
有攸往，主人有言	Has Easy Destination, The Master Has Notices
象曰 *(孔子)* ：	*LinerSign Says (Kongzi)* :
君子于行，義不食也	Junzi On the Run, Upright Not Eating that's

Comments:
Bird with drooping wings signify injury and persecution of the Enlighten-Hurt on flight.
Righteous Junzi on the move to exile similarly suffers hunger and marching orders.

六二：	**Sixer2:**
明夷，夷于左股	Enlighten-Hurt, Injured In Left Thigh
用拯馬壯，吉	Make Rescue, use Strong Horses, Auspicious
象曰 *(孔子)* ：	*LinerSign Says (Kongzi)* :
六二之吉	Sixer2, Its Auspiciousness
順以則也	Docile On Principles, that's

Comments:
Injured left thigh symbolic of Enlighten King Wen's (文王) imprisonment by evil King Zhou.
Wen's ministers offering treasures, beauties and great horses for his release, Auspicious.
(Xu:股88髀也)

九三：	**Niner3:**
明夷于南狩	Enlighten-Hurt On Southern Hunt
得其大首	Capturing The Great Leader
不可疾貞	Not Allow Rushed Integrity
象曰 *(孔子)* ：	*LinerSign Says (Kongzi)* :
南狩之志，乃大得也	Southern Hunt Its Aspiration, Is Great Achievement that's

Comments:
Niner3, Yang, top of Fire Trigram, liken to King Wu (武王) leading army in the South.
The son of Wen is cautioned not rush in the name of Integrity to overthrow the evil King Zhou.
(Xu: 狩205犬田也, 易曰明夷于南狩！)

六四：	**Sixer4:**
入于左腹	Entering Through Left Belly
獲明夷之心	Capture Enlighten-Hurt's Heart (feeling)
于出門庭	For Out-Door of Court (deciding to go into exile)
象曰 *(孔子)* ：	*LinerSign Says (Kongzi)* :
入于左腹	Entering Through Left Belly (closed consultation)
獲心意也	Get Heart-felt Decision, that's

Comments:
Entering through belly to reach heart, symbolising Weizi (微子) consultation with his uncles.
This led to his decision of self-exile to escape persecution from evil brother, King Zhou.
(Xu: 腹87厚也)

六五：	**Sixer5:**
箕子之明夷	Jizi's Enlighten-Hurt
利貞	Favors Integrity
象曰 *(孔子)：*	*LinerSign Says (Kongzi) :*
箕子之貞	Jizi's Integrity
明不可息也	Enlightenment Not Be Extinguished, that's

Comments:
Jizi (箕子), only proper name in *Yijing* that helps explain situation descriptions in this Hexagram
That reflect Characters important in: " Saga of the Fall of Shang and the Rise of Zhou Dynasty".
After Shang, Jizi went far East, established state of Korea (朝鮮), extending Chinese civilization.

上六：	**TopSixer:**
不明晦	Not Enlighten, Dim
初登于天	Initial Ascension To Heaven
後入于地	Afterwards Enter Into Earth
象曰 *(孔子)：*	*LinerSign Says (Kongzi) :*
初登于天	Initial Ascension To Heaven
照四國也	Illuminating 4 States that's (of 4 corners),
後入于地，失則也	Later Entering Into Earth (hell), Lost Principles (virtues) that's

Comments:
TopSixer description symbolic of tyrant King Zhou's (紂王) reign (last king of Shang Dynasty).
Like the Sun shining, Enlighten when enthroned, then later fallen into hell as evil tyrant.

Conclusions:
Enlighten-Hurt (Hexagram 36): Fire Trigram below and Earth Trigram above
Image: Fire beneath Earth, is like the Sun going into Earth, being obscured cover-up.
Symbolic: Of the Enlightened Jizi (箕子) got threatened Hurt, and went into exile.

King Wen:
The Enlighten-Hurt, favorable to people who have Integrity even under difficult situations.

Zhougong:
The only proper name seen in the *Yijing*, Jizi puts this Hexagram in a clear perspective.
Reflecting the main players in the Saga of Dynasty change, the Fall of Shang and Rise of Zhou.
The last king of Shang Dynasty King Zhou, very capable when enthroned, dazzling all states.
He soon descended into tyranny, persecuting his uncles and brothers who dared to council him.
He imprisoned King Wen (State of Zhou), released only when bribed with beauties and horses.
His uncle Jizi had to fake madness and brothers went on self exile to avoid persecution, death.
King Wu son of Wen, later led a army to overthrow him, and established the Dynasty of Zhou.

Kongzi:
The Sun enters Earth, symbolic of the Enlighten-Hurt.
Junzi Enlightened, need to have humility when facing the people to gain acceptance .

(明夷：誅也，雜卦傳)	(Enlighten-Hurt : killing - Miscellaneous 10th 'Wing')

Lessons (Enlighten-Hurt Hex.36)
Enlightenment is not enough, as we must also have humility to gain acceptance of people

(第三十七卦) 家人　　　　　　**Family People (Hexagram 37)**

外		上九	________	**TopNiner**	external
巽 （風, 上卦）		九五	________	**Niner5**	**Xun (Wind, Trigram above)**
		六四	__ __	**Sixer4**	
		九三	________	**Niner3**	
離 （火, 下卦）		六二	__ __	**Sixer2**	**Li (Fire, Trigram below)**
	內	初九	________	**FirstNiner**	internal

卦辭 *(文王)* ：　　　　　*Hexagram Text (King Wen) :*

家人 ：　　　　　Family People :

利女貞　　　　　Favors Woman's Integrity

象曰 *(孔子)* ：　　　　*Tuan says (Kongzi explains) :*

家人　　　　　Family People

女正位乎內　　　　　Woman Correct Place that's Inside

男正位乎外　　　　　Man Correct Place that's Outside

男女正　﹨　　　　　Man Woman Correctness

天地之大義也　　　　　Heaven Earth Their Great Uprightness that's

家人有嚴君焉　　　　　Family People Has Stern Lords that's

父母之謂也　　　　　Father Mother Their Salutation that's

父父，子子　　　　　Father Father, Son Son

兄兄，弟弟　　　　　Elder-brother Elder-brother, Young-brother Young-brother

夫夫，婦婦　　　　　Husband Husband, Wife Wife

而家道正　　　　　The Family Way in Proper-order

正家而天下定矣　　　　　Proper-ordered Families Then The World Stable indeed

Comments:
Image: Fire below, and Wind above taking Smoke coming out of Chimney, Family People.
Wen: Family People, Highlights the Importance of Woman and her Having Integrity.
Kongzi: Man outside, Woman inside, Father, Son, each has Role, stable Families, stable World.

[Xu:家150居也 ；人161天地之性最貴者也 ；性217人之陽气性善者也 ；君32尊也,從尹發號從口]

象曰 *(孔子)* ：　　　　*HexagramSign says (Kongzi) :*

風自火出，家人　　　　　Wind From Fire Emerge, Family People

君子以言有物　　　　　Junzi With Speech Has Substance

而行有恆　　　　　And Action Has Sustainability

Comments:
Wind coming out of Fire like Smoke from Chimney, image of Family People.
Junzi in Speech has Substance, in Actions has Lasting-Effects.

爻辭 *(周公)* ：	*Liner Text (Zhougong)* ：

初九：   **FirstNiner:**

閑有家，悔亡   Exclusion Has Family, Regrets Lost

象曰 *(孔子)* ：   *LinerSign Says (Kongzi)* ：

閑有家，志未變也   Exclusion Has Family, Wills Not Change that's

Comments:

Boy and Girl, initial Wills not changed, so gentle exclusion of others to start a Family.
Feeling not nice hurting third parties in marriage, however soon, such Regrets Lost.

[Xu: 閑248闌也；闌248門遮也；遮41遏也；遏41微止也]

六二：   **Sixer2:**

无攸遂   No Gentle Run-around (outside)

在中饋，貞吉   On Centre, Food, Integrity Auspicious

象曰 *(孔子)* ：   *LinerSign Says (Kongzi)* ：

六二之吉，順以巽也   Sixer2, Its Auspiciousness, Orderly With Docility that's

Comments:

Sixer2, gentle, Upright in Centre position, no gentle Run-around outside of home.
At Home, Orderly care of Family Food and lodging, with Integrity Auspicious.

[Xu: 遂41亼也；亡267亼, 逃也；饋107餉也]

九三：   **Niner3:**

家人嗃嗃   Family People He'He'

悔厲吉   Regrets, Grave, Auspicious

婦子嘻嘻，終吝   Wife Children Xi'Xi', Finally Painful

象曰 *(孔子)* ：   *LinerSign Says (Kongzi)* ：

家人嗃嗃\   Family People He'He'

未失也   Not Loss (principles) that's

婦子嘻嘻   Wife Children Xi'Xi'

失家節也   Lost Family Regulation that's

Comments:

Family members reprimanding voices, principles not lost, Grave, Regrets, remain Auspicious.
Wife and children frivolous laughters, Family Regulation lost, Ending Painful.

[Xu: 節95竹約也]

六四：   **Sixer4:**

富家，大吉   Wealthy Family, Greatly Auspicious

象曰 *(孔子)* ：   *LinerSign Says (Kongzi)* ：

富家大吉   Wealthy Family Greatly Auspicious

順在位也   Orders In Place that's

Comments:

Sixer4, Yin in Yin position, gentle centre Upright and in upper Trigram of authority.
Has ability and in place to build a wealthy Family, Auspicious.

[Xu: 富150備也，一日厚也]

九五：	Niner5:
王假有家	King's Arrival Has Families
勿恤，吉	Don't Worry, Auspicious
象曰 *(孔子)*：	*LinerSign Says (Kongzi) :*
王假有家	King's Arrival Has Families
交相爱也	Interaction Mutual Love, that's

Comments:
King's Arrival of age, has many Families, to ensure having a suitable heir to the throne.
All interactions have mutual love and care, so not to worry, Auspicious.
[Xu: 假165非真也，一曰至也；恤219憂也；交214交脛也；腳88脛也]

上九：	TopNiner:
有孚威如	Have Trust, Respect Like
終吉	Finally Auspicious
象曰 *(孔子)*：	*LinerSign Says (Kongzi) :*
威如之吉	Respect Like, Its Auspiciousness
反身之謂也	This is Saying, Reflect on Self that's

Comments:
Family Elder, Reflect on Self, whether has conduct and ability worthy of Trust and Respect.
Then having Trust and Respect from other Family People, finally Auspicious.
[Xu: 孚63卵子也, 一曰信也；威259姑也；姑259夫母也]

Conclusions:
Family People (Hexagram 37): Fire Trigram below and Wind Trigram above.
Image: Fire below, Wind above, like seeing smoke rising out of Chimney, Family People.

King Wen:
The Importance of Women among Family People is highlighted, favors having Integrity.

Zhougong:
FirstNiner: exclusively forms Family with partner Sixer4, as Wills unchanged, Regrets Lost.
Sixer2: orderly care of Family Home, docile, not running lost outside, Integrity, Auspicious.
Niner3: Family Disputes Grave but Auspicious; Wife and Children's frivolous noises, Painful.
Sixer4: docile Yin position, correctly placed to build-up Family Wealth, Greatly Auspicious.
Niner5: King's Families to ensure a suitable heir, has love and care, No Worries, Auspicious.
TopNiner: Elder in Family, self-reflect to see if worthy of Trust and Respects, finally Auspicious.
Family People: has good advice for all Family People, young and old, commoners and Kings.
Kongzi:
The Rule of Heaven and Earth, Woman's Role Inside, Man's Role Outside of Family
Father as father, Son as son, each playing own Role, then Stable Families, Stable World.

(家人：內也，雜卦傳)   (Family People : internal that's - Miscellaneous 10th 'Wing')

Lessons (Family People Hex.37)
Junzi' in Speech has Substance, in Action has Sustainability.

(第三十八卦) 睽　　　　　　　　Visions (Hexagram 38)

外	上九	________	Top Niner		external
離 (火，上卦)	六五	__ __	Sixer 5	Li (Fire, Trigram above)	
	九四	________	Niner 4		
	六三	__ __	Sixer 3		
兌 (澤，下卦)	九二	________	Niner 2	Dui (Wetland, Trigram below)	
內	九一	________	First Niner		internal

卦辭 *(文王)* ：　　　　　　*Hexagram Text (King Wen) :*
睽 ：　　　　　　　　　　Visions :
小事吉　　　　　　　　　Small Matters Auspicious

象曰 *(孔子)* ：　　　　　　*Tuan Says (Kongzi explains) :*
睽 ：　　　　　　　　　　Visions :
火動而上　　　　　　　　Fire Action Is Upward
澤動而下　　　　　　　　Wetland Action is Downward
二女同居　　　　　　　　2 daughters Together Staying
其志不同行　　　　　　　Their Wills Not Together Traveling
說，而麗乎明　　　　　　Joy, Then Bright And Enlightened
柔進而上行　　　　　　　Yin (Sixer4 of Hex.61 Core Trust) Forward And Upward Moving
得中而應乎剛　　　　　　Gain Centre (as Sixer5) And Respond To Yang (Niner2)
是以小事吉　　　　　　　Therefore Small Matters, Auspicious
天地睽而其事同也　　　　Heaven's Earth's Visions, And The Affairs Similar that's
男女睽而其志通也　　　　Male's Female's Visions, And The Wills Connected that's
萬物睽而其事類也　　　　All Matters' Visions, And The Tasks Categorised that's
睽之時用大矣哉　　　　　Time of Visions, Usage Great Indeed that's
Comments:
Image: Wetland (Young daughter) drains, Fire (Middle daughter) rises, has different Visions.
Wen: Visions, Sixer5 weak, Yin in Premier position, hence for Small Matters Auspicious.
Kongzi: Different Visions, of Heaven/Earth, Male/Female, All Matters together, Usage Great.
[Xu: 睽72目不相聲也，聽250聆也]

象曰 *(孔子)* ：　　　　　　*HexagramSign Says (Kongzi) :*
上火下澤，睽　　　　　　Above Fire, Below Wetland, Visions
君子以同而異　　　　　　Junzi With Similarities Knows Differences
Comments:
Fire burning upward and Wetland draining downward, Visions different.
Junzi understand the Similarities in order to appreciate the Differences.

爻辭 *(周公)* :	*Liner Text (Zhougong) :*
初九：	**FirstNiner:**
悔亡	Regrets Lost
喪馬勿逐自復	Lost Horse Don't Chase, will Self Return
見惡人，无咎	Seeing Fierce Person, No Faults
象曰 *(孔子)* :	*LinerSign Says (Kongzi) :*
見惡人，以辟咎也	Seeing Fierce Person, To Dispel Faults that's

Comments:
With Niner4, not partner, but has accord of Wills, so no more Regrets.
In time of Visions, seeing fierce person for exchange of views, to dispel ill-wills, No Faults.
[Xu:　辟....]

九二：	**Niner2:**
遇主于巷，无咎	Meeting Master At Alley-way, No Faults
象曰 *(孔子)* :	*LinerSign Says (Kongzi) :*
遇主于	Meeting Master At Alley-way
未失道也	Not Lost Way that's

Comments:
Niner2 meets partner Sixer5 Premier at Alley-way.
Visions different from above and below, but has not lost his Way, so No Faults.

六三：	**Sixer3:**
見輿曳	Sees Cart Mired
其牛掣	The Oxen Obstructed
其人天且劓	The Person Heaven Given Nose-cut
无初有終	No Beginning Has Ending
象曰 *(孔子)* :	*LinerSign Says (Kongzi) :*
見輿曳，位不當也	Sees Cart Mired, Position Not Appropriate that's
无初有終，遇剛也	No Beginning Has Ending, Meeting Yang (TopNiner) that's

Comments:
Sixer3 weak in Yang position, Visions distorted seeing Ox-cart mired, driver Person multilated.
Not Upright, no Beginning as doubts between 2 Yangs, meeting partner TopNiner has Closure.
[Xu: 且299薦也；曳311曳曳；曳311束縛挬抴]

九四：	**Niner4:**
睽孤	Visions Lonely
遇元夫，交乎	Meeting Primal Person, Interaction that's (FirstNiner)
厲无咎	Grave, No Faults
象曰 *(孔子)* :	*LinerSign Says (Kongzi) :*
交孚无咎	Interaction Trusting, No Faults
志行也	Wills Moving (in accord) that's

Comments:
Niner4 Lonely Visions, interaction with Yang corresponder FirstNiner, Grave but No Faults.
The friendship has Trust, as Wills are in accord, and Visions similar.

六五：	**Sixer5:**
悔亡，厥宗噬膚	Regrets Lost, Tracing Family-roots Biting Skin
往何咎	Going-forth What Faults?
象曰 *(孔子)：*	***LinerSign Says (Kongzi) :***
厥宗噬膚	Tracing Family-Roots Biting Skin,
往有慶也	Going-forth Has Celebration that's

Comments:
Sixer5, has Regrets as Yin in Yang position, then has partner Niner2 so Regrets Lost.
Tracing Family-Roots back to Niner2 below, finds Skin Biting intimacy so What Faults?
[Xu: 厥193發石也；宗151尊祖廟也]

上九：	**TopNiner:**
睽孤	Visions Lonely
見豕負塗，載鬼一車	Sees Pigs Covered with Mud, Carrying Devils 1 Cartload
先張之弧，後說之弧	First Stretching The Bow, Afterward Loosen The Bow
匪寇婚媾	Not Bandits Marriage Party
往遇雨則吉	Going-forth Meeting Rain Then Auspicious
象曰 *(孔子)：*	***LinerSign Says (Kongzi) :***
遇雨之吉	Meeting Rain Its Auspiciousness,
羣疑亡也	Crowding Suspicions Lost (wash away), that's

Comments:
TopNiner, Lonely Visions, hallucinating Muddy Pigs, Cartload of Devils, Bandits, stretched Bow.
Then Going-forth, meeting partner Sixer3 in the Rain, all suspicions wash-off, Auspicious.

Conclusions:
Visions (Hexagram 38): Wetland Trigram below and Fire Trigram above.
Image: Wetland below draining downward, Fire above burning upward, different Visions.
Symbolic: Wetland (Young-daughter) below, Fire (Middle-daughter) above, Visions differ.

King Wen:
Visions, Premier Sixer5, weak Yin, needs support of partner, Small Matters Auspicious.

Zhougong:
FirstNiner: Strong, Horse self-return, meeting Fierce Person to share Visions, No Faults.
Niner2: Wrong position but centre Upright, no lost of Way, meet Master at Alley, No Faults.
Sixer3: Visions distorted, sees mired Ox-cart Mutilation, meet partner TopNiner has Closure.
Niner4: Visions lonely, not partner, Trusted friend of FirstNiner, same Wills, Grave, No Faults.
Sixer5: Yang position, Regrets, tracing Roots to Niner2, finds Skin-biting intimacy, What Fault?
TopNiner: Visions, muddy pigs devils bandits, meet partner in Rain, doubts wash-off Auspicious.
Visions: Describes Visions that are discovered, shared, distorted by stress, suspicions, ...

Kongzi:
Visions differ, yet Heaven Earth are partners, Male Female connects, All Matters likewise.
In Visions, Junzi knows the similarities in order to appreciate the differences.

(睽：外也，雜卦傳)	(Visions : external - Miscellaneous 10th Wing)

Lessons (Visions Hex.38)
Junzi learns the Similarities in order to appreciate the differences in Visions of things.
This Visions philosophy is suited to resolving the different world views of USA and China today.

（第三十九卦）蹇　　　　　　　　**Limp　(Hexagram 39)**

<table>
<tr><td>外</td><td>上六</td><td>__ __</td><td>**Top Sixer**</td><td>**external**</td></tr>
<tr><td>坎　(水，上卦)</td><td>九五</td><td>________</td><td>**Niner 5**</td><td>**Kan　(Water, Trigram above)**</td></tr>
<tr><td></td><td>六四</td><td>__ __</td><td>**Sixer 4**</td><td></td></tr>
<tr><td></td><td>九三</td><td>________</td><td>**Niner 3**</td><td></td></tr>
<tr><td>艮　(山，下卦)</td><td>六二</td><td>__ __</td><td>**Sixer 2**</td><td>**Gen　(Mountain, Trigram below)**</td></tr>
<tr><td>內</td><td>初六</td><td>__ __</td><td>**First Sixer**</td><td>**internal**</td></tr>
</table>

卦辭 *(文王)*：	*Hexagram Text (King Wen) :*
蹇：	Limp :
利西南	Favors West South
不利東北	Not Favoring East North
利見大人，貞吉	Favors Seeing Great Person, Integrity Auspicious

象曰 *(孔子) :*	*Tuan Says (Kongzi explains) :*
蹇，難也	Limp, Difficulty that's
險在前也	Danger In Front that's
見險而能止	Seeing Danger And Able to Halt
知矣哉	Knowledge Indeed that's
蹇利西南	Limp, Favors West South
往得中也	Go-forth Gets Centre that's
不利東北	Not Favoring East North
其道窮也	Its Way Terminal that's
利見大人	Favors Seeing Great Person
往有功也	Go-forth Has Success that's
當位貞吉	Correct Position, Integrity Auspicious
以正邦也	To Upright States that's
蹇之時用大矣哉	Limp Its Timing and Usage, Great Indeed that's

Comments:
Limp, symbolic of Wen's handicap difficulty facing the tyranny of King Zhou from the East.
Limp favors West South, Wen's Homeland, where he ruled with Benevolence and Integrity.
When time of Limp is right, Great Wen in position will rise to set the States right, Auspicious.

(Xu: 蹇47跛也 ; 跛47行不正也 ; 脩89脯也 ; 脯89乾肉也)

象曰 *(孔子) :*	*HexagramSign Says (Kongzi) :*
山上有水，蹇	Mountain (halt) Above Has Water(danger), Limp
君子以反身脩德	Junzi To Turn-back Self, Cultivate Virtues

Comments:
Below Mountain (block), Above Water (danger), walking difficulty Limp.
Junzi meeting difficulty halt, turn-back to self-examine and to improve with self-cultivation.

爻辭 *(周公)* ：	*Liner Text (Zhougong) :*

初六 ：　　　　　　　　FirstSixer:
往蹇　　　　　　　　　Forward, Limp
來譽　　　　　　　　　Come, Praised
象曰 *(孔子)* ：　　　　*LinerSign Says (Kongzi) :*
往蹇來譽　　　　　　　Forward Difficult, Come be Praised
宜待也　　　　　　　　Appropriate to Wait that's
Comments:
FirstSixer is lowly, Limp forward difficult, stay back to await better timing for action, Praised.
(Xu: 譽5稱也；匪268器似竹筐；躬？)

六二 ：　　　　　　　　**Sixer2:**
王臣蹇蹇　　　　　　　King's Minister Limp Limp
匪躬之故　　　　　　　Not Self (serving), The Reason
象曰 *(孔子)* ：　　　　*LinerSign Says (Kongzi) :*
王臣蹇蹇　　　　　　　King's Minister, Difficulty upon Difficulty
终无尤也　　　　　　　Finally No Worries, that's
Comments:
Sixer2, loyal Minister faraway, braving double difficulties in service of King in distress.
In Limp Limp conditions, actions not in self-service, hence success or failure has No Worries.
(Xu: 尤308異也)

九三 ：　　　　　　　　**Niner3:**
往蹇　　　　　　　　　Forward Limp
來反　　　　　　　　　Come Turn-back
象曰 *(孔子)* ：　　　　*LinerSign Says (Kongzi) :*
往蹇來反　　　　　　　Forward Limp (Difficulty), Come Back
内喜之也　　　　　　　Inside (family) Happy of This that's
Comments:
Niner3 strong for action, but Forward Limp going into Water Hexagram, danger zone.
Safer Coming back in favor of Sixer2, and having him back is Happiness at home.

六四 ：　　　　　　　　**Sixer4:**
往蹇　　　　　　　　　Forward LImp
來連　　　　　　　　　Come-back Connection
象曰 *(孔子)* ：　　　　*LinerSign Says (Kongzi) :*
往蹇來連　　　　　　　Forward Limp, Come-back to Connect
當位實也　　　　　　　Correct Position, Solid that's (support)
Comments:
Sixer4, Forward Limp, facing difficulty going forward to help Sixer5 who is in Great Difficulty.
Come to Connect with Niner3 for Solid support for further actions, Sixer4 in Correct position.
(Xu: 連41員連也；員129物數也；實150富也)

九五：	**Niner5:**
大蹇，朋來	Big Limp, Friends Come
象曰 (孔子) :	*LinerSign Says (Kongzi) :*
大蹇朋來	Big Limp (Difficulty), Friends Coming (to help)
以中節也	With Upright and Principled-conduct that's

Comments:
King in Big Limp (big trouble), and Friends are coming with Help.
This is because King is Upright and Principled in conduct, a worthy King that's.
(Xu: 節95竹約；約272纏束也；束128縛也)

上六：	**TopSixer:**
往蹇	Forward Limp
來碩，吉	Come Success, Auspicious
利見大人	Favors Seeing Great Person
象曰 (孔子) :	*LinerSign Says (Kongzi) :*
往蹇來碩	Forward Limp Come Success
志在內也	Wishes Are Inward that's
利見大人，以從貴也	Favors Seeing Great Person, To Follow the Noble that's

Comments
TopSixer, Forward Limp to nowhere, come inward to Follow Noble Niner5, Success Auspicious.
(Xu: 碩182頭大也；頭181首也；從169隨行也；貴131物不賤也；賤131賈少也)

Conclusions:
Limp (Hexagram 39): Mountain Trigram below and Water Trigram above.
Image: of Limp, difficulty tracking Mountain (block), and treading Water (danger).
Symbolic: of Wen's difficulty facing the tyrant King Zhou of Shang Dynasty to the East North.

King Wen:
Naming this Hexagram Limp, reflects his handicap struggle against King Zhou in the East North.
Upright with Integrity, home in West South, bidding time for actions with friends, Auspicious.

Zhougong:
FirstSixer: Weak in Yang position, Forward Limp, Come to await for better timing, Praised.
Sixer2: Loyal minister, Double Limp difficulties in service of King, No Self-interest No Worries.
Niner3: Strong, Forward Limp, difficulty, Turn Inward to Sixer2, who receives him Happily.
Sixer4: Forward Limp, difficulty, Turn-back to Join Niner3, solves problems with Solid-support.
Niner5: Big Limp big difficulty, Friends coming as King is an Upright and Principled person.
TopSixer: Forward Limp nowhere, come back to follow Noble Niner5, great success Auspicious.
Limp: Liners above FirstSixer are all in Correct position, stable, to halt in face of Difficulties.

Kongzi:
Mountain (Halt), ahead has Water (Danger), image of walking difficulty, Limp.
Junzi facing difficulties halt, turn-back to consolidate, and to self-cultivate more Virtues.
(蹇：難也，雜卦傳)   (Limp : difficulty that's - Miscellaneous 10th 'Wing')

Lessons (Limp Hex.39)
Junzi handicapped, to halt, no blaming, turn-back to self-examine and for more self-improvement.

外	上六	___ ___	**Top Sixer**		eternal
震 （雷，上卦）	六五	___ ___	**Sixer 5**	**Zhen (Thunder, Trigram above)**	
	九四	_______	**Niner 4**		
內	六三	___ ___	**Sixer 3**		
坎 （水，下卦）	九二	_______	**Niner 2**	**Kan (Water, Trigram below)**	
	初六	___ ___	**First Sixer**		internal

卦辭 *(文王)* ：	***Hexagram Text (King Wen) :***
解：	Resolving:
利西南	Favoring West South
无所往	No Purpose Going-there
其來復吉	Then Come Back, Auspicious
有攸往	Have Purpose Going-there
夙吉	Earlier Auspicious

彖曰 *(孔子)* ：	***Tuan says (Kongzi explains) :***
解，險以動	Resolving, Danger Hence Action
動而免乎險，解	Action To Avoid The Danger, Resolving
解利西南	Resolving Favors West-South
往得衆也	Forward Gain Masses that's (transformation of Hex.46)
其來復吉	Then Come Back Auspicious
乃得中也	Still Gain Centre (Niner2) that's
有攸往夙吉	Has Gentle Progress, Earlier Auspicious
往有功也	Forward Has Achievement that's
天地解而雷雨作	Heaven Earth Resolving and Thunder Rain Actions
雷雨作	Thunder Rain Actions
而百果草木皆甲坼	And All Fruits, Grasses, Trees, Together Sprouting Emerging
解之時大矣哉	Time Of Resolving, Great Indeed that's

Comments:

Image: Water (Danger) and Thunder (Action) getting away, thus Resolving the Danger situation.
King Wen: No purpose then come back, Auspicious; else has purpose, go Earlier for Resolving.
Kongzi: Heaven-Earth Resolving issues, bringing on Thunder and Rain for growth of all Plants.

[Xu: 解94判也 ；夙 ... ；險304阻難也 ；甲308東方孟陽气萌動 ；坼289裂也]

象曰 *(孔子)* ：	***HexagramSign says (Kongzi) :***
雷雨作，解	Thunder Rain in-Action, Resolving
君子以赦過宥罪	CulturedOne By Forgiving Wrong, Pardoning Crimes

Comments:

Nature Resolving Crisis of famine, brings on Thunder and Rain for all plants
CulturedOne Resolving Wrongs and Crimes with forgiveness and compassionate punishment.

[Xu: 赦68置也 ；宥151寬也]

爻辭 (周公) :	*Liner Text (Zhougong) :*

初六： — **FirstSixer:**

无咎 — No Faults

象曰 (孔子) : — *LinerSign Says (Kongzi) :*

剛柔之際 — Strong (Yang), Gentle (Yin) Their Meeting-place

義无咎也 — Uprightness No Faults that's

Comments:
Early in Resolving, FirstSixer (Yin) meeting partner Niner4 (Yang), No Faults.
[Xu: 際306壁會也]

九二： — **Niner2:**

田獲三狐 — Fields, Catches 3 Foxes

得黄矢，貞吉 — Gain Yellow Arrow (king's gift), Integrity Auspicious

象曰 (孔子) : — *LinerSign Says (Kongzi) :*

九二貞吉 — Niner2 Has Integrity Auspicious

得中道也 — Takes Centre (Upright) Path that's

Comments:
The 3 Foxes symbolic of 3 Yins (evil forces) in Resolving Hexagram (premier Sixer5 excluded).
Niner2 Upright with Integrity, removes them successfully, awarded Yellow Arrow Auspicious.

六三： — **Sixer3:**

負且乘 — Burden, Also Riding

致寇至，貞吝 — Attracts Bandits A-Come, Integrity Painful

象曰 (孔子) : — *LinerSign Says (Kongzi) :*

負且乘 — Burden (with rich Goods) And Riding (nice Carriage)

亦可醜也 — Also Can be Ashamed that's

自我致戎 — Own Self Attracts Robbery

又誰咎也 — Then Whose Faults that's

Comments:
Sixer3 has Integrity amassing Wealth, but Riding Grand Carriage in public attracts Bandits.
Hence has Painful experience suffering robbery, but Whose Faults.
(Kongzi further elaborates when question by disciples - Attached Upper Commentary para.8)
[Xu: 負130恃也从人,守貝有所恃]

九四： — **Niner4:**

解而拇 — Resolving At Thumb-level

朋至斯孚 — Friends Arrive Then Trusted

象曰 (孔子) : — *LinerSign says (Kongzi) :*

解而拇 — Resolving At Thumb-level (with FirstSixer)

未當位也 — Not in Right Position, that's

Comments:
Niner4, Yin position, FirstSixer in Yang position, both not correctly place.
Resolving such relationship at Thumb-level, from friends who came Niner4 gains Trust.
{Xu: 拇250將指也；斯300析也}

六五：	**Sixer5:**
君子維有解，吉	Junzi Inclusively Has Resolutions, Auspicious
有孚于小人	Has Trust From Small People
象曰 *(孔子)：*	***LinerSign says (Kongzi) :***
君子有解	Junzi (Gentleman) Has Resolutions
小人退也	Small People Retreat that's

Comments:
Junzi (Gentleman), in Premier position, has power for Resolving all problems, Auspicious.
Able to gains Trust from Small people who retreat and give no more troubles.
[Xu: 維276車蓋維也]

上六 ：	TopSixer:
公用射	Lord's Action Shooting
隼于高墉之上	Quail At High City-Wall Above
獲之无不利	Catching It Not Unfavorable
象曰 *(孔子)：*	***LinerSign says (Kongzi) :***
公用射隼	Lord's Action Shooting Quail
以解悖也	For Resolving Discord, that's

Comments:
Lord on High, no Authority, try Shooting Quail above City-Wall to help Resolving Discords.
(Kongzi further elaborates when question by disciples - Attached Lower Commentary para.5)
[Xu: 隼79一日鶉字 ；墉288城垣也 ； 獲205獵所獲也 ；悖 …]

Conclusions:
Resolving (Hexagram 40): Water Trigram below and Thunder Trigram above.
Image: below in Danger (Water), above in Action (Thunder) breaking out of danger, Resolving.

King Wen:
With Purpose, to go early for Resolving, Auspicious; else come back, do not linger in Danger.

Zhougong:
FirstSixer: Meeting partner Niner4 early in Time of Resolving with Uprightness, no Faults.
Niner2: Upright, Resolving Yin forces (catches 3 foxes), gains Yellow Arrow award, Auspicious.
Sixer3: Flouting Wealth in public, riding Grand Carriage, attracts Bandits, only Self to Blame.
Niner4: Resolving wrongly placed relationship with FirstSixer, then friends come with Trust .
Sixer5: Authority, has Resolving power, gains Trust of Small people, who retreat, Auspicious.
TopSixer: Honored, no Authority, uses skill with Arrow to help Resolving Discords, Favorable.
Resolving: Great Time indeed with most problems resolved.

Kongzi:
Heaven and Earth Resolving Differences, bring Thunder and Rain, Nurturing Plants, all Lives.
Junzi to emulate, Resolving Crimes and Wrongs with Compassion and Forgiveness.

(解：緩，雜卦傳)   (Resolving : relieving - Miscellaneous 10th 'Wing')

Lessons (Resolving Hex.40)
Junzi (Gentleman) Resolving Crimes and Grievances with Compassion and Forgiveness.

(第四十一卦) 損　　　　　**Reduction　(Hexagram 41)**

外	上九	▬▬▬	TopNiner	eternal
艮 (山，上卦) 六五		▬ ▬	Sixer5	Gen (Mountain, Trigram above)
	六四	▬ ▬	Sixer4	
	六三	▬ ▬	Sixer3	
兌 (澤，下卦) 九二		▬▬▬	Niner2	Dui (Wetland, Trigram below)
內	初九	▬▬▬	FirstNiner	internal

卦辭 *(文王)*：	*Hexagram Text (King Wen) :*
損：	Reduction:
有孚，元吉	Has Trust, Primaly Auspicious
无咎，可貞	No Faults, Can Persevere
利有攸往	Favors Having Gentle Progress
曷之用	Whoever Is Using
二簋可用享	2 Rite-vessels Can Make Offerings

象曰 *(孔子)*：	*Tuan Says (Kongzi explains) :*
損：	Reduction:
損下益上	Reduction Below, Benefiting Above
其道上行	The Way is Upward Action
損而有孚，元吉	Reduction But Has Trust, Primally Auspicious
无咎，可貞，利有攸往	No Faults, Can Persevere, Favors Having Gentle Progress
曷之用，二簋可用享	Whoever Is Using, 2 Rite-vessels Can Make Offerings
二簋應有時	2 Rite-vessels Correctly Has Timing
損剛益柔有時	Reducing Yang, Benefiting Yin Has Timing
損益盈虛	Reduction / Benefits, Fullness / Emptiness
與時偕行	With Time Together Progress

Comments:
Image: Reduction of groups of 3 Yangs and 3 Yins of Hex.11 with Niner3/TopSixer interchange.
Wen: Reduction to using 2 Rite-vessels Offerings only, but with Sincerity, no Faults, Auspicious.
Kongzi: There is timing in the progression of Reduction, Benefits, Fullness and Emptiness.
(Xu: 損254減也 ；曷100何也 ；何163誰何之何 ；應217當也 ；偕164一曰俱也)

象曰 *(孔子)*：	*HexagramSign Says (Kongzi) :*
山下有澤，損	Mountain, Below Has Wetland, Reduction
君子以懲忿窒欲	Junzi To Suppress Sadness, Block Desires

Comments:
Mountain, below has Wetland, image of Reduction below to benefit height of mountain above.
In time of Reduction Junzi (Gentleman) self-cultivates, suppresses Sadness, blocks Desires.
[Xu: 忿221一曰憂也 ；窒153塞也 ；欲179貪欲也)

爻辭 *(周公)* :	*Liner Text (Zhougong) :*

初九：	**FirstNiner:**
巳事遄往，无咎	Committed Task, Trips to Go-visiting, No Faults
酌損之	Consider The Reduction
象曰 *(孔子)* :	*LinerSign Says (Kongzi) :*
巳事遄往	Committed Task, Trips Go-visiting
尚合志也	Above (Sixer4) in Accord of Wills, that's

Comments:
FirstNiner, Wills in accord with partner Sixer4, to help with regularly visiting, No Faults.
But needs to consider level of Reduction of own health, i.e. be discretional in helping.
(Xu: 巳311實也；遄40往來數也；酌312盛酒行觴；尚38曾也, 庶幾也；曾28詞之舒也)

九二：	**Niner2:**
利貞，征凶	Favors Integrity, Campaign Ominous
弗損益之	No Reduction to Benefit That
象曰 *(孔子)* :	*LinerSign Says (Kongzi) :*
九二利貞	Niner2, Favors having Integrity
中以爲志也	Centre (Uprightness) Be The Will, that's

Comments:
Niner2, in wrong Yin position, no Reduction of self to help like going on campaign, Ominous.
Favors having Integrity, with the Will to hold on to centre position of Uprightness.
(Xu: 益104饒也；饒108飽也；志217意也)

六三：	**Sixer3:**
三人行，則損一人	3 Persons Walking, Then Reduction of 1 Person
一人行，則得其友	1 Person Walking, Then Acquires A Friend
象曰 *(孔子)* :	*LinerSign Says (Kongzi) :*
一人行，三則疑也	1 Person Walking, 3 Then Suspicion (arise) that's

Comments:
Reduction of groups of 3 Yangs and 3 Yins in Hex.11 with Niner3 and TopSixer interchanged.
Suspicion easily arise in a group of 3, whereas walking alone has freedom, easy to find friends.
(Xu: 疑310惑也；惑221亂也)

六四：	**Sixer4:**
損其疾	Reducing Her Sickness
使遄有喜，无咎	Enabling Trips Has Joy, No Faults
象曰 *(孔子)* :	*LinerSign Says (Kongzi) :*
損其疾	Reduction of Her Sickness
亦可喜也	Also Can Celebrate that's

Comments:
Sixer4, feeling joy with Partner FirstNiner committed to visiting her regularly.
Has Reduction of her melancholy sickness, a thing to be celebrated, No Faults.
(Xu: 使165伶也；伶165弄也；弄59玩也, 从廾持玉；疾154病也；喜10樂也)

六五：	**Sixer5:**
或益之十朋之龜	Or Benefited with 10-Peng Turtle (divine)
弗克違，元吉	No Authority to Reject, Primally Auspicious
象曰 *(孔子)：*	***LinerSign Says (Kongzi) :***
六五元吉	Sixer5, Primally Auspicious
自上祐也	Even High (Heaven) is Helping, that's

Comments:
Sixer5 gentle, upright in premier position, is so good that even the Heaven helps her.
Receiving gift of 10-Peng *divine* Turtles that she cannot reject, Primally Auspicious.
(Xu: 克143肩也, 日肩任也，通能勝此物；違41離也；祐7助也)

上九：	**TopNiner:**
弗損益之，无咎	No Reduction to Benefit Others, No Faults
貞吉，利有攸往	Integrity Auspicious, Favors Having Gentle Progress
得臣无家	Win-over Citizens, No Family (being left out)
象曰 *(孔子)：*	***LinerSign Says (Kongzi) :***
弗損益之	No Reduction (self) to Benefits Others
大得志也	Great Achievement of Will, that's

Comments:
TopNiner on high, has power to benefit everyone with good governance, without self Reduction.
Citizens benefited, no family is left out, a great achievement of personal Will, Truly Auspicious.
(Xu: 臣66牽也, 事君也)

Conclusions:
Reduction (Hexagram 41): Wetland Hexagram below and Mountain Hexagram above.
Image: Reduction of Wetland below, to benefit Mountain's height above.
Symbolic: From Reduction of Yangs' below, ie. Niner3 up/ TopSixer down of Hexagram 11.

King Wen:
Reduction to 2 Rite-vessels Offerings (from 9), but with Sincerity, Integrity, Primal Auspicious.

Zhougong:
FirstNiner: Helps partner Sixer4 with visits, mindful of Reduction of own time, No Faults.
Niner2: Wills to stay Upright, Yin position, no Reduction to help others campaign as Ominous.
Sixer3: In Reduction, lone Person comes down (TopSixer of Hex.11), meets Niner2, Befriended.
Sixer4: Enjoys regular visits from partner Niner2, hence Reduction of Melancholy, No Faults.
Sixer5: Upright, Heaven protects, and citizens' gift of 'divine' Turtle, Greatly Auspicious.
TopNiner: Able to benefit without self Reduction, left no family behind, Achieved, No Faults.
Reduction: sounds negative, but is positively treated here, and Timing is important.

Kongzi:
Kongzi: Reduction is Timing, and Reduction Below is to support Above with beneficial Actions.
Reduction practice has proper Timing, like using only 2 Rite-vessels Offerings in poor harvest.
In Reduction Time, Junzi self-discipline to reduce Sadness and blocking Desires.
(損益：盛衰之始也，雜卦傳)   (Reduction : declining starts - Miscellaneous 10th Wing)

Lessons (Reduction Hex.41)
Junzi seeks self-improvement by Reduction of Sadness and Blocking bad Desires.

(第四十二卦) 益　　　　　　　　**Benefiting (Hexagram 42)**

<pre>
        外   上九   ________   TopNiner   external
  巽 (風,上卦) 九五   ________   Niner5   Xun (Wind, Trigram above)
               六四   __ __   Sixer4

               六三   __ __   Sixer3
  震 (雷,下卦) 六二   __ __   Sixer2   Zhen (Thunder, Trigram below)
        內   初九   ________   FirstNiner   internal
</pre>

卦辭 *(文王)* ：	***Hexagram Text (King Wen) :***
益：	Benefiting :
利有攸往	Favos Having Slow Progress
利涉大川	Favors Venturing Big Rivers

彖曰 *(孔子)* ：	***Tuan Says (Kongzi explains) :***
益：	Benefiting :
損上益下	Reduction Above (rulers) Benefiting Below (subjects)
民說，无疆	Citizens Happy, No Boundaries
自上下下，其道大光	From Top to Bottom Below, The Path Greatly Shining
利有攸往，中正有慶	Favors Having Slow Progress, Centre Correctness Has Celebration
利涉大川，木道乃行	Favors Venturing Big Rivers, Wood Way Still Operational
益動而巽，日進无疆	Benefiting Action And Orderly, Daily Advance No Boundaries
天施地生，其益无方	Heaven Bestows Earth Creating, This Benefiting No Borders
凡益之道，與時偕行	All Benefiting This Way, With Time Together Moving

Comments:
Image: Thunder action below, assisted by Wind above, Benefiting mutually.
Symbolic: From Hex.12, Niner4/ FirstSixer interchanged, i.e. reduction above Benefiting below.
Wen: Niner5 premier, all liners partnered, boat shape of hollow Yins, favors venturing big rivers.
Kongzi: Reduction above Benefiting citizens below, universal happiness, the Path shining.
[Xu: 益105饒 ；饒108飽也 ；畺291界也,或从彊土]

象曰 *(孔子)* ：	***HexagramSign Says (Kongzi) :***
風雷，益	Wdind Thunder, Benefiting
君子以見善則遷	Junzi With Seeing Goodness Then Migrate-over (be good)
有過則改	Has Mistakes Then Correct-over

Comments:
Wind and Thunder, two forces supplementing each other in action, Benefiting.
Junzi sees Goodness changes self-conduct to embrace, has mistakes make corrections.

爻辭 (周公)：	*Liner Text (Zhougong)：*
初九：	**FirstNiner:**
利用爲大作	Favors Deployment For Big Tasks
元吉无咎	Primaly Auspicious, No Faults
象曰 (孔子)：	*LinerSign Says (Kongzi)：*
元吉无咎	Primal Auspiciousness No Faults
下不厚事也	Lowly Not for Big Affairs that's

Comments:
FirstNiner Benefiting from above, gets assignment of Big Tasks, hence Primally Auspicious.
As lowly in rank with less ability for big affairs, hence expectation lesser and easily No Fault.

六二：	**Sixer2:**
或益之十朋之龜	Or Benefiting It with 10-Peng Turtle (big turtle)
弗克違	Not Able to Reject
永貞吉	Everlasting Truth Auspicious
王用享于帝，吉	King Makes Offerings To Emperor (of Heaven) that's
象曰 (孔子)：	*LinerSign Says (Kongzi)：*
或益之	Or Benefiting It
自外來也	From Outside Cometh, that's (Niner5)

Comments:
Sixer2 Benefited with gift of Big Turtle, not able to reject, be Ever-Truthful, Auspicious.
To assist King Niner5 in Divining, to make Offerings to the Emperor of Heaven, Auspicious.
[Xu: 朋 …]

六三：	**Sixer3:**
益之用凶事，无咎	Benefiting It With Ominous Affairs, No Faults.
有孚中行	Has Trust, Centre (Upright) Conduct
告公用圭	Informing the Lord Using Jade-tablet
象曰 (孔子)：	*LinerSign Says (Kongzi)：*
益用凶事	Benefiting With Ominous Affairs
固有之也	Long-time Has These that's (occurrence of disasters)

Comments:
Sixer3 misplaced, gets Benefiting when natural disasters strike i.e. famine, earthquakes, ...
The Lord informs with the Jade-tablet, authorising the opening of Granaries for disaster-relief.
[Xu: 告30牛觸人角箸橫木以告人；圭289瑞玉也上圓下方公執桓圭九寸侯執信圭伯執躬圭
皆七寸子執穀璧男執蒲璧五寸以封諸侯]

六四：	**Sixer4:**
中行告公從	Centre (authority) Action Informed, Lord Obeyed
利用爲依遷國	Favors Using As Guide, Moving Kingdom
象曰 (孔子)：	*LinerSign Says (Kongzi)：*
告公從，以益志也	Informed, Lord Obeyed, For Benefiting Wills that's

Comments:
Authority informed, Lord obeyed orders, moved citizens of vanquished Kingdom of King Zhou.
Alluding to King Wu Benefiting the defeated citizens, not killed but moved them to a new place.

九五：	**Niner5:**
有孚惠心	Has Trust Kind Hearted
勿問元吉	Don't Ask, Primally Auspicious
有孚惠我德	Has Trust Comforting My Virtues
象曰 *(孔子)*：	***LinerSign Says (Kongzi)*:**
有孚惠心，勿問之矣	Has Trust Kind Hearted, Don't Ask of This that's
惠我德，大得志也	Appreciating My Virtues, Great Achievement of Wills that's

Comments:
Niner5 Premier, has Trust, Kind Hearted, Benefiting Citizens without being asked.
In turn Citizens has Trust, thankful of King's Virtues and Wills for great achievement.

上九：	**TopNiner:**
莫益之，或擊之	Not Benefiting It, Or Hitting It
立心勿恒，凶	Setting Heart Not Lasting , Ominous
象曰 *(孔子)*：	***LinerSign Says (Kongzi)* :**
莫益之偏辭也	Not Benefiting It, Words Aside that's
或擊之，自外來也	Or Hitting It, From Outside Cometh, that's

Comments:
TopNiner not Benefiting subjects any more, as heart resolution to do so not lasting, Ominous.
Thus when hit by outside forces, citizens will not come to his assistance.
(Kongzi further elaborates when question by disciples - Attached Lower Commentary para.5)
[Xu: 恒286常也]

Conclusions:
Benefiting (Hexagram 42): Thunder Trigram below and Wind Trigram above.
Image: Thunder actions below, Wind following above, mutually Benefiting for achievement.
Symbolic: Focus FirstNiner, a Benefit of Niner4 exchanging for FirstSixer in Hex.12.

King Wen:
Niner5, all partners balanced, hollow Yins inside, boat-shape favors venturing big rivers.

Zhougong:
FirstNiner: Benefited with Big Tasks, Auspicious; lowly with less ability to achieve, No Faults.
Sixer2: Benefit of 10-Peng Turtle, helps King in divination, makes Offerings, Twice Auspicious
Sixer3: misplaced, commonly Benefiting from Disaster-reliefs, Jade-tablet ordered, No Faults.
Sixer4: alluded, Benefiting King Zhou's citizens, migrated to new land, was King Wu's Wills.
Niner5: trusted King, Benefiting citizens who reciprocated, Wills achieved, Primally Auspicious.
TopNiner: lost resolution to Benefiting citizens, so no help if attack by outside forces, Ominous.
Benefiting: Bottom 3 liners Benefited, Sixer4 Niner5 Benefiting but not TopNiner Ominous.

Kongzi:
Reduction above to Benefiting subjects below, the Shining Path without boundaries.
Junzi sees Goodness migrates to Goodness, makes mistakes makes immediate corrections.
(損益：盛衰之始也，雜卦傳)(Reduction Benefiting: prosperity decline starts-Misc.10th Wing)

Lessons (Benefiting Hex.42)
Truly, reduction above to Benefiting subjects below, is the Shining Path forward for humankind.
Likewise, big businesses ought to take less profits and lower prices for Benefiting the masses.

(第四十三卦) 夬　　　　　　　　**Ostracism (Hexagram 43)**

	上六	▬▬　▬▬	**TopSixer**	external
兌 (澤, 上卦)	九五	▬▬▬▬▬	**Niner5**	**Dui (Wetland, Trigram above)**
	九四	▬▬▬▬▬	**Niner4**	
	九三	▬▬▬▬▬	**Niner3**	
乾 (天, 下卦)	九二	▬▬▬▬▬	**Niner2**	**Qian (Heaven, Trigram below)**
	初九	▬▬▬▬▬	**FirstNiner**	internal

卦辭 *(文王)* :　　　　　　　　*Hexagram Text (King Wen) :*

夬 :　　　　　　　　　　　　Ostracism:

揚于王庭　　　　　　　　　　Broadcast (evidence) In King's Court

孚號有厲　　　　　　　　　　Honestly Declaring, Has Seriousness

告自邑　　　　　　　　　　　Inform Own Countrymen

不利即戎，利有攸往　　　　　Not Favoring Resort To Violence, Favors Having Slow Advance

象曰 *(孔子)* :　　　　　　　*Tuan Says (Kongzi explains) :*

夬 : 決也　　　　　　　　　Ostracism: Cut-off that's

剛決柔也　　　　　　　　　　Yangs Cut-off Yin that's

健而說　　　　　　　　　　　Strength (Heaven) And Joy (Wetland)

決而和　　　　　　　　　　　Flow-separately And Harmoniously

揚于王庭，柔乘五剛也　　　　Announcing in King's Court, Yin Riding on 5 Yangs that's

孚號有厲　　　　　　　　　　Honest Declaration Has Serious (consequence)

其危乃光也　　　　　　　　　Its Dangerous Yet Shining that's

告自邑　　　　　　　　　　　Informing Own Countrymen

不利即戎　　　　　　　　　　Not Favoring Resort to Violence

所尚乃窮也　　　　　　　　　Whatever Aspiration Is Exhausted that's

利有攸往　　　　　　　　　　Favors Having Slow Progress

剛長乃終也　　　　　　　　　Yang's Growth Becomes Terminal that's (all Yangs)

Comments:
Image: TopSixer, a lone Yin sitting on 5 Yangs is the problem here, causing Ostracism in court.
Wen: Ostracism done openly in court, honestly inform all countrymen, no resort to violence.
Kongzi: Yangs Ostracizing Yin with Strength and Joy, harmoniously going their separate ways.
[Xu: 夬64分決也；號101呼；剛91疆斷；健163亢也；說53釋也；釋28解也；決233行流]

象曰 *(孔子)* :　　　　　　　*HexagramSign Says (Kongzi) :*

澤上於天，夬　　　　　　　　Wetland Atop On Heaven, Ostracism

君子以施祿及下　　　　　　　Junzi (Gentleman) By Giving Prosperity To Subordinates

居德則忌　　　　　　　　　　Claiming Virtuous (credit) Is Taboo

Comments:
Wetland atop of Heaven is symbolic of Ostracism.
TopSixer bestows prosperity on 5 Yangs subordinates, claims no credit else suffers Ostracism.

爻辭 *(周公)* ：	*Liner Text (Zhougong) :*
初九：	**FirstNiner:**
壯于前趾	Strong At Front Toe
往不勝爲咎	Forward but No Win Is Disastrous
象曰 *(孔子)* ：	*LinerSign Says (Kongzi) :*
不勝而往，咎也	Not Winning But Go-forth, Disastrous that's

Comments:
FirstNiner at Yang position is strong but advancing at toe level, too lowly to win, Disastrous.
[Xu: 爲63母猴也]

九二：	**Niner2:**
惕號	Respectful Declaration
莫夜有戎，勿恤	Dark Night Has Violence, Not Worry
象曰 *(孔子)* ：	*LinerSign Says (Kongzi) :*
有戎勿恤	Has Violence Not Worry
得中道也	Possess Centrist's Way that's

Comments:
Niner2 in Yin position and centre, practice centrism, hence no worry even in dark of night.
[Xu: 惕223敬也；恤21`9憂也收也；收69捕也]

九三：	**Niner3:**
壯于頄、有凶	Tough At Cheek-bone, Has Danger
君子夬夬	Junzi Ostracism Ostracism
獨行遇雨	Action Alone Encounter Rain
若濡有慍，无咎	If Drenched Has Anger but No Disaster
象曰 *(孔子)* ：	*LinerSign Says (Kongzi) :*
君子夬夬	Junzi (Gentleman) Ostracism Ostracism (firmly)
終无咎也	Finally No Disaster that's

Comments:
Niner3 in Yang position, with determined Ostracism shown on the face, hence has danger.
Only Yang partner of TopSixer, went alone got drenched head cleared, angry but no disaster.
[Xu: 濡228水出涿郡...；咎167災也；災209天火也

九四：	**Niner4:**
臀无膚	Buttocks No Skin
其行次且	Its Movement Has Difficulty
牽羊悔亡	Lead Goat (if follow), Regrets Lost
聞言不信	Heard Advice Not Believing
象曰 *(孔子)* ：	*LinerSign Says (Kongzi) :*
其行次且，位不當也	Its Movement Has Difficulty, Position Not Correct that's
聞言不信，聰不明也	Heard Advice Not Believing, Hearing but Not Enlightened that's

Comments:
Niner4, weak in Yin position has difficulty dealing with TopSixer.
Not following the lead of other Yangs in severing ties with TopSixer, is lacking enlightenment.

九五：	**Niner5:**
莧陸夬夬	Amaranth Land, Cut-off Cut-off
中行无咎	Centrism for Action, No Faults
象曰 *(孔子)：*	***LinerSign Says (Kongzi) :***
中行无咎	Centrism for Action, No Faults
中未光也	Zenith 1-3 pm Brightness that's

Comments:
Niner5, the authority acting with centrism, no disaster, as action transparent in broad daylight.

上六：	**TopSixer:**
无號	No Howling
终有凶	Ultimately Has Danger
象曰 *(孔子)：*	***LinerSign Says (Kongzi) :***
无號之凶	No Howling Its Danger
终不可長也	Finally Cannot Long (lasting) that's

Comments:
TopSixer, Yin the evil one at wits end, no voice to protest, finally has danger as cannot long last.

Conclusions:
Ostracism (Hexagram 43):   Heaven Trigram below and Wetland Trigram above
Image: 5 Yangs beneath chasing lone Yin above, Yangs Ostracizing Yin.
Symbolic: TopSixer a lone Yin sitting on top of 5 Yangs, fertile condition for Ostracism.

King Wen:
Open Ostracism in court, honestly, inform all countrymen, no resort to violence, favors progress.

Zhougong:
FirstNiner strong in Yang position, too lowly at toe level, hence in Ostracism action No Win.
Niner2 centre Upright in Ostracism exercise, hence violence in the dark of night No Worry.
Niner3 partner TopSixer, Ostracism in the face, go alone met rain, mind cleared but No Disaster.
Niner4 in Yin position, actions awkward, not following lead of other Yangs, Not Enlightened.
Niner5 central authority, practices centrism, Ostracism actions transparent in broad Daylight.
TopSixer sitting atop 5 Yangs, at wits end facing Ostracism, lost voice, and finally Succumbed.
Ostracism: varying, reflective of the 5 Yangs in status, strength and relationship with TopSixer.

Kongzi:
Yangs Ostracizing Yin with Strength and Joy, harmoniously going their separate ways.
TopSixer bestows prosperity on 5 Yangs subordinates, to claims no credit else suffers Ostracism.
(夬：決也剛決柔也，雜卦傳)   (Ostracism : Cut-off Yangs cut-off Yin- Misc.10th Wing)

Lessons (Ostracism Hex.43)
Ostracism be done honestly, openly, not resorting to violence, thus preserving harmony.
Ostracism to be avoided by taking no credit for benefits bestowed on subordinates below.

(第四十四卦)　姤　　　　　　Encounters (Hexagram 44)

外	上九	________	TopNiner		eternal
乾　(天,上卦)	九五	________	Niner5	Qian (Heaven, Trigram above)	
	九四	________	Niner4		
	九三	________	Niner3		
巽　(風,下卦)	九二	________	Niner2	Xun (Wind, Trigram below)	
內	初六	__　__	FirstSixer		internal

卦辭 *(文王)* ：	*Hexagram Text (King Wen) :*
姤:	Encounters:
女壯	Woman Strong (character)
勿用取女	Do Not Take-in Woman

彖曰 *(孔子)* ：	*Tuan Says (Kongzi explains) :*
姤，遇也	Encounters that's
柔遇剛也	Gentle (FirstSixer) Encounter the Strong (Yangs) that's
勿用取女	Do Not Take-in woman
不可與長也	Cannot With (her) has Development that's
天地相遇	Heaven and Earth Mutually Encounter
品物咸章也	Kinds and Matters All Perfection that's
剛遇中正	Yang (Niner5) Encountered, is Centrist Righteous
天下大行也	The World has Great Progress that's
姤之時	Encounters Its Time
義大矣哉	Uprightness Great Indeed that's

Comments:
Image: a lone Yin FirstSixer Encounters 5 strong Yangs above.
Wen: meeting 5 men, woman strong in character, likely loose in conduct, do not take-in as wife.
Kongzi: Niner5, righteous person in authority, achieving great progress, Positive Encounters.
[Xu: 姤265偶也 ；偶167桐人也 ；桐117榮也]

象曰 *(孔子)* ：	*HexagramSign Says (Kongzi) :*
天下有風，姤	Heaven Below Has Wind, Encounters
后以施命誥四方	Afterwards By Executive Orders, Announces to 4 Corners

Comments:
Heaven beneath has Wind, signifies free roaming with many Encounters.
Helping Authority of Perfection with a mission for progress, to spread the message worldwide.
[Xu: 施140旗兒 ；誥52告也 ；告30牛觸人角箸橫木所以告人也]

爻辭 *(周公) :*	*Liner Text (Zhougong) :*

初六：　　**FirstSixer:**

繫于金柅，貞吉　　Tethers To Gold Tree-pole, Augurs Good-fortune

有攸往，見凶　　Has Slow Progress, Sees Danger

羸豕孚蹢躅　　Thin Pig Nursing, not Moving Legs (fear stepping on youngsters)

象曰 *(孔子) :*　　*LinerSign Says (Kongzi) :*

繫于金柅　　Tethering To Golden Tree-pole

柔道牽也　　Gentle Way of Leading that's

Comments:

FirstSixer a lone woman Encounters 5 Yangs (males), moving forward sees Danger.
Best stay-put like nursing pig, not moving legs not stepping on youngsters, Auspicious.

[Xu: 柅116木也實如棃；攸68行水也；羸78瘦也；蹢47住足也；躅46蹢躅也]

九二：　　**Niner2:**

包有魚，无咎　　Embrace Has Fish (Yin), No Faults

不利賓　　Not Favourable to Respect

象曰 *(孔子) :*　　*LinerSign Says (Kongzi) :*

包有魚　　Embrace Has Fish (FirstSixer)

義不及賓也　　Rightly Not Amounting to Respect that's

Comments:

Niner2, neighbor embraces FirstSixer, No Faults.
But be warned of overdoing it with respect.

[Xu: 魚242水蟲也象形；賓130所敬也]

九三：　　**Niner3:**

臀无膚　　Buttock No Skin (restive)

其行次且，厲　　Its Actions Secondarily Recommended, Grave

无大咎　　No Big Faults

象曰 *(孔子) :*　　*LinerSign Says (Kongzi) :*

其行次且　　Its Actions Secondarily Recommended

行未牽也　　Actions Not Linked that's

Comments:

Niner3, strong Yang and in position for action, but no direct Encounter with FirstSixer.
Niner3 restive and actions awkward as no linkage with FirstSixer, but No Big Faults.

[Xu: 次180不前不精；且299薦从几足有二橫一其下地也]

九四：　　**Niner4:**

包无魚　　Embracing No Fish (FirstSixer)

象曰 *(孔子) :*　　*LinerSign Says (Kongzi) :*

无魚之凶，遠民也　　No Fish The Danger, Far-apart Citizen that's

Comments:

Niner4 and FirstSixer are partners, as both are bottom liners in respective Trigrams.
Apart Niner4 cannot embrace FirstSixer, but neighbor Niner2 can, animosity arises, Ominous.

九五：	**Niner5:**
以杞包瓜	With Qi (杞, a hardwood) Wrapping Melon (perishable)
含章，有隕自天	Embodiment of Perfection, Have Manna From Heaven
象曰 (孔子)：	***LinerSign Says (Kongzi) :***
九五含章，中正也	Niner5 Embodied Perfection, Centrist and Righteous that's
有隕自天	Like Manna descend From Heaven
志不舍命也	Resolution Not to Abandon Mission that's

Comments:
Niner5 is centrist and righteous, like manna descend from Heaven above, the PerfectOne.
In position of authority, resolves with a mission to bring salvation to all, including FirstSixer.
[Xu: 杞117枸杞子；含310嗛也口有所銜，隕305從高下也；志217意也；舍108市居也]

上九：	**TopNiner:**
姤其角，吝	Encounters Its Horn (farthest tip), Painful
无咎	No Faults
象曰 (孔子)：	***LinerSign Says (Kongzi) :***
姤其角，上窮吝也	Encounters Its Horn, Upper Limit Painful that's

Comments:
TopNiner at upper limit, is farthest from FirstSixer and not a chance of an Encounter.
Hence feeling of resentment and Painful.
[Xu: 吝34恨惜也；恨221怨也；惜222痛也；窮153極也]

Conclusions:
Encounters (Hexagram 44): Wind Trigram below and Heaven Trigram above.
Image: Heaven beneath has Wind, going all places making Encounters.
Symbolic: Lone Yin FirstSixer appearing, making Encounters with 5 Yangs above.

King Wen:
Alone and Lowly, Encountering with 5 Yangs, FirstSixer is a woman of very strong character.
Wen is cautious of such Encounters, warns that woman may not be accepted or taken-in.

Zhougong:
FirstSixer, lowly like thin nursing pig, safe be tethered, not moving, Auspicious else Ominous.
Niner2, the neighbor may embrace FirstSixer but not to Over-Respecting her, No Faults,
Niner3 in Yang position is restive, as separated with no direct involvement, No Big Faults.
Niner4 apart fail to embrace FirstSixer, animosity with Niner2 who can as neighbor, Ominous.
Niner5, authority on a mission of salvation for all, like manna from Heaven, the PerfectOne.
TopNiner, up in the 'Horn' farthest from an encounter with FirstSixer suffers resentment Pain.
Encounters: warns of amorous Encounters, but may also Encounter the PerfectOne!

Kongzi:
Highlight positive Encounter with PerfectOne in authority, like manna from above.
Junzi helping Authority with a mission for progress, to spread the message worldwide.
(姤：遇也，柔遇剛也 - 雜卦傳)(Encounters : meetings, Yin with Yangs - Misc.10th 'Wing')

Lessons (Encounters Hex.44)
Amorous Encounters should be guarded, and rightly so, as sexual harassments are common.
Encountering PerfectOne in authority is like manna from Heaven above, sadly not so common.

(第四十五卦) 萃　　　　　　　**Grassland (Hexagram 45)**

外	上六	___ ___	**TopSixer**	**external**
兌 (澤，上卦)	九五	_______	**Niner5**	**Dui (Wetland, Trigram above)**
	九四	_______	**Niner4**	
	六三	___ ___	**Sixer3**	
坤 (地，下卦)	六二	___ ___	**Sixer2**	**Kun (Earth, Trigram below)**
內	初六	___ ___	**FirstSixer**	**internal**

卦辭 *(文王)* ：	*Hexagram Text (King Wen) :*
萃：	Grassland :
亨，王假有廟	Prosperity, King's Arrival Has Temple
利見大人，亨	Favors Seeing Great Person, Prosperity
利貞，用大牲吉	Favors Truth, Using Big Animal (sacrificial), Auspicious
利有攸往	Favors Having Soft Venture

象曰 *(孔子)* ：	*Tuan Says (Kongzi explains) :*
萃，聚也	Grassland, Gathering that's (of grass plants)
順以兌	Supportive (Earth) With Joy (Wetland)
剛中而應	Yang (Niner5) Centre And Responder (Sixer2)
故聚也	Hence Gathering that's
王假有廟，致孝享也	King Arrival Has Temple, Attains Filial-piety, Prosperity
利見大人亨	Favors Seeing Great Person Prosperity,
聚以正也	Gathering For Correct (reasons) that's
用大牲吉	Using Big Animal Auspicious (sacrificial)
利有攸往	Favors Having Slow Venture
順天命也	Accords with Heaven's Order that's
觀其所聚	Observes The Purpose for Gathering
而天地萬物之情可見矣	Thus Heaven Earth All Matters, Their Desires Can be Seen that's

Comments:
Image: Below Earth (Support), above Wetland (Joy), Grassland a Gathering of growth.
Wen: Prosperity, King makes sacrificial offerings in Ancestral Temple Gathering, Auspicious.
Kongzi: Gathering in Ancestral Temple, makes Offerings, rightful purpose accords with Heaven.
[Xu: 萃23艸(兒)；艸15百艸也；聚169會也；情217人之陰气有欲者)

象曰 *(孔子)* ：	*HexagramSign Says (Kongzi) :*
澤上於地，萃	Wetland Rises On Earth, Grassland (Gathering)
君子以除戎器戒不虞	Junzi With Removal of Weapon Tools, Unkind Militants

Comments:
In Gathering, Junzi mindful of safety, removes weapons and keeps undesirables away.
[Xu: 除306殿陛;陛306升高階;戎266兵也;虞103騶虞也,白虎黑文尾長於身,仁獸食自死之肉]

爻辭 *(周公)* :	*Liner Text (Zhougong) :*

初六： — **FirstSixer:**

有孚不終	Has Trust, No Ending
乃亂乃萃	Its Confusion Its Grassland
若號	Or A-calling
一握爲笑	1 Hand-hold, Being Laugh at
勿恤，往无咎	Don't Worry, Venture No Faults

象曰 *(孔子)* :	*LinerSign Says (Kongzi) :*
乃亂乃萃	Its Confusion Its Grassland (Gathering)
其志亂也	The Wills Confused that's

Comments:
FirstSixer, separated by 2 Yins, go a-calling for partner Niner4 to come join hands Together.
Others laugh, Trust shaken, but in Gathering time, not to worry, go-forth, No Faults.
[Xu: 握252搤持也]

六二： — **Sixer2:**

引吉	Leading, Auspicious (from Niner5)
无咎	No Faults
孚乃利用禴	Trust Thus Favors Using Simple-rites

象曰 *(孔子)* :	*LinerSign Says (Kongzi) :*
引吉无咎	Leading, Auspicious No Faults
中未變也	Centres No Changes that's (both Upright)

Comments:
In time of Gathering, both Sixer2 and partner are Centres with Trust Unchanged, Auspicious.
Sandwiched by 2 Yins, Sixer2 needs Niner5's Leading with simple Music-rites, No Faults.
[Xu: 龠48樂之竹管三孔以和眾聲]

六三： — **Sixer3:**

| 萃如嗟如，无攸利 | Gathering Like Sighing Like, No Easy Gain |
| 往无咎，小吝 | Venture No Fault, Small Insult |

| 象曰 *(孔子)* : | *LinerSign Says (Kongzi) :* |
| 往无咎，上巽也 | Venture No Fault, TopSixer Docile, that's |

Comments:
Sixer3 sighing as no easy gain when Gathering with Niner4 a neighbor not rightful partner.
Venture to Gathering with partner TopSixer No Fault, but also a Yin, hence a Small Insult.
[Xu: 巽99具也,庶物皆具丌以薦之；具59共置也]

九四： — **Niner4:**

| 大吉，无咎 | Greatly Auspicious, No Fault |

| 象曰 *(孔子)* : | *LinerSign Says (Kongzi) :* |
| 大吉无咎，位不當也 | Greatly Auspicious, No Fault, Position Not Proper that's |

Comments:
In Gathering, Niner4 next to Premier, supported by 3 Yin subjects below, Greatly Auspicious.
However Yang in Yin position, authority checked by Niner5, hence has Regrets but No Fault.

九五:	Niner5:
萃有位，无咎	Grassland (Gathering) Has Position, No Fault
匪孚，元永貞	Not Trusted, Primal Everlasting Integrity
悔亡	Regrets Lost
象曰 *(孔子)*:	*LinerSign Says (Kongzi)*:
萃有位	Grassland (Gathering) Has Position
志未光也	Wills Yet to Shine that's

Comments:
Niner5 Yang Premier, has position No Fault, Gathering no Trust from Yins as Wills yet to show.
Hold to Primal Integrity Everlasting to win Trust then no more Regrets .

上六:	TopSixer:
齎咨涕洟	Lost Advisory-Gathering, Sobbing Snivelling
无咎	No Faults
象曰 *(孔子)*:	*LinerSign Says (Kongzi)*:
齎咨涕洟	Lost Advisory-Gathering, Sobbing Snivelling
未安上也	Not Secure On-top that's

Comments:
End of Gathering, TopSixer laments lost of Advisory-group, insecure at Top-level, No Faults.
[Xu: 齎130持遺；遺41匕也；咨32謀事曰咨；涕237泣；泣237無聲出涕；洟237鼻液也]

Conclusions:
Grassland (Hexagram 45): Earth Trigram below and Wetland Trigram above.
Image: Earth (Support), above Wetland (Joy), Grassland, Gathering of community growth.
Symbolic: Support and Joy, Gathering for Ancestral Offerings and meet-up of Individuals.

King Wen:
Temple Gathering, honoring Ancestors, Prosperity, Favors Ventures with Truth, Auspicious.

Zhougong:
FirstSixer: above 2 Yins laughed, Confused, Niner4 called for Gathering, No Worry, No Fault.
Sixer2: between 2 Yins, needs Niner5 to Lead Gathering with simple Music-rites, Auspicious.
Sixer 3: sigh, misses strong Niner4 for Gathering No Fault, partner TopSixer a Yin, Small Insult.
Niner4: Regrets Yin position, next to Premier, with support of Yins subjects below, Auspicious.
Niner5: Gathering no Trust from Yins, holds everlastingly to Primal Integrity, then Regrets Lost.
TopSixer: End of Gathering, weak, Lamenting Lost of Advisory Group, insecure No Faults.
Grassland: Describes trials and tribulations of individuals of different status getting Together.

Kongzi:
Gathering in Ancestral Temple, make Offerings, rightful purpose, accord with Heaven.
In large Gathering, Junzi concerns for security, checks for likely weapons, barring Undesirables.
(萃：聚，雜卦傳)　　　　　(Grassland : gathering - Miscellaneous 10th Wing)

Lessons (Grassland-Gathering Hex.45)
For large Gathering, Junzi's concern for security, checks for weapons, barring Undesirables.
Today, security concern still here with more electronic surveillance cameras, Entry-checks.

（第卦四十六） 升　　　　　　　**Rising (Hexagram 46)**

<pre>
      外   上六   __ __   TopSixer   external
坤 （地，上卦） 六五   __ __   Sixer5   Kun (Earth, Trigram above)
              六四   __ __   Sixer4

              九三   _______ Niner3
巽 （風，下卦） 九二   _______ Niner2   Xun (Wind, Trigram below)
      內   初六   __ __   FirstSixer   internal
</pre>

卦辭 *(文王)* ：	***Hexagram Text (King Wen)*** *:*
升 ：	Rising:
元亨	Primal Prosperity
用見大人，勿恤	Action to See Great Person, No Worries
南征吉	Southward Expedition, Auspicious

象曰 *(孔子)：*	***Tuan Says (Kongzi explains)*** *:*
柔以時升	Yins (gentle) with Time Rising
巽而順	Wind (conform) Then Earth (supportive)
剛中而應	Yang (Niner2) Centre (Upright) And Respond (to Sixer5)
是以大亨	Therefore Great Prosperity
用見大人勿恤	Action to See Great Person No Worries
有慶也	Have Celebrations that's
南征吉	Southward Expedition Auspicious
志行也	Ambitions Fulfilling, that's

Comments:

Image: Rising of the 3 gentle Yins to the top Earth Trigram, dominating and above the 2 Yangs.

Wen: sees state of Zhou's Rising Primal Prosperity and Southward Expedition Auspiciousness.

Kongzi: Alluding to Wen (Sixer5) and partner Niner2, southward expedition and success.

[Xu:升300十龠也从斗；斗300十升；德43升也；巽99具也从丌；丌99下基也薦物之丌象]

象曰 *(孔子)：*	***HexagramSign Says (Kongzi)*** *:*
地中生木，升	Earth Inside, Growing Wood (Wind is wood), Rising
君子以順德	Junzi (Gentleman) By Docile Virtues
積小以高大	Accumulates Small (acts of Virtue) to Be Great (Sage)

Comments:

Wind (wood) below Earth, Image of Acorn emerging from ground, Rising to be a forest giant.
Likewise, conforming Junzi accumulates little acts of virtues, becoming Great Sage.

| 爻辭 *(周公)* :| *Liner Text (Zhougong) :* |

初六：　　**FirstSixer:**
允升　　Accord Rising
大吉　　Greatly Auspicious
象曰 *(孔子)* :　　*LinerSign Says (Kongzi) :*
允升大吉　　Accord Rising, Greatly Auspicious
上合志也　　Above, Accord of Wills that's

Comments:
FirstSixer, gentle Yin, with Wills in accord with the 2 Yangs above, hence Greatly Auspicious.
[Xu: 允176信也从儿；儿176仁人也古文奇字人也象形]

九二：　　**Niner2:**
孚乃利用禴　　Trust, Thus Favorable Using Ceremonial-rites
无咎　　No Faults
象曰 *(孔子)* :　　*LinerSign Says (Kongzi) :*
九二之孚　　Niner2, Its Trust
有喜也　　Have Good-news, that's

Comments:
Niner2, in Yin position, gentle, Upright, wins Trust of partner Sixer5.
With Glad-tidings coming, celebrates using ceremonial-rites, No Faults.
[Xu: 礻禴....；禴48樂之竹管三孔以和眾聲也]

九三：　　**Niner3:**
升虛邑　　Rising, Empty Land
象曰 *(孔子)* :　　*LinerSign Says (Kongzi) :*
升虛邑.　　Rising, Unoccupied Land
无所疑也　　No Reason to Doubts that's

Comments:
Facing 3 Yins (Earth Trigram) above, Image of unoccupied land, can expect No Resistance.
Thus Niner3, Rising into such territory has no Doubts of taking-over Successfully.
[Xu: 虛169大丘也崑崙謂之崑崙虛古者有九夫爲井四井爲邑四邑爲丘丘爲之虛;邑131國也]

六四：　　**Sixer4:**
王用亨于岐山　　King Makes Feast At Mount Qi
吉，无咎　　Auspicious, No Faults
象曰 *(孔子)* :　　*LinerSign Says (Kongzi) :*
王用亨于岐山　　King Makes Feast At Mount Qi
順事也　　Orderly Affairs, that's

Comments:
State's affairs peaceful and prosper, King makes Offerings at Mount Qi, no Faults Auspicious.
Mount Qi is located in the Kingdom of King Wen in the West.

六五：	**Sixer5:**
貞吉	Integrity Auspicious
升階	Rising up the Steps
象曰 *(孔子)：*	***LinerSign Says (Kongzi) :***
貞吉升階	Integrity Auspicious, Rising in Status
大得志也	Great Fulfilling of Ambitions that's

Comments:
Sixer5, weak Yin with Integrity, Rising into Kingship with Great Achievements Auspicious.
[Xu: 階306陛也；陛306升高階]

上六：	**TopSixer:**
冥升	Dark Rising
利于不息之貞	Favors To Not Losing Its Integrity
象曰 *(孔子)：*	***LinerSign Says (Kongzi) :***
冥升在上	Dark Rising On High
消不富也	Loss (Integrity) Not Prosper that's

Comments:
Dark Rising, upper limit, to keep the High status, better not to lose Integrity.
[Xu: 冥141幽也从日从六从冖；幽84隱也从山中；消235盡也从水]

Conclusions:
Rising (Hexagram 46): Wind Trigram below and Earth Trigram above.
Image: 3 of 4 gentle Yins Rising above the 2 Yangs, to Kingship and dominant positions.
Symbolic: Wind (wood) below Earth, an acorn emerges from Earth, Rising into a forest giant.

King Wen:
A kindly person, sees his Zhou State Rising like the gentle Yins, predicting Primal Prosperity.
Southward expansion and fulfillment of his ambition to establish a Zhou Dynasty, Auspicious.

Zhougong:
FirstSixer: gentle, serving the 2 Yangs above on Accord Rising, Greatly Auspicious.
Niner2: gentle Upright, Trusted by Premier partner, Good-news Rejoice No Faults.
Niner3: strong in position, Expedition into land of no resistance above, successes No Doubt.
Sixer4: kindly King Rising to Mount Qi, making Offerings for prosperity, No Faults Auspicious.
Sixer5: Rising Steps to Kingship with Great Achievement, has Integrity, Auspicious.
TopSixer: Dark Rising top limit, to keep high status and wealth, advise not to lose Integrity.
Rising: seems good generally and alluding to the Rising of King Wen over evil King Zhou.

Kongzi:
Wind (wood) beneath Earth, like an acorn Rising from the ground, growing into a forest giant.
Junzi likewise may accumulate Small Acts of Virtue to become a Great Sage.

(升：不來也，雜卦傳)　　　　　　　(Rising : not coming that's - Misc.10th 'Wing')

Lessons (Rising Hex.46)
Like Acorn Rising, Junzi (Gentleman) to accumulate small virtues and be a Great Sage.

(第四十七卦) 困　　　　　　　**Trapped (Hexagram 47)**

外	上六	___ ___	**TopSixer**	**external**
兑　(澤,上卦)	九五	_______	**Niner5**	**Dui (Wetland, Trigram above)**
	九四	_______	**Niner4**	
	六三	___ ___	**Sixer3**	
坎　(水,下卦)	九二	_______	**Niner2**	**Kan (Water, Trigram below)**
内	初六	___ ___	**FirstSixer**	**internal**

卦辭*(文王)* ：	***Hexagram Text (King Wen) :***
困 ：	Trapped:
亨，貞	Prosperity, Integrity
大人吉	Great People Auspicious
无咎	No Faults
有言不信	Have Words Not Believed

象曰*(孔子) :*	***Tuan Says (Kongzi explains) :***
困	Trapped
剛揜也	Yangs Covered that's
險以說	Danger Be Happy
困而不失其所亨	Trapped And Not Lose Own Purpose of Prosperity
其唯君子乎	This Only Junzi (Gentleman) Can
貞大人吉	Integrity, Great People Auspicious
以剛中也	With Yang (Niner2) Centre that's
有言不信	Have Words Not Believed (by others)
尚口乃窮也	Valued Mouth (talks) Still Fail that's

Comments:
Image: Trapped, Niner2 between Yins, and so too are Niner4 and Niner5 between Yins.
Wen: Trapped, Great People has Integrity Auspicious; with sweet talks, others not believing.
Kongzi: Trapped yet can be Happy as Niner2 and Niner5 are Centres have Integrity.
[Xu: 困129故廬也从木在口中；揜253一日也覆]

象曰*(孔子) :*	***HexagramSign Says (Kongzi) :***
澤无水，困	Wetland No Water, Trapped
君子以致命遂志	Junzi (Gentleman) Is Ready to Die Chasing Life-mission

Comments:
Water beneath Wetland (water drained), Image of Trapped with no water.
Trapped in Danger, Junzi (Gentleman) is ready to die to fulfil Life-Mission.
[Xu: 遂41辵也；志217意也]

爻辭 *(周公)*：	*Liner Text (Zhougong) :*
初六：	**FirstSixer**
臀困于株木	Bottom Trapped in Roots of Trees
入于幽谷，三歲不覿	Entered Into Quiet Valley, 3 Years Not Seen
象曰 *(孔子)*：	*LinerSign Says (Kongzi) :*
入于幽谷，幽不明也	Entered Into Secluded Valley, Dim Not Bright that's

Comments:

FirstSixer, lowly lost in the forest, not rescued for 3 years as partner Niner4 also Trapped.
Outlook dim not bright that's.   [Xu: 株118木根也；覿178見也]

九二：	**Niner2:**
困于酒食	Trapped in Wining Dining
朱绂方來	Red Ribbons (Honors) A-coming (from above)
利用亨祀，征凶，无咎	Favor Making Festive Offerings, Expedition Ominous, No Faults
象曰 *(孔子)*：	*LinerSign Says (Kongzi) :*
困于酒食	Trapped in Wining Dining (excessive)
中有慶也	Centre (upright) Have Celebrations that's

Comments:

Niner2, centre Upright, appreciated by authority above, have gifts of Honors a-coming.
Trapped in Wining and Dining, making Offerings, no Faults; but leading Expedition Ominous.
[Xu: 朱118赤心木松柏屬；杞8祭無已也；绂 …]

六三：	**Sixer3:**
困于石	Trapped in Stone (Niner4)
據于蒺藜，入于其宫	Station in Thorny Bush (Niner2), Entering Into Own House
不見其妻，凶	Not Seen Own Wife, Ominous
象曰 *(孔子)*：	*LinerSign Says (Kongzi) :*
據于蒺藜，乘剛也	Station in Thorny Bushes, Sitting-on Yang (Niner2)
入于其宫	Entering Into Own House
不見其妻，不祥也	Not Seen Own Wife, Not Good-sign that's

Comments

Sixer3, in Yang position, restive, doing the wrong thing, sitting on top of Niner2 (thorny bush).
Also Trapped by Niner4 (stone above) means Danger to self and family, Ominous.
(Kongzi further elaborates when asked by disciples. Attached Lower Commentary, para.5)

九四：	**Niner4:**
來徐徐	Coming Quietly Quietly
困于金車，吝，有終	Trapped in Golden Carriage, Painful, Have Closure
象曰 *(孔子)*：	*LinerSign Says (Kongzi) :*
來徐徐	Coming Quietly Quietly (act in moderation)
志在下也	Wishes At Below that's (FirstSixer)
雖不當位，有與也	Though Not in Right Position, Has Help that's

Comments:

Niner4 partnership with FirstSixer blocked, Trapped by Niner2 (golden carriage), Painful.
Not in right position but has help, quietly resolved the impasse, with FirstSixer has final Closure.
[Xu: 徐43安行也]

九五 ：	**Niner5:**
劓刖	Nose-cut, Circumcision
困于赤绂，乃徐有説	Trapped in Regal Strappings, Still Quietly Has Joy
利用祭祀	Favorable making ritual Offerings
象曰 *(孔子)* ：	***LinerSign Says (Kongzi)* :**
劓刖，志未得也	Nose-cut, Circumcision, Ambitions Not Realised that's
乃徐有説，以中直也	Still Quietly Has Joy, Being Centre (Upright), Honest that's
利用祭祀，受福也	Favor Making Ritual Offerings, Receive Good-fortune that's

Comments:
Trapped in Regal conspiracy, even Niner5 in honored position suffers Nose-cut, Circumcision.
Upright and Honest, with help of Heaven (make offerings) quietly regains Joy and Good-fortune.
[Xu: 劓92刑鼻也 ；刖92絕也]

上六 ：	**TopSixer:**
困于葛藟，于臲卼	Trapped in Grass-Creepers, At Tottering Mast
曰動悔，有悔	Says Actions Regretted, Has Regrets
征吉	Expedition Auspicious
象曰 *(孔子)* ：	***LinerSign Says (Kongzi)* :**
困于葛藟，未當也	Trapped in Grass-Creepers, Not Right (position) that's
動悔有悔，吉行也	Actions Regretted Has Regrets, Auspicious Progress that's

Comments:
TopSixer at high place, Trapped in Entangling Affairs as not in right position (no authority).
From prior entangling actions wiser for further actions, has learned to Regrets Auspicious.

Conclusions:
Trapped (Hexagram 47): Water Trigram below and Wetland Trigram above.
Image: Water below, and draining from Wetland leaves no water above, Trapped.
Symbolic: Trapped, all 3 Yang-liners are enclosed between Yin-liners.

King Wen:
Trapped No Faults of Great people who live by Integrity, find ways to Prosperity, Auspicious.
When Trapped, your words are not believable, so 'Talking' your way out is a poor choice.
Zhougong:
FirstSixer: lowly, Trapped in Roots-forest, 3 years no help from Niner4, outlook Not Bright.
Niner2: Upright, gifts from authority no Faults, but Trapped in Wining and Dining Ominous.
Sixer3: Yin in Yang position, restive actions, Trapped by Yangs, self and family in Danger .
Niner4: Trapped by Niner2, acts with moderation, relationship with FirstSixer Has Closure.
Niner5: Trapped by Regal Status gets mutilated; Upright with Offerings, regains Good-fortune.
TopSixer: no authority, Trapped in entangling affairs, has regrets and wiser, Auspicious.
Trapped: situations inherited or by choice, resolve with Upright Honesty, learning from Regrets.

Kongzi:
Trapped in Danger, Junzi (Gentleman) are ready to sacrifice for a Good Course.
(困：而困相遇也，雜卦傳)   (Trapped : mutually met - Misc.10th 'Wing')

Lessons (Trapped Hex.47)
Trapped, Junzi (Gentleman) is ready to die for a Noble Course.
The world seems full of scams that never fail to Trap the unwary who expect free lunches.

（第四十八卦）井　　　　　　　**water-Well (Hexagram 48)**

外		上六	＿＿　＿＿	**TopSixer**	**external**
坎　(水, 上卦)		九五	＿＿＿＿＿	**Niner5**	**Kan (Water, Trigram above)**
		六四	＿＿　＿＿	**Sixer4**	
		九三	＿＿＿＿＿	**Niner3**	
巽　(風, 下卦)		九二	＿＿＿＿＿	**Niner2**	**Xun (Wind, Trigram below)**
内		初六	＿＿　＿＿	**FirstSixer**	**internal**

卦辭 (文王)：　　　　　　　　　*Hexagram Text (King Wen) :*

井：　　　　　　　　　　　　　water-Well :

改邑不改开　　　　　　　　　　Change City Not Change Water-Well

无喪无得　　　　　　　　　　　No Loss No Gain

往來井井　　　　　　　　　　　Forward Backward water-Well water-Well

汔至，亦未繘井　　　　　　　　Dry Up, Also No Rope water-Well

羸其瓶，凶　　　　　　　　　　Broke Its Vessel, Ominous

象曰 (孔子)：　　　　　　　　　*Tuan Says (Kongzi explains) :*

巽乎水而上木，井　　　　　　　Xun (Wood) That's Water Is In Wood (bucket), water-Well

井養而不窮也　　　　　　　　　water-Well Nourishes And Not Depleted that's

改邑不改井　　　　　　　　　　Change City Not Change water-Well

乃以剛中也　　　　　　　　　　Still With Yangs as Centres that's (Niner2, Niner5)

汔至亦未繘井　　　　　　　　　Dry Up, Also No Rope Water-Well

未有功也　　　　　　　　　　　Prior Having Success that's

羸其瓶　　　　　　　　　　　　Broke Its Vessel

是以凶也　　　　　　　　　　　This Is Ominous that's

Comments:
Image: Xun (wood) below Water, bucket drawing Water above, water-Well; 2 Yang Centres.
Wen: City can move not water-Well, serving non-stop until dry up, Ominous.
Kongzi: water-Well not depleted, maintain rope and bucket for successful use, else Ominous.
[Xu: 井106八家一井 ; 邑131國也 ; 汔235水涸; 涸235渴; 渴235盡; (繘)276绠也; 羸178瘦也]

象曰 (孔子)：　　　　　　　　　*HexagramSign Says (Kongzi) :*

木上有水，井　　　　　　　　　Wood (bucket) Above Has Water, Water-Well

君子以勞民勸相　　　　　　　　Junzi With Appreciation of Citizens, Encourage Mutually

Comments:
Wood (bucket) above has water, water-Well image.
Junzi watches Citizens flooding the padi fields, appreciates their labor and productivity.
[Xu: 勸292勉也 ; 勉292彊也 ; 相72省視也 ; 省74視也]

爻辭 (周公)：	*Liner Text (Zhougong)*:
初六：	**FirstSixer:**
井泥不食	water-Well Mud Not Edible
舊井无禽	Old water-Well No Birds
象曰 (孔子)：	*LinerSign Says (Kongzi)*:
井泥不食，下也	water-Well Mud Not Food, Bottom that's
舊井无禽，時舍也	Old water-Well No Birds, Time Abandoned that's

Comments:
FirstSixer at bottom of Water-Well, has Mud not Food.
Like an abandoned old water-Well that even Birds will not fly over for water.

九二：	**Niner2:**
井谷射鮒	water-Well Mouth-edge Shooting Fish-fries
甕敝漏	Bucket Cracked Leaking
象曰 (孔子)：	*LinerSign Says (Kongzi)*:
井谷射鮒	water-Well Mouth-edge Shooting Fish-fries
无與也	No Partner that's

Comments:
Niner2, Yang in Yin position misplaced, no partner above, neighbor of weak FirstSixer below.
Niner5 also Yang blocks, cannot rise for big tasks, collects small Fish among leaking bucket.
[Xu: 谷161口上阿；阿304大陵也；敝161..，一曰敗衣；漏237以銅受水刻節晝夜；與....]

九三：	**Niner3:**
井渫不食	water-Well Raised-up Not Drinking
爲我心惻	Becomes My Heart Pain
可用汲	Can Be Drawn (water)
王明並受其福	King Enlightened, Together Receive Its Good-fortune
象曰 (孔子)：	*LinerSign Says (Kongzi)*:
井渫不食	water-Well Raised-level (taxes) Not Drinking
行惻也	Administering Compassion that's
求王明，受福也	Request Enlightened King, Bestows Good-fortune that's

Comments:
Local officials raised taxation on water drawn, water-Well not use, pains Niner3's heart.
Niner3 strong, request King's compassion for free usage, thus bestowing Good-fortune to all.
[Xu: 渫237除去也；除306殿陛；陛306升高階；惻222痛也]

六四：	**Sixer4:**
井甃无咎	water-Well inner-Walled, No Fault
象曰 (孔子)：	*LinerSign Says (Kongzi)*:
井甃无咎	water-Well inner-Walled No Fault
脩井也	Repair of water-Well that's

Comments:
Sixer4, a Yin in placed, benevolent, position next to Premier.
As high official helps repairing inner-wall of Water-Well, No Faults.
[Xu: 甃269井壁也]

九五：	**Niner5:**
井冽	water-Well Clear
寒泉食	Cool Spring Food
象曰 *(孔子)：*	***LinerSign Says (Kongzi) :***
寒泉之食	Cool Spring Its Food (Water)
中正也	Centre Upright that's

Comments:
Niner5 King, centre Upright, correct Yang in Yang Position, is like a cool-Spring.
His administration is like a cool-Spring water-Well that all citizens can Enjoy.
[Xu: 冽230水清也]

上六：	**TopSixer:**
井收勿幕	water-Well Collection, Don't Cover
有孚元吉	Has Trust, Primal Auspiciousness
象曰 *(孔子)：*	***LinerSign Says (Kongzi) :***
元吉在上	Primal Auspiciousness On Top
大成也	Great Achievement that's

Comments:
TopSixer atop water-Well, not covering it, allowing free collection of water by all people.
Has Trust that water constantly flow, Great Achievement, Primal Auspiciousness.
[Xu: 收69捕也 ；幕159帷在上,日幕覆食案亦曰幕]

Conclusions:
water-Well (Hexagram 48): Wind Trigram below and Water Trigram above.
Image: Xun (wood) below Water, bucket drawing Water above, water-Well; Yang Centres.

King Wen:
water-Well immovable, where it sits Prosperity , when runs dry City must move on, Ominous.

Zhougong:
FirstSixer: bottom, old water-Well, time abandoned, mud only, not edible, fly-over No Birds .
Niner2: Yang Niner5 not partner, with neighbor FirstSixer shoot fish in water-Well, small Gain.
Niner3: right position, strong, Requested King, no charges for water-Well for all, Good-fortune.
Sixer4: right placing, not centre, supports King above, repairs walls of water-Well, No Faults.
Niner5: right positioned King, to citizens his administration is like a cool-Spring water-Well.
TopSixer: kind, water-Well Top, Not-covered and free, Great Achievement, Primally Auspicious.
water-Well: needs maintenance, immovable and when depleted, population must move on.

Kongzi:
water-Well not depleted, to manage well rope and bucket for successful use, else Ominous.
Junzi observes flooded padi fields, appreciates citizens' labors, productivity with water-Well.
(井：通，雜卦傳)　　　　　　　(water-Well : connecting - Miscellaneous 10th 'Wing')

Lessons (water-Well Hex. 48)
water-Well freely serving everybody also needs to repair walls, renewal of bucket and rope.
Fresh water-Well not movable, and when runs dry City needs move to new sources.

(第四十九卦) 革　　　　　　　　Changes　(Hexagram 49)

外	上六	▬　▬	**TopSixer**		external
兌　(澤，上卦)	九五	▬▬▬	**Niner5**	**Dui　(Wetland, Trigram above)**	
	九四	▬▬▬	**Niner4**		
	九三	▬▬▬	**Niner3**		
離　(火，下卦)	六二	▬　▬	**Sixer2**	**Li　(Fire, Trigram below)**	
内	初九	▬▬▬	**FirstNiner**		internal

卦辭 *(文王)* ：	*Hexagram Text (King Wen) :*
革：	Changes :
已日乃孚	Already Days Then Trusting
元亨，利貞	Primal Prosperity, Favors Integrity
悔亡	Regrets Lost

彖曰 *(孔子)* ：	*Tuan Says (Kongzi explains) :*
革：水火相息	Changes : Water Fire Mutual Antagonistic
二女同居	2 Daughters Staying Together
其志不相得，曰革	Their Wills Not Mutually Accorded, Call it Changes
巳日乃孚	Already Days Then Trusting
革而信之	Changes And Believing It
文明以說	Civil Enlightenment (Fire) With Joy (Wetland)
大亨以正	Great Prosperity With Uprightness
革而當，其悔乃亡	Changes Are Correct, Its Regrets Then Lost (no more)
天地革而四時成	Heaven Earth Changes And 4 Seasons Formations
湯武革命	Tang Wu (King) Orders of Changes (to overthrow Xia Dynasty)
順乎天而應乎人	Accord With Heaven And Resonate With People
革之時大矣哉	Time of Changes Great Indeed that's

Comments:
Image: Fire, above Wetland; Fire evaporates water above, Water douses Fire below, Changes.
Wen: Changes need Days to build Trust, Primal Prosperity favors Integrity, then no Regrets.
Kongzi: Changes, Heaven Earth Changes in 4 Seasons, King Tang Wu overthrown Xia Dynasty.
[Xu:革60獸皮治去其毛,革更之象 ；已310四月陽气巴出陰气巳藏,萬物見成文章故巳; 息217
喘也 ；喘31疾息也 ；疾154病也 ；信52誠也 ；當291田相值也 ；命32使也]

象曰 *(孔子)* ：	*HexagramSign Says (Kongzi) :*
澤中有火，革	Wetland Inside Has Fire, Changes
君子以治歷明時	Junzi With Governing History, Understand Time

Comments:
Junzi, looking into the past history of Changes, learns to understand present time affairs.
[Xu:治227水出東萊曲城... ；歷38過也]

爻辭 *(周公)* ：	***Liner Text (Zhougong) :***
初九：	**FirstNiner:**
鞏用黃牛之革	Secure With Yellow Oxen Leather
象曰 *(孔子)* ：	***LinerSign Says (Kongzi) :***
鞏用黃牛	Secure With Yellow Oxen
不可以有爲也	Not Allow To Have Action that's

Comments:

In Changes, any action means changing the established Norms with serious consequences. FirstNiner, no partner, no consultation, early Changes not allow, needs leather to secure him.

[Xu: 鞏60以韋束也；韋113相背也,... 獸皮之韋可以束枉.....]

六二：	**Sixer2:**
巳日乃革之	Already Days Then Changes It
征吉，无咎	Campaign Auspicious, No Faults
象曰 *(孔子)* ：	***LinerSign Says (Kongzi) :***
巳日革之	Already Days Changes It
行有嘉也	Actions Has Praises that's

Comments:

Sixer2, right position, gentle, centre of Fire (enlightenment), has partner, days of consultation. Actions for Changes, earn Praises, hence Changes Auspicious, No Faults.

九三：	**Niner3:**
征凶，貞厲	Campaign Danger, Truly Grave
革言三就，有孚	Changes Consultation 3 Agreements, Has Trust
象曰 *(孔子)* ：	***LinerSign Says (Kongzi) :***
革言三就	Changes Consultation 3 Agreements
又何之矣	Else How Do-it that's

Comments:

Niner3, top of Fire, too strong, rash, rush to act, Danger, Truly Grave. Changes need consultation, 3 levels of agreement (king, lords, commoners), or how else?

[Xu: 就111就高也；尤308異也；異59分也]

九四：	**Niner4:**
悔亡，有孚	Regrets Lost, Has Trust
改命吉	Changing Orders Auspicious
象曰 *(孔子)* ：	***LinerSign Says (Kongzi) :***
改命之吉	Changing Orders Its Auspiciousness
信志也	Honesty Wills that's

Comments:

Niner4, regrets Yin position, where Fire meets Water, time for Changes, Regrets Lost. Niner4, with Will of Honesty gains Trust, Changing Orders of the day, Auspicious.

[Xu:命32使也]

九五：	**Niner5:**
大人虎變	Great Person Tiger Changes
未占有孚	Before Divination Has Trust
象曰 *(孔子)* ：	***LinerSign Says (Kongzi)* :**
大人虎變	Great Person Tiger Changes
其文炳也	Its Marking-stripes Shining that's

Comments:
Niner5 king position, Great Person initiating Changes with authority in the kingdom.
With Shining marks of Achievements, even before divine consultation, citizens has full Trust.
[Xu: 變68更也；炳209明也]

上六：	**TopSixer:**
君子豹變	Junzi Leopard Changes
小人革面	Small People Changes Face
征凶，居貞吉	Campaign Danger, Stay-put Truly Auspicious
象曰 *(孔子)* ：	***LinerSign Says (Kongzi)* :**
君子豹變，其文蔚也	Junzi Leopard Changes, Its Marking-spots Subtle that's
小人革面，順以從君也	Small Person Changes Face, Docile To Follow the Lord that's

Comments:
Junzi's Leopard-sports Changes, commoners' Changes Facial only, to follow lead of the Lord.
At the upper limit of Changes, further Changes is Danger, Stay-put truly Auspicious.
[Xu: 蔚20牡蒿；牡29畜父也；尉208从上案下..又持火以尉申繒也；申311神；繒273帛也]

Conclusions:
Changes (Hexagram 49): Fire Trigram below and Wetland Trigram above.
Image: Changes, Wetland dousing Fire from above, and Fire evaporating Water from below.
Symbolic: Fire (middle daughter), Wetland (young daughter) above, Changes of Wills.

King Wen:
Stresses need for time to build Trust for Changes, then Primal Prosperity, No Regrets.

Zhougong:
FirstNiner: no partner, too early for Changes, secure with Oxen leather, Actions not allow.
Sixer2: Yin placed, centre, has partner, days of consultation, No Faults, Changes Auspicious.
NIner3: too strong, rash, needs 3 consultation levels for Trust in Changes, else Ominous.
Niner4: Yin position, fire meet water, time for Changes No Regrets, Honest Will, Auspicious.
Niner5: with shining Tiger-Stripes credential, kingdom trusted Changes even before Divination.
TopSixer: Junzi's Leopard-Spots Changes subtle, citizens' Changes facial, Stay-put Auspicious.
Changes: time for study, consultations, credentials are important to gain Trust for Changes.

Kongzi:
King Tang Wu Changes Orders overthrown the Sia Dynasty in accord of Heaven and People.
Calls for study, to learn from history, to understand the present for effective Changes.
(革：去故也，雜卦傳)   (Changes : discard old-stuffs - Misc.10th 'Wing')

Lessons (Changes Hex.49)
Take time to study history, understand the present, with consultation gain Trust, then no regrets.

（第五十卦）鼎　　　　　　　**Tripod　(Hexagram 50)**

	上九	＿＿＿＿	**TopNiner**	external
離　（火，上卦）	六五	＿＿　＿＿	**Sixer5**　Li (Fire, Trigram above)	
	九四	＿＿＿＿	**Niner4**	
	九三	＿＿＿＿	**Niner3**	
巽　（風，下卦）	九二	＿＿＿＿	**Niner2**　Xun (Wind, Trigram below)	
	初六	＿＿　＿＿	**FirstSixer**	internal

卦辭 *(文王)* ：	***Hexagram Text (King Wen)*** ：
鼎 ：	Tripod ：
元吉，亨	Primaly Auspicious, Prosperity

象曰 *(孔子)*：	***Tuan Says (Kongzi explains)*** ：
鼎	Tripod
象也	Image that's
以木巽火	With Wood Wind (following) Fire
亨飪也	Prosperity Cooking that's
聖人亨	Sage Person Cooking
以享上帝	For Offerings Above Emperor (of Heaven)
而大亨以養聖賢	And Big Cooking For Nurturing Sages and the Virtuous
巽而耳目聰明	Xun (Wind) For Ears Eyes, Sensitive (hearing) Clear (seeing)
柔進而上行	Yin Advance And Upward Move (ref. Sixer5)
得中而應乎剛	Gain Centre And Responding With Yang (ref. Niner2)
是以元亨	Therefore Primal Prosperity

Comments:
Image: Wind (Wood) below feeding Fire above, Cooking food in the Tripod.
Symbolic: Of a Tripod, FirstSixer the Legs, Niner2,-3,-4 the Body and Niner5 the Ears.
Wen: Tripod (ancient symbol of legitimacy of the ruling King), Prosperity, Primally Auspicious.
Kongzi: Holding food in Offerings to Emperor of Heaven, Feasting the Sages and the Virtuous.
[Xu: 鼎143三足两耳和五味之寶器也 ；亨... ；享... ；聰250察也 ；明141照也]

象曰 *(孔子)*：	***HexagramSign Says (Kongzi)*** ：
木上有火，鼎	Wood Above Has Fire, Tripod
君子以正位凝命	Junzi With Correct Positioning, Concentrates to achieve Mission.

Comments:
Tripod with correct positioning before holding food for proper cooking.
Likewise, Junzi First be in Correct Position, then able to Concentrate on achieving Life-mission.
[Xu: 凝240310惑也从子]

爻辭 *(周公)* : **Liner Text (Zhougong) :**

初六 : **FirstSixer:**

鼎顛趾，利出否 Tripod Top-over Toes, Favors Out-pouring Residuals

得妾以其子，无咎 Gain Concubine For Her son, No Faults

象曰 *(孔子)* : **LinerSign Says (Kongzi) :**

鼎顛趾，未悖也 Tripod Top-over Toes (legs), Not Paradoxical that's

利出否，以從貴也 Favors Out-pouring Residuals, To Follow the Noble (Niner4)

Comments:

FirstSixer, lowly concubine with a son, opted to follow noble partner Niner4 above, No Faults.
Thus gaining respect, discarding her lowly life like Tripod bottom-up to clear residuals inside.

[Xu: 顛181頂也；悖...]

九二 : **Niner2:**

鼎有實 Tripod Has Solid

我仇有疾 My Neighbor Has Sickness

不我能即，吉 Not Me Able to Accommodate, Auspicious

象曰 *(孔子)* : **LinerSign Says (Kongzi) :**

鼎有實，慎所之也 Tripod Has Solid, Caution Results Of that's

我仇有疾 My Neighbor Has Sickness (ref. FirstSixer)

終无尤也 Finally No Worries, that's

Comments:

Niner2, Yang like Tripod Solid body, centre Upright, Auspicious.
Steadfast, cautious, resisting neighbor FirstSixer's advances, finally No Worries.

[Xu: 仇167讎也；讎51猶讐以言對也；即106即食也；慎217謹也；所300伐木聲]

九三 : **Niner3:**

鼎耳革，其行塞 Tripod Ears Changes, Its Journey Blocked

雉膏不食 Pheasant Meat Not Eaten

方雨虧悔，終吉 Been Raining Losing Regrets, Finally Auspicious

象曰 *(孔子)* : **LinerSign Says (Kongzi) :**

鼎耳革 Tripod Ears Changes (ref. Sixer5)

失其義也 Lost Its Uprightness that's

Comments:

Niner3, Journey to responder TopNiner blocked by Changes of Sixer5 (Tripod Ears), Regrets.
Not centre, rash, no mood for Pheasant food, rain cleared mind on the way, finally Auspicious.

[Xu: 革60獸皮治去其毛革更之象; 塞288隔305障; 雉76有十四種盧諸雉,喬雉,.; 膏87肥也]

九四 : **Niner4:**

鼎折足，覆公餗 Tripod Broken Leg, Overturn Lord's Food

其形渥，凶 The Condition Messy, Ominous

象曰 *(孔子)* : **LinerSign Says (Kongzi) :**

覆公餗，信如何也 Overturn Lord's Food, Trustworthiness How About that's

Comments:

Niner4 next to Premier, important duties, has partner FirstSixer like a Tripod Broken Leg.
Weak incapable, mess up affairs, like spilling Lord's food, so where is the Trust, Ominous.

[Xu: 覆158覂也一日蓋也；覂158反覆也；餗...；渥234霑也；沾226一日益也]

六五：	**Sixer5:**
鼎黃耳	Tripod Yellow Ears
金鉉，利貞	Gold Carry-rod, Favors Truthfullness
象曰 *(孔子)*：	***LinerSign Says (Kongzi)*** :
鼎黃耳	Tripod Yellow Ears (soft color)
中以爲實也	Centre To Be Solid that's (ref. Niner2)

Comments:
Sixer5 is Tripod Yellow Ears, Yin gentle in Yang position, favors having Truthfulness.
Has support of partner Niner2, Solid Yang, centre Upright, like Gold Carry-rod.
[Xu: 鉉295舉鼎也]

上九：	**TopNiner:**
鼎玉鉉	Tripod Jaded Carry-rod
大吉无不利	Greatly Auspicious None Not Favorable
象曰 *(孔子)*：	***LinerSign Says (Kongzi)*** :
玉鉉在上	Jaded Carry-rod On Top
剛柔節也	Yang Yin Controlled that's

Comments:
TopNiner like Jaded Carry-rod on top of Tripod, Greatly Auspicious.
TopNiner, Yang in Yin position is gentle like Jade, in control on top, hence all affairs favorable.

Conclusions:
Tripod (Hexagram 50): Wind Trigram below and Fire Trigram above.
Image: Xun is Wind, is Wood feeding Fire above, for cooking food in the Tripod.
Symbolic: of the Tripod, FirstSixer the legs, Niner2, -3, -4 the body and Sixer5 the Ears.

King Wen:
Tripod upright, ancient image of legitimacy of Kingship, Primally Auspicious, Prosperity.

Zhougong:
FirstSixer: Tripod Toes, bottom-up to empty residuals, concubine has son, respected No Fault.
Niner2: Tripod Solid centre, steadfast against advances of neighbor FirstSixer, Auspicious.
Niner3: rash journey to TopNiner, blocks at Tripod Ears, Rain clears mind, Finally Auspicious.
Niner4: partner FirstSixer like Tripod broken leg, spills Lord's food, not Trustworthy, Ominous.
Sixer5: gentle Tripod Yellow Ears, has partner Niner2 and TopNiner support, favors Truthfulness.
TopNiner: is Jaded Carry-rod, Yang tempered in Yin position, all favorable, Greatly Auspicious.
Tripod: has 3 Auspiciousness, 1 Ominous, and No Faults with self-renewal at bottom level.

Kongzi:
Tripod, image of steady uprightness, suitable holding food Offerings for Emperor of Heaven.
Likewise, Junzi first be in correct position, then able to concentrate on achieving Life-mission.

(鼎：取新也，雜卦傳)　　　　　　　　(Tripod : acquire new stuffs - Misc.10th 'Wing')

Lessons (Tripod Hex.50)
Like Tripod, upright in proper position before trying to achieve life-mission.
Like Tripod when bottom-up, time to empty the rubbish in self and start a self-renewal.

(第五十一卦) 震　　　　　　　**Thunder (Hexagram 51)**

外	上六	＿ ＿	**TopSixer**	external
震 (雷, 上卦)	六五	＿ ＿	**Sixer5**	**Zhen (Thunder, Trigram above)**
	九四	＿＿＿	**Niner4**	
	六三	＿ ＿	**Sixer3**	
震 (雷, 下卦)	六二	＿ ＿	**Sixer2**	**Zhen (Thunder, trigram below)**
內	初九	＿＿＿	**FirstNiner**	internal

卦辭 *(文王)* :	***Hexagram Text (King Wen) :***
震：	Zhen (Thunder) :
亨	Prosperity
震來虩虩	Thunder Cometh Startling Threatening
笑言啞啞	Laughing Talking Ya Ya
震驚百里	Thunder Alarming 100 Miles
不喪匕鬯	Not Losing Instruments of Incense-rites (worshipping)

象曰 *(孔子)* :	***Tuan Says (Kongzi explains) :***
震，亨	Zhen (Thunder), Prosperity
震來虩虩	Thunder Cometh Startling Threatening
恐致福也	Alarm Extending to Good-fortune that's
笑言啞啞	Laughing Talking Ya Ya
後有則也	Afterwards Has Regularity that's
震驚百里	Thunder Alarming 100 Miles
驚遠而懼邇也	Alarming Faraway And Threatening Vicinity that's
出可以守宗廟社稷	Emerging, Able To Guard Temple and Society
以爲祭主也	To Be Master of Worship that's (Elder-son Thunder)

Comments:
Image: Thunder below Thunder above, successive Thunders, Yangs action beneath 2 Yins.
Symbolic: Focus FirstNiner, Thunder is Elder-son in the family of 8 Trigrams.
Wen: Thunder Startle 100 mile, Elder-son happy, steadfast master of Offering Rites, Prosperity.
Kongzi: Thunders alarm, be alert, happy guarding Temple Rites Society Orders, Good-fortune.
[Xu: 震241劈歷振物者; 虩103..恐懼; 匕168...亦所以用比取飯; 鬯106以秬釀..芬芳以降神]

象曰 *(孔子)* :	***HexagramSign Says (Kongzi) :***
洊雷，震	Successive Thunders, Thunderous
君子以恐懼脩省	Junzi With Alarm and Fear, Cultivates Awareness (of Faults)

Comments:
Thunderous Thunder igniting alarm and fear of retribution from Heaven and society.
Junzi is alerted to the need to cultivate self awareness and correction of faults.

[Xu: 洊 ... ; 省74視也通識也]

爻辭 *(周公)* ：	*Liner Text (Zhougong) :*
初九：	**FirstNiner:**
震來虩虩	Thunder Cometh Alarming Alarming
後笑言啞啞，吉	Afterwards Laughing Talking Ya Ya, Auspicious
象曰 *(孔子)* ：	*LinerSign Says (Kongzi) :*
震來虩虩	Thunder Cometh Alarm Alarming
恐致福也	Alarm Leading to Good-Fortune that's
笑言啞啞	Laughing Talking Ya Ya
後有則也.	Afterwards Has Orders that's

Comments:
Thunders startling, alarmed FirstNiner knows fear, careful to behave virtuously, Auspicious.
Good behaviour brings Orders and Good-fortune, hence afterwards laughter and happiness.

六二：	**Sixer2:**
震來厲	Thunder Cometh Grave
億喪貝	Calmly Losing Cowry-valuables
躋于九陵，勿逐	Climb Up 9 Hills, Don't Chase
七日得	7 Days Receive-back
象曰 *(孔子)* ：	*LinerSign Says (Kongzi) :*
震來厲，乘剛也	Thunder Cometh, Grave, On-top of Yang that's

Comments:
Thunders cometh, Sixer2 on-top of Yang FirstNiner Grave position, losing Cowry-valuables.
Sixer2, centre upright, calm with loss, climb the 9 hills, not chasing, received back after 7 days.
[Xu: 億165安也 ；具129海介蟲也古者貨貝而寶 ；躋45登也 ；陵304大陸山無石 ；逐41追也]

六三：	**Sixer3:**
震蘇蘇	Thunder Awakening Awakening
震行无眚	Thunder Actions, No Blur-vision
象曰 *(孔子)* ：	*LinerSign Says (Kongzi) :*
震蘇蘇	Thundering Half Awakening
位不當也	Position Not Proper that's

Comments:
Sixer3 Yin in Yang position misplaced, half awakened like a lost soul.
Take virtuous Thunder action in fear of retribution, No Blurred-vision.
[Xu: 蘇15桂荏也 ；桂115江南木百藥之長 ；荏15桂荏蘇从艸 ；眚73目病生翳]

九四：	**Niner4:**
震遂泥	Thunder Escaping Mud
象曰 *(孔子)* ：	*LinerSign Says (Kongzi) :*
震遂泥	Thunder Escaping Mud
未光也	Prior Shining that's

Comments:
Niner4, Yin position, not centre, actions between 2 Yins, like Thunder mired in Mud.
Niner4 is not capable of self-action prior to success in escape, Not Shining.
[Xu: 遂41亾也 ；亾267逃也]

六五：	**Sixer5:**
震往來，厲	Thunder Going Coming, Grave
億无喪有事	Calm No Loss, Has Affairs
象曰 (孔子)*:*	***LinerSign Says (Kongzi) :***
震往來厲，危行也	Thunder Going Coming Grave, Dangerous Actions that's
其事在中，大无喪也	Its Affairs In Centre, Great No Loss that's

Comments:
In time of Thunder, Sixer5 Yin in Premier position, is in constant danger.
If able to keep centre and upright in affairs, then No Great Loss that's.

上六：	**TopSixer:**
震索索	Thunder Hesitant Hesitant
視矍矍，征凶	Vision Downcast, Campaign Ominous
震不于其躬于其鄰	Thundering Not On The Body On The Neighbor
无咎，婚媾有言	No Faults, Marriage Consultation Has Words
象曰 (孔子)*:*	***LinerSign Says (Kongzi) :***
震索索，中未得也	Thunder Hesitant Hesitant, Centre Not Acquired that's
雖凶无咎	Althought Ominous, No Faults
畏鄰戒也	Afraid of Neighbor, be Guarded that's

Comments:
TopSixer at limit of Thunder Hesitant with vision downcast, campaign Ominous.
Marriage has argument, so be on guard of affected neighbors, No Faults.
[Xu: 索 .. ；矍79一曰視遽兒 ；遽42傳也,一曰窘也]

Conclusions:
Thunder (Hexagram 51): Thunder Trigram below and Thunder Trigram above.
*Image:*Thunder after Thunder, Actions; FirstNiner and Niner4, actions beneath the Yins.
Symbolic: Thunder startling, instilling fear of retribution and self-correction.

King Wen:
Thunder startle 100 mile, Elder-son happy, steadfast master of Offering Rites, Prosperity.

Zhougong:
FirstNiner: Thunder Alarm cause fear, bring good behaviour, then laughters and Good-fortune.
Sixer2: Thunder Grave, atop Yang lost savings, centre calmly not chasing, 7 days Recovered.
Sixer3: Thunder Awakening lost soul, virtuous actions for fear of retribution, No Blurred-vision.
Niner4: Thunder in Mud, mired between Yins actions not free prior to escape, Not Shining.
Sixer5: Thunder back and forth, Grave position, centre actions Upright, No Great Loss.
TopSixer: Thunder Hesitant wedding dispute, fear neighbors Ominous, be guarded No Faults.
Thunder: startling fear, be virtuous brings good-fortune afterwards No Faults.

Kongzi:
Thunder alarm, be alert, happy guarding Temple Rites Societal Orders, Good-fortune.
Thunder alert Junzi to the need for self-awareness, self-correction and self-cultivation.

(震：起也，雜卦傳)　　　　　　　　(Thunder {Zhen} : rising that's - Misc.10th 'Wing')

Lessons (Thunder Hex.51)
Startling Thunder instills fear, threaten retribution, awaken self-awareness and self-cultivation.

（第五十二卦） 艮　　　　　　　**Mountains (Hexagram 52)**

	上九	———	**TopNiner**		external
艮 （山，上卦）	六五	__ __	**Sixer5**	**Gen (Mountain, Trigram above)**	
	六四	__ __	**Sixer4**		
	九三	———	**Niner3**		
艮 （山，下卦）	六二	__ __	**Sixer2**	**Gen (Mountain, Trigram below)**	
	初六	__ __	**FirstSixer**		internal

卦辭 *(文王)* ：　　　　　　　　*Hexagram Text (King Wen) :*
艮其背　　　　　　　　　　　Mountains, The Back
不獲其身　　　　　　　　　　Not Capture The Body
行其庭　　　　　　　　　　　Moving In Courtyard
不見其人，无咎　　　　　　　Not See The Person, No Fault

象曰 *(孔子) :*　　　　　　　　*Tuan Says (Kongzi explains) :*
艮，止也　　　　　　　　　　Mountains, Stop that's
時止則止　　　　　　　　　　Time to Stop Then Stop
時行則行　　　　　　　　　　Time to Move Then Move
動靜不失其時　　　　　　　　Action and Stillness, Not Lost The Timing
其道光明　　　　　　　　　　The Path-way is Bright and Enlightened
艮其止　　　　　　　　　　　Mountains The Block
止其所也　　　　　　　　　　Blocking Whatever that's
上下敵應　　　　　　　　　　Above and Below Enemy-like Responses
不相與也　　　　　　　　　　Not Mutually Engaging that's
是以不獲其身　　　　　　　　Therefore, Not Capturing The Body
行其庭　　　　　　　　　　　Moving In Courtyard
不見其人，无咎也　　　　　　Not See The Person, No Fault that's
Comments:
Image: Mountains block, moving inside like seeing only backs of mountains, not whole body.
Wen: Great Person with Humility may not be recognised walking in courtyard, No Fault.
Kongzi: Time to stop, Time for action, with right timing, Life-Path is bright, No Fault.
(Xu: 艮168很也；很43一日行難也；獲205獵所獲；止38下基也；與59薰與)

象曰 *(孔子) :*　　　　　　　　*HexagramSign Says (Kongzi) :*
兼山艮　　　　　　　　　　　Double Mountains, Blocking
君子以思不出其位　　　　　　Junzi In Thinking Not Out Of Position
Comments:
Like Mountains solid in position, Junzi in thoughts confine to own area of responsibility.
(Xu: 兼146幷也；思216容也；容150盛也)

| 爻辭 (周公) : | *Liner Text (Zhougong) :* |

初六： — **FirstSixer:**

艮其趾，无咎 — Blocking At Toes, No Fault
利永貞 — Favors Everlasting Integrity

象曰 (孔子) : — *LinerSign Says (Kongzi) :*

艮其趾，未失正也 — Block At Toes, Not Lost Correctness, that's

Comments:
FirstSixer, lowly, Block at Toe level, No Fault.
Life quality will be favored provided Everlasting Integrity is maintained.

六二： — **Sixer2:**

艮其腓 — Block At Calf (leg)
不拯其隨 — Not Helping The Follower
其心不快 — The Heart Not Happy

象曰 (孔子) : — *LinerSign Says (Kongzi) :*

不拯其隨 — Not Helping The Follower
未退聽也 — Hasn't Fall-back to Listen that's

Comments:
Sixer2, a gentle Yin, Upright at Centre site, follower of Niner3.
Mountains Block, Niner3 has not fall-back to help and consult with her, hence Not Happy.
(Xu: 拯....)

九三： — **Niner3:**

艮其限 — Block At Waist
列其夤，厲熏心 — Break At Midriff, Grave Smoking Heart

象曰 (孔子) : — *LinerSign Says (Kongzi) :*

艮其限 — Blocking At Waist
危熏心也 — Danger Smoking Heart that's

Comments:
Niner3 Yang, top of lower Trigram, at Mid-life raring to climb high.
Like Blocked at threshold of career, like suffering Heart filled with Smoke, Grave.
(Xu: 限304阻也,一曰門橛 ；列91分解 ；夤142敬惕也 ；熏15火煙上出也 ；危194在高而懼)

六四： — **Sixer4:**

艮其身 — Block The Body
无咎 — No Faults

象曰 (孔子) : — *LinerSign Says (Kongzi) :*

艮其身 — Block The Body
止諸躬也 — Stop All Body-expression that's

Comments:
Block the Body, Stop all Body-expression, that is can start/stop action at will.
Sixer4, correct position, gentle, kind, in control of all relationships, No Faults.

(Xu: 諸51辨也 ；辨309治也 ；治227水出東萊曲城... ；躬....)

六五：	**Sixer5:**
艮其輔	Block The Cheek-bones
言有序	Speech Has Order
悔亡	Regrets Lost
象曰 *(孔子)：*	***LinerSign Says (Kongzi)：***
艮其輔	Block The Cheek-bones
以中正也	With Centre Correctness, that's

Comments:
Block the Cheek-bones from over-expression at face level.
Sixer5, Premier position, able to speak Orderly, though Yin in Yang role has no more Regrets.
[Xu: 輔303人頰車也；頰182面旁；序192東西牆)

上九：	**TopNiner:**
敦艮	Sincere Blocking
吉	Auspicious
象曰 *(孔子)：*	***LinerSign Says (Kongzi)：***
敦艮之吉	Sincere Blocking, Its Auspiciousness
以厚終	With Solid Ending, that's

Comments:
TopNiner at top limit, Sincere Blocking, like relinquishing power at retirement, Auspicious.
(Xu: 敦68怒也詆也一曰誰可也；詆57苛也一曰訶也；訶56大言而怒也)

Conclusions:
Mountains (Hexagram 52): Mountain Trigram below and Mountain Trigram above.
Image: Mountain upon Mountain, Back to Back, Blocking, Stopping.
Symbolism: Corresponding liners are opposing, enemy-like, each seeing the back of the other.

King Wen:
Mountains upon Mountains, walking inside, like seeing only there backs, not the bodies.
Person of Great Humility walking in the Courtyard, see back only, not recognise, No Faults.

Zhougong:
FirstSixer: Block at Toe level, lowly Yin, but with Everlasting Integrity, Faultless.
Sixer2: Block at leg-Calf level, Upright follower, but Niner3 not turn-back to consult, Unhappy.
Niner3: Block at Waist, cannot advance in mid-life, suffered like Heart Smoking, Danger.
Sixer4: Block Body, Yin position, kind, control all parts of body expression, No Faults.
Sixer5: Block the Cheek-bones for Orderly Speech, Upright, Yin in Yang role, No Regrets.
TopNiner: Sincere Block at top, like relinquishing power at retirement, Solid Ending, Auspicious.
Mountains: symbolic of Block, timely Blocks in Life-path and their consequences.

Kongzi:
Time to stop, time for actions, right timing brings bright and enlightened life experience.
Junzi should have thoughts Stopping in own positions, not outside area of authority.
(艮：止也，雜卦傳)   (Mountains : stop that's - Misc.10th 'Wing')

Lessons (Mountains Hex.52)
Block, Junzi to think in own area of responsibility, not threatening the authority of others.
Good advice for everybody for maintaining harmony at home and in the workplace.

(第五十三卦) 漸　　　　　　**Progress　(Hexagram 53)**

外	上九	________	**Top Niner**	**external**
巽 (風, 上卦)	九五	________	**Niner 5**	**Xun　(Wind, Trigram above)**
	六四	__ __	**Sixer 4**	
	九三	________	**Niner 3**	
艮 (山, 下卦)	六二	__ __	**Sixer 2**	**Gen　(Mountain, Trigram below)**
内	初六	__ __	**First Sixer**	**internal**

卦辭 *(文王)*：　　　　　　*Hexagram Text (King Wen) :*

漸：　　　　　　Progress:

女歸，吉　　　　　　Girls Homing, Auspicious

利貞　　　　　　Favors Integrity

彖曰 *(孔子)*：　　　　　　*Tuan Says (Kongzi explains) :*

漸之進也　　　　　　Progress Its Advance that's

女歸吉也　　　　　　Girls Homing Auspicious that's (marriage)

進得位　　　　　　Advance Gain Position (Niner5)

往有功也　　　　　　Forward Has Success that's

進以正　　　　　　Advance With Uprightness

可以正邦也　　　　　　Can Be Uprighting States that's

其位，剛得中也　　　　　　Its Positions, Strong (Yang) Gain Centre-stage that's

止而巽　　　　　　Halt (Mountain) Then Xun (Wind)

動不窮也　　　　　　Action Not Exhausting that's

Comments:

Image: Mountain (Halt) below, then Wind (ceaseless motion) above, Gradual Progress.

Wen: Girls (Yins) Homing (marriage) below Yangs in support, with Integrity, Auspicious.

Kongzi: is alluding to Wen's success in Uprighting states, finally establishing the Zhou Dynasty.

[Xu: 漸226水出丹陽.. ; 歸38女嫁也 ; 巽99具也，易爲長女爲風者]

象曰 *(孔子)*：　　　　　　*HexagramSign Says (Kongzi) :*

山上有木，漸　　　　　　Mountain, Above Has Wood, Progress

君子以居賢德善俗　　　　　　Junzi By Dwelling with Talented Virtuous Improves Conduct.

Comments:

Mountain below, Wood (Xun is Wood) above, trees' gradual growth on mountain, Progress .

Junzi by dwelling among the Talented and Virtuous, has gradual progress in Good-conduct.

[Xu: 德42升也 ; 善58吉也 ; 俗165習也]

爻辭 (周公) ：	**Liner Text (Zhougong) :**
初六：	**First Sixer:**
鴻漸于干	Geese Progress To Shore
小子厲，有言，无咎	Small Person Grave, Has Comment, No Faults
象曰 (孔子) ：	**LinerSign Says (Kongzi) :**
小子之厲，義无咎也	Small Person The Warning, Uprightness No Faults that's

Comments:
Like geese has order of flight, gradual Progress towards shore.
Small person Progressing at bottom level suffers comments, with Uprightness No Faults.
[Xu: 干50犯也；犯205侵也；侵165漸進也]

六二：	**Sixer 2:**
鴻漸于磐	Geese Progress Towards Rock-cliff
飲食衎衎，吉	Drinking Feeding Happily, Auspicious
象曰 (孔子) ：	**LinerSign Says (Kongzi) :**
飲食衎衎，不素飽也	Drinking Feeding Happily, No 'Plain' Feeding, that's

Comments:
Geese Progress onto Rock-cliff, feeding happily by own efforts in finding food, Auspicious.
[Xu: 磐195堅也；衎44行喜兒]

九三：	**Niner 3:**
鴻漸于陸	Geese Progress To Flatland
夫征不復	Person on Expedition No Return
婦孕不育，凶	Woman Pregnancy Not Productive, Danger
利禦寇	Favors Resisting Bandits
象曰 (孔子) ：	**LinerSign Says (Kongzi) :**
夫征不復	Person on Expedition Not Returning
離羣醜也	Leaving Group Shameful that's
婦孕不育	Woman Pregnancy Not Productive (miscarriage)
失其道也	Lost Her Virtues that's
利用禦寇，順相保也	Favors For Resisting Bandits, In-line for Mutual Protection

Comments:
Progress to Flatland not suitable for water bird, augurs no return for man on expedition Ominous.
For woman miscarriage; Niner3 strong, thus favors resisting bandits for mutual protection.
[Xu: 陸304高平地；復43往來也；禦9祀也；寇68暴也；孕310裹子也；育310養子使作善]

六四：	**Sixer 4:**
鴻漸于木	Geese Progress To Wood (forest)
或得其桷，无咎	May Find The Jue-tree, No Fault
象曰 (孔子) ：	**LinerSign Says (Kongzi) :**
或得其桷	May Find The Jue-tree (broad-branched)
順以巽也	Smoothly As Xun (Wind) that's

Comments:
Geese Progress onward to Forest area, will smoothly find the broad-branched Jue-trees.
Geese, water-bird, webbed feet need broad branches for standing-space, No Faults.
[Xu: 桷120榱也,椽方曰桷]

九五：	**Niner 5:**

鴻漸于陵　　Geese Progress To Highland
婦三歲不孕　　Woman 3 Years No Pregnancy
終莫之勝也，吉　　Finally None Defeat Her that's, Auspicious
象曰 (孔子) ：　　*LinerSign Says (Kongzi) :*
終莫之勝吉　　Finally None Defeat Her, Auspicious
得所願也　　Gain What she Wishes that's

Comments:
Like geese Progress on to Highland, Sixer2 realised her wish to marry partner Niner5.
Overcoming the separation by Niner3 and Sixer4 and no pregnancy for 3 years, Auspicious.
[Xu: 陵304大阜；阜304大陸山無石者]

上九：　　**Top Niner:**
鴻漸于逵　　Geese Progress To Path-in-cloud
其羽可用爲儀，吉　　Its Feathers Can be Used For Ceremonials, Auspicious
象曰 (孔子) ：　　*LinerSign Says (Kongzi) :*
其羽可用爲儀，吉　　Its Feathers Can be Used For Ceremonials, Auspicious
不可亂也　　Not Allowed be Ruffled, that's

Comments:
Finally, geese Progress to Path-in-cloud, with feathers unruffled, still good for Ceremonial use.
Alluding to Wen's Integrity till death, finally honored by son as founder King of Zhou Dynasty.
[Xu: 逵..... ！]

Conclusions:
Progress (Hexagram 53): Mountain Trigram below and Wind Trigram above.
Image: Mountain beneath, gradual growth of trees (Xun is Wood) above, Progress.
Symbolic: of Girls Homing, with all Yins coming below to support Yangs in both Trigrams.

King Wen:
Girls Homing marriage in support of husbands and with Integrity, Auspicious.

Zhougong:
FirstSixer: Geese to shore, weak, Progress at bottom, suffers comments, Warning No Fault.
Sixer2: Geese Progress to Rock-cliff, find own food, feeding happily, Auspicious.
Niner3: Progress to Flatland not for water-bird, man no return, woman unproductive, Ominous.
Sixer4: Progress to Forest, need to find the Jue-trees, water-bird landing-space, No Fault.
Niner5: Progress to Highland, Sixer2 surmount obstacles with partner as wished, Auspicious.
TopNiner: Progress to Path-in-cloud, feathers still unruffled, for Ceremonial Usage, Auspicious.
Progress: reflecting gradual Progress of King Wen's life story and success, Uprighting States.

Kongzi:
Sixer2 to Niner5, all correctly positioned, alluding to King Wen's Integrity for Uprighting States.
Cultivating Virtues is gradual Progress, thus Junzi needs to dwell among the Virtuous-talented.
(漸: 女歸代男行也，雜卦傳) (Progress : woman return awaits man's action-Misc.10th 'Wing')

Lessons (Progress Hex.53)
A good environment is important for the Progressive development of good character.

(第五十四卦) 歸妹 **Married Maid (Hexagram 54)**

外	上六	___ ___	**TopSixer**	**external**
震 (雷, 上卦)	六五	___ ___	**Sixer5**	**Zhen (Thunder, Trigram above)**
	九四	________	**Niner4**	
	六三	___ ___	**Sixer3**	
兌 (澤, 下卦)	九二	________	**Niner2**	**Dui (Wetland, Trigram below)**
內	初九	________	**FirstNiner**	**internal**

卦辭 *(文王)* :	***Hexagram Text (King Wen) :***
歸妹	Married Maid
征凶，无攸利	Campaign Danger, No Easy Gain

彖曰 *(孔子)* :	***Tuan Says (Kongzi explains) :***
歸妹	Married Maid
天地之大義也	Heaven Earth Their Great Purpose that's
天地不交而萬物不興	Heaven Earth Not Interact Then All Matters Not Prosper
歸妹，人之終始也	Married Maid, People's Endings Beginnings that's
說以動	Joy For Action
所歸, 妹也	Already Married, Maid that's (on maid initiative)
征凶，位不當也	Campaign Danger, Position Not Correct that's
无攸利	No Easy Gain
柔乘剛也	Yins A-top of Yangs that's

Comments:
Inage: Wetland (young daughter), Thunder (elder son), Joy for Action, Married Maid.
Symbolic: Niner2 to Sixer5, all 4 not in proper positions, also Yins sitting atop of Yangs.
Wen: Married Maid, maid already married (interacted), campaign Danger, No Easy Gain.
Kongzi: Joy for Action, Elopement, reverse of end-beginning, positions incorrect, Ominous.
[Xu: 歸38女嫁也，妹259女弟也，所300伐木聲]

象曰 *(孔子)* :	***HexagramSign Says (Kongzi) :***
澤上有雷，歸妹	Wetland Above Has Thunder, Married Maid
君子以永終知敝	Junzi With Established Endings Knows Faults

Comments:
Wetland (young daughter, Joy), above Thunder (elder son, Action), Married Maid elopement.
From past established endings, Junzi knows such elopement is faulty from the beginning.
[Xu: 終278綵絲也，綵272急也，敝161一曰敗衣；永240長也象水巠里之長]

爻辭 (周公)：	*Liner Text (Zhougong) :*
初九：	**FirstNiner:**
歸妹以娣	Married Maid As Concubine
跛能履，征吉	Lame Can Walk, Campaign Auspicious
象曰 (孔子)：	*LinerSign Says (Kongzi) :*
歸妹以娣	Married Maid As Concubine
以恆也	For Everlasting that's
跛能履吉	Lame Can Walk Auspicious
相承也	Mutually Supportive that's

Comments:
FirstNiner, Married Maid can be a concubine permanently.
A strong Yang, lowly like lame can still walk and be supportive of husband, Auspicious.
[Xu: 娣258女弟也，跛47行不正也；履175足所依也；扉174履也　]

九二：	**Niner2:**
眇能視	One-eyed Can See
利幽人之貞	Favors Quiet Person's Integrity
象曰 (孔子)：	*LinerSign Says (Kongzi) :*
利幽人之貞	Favors Quiet Person's Integrity
未變常也	Not Changing Norms that's

Comments:
Niner2, Centre Upright maid, but partner Sixer5 is no good as wrongly in Yang position.
Like a half-blind handicapped, not to change the norms in life keep her quietude, has Integrity.
[Xu: 眇73－目小也]

六三：	**Sixer3:**
歸妹以須	Married Maid With Hairy-face
反歸以娣	Return Marriage As Concubine
象曰 (孔子)：	*LinerSign Says (Kongzi) :*
歸妹以須，未當也	Married Maid With Hairy-face, Not Correctly (positioned) that's

Comments:
Sixer3, a Yin in Yang position and not centre, thus has Hairy-face.
Married Maid can only returned as Concubine, suffering the consequences of Wrong Position.
[Xu: 須84面毛也]

九四：	**Niner4:**
歸妹愆期	Married Maid Passed Period
遲歸有時	Late Marriage Has Timing
象曰 (孔子)：	*LinerSign Says (Kongzi) :*
愆期之志	Passed Period, Its Will
有待而行也	Has Expectation (fulfilled) Then Action that's

Comments:
Niner4, Yang, a strong maid of upper class, with no partner, not compromising, Has Timing.
She has the Will to wait pass the ideal marriage period for the right person before marrying.
[Xu: 愆221過也；過39度也；度65法制也]

六五：	**Sixer5:**
帝乙歸妹，其君之袂	Emperor Yi Marrying Daughter, The Bride's Sleeves
不如其娣之袂良	Not Comparable To Concubines' Superior Sleeves
月幾望，吉	Moon Nearly Full, Auspicious
象曰 *(孔子)*：	***LinerSign Says (Kongzi) :***
帝乙歸妹	Emperor Yi Marrying Daughter
不如其娣之袂良也	Not Comparable to Concubines' Sleeves Standard that's
其位在中，以貴行也	Her Position In Centre, With Noble Conduct that's

Comments:
Emperor Yi marrying daughter in gown not comparable with his concubines, Auspicious.
Princess marrying commoner Niner2, not in pomp, but in white purity, like the Full-moon.
[Xu: 袂171袖也；良111喜也；幾24微也殆也，貴131物不賤也]

上六：	**TopSixer:**
女承筐无實	Maid Offers Bamboo-vessel No Substance
士刲羊无血，无攸利	Scholar Pierces Goat No Blood, No Easy Gain
象曰 *(孔子)*：	***LinerSign Says (Kongzi) :.***
上六无實，承虛筐也	TopSixer No Substance, Offers Empty Bamboo-vessel

Comments:
TopSixer, very late in marriage, has all the bad signs in rites, hence No Easy Gain.
Empty vessel symbolic of maid's infertility, no blood signifies scholar's blood-line not flowing!
[Xu: 實150富也；富150備也，一曰厚也 ；刲92刺也；承253奉也受也；虛169大丘也, 堨崘丘謂之崐崘虛；筐268匡,器似竹筐]

Conclusions:
Married Maid (Hexagram 54): Wetland Trigram below and Thunder Trigram above.
Image: Wetland (Young-daughter), above Thunder (Elder-son), Elopement, Married Maid.
Symbolic: Niner2 to Sixer5, all 4 liners in wrong positions, Yins atop of Yangs, Ominous.

King Wen:
Maid already married, Young-daughter's Joy with Elder-son's Action, no easy gain, Ominous.

Zhougong:
TopNiner: Married Maid, no partner, Yang maid, lamed can walk, as concubine, Auspicious.
Niner2: Partner Sixer5 above, handicapped like one-eyed, can see, keeps Quietude Integrity.
Sixer3: Married Maid with Hairy-faced, returned marriage as concubine, Wrong Position.
Niner4: Married Maid, passed ideal age, has Expectation, Wills to wait for right person, Timing.
Sixer5: Emperor Marrying daughter to partner Niner2, not in pomp, like Full-moon, Auspicious.
TopSixer: late marriage, rite-vessel empty sign of infertility, goat no blood flow no blood-line.
Married Maid: all about maids in different situations, Yins are maids, Yangs are strong maids.
Kongzi:
Heaven and Earth, interaction has Great Purpose, the prosperity of all matters.
Marriage based on Joy not proper Love, from past end results, we know the Faults.
(歸妹：女之終也，雜卦傳) (Married Maid : girl's closure that's - Misc.10th 'Wing')

Lessons (Married Maid Hex.54)
Junzi, from past results knows faults, proper arrangement for proper marriage, not elopement.
Highlighted low expectation in poor conditions, infertility problem in late marriage, and others.

(第五十五卦) 豐　　　　　　　　**Expansion (Hexagram 55)**

外	上六	▬▬ ▬▬	**TopSixer**	**external**
震 （雷，上卦）	六五	▬▬ ▬▬	**Sixer5**	**Zhen (Thunder, Trigram above)**
	九四	▬▬▬▬	**Niner4**	
	九三	▬▬▬▬	**Niner3**	
離 （火，下卦）	六二	▬▬ ▬▬	**Sixer2**	**Li (Fire, Trigram below)**
内	初九	▬▬▬▬	**FirstNiner**	**internal**

卦辭 *(文王)*：	*Hexagram Text (King Wen) :*
豐：亨	Expansion : Prosperity
王假之，勿憂	King Achieves It, Don't Worry
宜日中	Proper, Sun at Zenith

[Xu: 豐103豆之豐滿者也；假165非真也，一日至也；宜151所安也]

象曰 *(孔子)*：	*Tuan Says (Kongzi explains) :*
豐，大也	Expansion, Big that's
明以動，故豐	Enlighten For Action, hence Expansion
王假之，尚大也	King Achieves It, Aspiring be Big that's
勿憂，宜日中	Don't Worry, Proper be Sun at Zenith (Upright, non-bias)
宜照天下也	Proper to Light-up World that's
日中則昃	Sun Zenith Then West-setting
月盈則食	Moon Full Then Eaten (Waning)
天地盈虛	Heaven Earth Full / Empty
與時消息也	With Time Expire /Alive) that's
而況於人乎	Then Same-way For People, No?
況於鬼神乎	Same-way For Devils Spirits, No?

Comments:
Image: Fire (light) meeting Thunder (action) above, Enlighten Action for Expansion.
Wen: Expansion,Prosperity, King achieves it, no worry of decline, be Upright like Sun at Zenith.
Kongzi: Sun Zenith--Setting, Moon Full--Waning, naturally also for People, Devils & Spirits.

[Xu: 昃138日在西方時側也；消235盡也；息217喘也；況229寒水也]

象曰 *(孔子)*：	*HexagramSign says (Kongzi) :*
雷電皆至，豐	Thunder Lightning Both Arrive, Expansion
君子以折獄致刑	Junzi With Breaking Dungeons, Achieves Punishment.

Comments:
Lightning Thunder together arrive, Enlighten Action for Expansion.
Junzi with Expansion and Prosperity, breaks need for Dungeons, reduces need for Punishment.

[Xu: 致…；至247鳥飛从高下地也]

爻辭 *(周公)* :	*Liner Text (Zhougong)* :
初九：	**FirstNiner:**
遇其配主	Meet The Partner Master (Niner4)
雖旬无咎，往有尚	Though Equal No Faults, Go-forth Has Aspiration
象曰 *(孔子)* :	*LinerSign Says (Kongzi)* :
雖旬无咎，過旬災也	Though Equal (also Yang) No Faults, Over Equal, Disaster that's

Comments:

FirstNiner, has aspiration, meets partner master Niner4, Yang meets Yang, No Faults.
Be warned not to show Self-Expansion, to exert superiority over partner then Disastrous.

[Xu: 旬188徧也, 十日爲旬；徧43帀也；帀127周也；周33密也；雖279似蜥蜴而大]

六二：	**Sixer2:**
豐其蔀	Expansion Of Forestland
日中見斗，往得疑疾	Sun Zenith, See Big-Dipper (Sixer5), Go-forth Suspicion Sickness
有孚發若，吉	Has Trust Display Judiciously, Auspicious
象曰 *(孔子)* :	*LinerSign Says (Kongzi)* :
有孚發若，信之發志也	Has Trust Display Judiciously, Honesty Its Display of Will that's

Comments:

Won Forestland in Expansionism, with Uprightness like Sun Zenith meeting King Sixer5.
As go-forth arouses suspicion, hence needs to display Will of Honesty in serving the King.

[Xu: 蔀.... ，發270躾發也；躾110弓弩發於身而中於遠也；若24擇菜也]

九三：	**Niner3:**
豐其沛，日中見沫	Expansion Of Grassland, Sun Zenith See Small-Star (TopSixer)
折其右肱，无咎	Broke The Right Arm, No Fault
象曰 *(孔子)* :	*LinerSign Says (Kongzi)* :
豐其沛，不可大事也	Expansion Of Grassland, Not Capable of Big Tasks, that's
折其右肱，終不可用也	Broke The Right Arm, Finally Not Able to Use that's

Comments:

Niner3 strong, partner TopSixer weak, together not capable of big task in Expansionism.
Niner3 like a broken arm, finally not been used, No Faults.

[Xu: 沛228水出遼東...，沫237洒面也；洒236滌也；肱...]

九四：	**Niner4:**
豐其蔀	Expansion Of Forestland
日中見斗	Sun Zenith See Big-Dipper (King, Sixer5)
遇其夷主，吉	Meet The Equal Master (FirstNiner), Auspicious
象曰 *(孔子)* :	*LinerSign Says (Kongzi)* :
豐其蔀，位不當也	Expansion Of Forestland, Position Not Correct that's
日中見斗，幽不明也	Sun Zenith See Big-Dipper (Sixer5), Dim Not Bright that's
遇其夷主，吉行也	Meeting The Equal Master (FirstNiner), Auspicious Trip that's

Comments:

In Expansion tasks, Niner4 not strong in Yin position, but Upright like Sun Zenith, serving King.
Sixer5, a dim Yin, not capable, hence better working with Equal Master FirstNiner, Auspicious .

[Xu: 斗300十升也；夷213平也,東方之人也]

六五：	**Sixer5:**
來章	Comes Distinction
有慶譽，吉	Has Celebrated Reputation, Auspicious
象曰 (孔子)：	*LinerSign Says (Kongzi)* :
六五之吉，有慶也	Sixer 5 Its Auspiciousness, Has Celebration that's

Comments:
Partner Sixer2, at Centre of Li Trigram, with great enlightenment, comes help with Expansion.
With success expected hence has celebrations, Auspicious.
[Xu: 章58樂竟爲一章,从音从十,十數之終也]

上六：	**TopSixer:**
豐其屋，蔀其家	Expansion Of House, Forested-screen The Home
闚其戶，闃其无	Observes The Door, Quiet There are No People
三歲不覿，凶	3 Years Not Seen, Ominous
象曰 (孔子)：	*LinerSign Says (Kongzi)* :
豐其屋，天際翔也	Expansion Of House, Floating at Heaven's Edge that's
闚其戶	Observes The Door
闃其无人，自藏也	Quiet There are No People, Self Hiding that's

Comments:
TopSixer, Expansion of House to maximum, grand like building a castle in the air.
Forest-screened, no body seen around for 3 years, like self-hidden, Ominous.
[Xu: 闚249閃也 ；闃249静也 ；覿178見也 ；翔75回飛 ；戶247護也,半門曰戶]

Conclusions:
Expansion (Hexagram 55):   Fire Trigram below and Thunder Trigram above.
Image: Fire (Light) below meeting Thunder (Action) above, enlighten action for Expansion.

King Wen:
Expansion, Prosperity, King achieved, fears decline, be Sun Zenith, unbiased, then No Worries.

Zhougong:
FirstNiner: meets partner Master Niner4, No Faults, Self-Expansion in superiority, Disastrous.
Sixer2: Forestland Expansion, sees Dipper Sixer5, shows Trust allays Suspicion, Auspicious.
Niner 3: Grassland Expansion, sees Small-star TopSixer, like broken arm, not be used, NoFaults.
Niner4: Forestland Expansion, King Dipper dim, meets Equal Master FirstNiner Auspicious.
Sixer5: Weak King, Enlightened Sixer2 coming to assists Expansion, Celebrations Auspicious.
TopSixer: Over Expansion of House, like castle in the air, House Quiet, nobody seen, Ominous.
Expansion: Thrice Auspicious, also warns of danger of Self-Expansion and Over-Expansion.

Kongzi:
Sun Zenith--Setting, Moon Full--Waning, likewise with people and Spirits, Expansion-Decline.
Fire and Thunder for Enlightened Action, Junzi works to break Dungeons reduce Punishment.
(豐：多故也，雜卦傳)   (Expansion : many old friends - Misc.10th 'Wing')

Lessons (Expansion Hex.55)
Expansion like Sun has Zenith point, Over-the-top is Decline, Seclusion and Oblivion.
Old mansions are oft seen lifeless in seclusion, owners not enjoying fruit of over-Expansion!

（第五十六卦）旅　　　　　　　　　　**Traveling (Hexagram 56)**

<table>
<tr><td>　</td><td>外</td><td>上九</td><td>_______</td><td>**TopNiner**</td><td>**external**</td></tr>
<tr><td>離 （火，上卦）</td><td></td><td>六五</td><td>__　__</td><td>**Sixer5**</td><td>**Li (Fire, Trigram above)**</td></tr>
<tr><td></td><td></td><td>九四</td><td>_______</td><td>**Niner4**</td><td></td></tr>
<tr><td></td><td></td><td>九三</td><td>_______</td><td>**Niner3**</td><td></td></tr>
<tr><td>艮 （山，下卦）</td><td></td><td>六二</td><td>__　__</td><td>**Sixer2**</td><td>**Gen (Mountain, Trigram below)**</td></tr>
<tr><td>　</td><td>内</td><td>初六</td><td>__　__</td><td>**FirstSixer**</td><td>**internal**</td></tr>
</table>

卦辭 *(文王)* ：	*Hexagram Text (King Wen) :*
旅：	Traveling:
小亨	Small Prosperity
旅貞吉	Traveling, Integrity, Auspicious

彖曰 *(孔子) :*	*Tuan Says (Kongzi explains) :*
旅：	Traveling :
小亨	Small Prosperity
柔得中乎	Yin Has Centre that's (Sixer5)
外而順乎剛	Outside Is Docile To Yangs (Niner4, TopNiner)
止而麗乎明	Stop (Mountain) And Shine (Fire) To Enlighten
是以小亨	This Is Small Prosperity
旅貞吉也	Traveling with Integrity Auspicious that's
旅之時義大矣哉	Time of Traveling, Uprightness Great Indeed tthat's

Comments:
Traveling bringing Small Prosperity, Traveling with Integrity, Auspicious.
When Traveling, kindness, upright and such enlightened conducts are great for welfare, safety.

[Xu: 旅141軍之五百人 ；麗203旅行也, 鹿性 ；順182理也 ；剛91彊斷也; 義167己之威義也]

象曰 *(孔子) :*	*HexagramSign Says (Kongzi) :*
山上有火，旅	Mountain, Above Has Fire, go Traveling
君子以明慎用刑	Junzi With Enlightened Care Uses Punishment
而不留獄	And Not Stop at Imprisonment

Comments:
Mountain above has Fire, symbolic of a place not for staying, like a prison.
Junzi with enlightenment punishes with care and not just stop at imprisonment.

(Xu: 慎217謹也 ；刑92到也 ；留291止也 ；獄206确石195堅也)

爻辭 (周公)：	*Liner Text (Zhougong):*
初六：	**FirstSixer:**
旅瑣瑣	Traveling Jade clinking
斯其所取災	Breaking in-Doors to Seize, Disaster
象曰 (孔子)：	*LinerSign Says (Kongzi):*
旅瑣瑣	Traveling Jade clinking
志窮災也	Wills Lost (after robbery), Disaster that's

Comments:
FirstSixer, weak and inexperienced, Traveling with wealth exposed, suffered robbery, Disaster.
(Xu: 瑣12玉聲；斯300析也，曰斧以斯之；所300伐木聲也；取64捕取也)

六二：	**Sixer2:**
旅即次	Traveling Check-in Accommodation
懷其資	Bosom-carried Own Wealth
得童僕貞	Acquired Child Servant with Integrity
象曰 (孔子)：	*LinerSign Says (Kongzi):*
得童僕貞	Acquired Child Servant with Integrity
終无尤也	Finally No Worries that's

Comments:
Traveling with Wealth, accepted temporary accommodation, acquired child servant.
Treating servant well with Integrity, having help and good company, so No Worries
(Xu: 即106就也，即食也；次180不前不精也)

九三：	**Niner3:**
旅焚其次	Traveling Accommodation Got Burnt
喪其童僕，貞屬	Lost own Child Servant, Truly Grave
象曰 (孔子)：	*LinerSign Says (Kongzi):*
旅焚其次	Traveling Accommodation Got Burnt
亦以傷矣	Also Been Harmed that's
以旅與下	On Travel Dealing with Servant
其義喪也	The Uprightness Lost that's

Comments:
Niner3, Yang and not Centre (not Upright), top of bottom trigram, too strong and fierce.
Unfair dealing with servant who burnt accommodation and left, Truly Grave.

九四：	**Niner4:**
旅于處	Traveling At Place (outside)
得其資斧，我心不快	Gain Own Wealth Axe, My Heart Not Happy
象曰 (孔子)：	*LinerSign Says (Kongzi):*
旅于處，未得位也	Traveling At Place (not at home), Not Has Position that's
得其資斧，心未快也	Gain Own Wealth Axe, Heart (feeling) not Happy that's

Comments:
Niner4, Yang , kind, accumulates Wealth, has Security with weapon for defence.
Still feeling unhappy at heart, as Traveling outside at work, and has not return home!
(Xu: 處299止也；尻299處也从尸得几而止孝經曰仲尼尻尻謂閒居如此]

六五：	**Sixer5:**
射雉	Shot Pheasant
一矢亡	One Arrow Killed
終以譽命	Finally With Honored Appointment
象曰 *(孔子)：*	***LinerSign Says (Kongzi) :***
終以譽命	Finally With Honored Appointment
上逮也	Above Reached (informed) that's

Comments:
Sixer5, in honored position, kind, upright, in Traveling killed Pheasant with a single shot.
Prowess news reached authority above, finally gained recognition and Honored Appointment.
[Xu: 命32使也；逮40唐逮及也]

上九：	**TopNiner:**
鳥焚其巢	Bird, Burnt Its Nest
旅人先笑後號咷	Traveling Person First Laugh, later howling Wailing
喪牛于易，凶	Lost Cow At Market, Ominous
象曰 *(孔子)：*	***LinerSign Says (Kongzi) :***
以旅在上，其義焚也	As Traveling On High, Its Uprightness Burnt that's
喪牛于易，終莫之聞也	Lost Cow At Market, Finally Not Been Heard that's

Comments:
TopNiner, Traveling on High, too strong and frivolous, like burning Bird's nest for a laugh.
With Lost of Uprightness conduct, also lost wealth at market place, finally gone into Oblivion.

Conclusions:
Traveling (Hexagram 56): Mountain Trigram below and Fire Trigram above.
Image: Mountain below with Fire above, volcano; not a place to stay so go Traveling.

King Wen:
Traveling, Small Prosperity, maintain Integrity along the way, Auspicious.

Zhougong:
FirstSixer: Early in Traveling, inexperience, exposed wealth, attracting robbers, Disastrous.
Sixer2: Upright, Traveling with Wealth, has honest child servant for company, No Worries.
Niner3: strong headed, ill treated servant who burnt hotel and left, Integrity Compromised.
Niner4: kind, working, Traveling, amassed wealth, achieved security, not at home, feeling Sad.
Sixer5: honored position, Traveling, killed bird with 1 shot, prowess recognised, finally Honored.
TopNiner: too strong on top, burnt bird's nest, frivolous, lost fortune at market, fell intoOblivion.
Traveling: exciting characters found on the traveling-trail, also care and conduct to be observe.

Kongzi:
Fire above Mountain, not a place to stay, go Traveling.
Junzi, compassionate in Judgement, not imprisonment but banishment to Travel far-away.
(豐：多故也，雜卦傳)   (Expansion : many old friends - Misc.10th 'Wing')

Lessons (Traveling Hex.56)
For safe Traveling, do not expose wealth, always have Integrity and goodwill treating others.
We should be compassionate in Punishment, replace Prison with Traveling for Rehabilitation!

(第五十七卦) 巽   **Wind (Hexagram 57)**

外	上九	________	**TopNiner**	**external**
巽 （風, 上卦）	九五	________	**Niner5**	**Xun (Wind, Trigram above)**
	六四	__ __	**Sixer4**	
	九三	________	**Niner3**	
巽 （風, 下卦）	九二	________	**Niner2**	**Xun (Wind, Trigram below)**
内	初六	__ __	**FirstSixer**	**internal**

卦辭 (文王) ：   ***Hexagram Text (King Wen) :***

巽：	Wind
小亨	Small Prosperity
利有攸往	Favors Having Gentle Venture
利見大人	Favors Seeing Great Person

象曰 (孔子) ：   ***Tuan Says (Kongzi explains) :***

重巽以申命	Double Xun (Conformity) For Implementing Orders
剛巽乎中正而志行	Yang Conformity that's Centre Right And Wills Achieved
柔皆順乎剛	Yins All Submissive To Yangs
是以小亨	Therefore Small Prosperity
利有攸往	Favors Having Gentle Venture
利見大人	Favors Seeing Great Person

Comments:
Image: Wind following Wind, Conformity (all liners, no pairing partners).
Symbolic: Focus on Yins, actions below the Yangs Conformity, hence Small Prosperity.
Wen: Conformity of Yins, favors gentle Venture, seeing Great Person, Small Prosperity.
Kongzi: Yangs centres Will done, Small Yins all obedient, favors seeing Great Person.
[Xu: 巽99具也从丌庶物皆具丌以爲之]

象曰 (孔子) ：   ***HexagramSign Says (Kongzi) :***

隨風，巽	Following Wind, Conformity
君子以申命行事.	Junzi for Implementing Orders, Take Actions.

Comments:
Wind following Wind, Wind-conformity.
Like Wind, Junzi obediently takes actions in all affairs, with Will to fulfilling Destiny.
[Xu: 申311神也七月陰气成體自申束从臼自持也吏臣舖時聽事申旦政也]

爻辭 *(周公)* :	*Liner Text (Zhougong) :*

初六： — **FirstSixer:**

進退	Forward Backward
利武人之貞.	Favors Soldier Person's Truthfulness

象曰 *(孔子)* :	*LinerSign Says (Kongzi) :*
進退，志疑也	Forward Backward, Wills Doubtful that's
利武人之貞	Favors Soldier Person's Truthfulness
志治也	Wills Achieved that's

Comments:
FirstSixer, weak, lowly in Wind-conform, Wills uncertain, wavering in actions.
If FirstSixer has spirit of a soldier with Truthfulness, then Wills will be achieved.
[Xu: 治227水出東萊田城...]

九二： — **Niner2:**

巽在牀下	Wind-conform At Sit-stool Beneath
用史巫紛若	Usage of Official Witch Talisman Fragrant-Grass,
吉，无咎	Auspicious, No Faults

象曰 *(孔子)* :	*LinerSign Says (Kongzi) :*
紛若之吉，得中也	Talisman Fragrant-Grass, Auspicious, Gain Centre that's

Comments:
Niner2, in Yin position in lower trigram, uncomfortable, like Conformity beneath Sit-stool.
At Centre able to Conform hence No Faults, has Witch to make Offerings, Auspicious.
[Xu: 牀121安身之坐者；史65記事者也又持中,中正也；巫100祝也女能事無形以舞降神者
也；紛276馬尾韜；若24擇菜,一曰杜若香]

九三： — **Niner3:**

頻巽，吝	Repeat Conformity, Shame

象曰 *(孔子)* :	*LinerSign Says (Kongzi) :*
頻巽之吝	Repeated Conformity Its Shame
志窮也	Wills Exhausted that's

Comments:
Niner3, Yang in Yang position, top position of lower trigram, too strong for Conformity
Repeated Wind-conformity efforts to gain acceptance, Wills exhausted, what a Shame.
[Xu: 頻 ...]

六四： — **Sixer4:**

悔亡	Regrets Lost
田獲三品	Fields Capture 3 Kinds

象曰 *(孔子)* :	*LinerSign Says (Kongzi) :*
田獲三品，有功也	Fields Capture 3 Kinds, Has Success that's

Comments:
Sixer4, no partner, trapped in Wind-conformity between Yangs, has Regrets.
In correct position, and in the fields has successes capturing 3 kinds, Regrets Lost.
[Xu: 品48眾庶也；庶193屋下眾也]

九五：	Niner5:
貞吉	Truthfulness Auspicious
悔亡无不利	Regrets Lost None Not Favorable
无初有終，先庚三日	No Beginning Has Ending, Before Harvest 3 Days
後庚三日，吉	After Harvest 3 Days, Auspicious
象曰 *(孔子)* ：	*LinerSign Says (Kongzi) :*
九五之吉	Niner5 Its Auspiciousness
位正中也	Position Correct and Centre that's

Comments:
Niner5, Yang Premier, Centre, too strong for Wind-conformity, in the Beginning has Regrets.
Right position, make changes, peaceful 3 days before, fruitful 3 days after, Doubly Auspicious.
[Xu: 庚309位西方象秋時萬物庚,庚有實也]

上九：	TopNiner:
巽在牀下	Wind-conformity At Sit-stool Beneath
喪其資斧，貞凶	Lost Its Resource Axe, Truly Ominous
象曰 *(孔子)* ：	*LinerSign Says (Kongzi) :*
巽在牀下，上窮也	Wind-conformity At Sit-stool Beneath　, Top Exhausted that's
喪其資斧，正乎凶也	Lost Its Resource Axe, Correctly That's Ominous that's

Comments:
TopNiner at top yet Wind-comformity at Sit-stool level, overly Conforming.
No partner, exhausted, loosing resources and axe security, Truly Ominous.

Conclusions:
Wind-conform (Hexagram 57): Wind Trigram below and Wind Trigram above.
Image: Wind following Wind, Wind-conformity, no partner pairing for all liners here.
Symbolic: Focus Yins, each Conforming beneath 2 Yangs, favors Venture, Small Prosperity.

King Wen:
Conformity of Yins, hence Small Prosperity, favors Venture, favors Seeing Great Person.

Zhougong:
FirstSixer: low in Conformity wavering doubts, if has spirit of a Soldier Truthful, Wills be done.
Niner2: lowly Conformity beneath Sit-stool No Faults, Witch helps make Offerings, Auspicious.
Niner3: Yang in right position, too Strong to be Conforming, trying exhausted, what a Shame.
Sixer4: Conformity between 2 Yangs Regrets, right position and has successes, Regrets Lost.
Niner5: Yang regrets Conformity, but Upright, Changes fruitful in 3 days, Doubly Auspicious.
TopNiner: top limit, no partner, overly Conforming, lost resources protection, Truly Ominous.
Wind-conform: generally resisted and regretted at all levels, and at top level Ominous.

Kongzi:
Yangs centres, Wills done, Small Yins all obedient, favors seeing Great Person.
Wind-conformity, Junzi obediently takes actions in all affairs, with Wills to fulfil Destiny.

(巽：伏也，雜卦傳)　　　(Xun (Wind) : low-lying that's - Miscellaneous 10th 'Wing')

Lessons (Wind-conform Hex.57)
The weak following the strong, Conformity favors fulfilling orders, having small prosperity.
Wind-conform favors at ground level, but Conformity at top level like populism is disastrous.

(第五十八卦) 兌　　　　　　**Wetland (Hexagram 58)**

外	上六	___ ___	**TopSixer**		**external**
兌 (澤，上卦)	九五	_______	**Niner5**	**Dui (Wetland, Trigram above)**	
	九四	_______	**Niner4**		
	六三	___ ___	**Sixer3**		
兌 (澤，下卦)	九二	_______	**Niner2**	**Dui (Wetland, Trigram below)**	
內	初九	_______	**FirstNiner**		**internal**

卦辭 *(文王)* ：　　　　　　***Hexagram Text (King Wen) :***
兌：　　　　　　Wetland :
亨，利貞　　　　　　Prosperity, Favors Integrity

象曰 *(孔子)* ：　　　　　　***Tuan Says (Kongzi explains) :***
兌，說也　　　　　　Wetland, Joy (speechless) that's
剛中而柔外，說　　　　　　Strong (Yangs) Centre And Gentle (Yins) Outward, Joy
以利貞　　　　　　To Favors Integrity
是以順乎天而應乎人　　　　　　Therefore in Accord With Heaven And in Response To People
說以先民，民忘其勞　　　　　　Joy First For Citizens, Citizens Forget The (sweat of) Labor
說以犯難，民忘其死　　　　　　Joy To Tackle Difficulty, Citizens Forget The (fear of) Death
說之大，民勸矣哉　　　　　　Joy Is Great, Citizens Persuaded indeed, that's
Comments:
Image: Wetland above, Wetland below, double Joy (speechless Happiness)
Symbolic: Have Trust centres (Niner2, Niner5) and Gentleness outside (Sixer3, TopSixer), Joy.
Wen: Wetland-joy is Prosperity, however over-joy must be guarded with having Integrity.
Kongzi: Trust inside and Gentleness outside, accord with Heaven and responsive to People.
With Joy, Citizens will not fear Death and be persuaded to take-on difficult Tasks.
[Xu: 兌176說也從儿 ；儿176仁人也 ；說53說釋也 ；順182理也 ；忘220不識也 ；犯205浸也 ；
難80鳥也 ；勸292勉也]

象曰 *(孔子)* ：　　　　　　***HexagramSign Says (Kongzi) :***
麗澤，兌　　　　　　Beautiful Wetland, Joy
君子以朋友講習　　　　　　Junzi With Friends Discusses and Practices
Comments:
Beautiful Wetland, Joy of speechless happiness.
Junzi, one of life's Joy is meeting with friends for discussion and practices.
[Xu: 麗203旅行也, 鹿性見食急必旅行 ；講53和解也 ；習74數飛也]

爻辭 *(周公)* :	*Liner Text (Zhougong)* :

初九 :	**FirstNiner:**
和兌	Harmonious Joy
吉	Auspicious
象曰 *(孔子)* :	*LinerSign Says (Kongzi)* :
和兌之吉	Harmonious Joy, Its Auspiciousness
行未疑也	Actions has No Doubts that's

Comments:
FirstNiner at bottom of Joy, only Yang with no Yin as neighbor.
No complicated human relationship experiences, hence in all Actions, no Doubts, Auspicious.
[Xu: 和32相(雁言)也；疑从子从止；310惑也]

九二 :	**Niner2:**
孚兌	Trusting Joy
吉，悔亡	Auspicious, Regrets Lost
象曰 *(孔子)* :	*LinerSign Says (Kongzi)* :
孚兌之吉	Trusting Joy Its Auspiciousness
信志也	Honest Will that's

Comments:
Niner2, Yang in Yin placing has regrets, but also in centre Trust position, hence regrets lost.
Niner2 has Will of Honesty, facing the untrustworthy Sixer3 with Trusting Joy, Auspicious.
[Xu: 孚63卵子也, 从爪从子, 一曰信也；信52誠也；志217意也]

六三 :	**Sixer3:**
來兌	Coming Joy
凶	Ominous
象曰 *(孔子)* :	*LinerSign Says (Kongzi)* :
來兌之凶	Coming Joy, Its Ominousness
位不當也	Position Not Correct that's

Comments:
Sixer3, Yin in Yang position, not centre, and without partner, not the best of person.
Top of Trigram, stooping to bring Joy to Niner2, Ominous.
[Xu: 來111周所受瑞麥來麰…故爲行來之來；當291田相值]

九四 :	**Niner4:**
商兌未寧	Business Joy Not Settled
介疾有喜	In-between Sickness Has Good-news
象曰 *(孔子)* :	*LinerSign Says (Kongzi)* :
九四之喜	Niner4 The Good-news
有慶也	Has Celebration that's

Comments:
Niner4 may befriend soft Sixer3 or help king Niner5, hence Business Joy not settled.
Niner4 correct positioned, resolves to help kingdom prosper, Celebrations.
[Xu: 商…；寧150安也；介28畫也, 从八从人, 人各有介]

九五：	**Niner5:**
孚于剝	Trusting The Usurper
有厲	Has Gravity
象曰 *(孔子)：*	***LinerSign Says (Kongzi) :***
孚于剝	Trusting The Usurper (TopSixer)
位正當也	Position Centre and Correct that's

Comments:
Niner5 in Yang placing, king in centre position, thus Niner5 is very strong.
Trusting Joy for TopSixer the Usurper no danger, but situation Grave.
[Xu: 剝91裂也, 刻割也 ；彔144刻木彔彔]

上六：	**TopSixer:**
引兌	Leading Joy
象曰 *(孔子)：*	***LinerSign Says (Kongzi) :***
上六引兌	TopSixer Leading Joy
未光也	Not Enlightening that's

Comments:
TopSixer is the Leading Joy of Niner5 who neglects the kingdom.
This form of conduct Not Enlightening.
[Xu: 引270開弓也]

Conclusions:
Wetland-joy (Hexagram 58): Wetland Trigram below and Wetland Trigram above.
Image: Wetland below, Wetland above, double Wetland Jjoy.
Symbolic: Yangs Centres (Trust) and Yins (Gentleness) outward, Joy.

King Wen:
Wetland-joy is Prosperity, over-joy best be guarded with having Integrity.

Zhougong:
FirstNiner: the only Yang isolated from Yins, Harmonious Joy, as has No Doubts, Auspicious.
Niner2: Trusting Joy with Sixer3, Regrets in Yin place, but Centre of Honest Wills, Auspicious.
Sixer3: Yang placing, not Centre, no partner, not trustworthy, brings Joy to Niner2, Ominous.
Niner4: Business Joy option, supports Niner5, cut-off Sixer3 ill-will, Prosperity, Celebrations.
Niner5: Yang king, strong no danger, but Trusting Joy for Usurper TopSixer, situation Grave.
TopSixer: Leading Joy for Niner5 who thus neglects kingdom, conduct Not Luminous.
Wetland-joy: Joy is prosperity, but over-joy must be guarded with having Integrity.

Kongzi:
Bring Universal Joy to Citizens, then people are not tired in Labor, or fear Death in War.
Joy of Life for the Junzi is meeting with friends for discussions and practices.

(兌：見也，雜卦傳)　　　　　　　　(Joy : visible that's - Misc.10th Wing)

Lessons (Wetland Hex.58)
First, leaders must bring Joy and Prosperity before requesting citizens to labor and to fight.
Junzi, Joy of life is meeting friends for discussions and practices.

(第五十九卦) 渙　　　　　　　　**Dispersion　(Hexagram 59)**

<table>
<tr><td>外</td><td>上九</td><td>________</td><td>TopNiner</td><td>external</td></tr>
<tr><td>巽　(風，上卦)</td><td>九五</td><td>________</td><td>Niner5</td><td>Xun　(Wind, Trigram above)</td></tr>
<tr><td></td><td>六四</td><td>__　__</td><td>Sixer4</td><td></td></tr>
<tr><td></td><td>六三</td><td>__　__</td><td>Sixer3</td><td></td></tr>
<tr><td>坎　(水，下卦)</td><td>九二</td><td>________</td><td>Niner2</td><td>Kan　(Water, Trigram below)</td></tr>
<tr><td>內</td><td>初六</td><td>__　__</td><td>FirstSixer</td><td>internal</td></tr>
</table>

卦辭 *(文王)*：	***Hexagram Text (King Wen) :***
渙：	Dispersion :
亨，王假有廟	Prosperity, King Arrival Has Temple
利涉大川	Favors Venture Big River
利貞	Favors Truthfulness

彖曰 *(孔子)*：	***Tuan Says (Kongzi explains) :***
渙，亨	Dispersion, Prosperity
剛來而不窮	Yang (Niner2) Cometh And Not Dead-end (at Centre)
柔得位乎外而上同	Yin (Sixer4) Gain Position that's Outside And Above Accorded
王假有廟	King Arrival Has Temple
王乃在中也	King Still In Centre that's (Niner5)
利涉大川	Favors Venturing Big River
乘木有功也	Riding Wood (boat) Has Success that's

Comments:
Image: Wind blowing above Water, Dispersion.
Symbolic: Dispersion of Yin Yang in Hex.12 Isolation, Sixer2 and Niner4 exchanging place.
Wen: Sees Prosperity, King has Temple, unites citizens in ancestral spirit for Truthful Venture.
Kongzi: King (Niner5) Centre of Xun (Wind, is wood), leads in boats has success in Dispersion.
[Xu: 渙229流散也；亨......；廟193尊先祖兒也]

象曰 *(孔子)*：	***HexagramSign Says (Kongzi) :***
風行水上，渙	Wind Moving Water Above, Dispersion
先王以享于帝立廟	Past Kings With Offerings To Ancestors Set-up Temple

Comments:
Wind moving above Water, Dispersion (of the living and the dead into separate worlds).
Past Kings built Temple for Ancestral Offerings, uniting Citizens in past Pioneering Spirit.

爻辭 *(周公)* :	*Liner Text (Zhougong)* :

初六：	**FirstSixer**
用拯	Action Rescue
馬壯，吉	Horse Strong, Auspicious
象曰 *(孔子)* :	*LinerSign Says (Kongzi)* :
初六之吉	FirstSixer Its Auspiciousness
順也	Obedience that's

Comments:
In Dispersion, FirstSixer wishes to save the situation, team-up with Niner2 (strong horse).
FirstSixer, Yin at the bottom, weak, limited strength, but obedient to Niner2, hence Auspicious.
[Xu: 拯......]

九二：	**Niner2:**
渙奔其机，悔亡	Dispersion Gallop The Woods, Regrets Lost
象曰 *(孔子)* :	*LinerSign Says (Kongzi)* :
渙奔其机	Dispersion Gallop The Woods (Boats)
得願也	Achieves Wills that's

Comments:
Niner2 in Yin position has Regrets, Racing his boats in rescue, works hard to stop Dispersion.
With Responder Niner5 of the same Wills, achieve success, thus No Regrets.
[Xu: 奔215疾也从卉；机118木也]

六三：	**Sixer3:**
渙其躬	Dispersion The Body
无悔	No Regrets
象曰 *(孔子)* :	*LinerSign Says (Kongzi)* :
渙其躬，志在外也	Dispersion The Body, Wills On Outside that's

Comments
Sixer3, misplaced, not centre has regrets, helps with Dispersion of personal wealth.
Only one with external partner TopNiner, has Wills to go join him, hence Regrets no more.
[Xu: 躬152身也]

六四：	**Sixer4:**
渙其羣，元吉	Dispersing Its Crowd, Primal Auspiciousness
渙其丘，匪夷所思	Dispersion Its Hill, Not One-Can-Think-of (unthinkable)
象曰 *(孔子)* :	*LinerSign Says (Kongzi)* :
渙其羣元吉	Dispersing Its Crowd (Clique), Primal Auspiciousness
光大也	Shining Big that's

Comments:
Sixer4, fixer of Dispersion, Dispersing Own Clique of bad influences, Primaly Auspicious.
Right placed, to supports Niner5, regroup Hill-like Shining Clique, an act that's Unthinkable.
[Xu:羣78輩也 ；夷213平也,東方之人也]

九五：	**Niner5:**
渙汗其大號	Dispersing Sweat Its Great Rally-Call
渙王居，无咎	Dispersing King's Possession, No Faults
象曰 *(孔子)*：	***LinerSign Says (Kongzi) :***
王居无咎	King's Possession, No Fault
正位也	Proper Position that's

Comments:
Niner5, Yang King, Centre, like whole body-sweat, Dispersing His Rally-Call Kingdom-wide.
Premier position, Dispersing his possession to finance for greater achievement, No Faults.
[Xu: 汗237人液也；嘷34號也]

上九：	**TopNiner:**
渙其血	Dispersing Its Blood
去逖出，无咎	Away Far Out, No Faults
象曰 *(孔子)*：	***LinerSign Says (Kongzi) :***
渙其血	Dispersing Its Blood
遠害也	Distancing Harm that's

Comments:
TopNiner at end of Dispersion, to Disperse personal defects, getting rid of bad blood.
Distancing oneself of harmful habits in wining, dining, and non-virtuous conducts, No Faults.
[Xu: 逖42遠也]

Conclusions:
Dispersion (Hexagram 59): Water Trigram below and Wind Trigram above.
Image: Water moving above Wind, Dispersion.
Symbolic: Dispersion of Yangs and Yins in Hex.12 Isolation, with Sixer2 Niner4 inter-change.

King Wen:
King in Temple, Rally Citizens in Pioneering Ancestral Spirit for Truthful Ventures, Prosperity.

Zhougong:
FirstSixer: misplaced, weak, Rescue action with strong Horse Niner2, obedient, Auspicious.
Niner2: misplaced, Regrets, responder Niner5 same Wills, racing Boats to help, Regrets Lost.
Sixer3: Wills external with partner TopNiner, Dispersing Personal wealth to help, No Regrets.
Sixer4: Dispersing own Clique Auspicious, regroup for enlighten service, action Unthinkable!
Niner5: King Dispersing possession to finance Great Rally-call to all Citizens, No Faults.
TopNiner: top-end Dispersion of bad blood, bad conduct, keep away from Harm, No Faults.
Dispersion: contribute personal wealth to help, dismantle self-interests doing the Unthinkable!

Kongzi:
Time to rally around ancestral pioneering spirit, making personal sacrifices for Unity.
Past Kings built Temple for Ancestral Offerings, uniting Citizens in past Pioneering Spirit.
(渙：離，雜卦傳)　　　　　(Dispersion : is leaving - Misc.10th 'Wing')

Lessons (Dispersion Hex.59)
Time of Dispersion Crisis, important the King is still there to rally help, turn situation around.
Like in a sinking boat, important that Captain remains to direct rescue operation, reduce losses.

（第六十卦）節　　　　　　　　**Thrift (Hexagram 60)**

<table>
<tr><td>　</td><td>外</td><td>上六</td><td>__ __</td><td>**TopSixer**</td><td></td><td>**external**</td></tr>
<tr><td>坎</td><td>（水，上卦）</td><td>九五</td><td>______</td><td>**Niner5**</td><td>**Kan (Water, Trigram above)**</td><td></td></tr>
<tr><td>　</td><td>　</td><td>六四</td><td>__ __</td><td>**Sixer4**</td><td></td><td></td></tr>
<tr><td>　</td><td>　</td><td>六三</td><td>__ __</td><td>**Sixer3**</td><td></td><td></td></tr>
<tr><td>兌</td><td>（澤，下卦）</td><td>九二</td><td>______</td><td>**Niner2**</td><td>**Dui (Wetland, Trigram below)**</td><td></td></tr>
<tr><td>　</td><td>內</td><td>初九</td><td>______</td><td>**FirstNiner**</td><td></td><td>**internal**</td></tr>
</table>

卦辭 *(文王)* ：	***Hexagram Text (King Wen)*** ：
節，亨	Thrift, Prosperity
苦節不可貞	Bitter Thrift Not Be Affirmed

彖曰 *(孔子)* ：	***Tuan Says (Kongzi explains)*** ：
節亨	Thrift Prosperity
剛柔分而剛得中	Yin (Sixer3) Yang (Niner5) Separated And Yang Get Centre
苦節不可貞	Bitter Thrift Not be Affirmed
其道窮也	Its Way Limited that's
說以行險	Joy To Tread Danger
當位以節	Correct Position For Thrift (Niner5)
中正以通	Centre, Upright For Connectivity (Niner2)
天地節而四時成	Heaven Earth Thrifty Then 4 Seasons Formed
節以制度	Thrift With Principled Measures
不傷財	Not Hurting Economy
不害民	Not Harming Citizens

Comments:
Image: Wetland, above has Water, Thrift; arise from Yin Yang separation in Hex.11 Interaction.
Wen: Thrift is Prosperity, but extreme Bitter Thrift not be lauded.
Kongzi: Thrift with measured degree, not hurting the Economy, not harming Citizens.
[Xu: 節95竹約也；約272纏也；窮153極也]

象曰 *(孔子)* ：	*HexagramSign Says (Kongzi)* ：
澤上有水，節	Wetland Above Has Water, Thrift
君子以制數度	Junzi With Principled Accounting Rules
議德行	Discuss Virtuous Conduct

Comments:
Wetland (limiting capacity to hold water), above has Water, Thrift.
Junzi judges Virtuous Conduct by looking at the balance sheet (Thrifty or a miser)
[Xu: 制92裁也；數68計也；度65法制也，一曰止也；議52語也；語51論也；德43升也]

爻辭 *(周公)* :	*Liner Text (Zhougong)* :

初九：	**FirstNiner:**
不出戶庭	Not Stepping-out Homestead Courtyard
无咎	No Faults
象曰 *(孔子)* :	*LinerSign Says (Kongzi)* :
不出戶庭	Not Stepping-out Homestead Courtyard
知通塞也	Knows Free-flowing or Blocked, that's

Comments:
FirstNiner, early Thrift, not venturing out, No Faults.
As Yang in Yang position knows external situation well, whether Free-flowing or Blocked.
(Kongzi has elaboration when asked by disciples, Attached Upper Commentary, para.8.)
[Xu: 戶247護也]

九二：	**Niner2:**
不出門庭	Not Stepping-out In-door Compound
凶	Ominous
象曰 *(孔子)* :	*LinerSign Says (Kongzi)* :
不出門庭凶	Not Stepping-out Indoor Compound, Ominous
失時極也	Miss Timing to the Extreme, that's

Comment
Niner2, not even stepping-out Indoor Compound, misses Timing to the Extreme
Centre position, strong Yang, young no action, knows Thrift but not Opportunities, Ominous.

六三：	**Sixer3:**
不節若	Not Thrifty Like
則嗟若，无咎	Then Sighing Like, No Faults
象曰 *(孔子)* :	*LinerSign Says (Kongzi)* :
不節之嗟	Not Thrifty The Sighing
又誰咎也	Then Whose Faults that's?

Comments:
Sixer3, weak Yin in Yang position, not centre, cannot naturally be Thrifty, No Faults.
If Faults be allocated, then Whose Faults as Sixer3 is born that way naturally?

六四：	**Sixer4:**
安節	Quiet Thrift
亨	Prosperity
象曰 *(孔子)* :	*LinerSign Says (Kongzi)* :
安節之亨	Quiet Thrift Its Prosperity
承上道也	Support Above Virtuous-way that's

Comments:
Sixer4, correct in Yin position, with Quiet Thrift, supportive of Niner5 above, Prosperity.
[Xu: 安150靜也]

九五：	**Niner5:**
甘節，吉	Beautiful Thrift, Auspicious
往有尚	Going-forth Has Aspirations
象曰 *(孔子)：*	***LinerSign Says (Kongzi):***
甘節之吉	Beautiful Thrift, Its Auspiciousness
居位中也	Occupied Position Central that's

Comments:
Niner5, King, strong Yang, in central position to achieve Aspirations, Auspicious.
Hence his is Beautiful Thrift, prosperity for the Kingdom and Citizens.
[Xu: 甘100美也；美78祥也；祥7福也；尚28曾也,庶幾也；曾28詞舒也；幾24微也殆也]

上六：	**TopSixer:**
苦節	Bitter Thrift
貞凶，悔亡	Truly Ominous, Regrets Lost
象曰 *(孔子)：*	***LinerSign Says (Kongzi):***
苦節貞凶	Bitter Thrift with Integrity Ominous
其道窮也	This Way Extreme that's

Comments:
Bitter Thrift is Extreme Thrift even with Integrity Ominous.
However Thrift is basically a good thing, hence No Regrets.
[Xu: 窮153極也]

Conclusions:
Thrift (Hexagram 60): Wetland Trigram below and Water Trigram above.
Image: Wetland, above Water, Joy below emerging to meet Danger above and halt, Thrift.
Symbolic: Thrift, formation from Yin (Sixer5) Yang (Niner3) exchange in Interaction (Hex.11) .

King Wen:
Thrift is Prosperity, but extreme Bitter Thrift is Dangerous and truly not be Lauded.

Zhougong:
FirstNiner: Early Thrift, not Stepping-out Courtyard, knows conditions Free/Blocked, No Faults.
Niner2: Centre strong, knows Thrift but not Opportunity, Not Stepping-out Compound,Ominous.
Sixer3: Weak in Yang position, not centre, not Thrifty, Sighing, No Faults, else whose Faults?
Sixer4: Gentle, right Yin position, supportive of Niner 5 with Quiet Thrift, Prosperity.
Niner5: Beautiful Thrift, Yang King, centre, go forth with Aspiration for Citizens, Auspicious.
TopSixer: top old, Bitter Thrift even with Integrity Ominous; but Thrift basically has No Regrets.
Thrift: practices to varying degree are described, good for reference and consultation.

Kongzi:
Heaven Earth have Thrift, and the four seasons established.
In Thrift, Regulations are judged by not hurting the Economy or harming Citizens.
(節：止也，雜卦傳)   (Thrift : limiting that's - Misc.10th 'Wing')

Lessons (Thrift Hex. 60)
In Thrift, Junzi set-up accounting measures to judge people by their virtues and conduct.
Stock Exchanges for honest liquidity exchanges; Unscrupulous manipulate it for selfish gains.

(第六十一卦) 中孚　　　　　　　**Core Trust (Hexagram 61)**

	上九	______	**TopNiner**	external
巽　(風, 上卦)	九五	______	**Niner5**	**Xun (Wind, Trigram above)**
	六四	__ __	**Sixer4**	
	六三	__ __	**Sixer3**	
兌　(澤, 下卦)	九二	______	**Niner2**	**Dui (Wetland, Trigram below)**
	初九	______	**FirstNiner**	internal

卦辭 *(文王)*：　　　　　　　　　*Hexagram Text (King Wen) :*
中孚：　　　　　　　　　　　　Core Trust :
豚魚吉　　　　　　　　　　　　Piglets Fish Auspicious
利涉大川　　　　　　　　　　　Favors Venture Big River
利貞　　　　　　　　　　　　　Favors Integrity

象曰 *(孔子)*：　　　　　　　　*Tuan Says (Kongzi explains) :*
中孚：　　　　　　　　　　　　Core Trust :
柔在内而剛得中　　　　　　　　Yins On Inside And Yangs Get Centres
說而巽　　　　　　　　　　　　Joy (Wetland) And Xun (Wind-conformity)
孚乃化邦也　　　　　　　　　　Trust That Transform Kingdoms that's
豚魚吉　　　　　　　　　　　　Piglets Fish Auspicious
信及豚魚也　　　　　　　　　　Trust Reaching Piglets and Fish that's
利涉大川　　　　　　　　　　　Favors Venture to Big River
乘木舟虛也　　　　　　　　　　Riding Wooden Boat Hollow that's
中孚以利　　　　　　　　　　　Core Trust With Advantages
乃應乎天也　　　　　　　　　　Which Respond To Heaven that's

Comments:
Image: Sixer3 Sixer4 at Hexagram Centre, Niner2, Niner5 at Trigram Centres, Core Trust.
Symbolic: Of a wooden boat (hollow centre) sailing the Wetland, Trusting the Wind above.
Wen: Core Trust that even piglets fishes can feel, favors venturing, with Integrity Auspicious.
Kongzi: Wetland Joy and Wind Conformity, Core Trust accorded Heaven, transform kingdoms.
[Xu: 孚63卵孚也从子从爪, 一曰信也；豚197小豕也]

象曰 *(孔子)*：　　　　　　　　*HexagramSign Says (Kongzi) :*
澤上有風，中孚　　　　　　　　Wetland Above Has Wind, Core Trust
君子以議獄緩死　　　　　　　　Junzi In Penal Judgement, Suspend Death (stays execution)

Comments:
Above Wetland has Wind, Joy meet Conformity, symbolic of Core Trust.
Junzi with Core Trust, careful in Penal Judgement, stays irreversible Execution.
[Xu: 議52語也；語51論也；獄206确也从言二犬所以守也；緩278(素卓)也；卓168高也]

爻辭 *(周公)* :	*Liner Text (Zhougong)* :
初九 :	FirstNiner:
虞吉	Yu Auspicious
有他不燕	Has Thirty-party No Quietude
象曰 *(孔子)* :	*LinerSign Says (Kongzi)* :
初九虞吉	FirstNiner, Yu (mythical animal) Auspicious
志未變也	Wills Not Changed that's

Comments:
FirstNiner, Benevolent Trust like Yu (mythical animal, not killing, only eat dead meat).
FirstNine and Sixer4 partner, no third-party, Wills not changed peace at home, Auspicious.
[Xu: 虞103(馬鋘)虞也, 白虎黑文尾長於身仁獸食自死之肉；燕245玄鳥也；玄84幽遠也]

九二 :	**Niner2:**
鳴鶴在陰	Calling Crane In the Shade (Niner2)
其子和之	Its Child Harmonizes With It
我有好爵，吾與爾靡之	I Have Good Goblet, I With You Enjoy It
象曰 *(孔子)* :	*LinerSign Says (Kongzi)* :
其子和之，中心願也	Its Child Harmonizes with It, Centre Heart Wishes that's

Comments:
Niner2 and child Niner5, Centre of each respective Trigram, responding in Harmony.
Both cranes, family Trust in each other, and if they can drink would share a goblet of wine!
(Kongzi elaborates further when asked by disciples, *Attached Upper Commentary para.8.*)

六三 :	**Sixer3:**
得敵	Acquired Enemy
或鼓或罷	Or Drumming, Or Beating (a retreat)
或泣或歌	Or Sobbing, Or Singing
象曰 *(孔子)* :	*LinerSign Says (Kongzi)* :
或鼓或罷	Or Drumming Or Beating (a retreat)
位不當也	Position Not Proper that's

Comments:
Partners Sixer3 and TopNiner, both not Centre, not correct in positions, No Trust in each other.
At end of Core Trust TopNiner is like an enemy, and Sixer3 knows not to cry or to laugh!
[Xu: 敵68仇；鼓69擊鼓 ；罷158遣有罪, 从网能言而賢能而入网而貫遣之; 泣237無聲出涕]

六四 :	**Sixer4:**
月幾望	Moon Nearly Full
馬匹亡，无咎	Horse Mate Run-away, No Faults
象曰 *(孔子)* :	*LinerSign Says (Kongzi)* :
馬匹亡	Horse Mate Run-away
絕類上也	Rejects Kindred, Upward-looking that's

Comments:
Partner FirstNiner like the full moon is far-away, and horse ran-away thus no transport to go.
Neighbor Niner5, King like the full moon that Sixer4 can look-up to with Full Trust, No Faults.
[Xu: 幾84微也殆也 ；望267出亡在外望其還 ；亡267逃也；絕271斷絲也；類205種類相似]

九五：	**Niner5:**
有孚攣如	Has Trust, Binding Like
无咎	No Faults
象曰 *(孔子)：*	*LinerSign Says (Kongzi) :*
有孚攣如	Has Trust Binding Like
位正當也	Position Upright and Proper that's

Comments:
Niner5, Yang in Yang Proper position, as King is Upright in Centre position.
Has Binding Trust with Citizenry, transforming Kingdoms, No Faults.
[Xu: 攣255係也；係167絜束也]

上九：	**TopNiner:**
翰音登于天	Rooster Crowing Rises To Heaven
貞凶	Integrity, yet Ominous
象曰 *(孔子)：*	*LinerSign Says (Kongzi) :*
翰音登于天	Rooster Crowing Rises To Heaven
何可長也	How Can be Sustained that's!

Comments:
TopNiner, weak in Yin position, like Rooster not built for high flight up the Heaven.
On high, trumpeting achievements, Over Trust in own ability, though has Integrity, Ominous.
[Xu: 翰75天雞赤羽也；音58聲也生於心有節於外]

Conclusions:
Core Trust (Hexagram 61): Wetland Trigram below and Wind Trigram above.
Image: Core Trust of a wooden dug-out, sailing the Wetland with a calm Wind following.
Symbolic: Wooden boat, Hexagram's hollow centre of Yins, Trigrams' solid centres of Yangs.

King Wen:
Core Trust that piglets, fishes can feel, favors venture for big tasks, with Integrity Auspicious.

Zhougong:
FirstNiner: benevolent like Yu, Trust in partner Sixer4, solid Wills, no thirty-party, Auspicious.
Niner2: apart, crane family a-calling, Trust from heart like sharing a goblet of wine, Harmony.
Sixer3: and TopNiner both not centre, wrong positions, partners turn enemies, No Trust.
Sixer4: no horse to FirstNiner below, Trust in Niner5 like Full-moon above, No Faults.
Niner5: King centre, right position, has Binding Trust, transform Kingdoms, No Faults.
TopNiner: weak in Yin position, crowing Rooster, Over self-Trust has Integrity, still Ominous.
Descriptions of the working of Core Trust between individuals in various life situations.
Core Trust: even bandits have Core Trust among themselves to share the spoils.

Kongzi:
With Core Trust, Junzi exercises care in penal judgement, stays irreversible execution.
(中孚：信也，雜卦傳)   (Core Trust : honesty that's - Misc.10th 'Wing')

Lessons (Core Trust Hex.61)
Junzi exercises extreme care in penal judgement, stays execution as this is irreversible.
Core Trust is the only pre-requisite needed for nations to sit together to settle differences.

(第六十二卦) 小過　　　　　　　　　**Small Excess (Hexagram 62)**

	上六	＿＿　＿＿	**TopSixer**		**external**
震　(雷, 上卦)	六五	＿＿　＿＿	**Sixer5**	**Zhen (Thunder, Trigram above)**	
	九四	＿＿＿＿＿	**Niner4**		
	九三	＿＿＿＿＿	**Niner3**		
艮　(山, 下卦)	六二	＿＿　＿＿	**Sixe 2**	**Gen (Mountain, Trigram below)**	
	初六	＿＿　＿＿	**FirstSixer**		**internal**

卦辭 *(文王) :*　　　　　　　　　　*Hexagram Text (King Wen) :*

小過：　亨，利貞　　　　　　Small Excess: Prosperity, Favors Integrity

可小事，不可大事　　　　　Allow for Small Matters, Not Allow for Big Matters

飛鳥遺之音　　　　　　　　Flying Bird Legacy of Sound

不宜上，宜下，大吉　　　　Not Suitable Upward, Suitable Downward, Greatly Auspicious

象曰 *(孔子) :*　　　　　　　　　*Tuan Says (Kongzi explains) :*

小過　　　　　　　　　　　Small Excess

小者過而亨也　　　　　　　Small (Yins) Excess And Prosper that's

過以利貞，與時行也　　　　Excess Which Favor Integrity, Marching With Time that's

柔得中　　　　　　　　　　Gentle (Yins) Get Centres (Sixer2 and Sixer5)

是以小事吉也　　　　　　　Therefore Small Matters Auspicious that's

剛失位而不中　　　　　　　StrongYangs Loss Positions And Not Centres (Niner3, Niner4)

是以不可大事也　　　　　　Therefore Not Allow Great Matters that's

有飛鳥之象焉　　　　　　　Has Flying Bird This Image that's

飛鳥遺之音　　　　　　　　Flying Bird Legacy of Sound (passing call)

不宜上宜下，大吉　　　　　Not Suitable Upward Suitable Downward, Greatly Auspicious

上逆而下順也　　　　　　　Upward Resistance Whereas Downward Gliding-easy that'

Comments:

Image: Flying Bird (centre-body of 2 strong Yangs, spread-wings of weak Yins, 2 on each side).

Symbolic: Yin is '"Small", 4 in numbers is "Excess" over the 2 Yangs, hence "Small Excess".

Wen: Sixer2 and Sixer5, Yins centre positions, hence suitable for achievement in small affairs.

Kongzi: Niner3 Niner4, Yangs in wrong positions, hence not suitable for success in big matters.

Flying-bird passing call, suited to be heard below, hence be humble Greatly Auspicious.

[Xu: 過39度也；遺41凶也]

象曰 *(孔子) :*　　　　　　　　　*HexagramSign Says (Kongzi) :*

山上有雷，小過　　　　　　Above Mountain Has Thunder, Small Excess

君子以行過乎恭　　　　　　Junzi With Conduct, Excess in Respect !

喪過乎哀　　　　　　　　　Bereavement, Excess in Sorrow !

用過乎儉　　　　　　　　　Expenditure, Excess in Thrift !

Comments:

Thunder rumbling softly high above the mountain, symbolic of Small Excess.

Junzi in conduct, to show Small Excess in Respect, Sorrow and Thrift, not excessively.

爻辭 *(周公) :*	***Liner Text (Zhougong) :***

初六 : — **FirstSixer:**

飛鳥以凶 — Flying Bird, Braving Danger

象曰 *(孔子) :* — ***LinerSign Says (Kongzi) :***

飛鳥以凶，不可如何也 — Flying Bird Braving Danger, Not Allow Then How that's

Comments:
FirstSixer, to reach partner Niner4 above, needs to fly upwards, braving Danger.
There is no other choice, is there?

六二 : — **Sixer2:**

過其祖，遇其妣 — Over The Patriarch, Meeting The Matriarch

不及其君，遇其臣，无咎 — Not Reaching The King, Meeting The Minister, No Fault

象曰 *(孔子) :* — ***LinerSign Says (Kongzi) :***

不及其君 — Not Reaching The King

臣不可過也 — Minister Not Allow Over that's (missing)

Comments:
Sixer2 trying to reach King Sixer5, is blocked by Niner3 (patriarch) and Niner4 (matriarch).
Try reaching the King but instead meeting the Matriarch, No Faults.

九三 : — **Niner3:**

弗過防之 — No Excess Defence against Them (Yins)

從或戕之，凶 — Accepting Or Killing Them, Ominous

象曰 *(孔子) :* — ***LinerSign Says (Kongzi) :***

從或戕之 — Accommodating Or Killing Them (Yins)

凶如何也 — Ominous Like How that's ?

Comments:
Niner3, strong in Yang position, confident, no excess defence against the 4 Yins (Small people).
In time of Small Excess, joining or opposing them, both ways Ominous.
[Xu: 戕266搶也, 他國臣來弒君曰戕；從169隨行也从从]

九四 : — **Niner4:**

无咎 — No Faults

弗過遇之 — No Excess Meeting Them

往屬必戒 — Go-forth Grave, Certain be Guarded

勿用永貞 — Don't Act, Lasting Integrity

象曰 *(孔子) :* — ***LinerSign Says (Kongzi) :***

弗過遇之，位不當也 — No Excess Meeting Them, Position Not Correct that's

往屬必戒 — Go-forth Grave, Certain be Guarded

終不可長也 — Finally Not Allow Development that's

Comments:
Niner4, weak position, not suited to overly reaching-out to the 4 Yins (Small people)
In time of Excess Yins, best be Guarded, take No Actions, and to maintain lasting Integrity.

六五：	**Sixer5:**
密雲不雨	Thick Clouds, No Rain
自我西郊	From My Western Suburb
公弋取彼在穴	Lord's Arrow (messenger) To-get That (talent) In Cave
象曰 *(孔子)*：	***LinerSign Says (Kongzi)*** *:*
密雲不雨	Thick Clouds, No Rain
已上也	Already High, that's

Comments:
Sixer5, King high with authority, try enlisting the help of Sixer2 for great achievement.
In time of Small Excess, Yins are Ineffective like thick clouds gathering producing no rain.
[Xu: 公28平分也 ；弋265象折木袤鋭著形, 象物挂之也 ；彼43往有所加也]

上六：	**TopSixer:**
弗遇過之	Not Meeting Excess (higher) than It
飛鳥離之，凶	Flying Bird Leaving It, Danger
是謂災眚	This is Disastrous Cataract
象曰 *(孔子)*：	***LinerSign Says (Kongzi)*** *:*
弗遇過之，已亢也	Not Meeting Higher than It, Already Over-top, that's

Comments:
TopSixer, the upper limit of Small Excess, a height where no bird will dwell and leave, Danger.
Yin at top of Yins Excess, is a disastrous situation, like having cataract that leads to blindness.
[Xu: 災209天火 ；眚73目病生翳也 ；亢215人頸也]

Conclusions:
Small Excess (Hexagram 62): Mountain Trigram below and Thunder Trigram above.
Image: Yins is "Small", 4 numbers of Yins is in "Excess" to the 2 Yangs, Small Excess.
Symbolic: Flying Bird's passing-call sinks (heard below) signifies Humility, Greatly Auspicious.

King Wen:
Small Excess augurs Prosperity, favors with Integrity, good for small tasks, not for big matters.
"Flying-bird passing-call", sound suited to descent symbolic of Humility, Greatly Auspicious.

Zhougong:
FirstSixer: lowly going up to partner Niner4 above, like Flying Bird going high, Risk Danger
Sixer2: past over Niner3 (Patriarch), met Niner4 (Matriarch), not reaching Sixer5, no Faults.
Niner3: no excess Defence, Accepting or Killing the 4 Yins (Small people), Braving Danger.
Niner4: in Small Excess, weak going forward Grave, certainly be guarded, don't act, No Faults.
Sixer5: King enlists Sixer2, Yins together ineffective like thick clouds gathered, No Rain.
TopSixer: top of Small Excess, a height Flying-bird do not dwell, like disastrous illness Danger.
Small Excess: dangerous time when Small People are in excess, thus be guarded at all time.

Kongzi:
Above Mountain has Thunder, symbolic of Small Excess; Junzi likewise may not be excessive.
Junzi, shows Small Excess in Respect, Sorrow in Bereavement, and Thrift, never excessive.

(小過：過也，雜卦傳)　　　　　　　　(Small Excess : excessive that's - Misc.10th 'Wing')

Lessons (Small Excess Hex.62)
Small Excess is bad and big Excess is worst with untold consequences, like the poverty gap.

(第六十三卦) 既濟　　　　　　**Completion (Hexagram 63)**

<pre>
        外   上六 __ __   TopSixer   external
坎 (水，上卦) 九五 ______ Niner5   Kan (Water, Trigram above)
        六四 __ __   Sixer4

        九三 ______ Niner3
離 (火，下卦) 六二 __ __   Sixer2   Li (Fire, Trigram below)
        內   初九 ______ FirstNiner   internal
</pre>

卦辭 *(文王)* ：	***Hexagram Text (King Wen) :***
既濟：	Completion :
亨，小，利貞	Prosperity, Small, Favors Integrity
初吉終亂	Initially Auspicious, Ending Turmoil
象曰 *(孔子)* ：	***Tuan Says (Kongzi explains) :***
既濟亨	Completion Prosperity
小者亨也	Small Kind Prosperity that's
利貞	Favors Integrity
剛柔正而位當也	Yang Yin Centres And Positions Correct that's
初吉	Initially Auspicious
柔得中也	Yin (Sixer2) Gain Centre that's
終止則亂	Ending Stop Then Turmoil
其道窮也	The Way Impoverished that's

Comments:
Image: Fire can evaporates Water above, Water can douses fire below, interaction Complete.
Wen: Completion, Prosperity also for Small Kind, Initially Auspicious, Finally Turmoil.
Kongzi: alluding to Wen's as Sixer2 initial Auspiciousness, King Zhou's as Niner5 final Turmoil.
[Xu: 既106小食也；濟228水出常山....]

象曰 *(孔子)* ：	***HexagramSign Says (Kongzi) :***
水在火上，既濟	Water On Fire Top, Completion
君子以思患而豫防之	Junzi With Thinking of Problems And Pre-empting Them

Comments:
Water above Fire, water douses fire, and fire evaporates Water, Completion of interaction.
Junzi thinking of worrying possibilities, takes precautionary measures.
[Xu: 患223憂也]

爻辭 (周公) :	*Liner Text (Zhougong) :*

初九：	**FirstNiner:**
曳其輪	Drag The Wheels
濡其尾，无咎	Immersed The Tail, No Faults
象曰 *(孔子) :*	*LinerSign Says (Kongzi) :*
曳其輪	Dragging The Wheels
義无咎也.	Uprightness No Faults that's

Comments:
Wheels below, Tail behind, warning of difficulties at low level.
Early in time of Completion, slow progress only, has Justice, so No Faults.
[Xu: 曳311曳曳也；曳311束縛捽...；濡228水出涿郡故....]

六二：	**Sixer2:**
婦喪其茀	Woman Lost The Carriage-curtain
勿逐	Don't Chase
七日得	7 Days Regain
象曰 *(孔子) :*	*LinerSign Says (Kongzi) :*
七日得，以中道也	7 Days Regain, With Upright Way that's

Comments:
In Completion, Niner5 complacent not inviting, hence Sixer2 lost reason to travel to join him.
Sixer2, correct position and Upright, warn not to chase, just wait awhile, situation will Resolve.
Xhu: 茀24道多艸,不何行；逐41追也]

九三：	**Niner3:**
高宗伐鬼方	Gao Zong (Emperor) Attacked Gui Land (barbarians to North)
三年克之	3 Years Conquer It
小人勿用	Small People Don't Use
象曰 *(孔子) :*	*LinerSign Says (Kongzi) :*
三年克之，憊也	3 Years Conquer It, Exhaustive that's

Comments:
Emperor Gao Zong pre-emptive attack on Gui Land to the North
Completion in 3 years, exhaustive campaign, so don't listen to Small People's advice.
[Xu: 伐167擊也；克143肩也,....通能勝此物謂之克；憊223...,(忄甫)也]

六四：	**Sixer4:**
繻有衣袽	Leak Has Clothes with Padding
終日戒	Whole Day Guarded
象曰 *(孔子) :*	*LinerSign Says (Kongzi) :*
終日戒，有所疑也	Whole Day Guarded, Has Whatever Worries, that's

Comments:
Sixer4, in Yin position, mindful in time of Completion safety, has preparation for Emergency.
Whole Day Alert, has Clothes with Paddings for plugging any leakage on-board.
[Xu: 繻274繒采色也；(衤如)....；繒273帛也；戒59警也]

九五：	Niner5:
東鄰殺牛	Eastern Neighbors Sacrificing Oxens
不如西鄰之禴祭	Not Comparable to Western Neighbors' Musical Offerings
實受其福	Solidly Receiving The Good-fortune
象曰 (孔子) ：	*LinerSign Says (Kongzi) :*
東鄰殺牛	Eastern Neighbors Sacrificing Oxen
不如西鄰之時也	Not Comparable to Western Neighbors' Timing, that's
實受其福	Solidly Receiving The Good-fortune
吉大來也	Auspiciousness Greatly Cometh, that's

Comments:
In Time of Completion, benevolent King Wen's Ritual Offerings for Good Harvest, Auspicious.
In contrast, evil King Zhou to the East made Grand Sacrificial Offerings of killing Oxen.
[Xu: (衤龠)......；龠48樂之竹管三孔以和眾聲]

上六：	TopSixer:
濡其首，厲	Immersed The Head, Grave
象曰 (孔子) ：	*LinerSign Says (Kongzi) :*
濡其首	Immersed The Head
何可久也	How Can Long-lasting that's ？

Comments:
TopSixer, weak at end of Completion Time, complacent careless Head immersed, Grave.

Conclusions:
Completion (Hexagram 63): Fire Trigram below and Water Trigram above.
Image: Fire below evaporates Water, Water above douses Fire, Completion of interaction.
Symbolic: Yin in Yin position, Yang in Yang position, all Liners in right place, Completion.

King Wen:
Prosperity, of Small Kind, favors Integrity, warns initially Auspicious, careless finally Turmoil.

Zhougong:
FirstNiner: drag Wheels, Immerse Tail, Completion early difficulties, be Righteous No Faults.
Sixer2: centre Upright, woman lost carriage-curtain, don't chase, can wait 7 days to Regain.
Niner3: Gao Zong attacked Gui Land, 3 years to Completion exhausted, SmallOne Don't Use.
Sixer4: Yin in Yin worry whole day, vigilant has cloth-paddings on-board to plug urgent Leak.
Niner5: Easterners sacrificial offerings, in contrast Westerner celebration rites Benevolent. Top-
Sixer: end of Completion, complacent careless, fox's head immersed situation Grave
Completion: warns of early difficulties, delays, ill-advice, emergency, careless at the very end.

Kongzi:
Alluding to Wen's Yin Sixer2 initially Auspicious, King Zhou's Yang Niner5 final Turmoil.
On Completion, Junzi thinks of possible emergency, takes pre-emptive measures.
(既濟：定也，雜卦傳)　　　　　　　(Completion : fixed-state that's - Misc.10th 'Wing')

Lessons (Completion Hex.63)
In Peace and Safety, one must also be vigilant of possible Dangers (居安思危).
On Completion of project, initial usage Auspicious then final Turmoil if careless in maintenance.

（第六十四卦）未濟　　　　　　　　　**Prior Completion (Hexagram 64)**

	上九 _______	**TopNiner**	external
離 （火，上卦）	六五 __ __	**Sixer5**	**Li (Fire, Trigram above)**
	九四 _______	**Niner4**	
	六三 __ __	**Sixer3**	
坎 （水，下卦）	九二 _______	**Niner2**	**Kan (Water, Trigram below)**
	初六 __ __	**FirstSixer**	internal

卦辭 *(文王)* ：　　　　　　　　　　*Hexagram Text (King Wen) :*

未濟：　　　　　　　　　　　　　Prior Completion :

亨　　　　　　　　　　　　　　　Prosperity

小狐汔濟　　　　　　　　　　　　Little Fox Ended Crossing

濡其尾，无攸利　　　　　　　　　Wet Its Tail, No Easy Gain

象曰 *(孔子)* ：　　　　　　　　　*Tuan Says (Kongzi explains) :*

未濟亨　　　　　　　　　　　　　Prior Completion Prosperity

柔得中也　　　　　　　　　　　　Yin Gain Centre that's (ref. Sixer5)

小狐汔濟　　　　　　　　　　　　Little Fox Ended Crossing (river)

未出中也　　　　　　　　　　　　Not Out of Centre that's

濡其尾，无攸利　　　　　　　　　Wet Its Tail, No Easy Gain

不續終也　　　　　　　　　　　　Not Continue till Finality that's

雖不當位，剛柔應也　　　　　　　Though Not Proper Position, Yangs Yins Responding that's

Comments:
Image: Water below drain downward, above Fire burn upward, no interaction, PriorCompletion.
Symbolic: Focus Sixer5, all Liners in wrong positions, though each has corresponding partners.
Wen: Sees Prosperity, warns son Wu, like little fox be careful at ending, gain kingdom not easy.
Kongzi: Sees Prosperity, alluding to Zhou Dynasty, not in positions but all responding, united.

[Xu: 未311昧也...象木重枝葉；齊143禾麥吐穗上平也；汔235水涸也,渴也,盡也；濡228水出...]

象曰 *(孔子)* ：　　　　　　　　　*HexagramSign Says (Kongzi) :*

火在水上，未濟　　　　　　　　　Fire On Water Above, Prior Completion

君子以慎辨物居方　　　　　　　　Junzi With Careful Examination Housing Categories

Comments:
Water drain downward, Fire above burn upward, separate entities, Prior Completion.
Likewise, Junzi carefully differentiate matters, housing them in separate categories.

[Xu: 慎217謹也；居174蹲也从尸,古者居从古]

爻辭 *(周公)* :	*Liner Text (Zhougong) :*

初六： **FirstSixer:**

濡其尾，吝　　Wet Its Tail, Shame

象曰 *(孔子)* : 　*LinerSign Says (Kongzi) :*

濡其尾　　Wet Its Tail

亦不知極也　　Also Not Knowing Finality that's

Comments:
FirstSixer, (young King Wu) beware of Finality of Completion in struggle against King Zhou.
Else like little fox, not careful till the end, wet its Tail Prior Completion of crossing river, Shame.
[Xu: 極....]

九二： **Niner2:**

曳其輪　　Clamp-down The Wheels

貞吉　　Truthfulness Auspicious

象曰 *(孔子)* : 　*LinerSign Says (Kongzi) :*

九二貞吉　　Niner2 Truthfulness Auspicious

中以行正也　　Centre For Action, Uprightness that's

Comments:
Prior Completion, Niner2, Yang strong for action, able to advance against weak Premier Sixer5.
Niner2, Centre Upright, self-control, Wheel-clamp of war chariots, stays Truthful, Auspicious.
{Xu: 曳311臾曳也 ；臾311束縛捽爲臾 ；輪303有輻曰輪]

六三： **Sixer3:**

未濟，征凶　　Prior Completion, Campaign Ominous

利涉大川　　Favor Venturing Big Rivers

象曰 *(孔子)* : 　*LinerSign Says (Kongzi) :*

未濟征凶　　Prior Completion Campaign Ominous

位不當也　　Position Not Proper that's

Comments:
Sixer3 weak Yin, misplaced in Yang position, Not Centre, Campaign Ominous.
Hence suspect there is a missing word 'Not' in front of "Favor Venturing Big Rivers".

九四： **Niner4:**

貞吉，悔亡　　Truthfulness Auspicious, Regrets Lost

震用伐鬼方　　Stirring Deployment Fighting Devils Region

三年有賞于大國　　3 Years Has Award Of Big Kingdom

象曰 *(孔子)* : 　*LinerSign Says (Kongzi) :*

貞吉悔亡　　Truthfulness Auspicious, Regrets Lost

志行也　　Ambitions Fulfilled that's

Comments:
Niner4 Regrets in Yin position, Stirringly Deployed to Fight the Devils Region, Regrets Lost.
Succeeded in 3 Years, Awarded Lordship of a Big kingdom, Ambitions fulfilled.

六五：	**Sixer5:**
貞吉，无悔	Truthfulness Auspicious, No Regrets
君子之光	Junzi His Shining
有孚，吉	Has Trust, Auspicious
象曰 *(孔子)*：	***LinerSign Says (Kongzi)*** *:*
君子之光	Junzi, The Light (of whole Kingdom)
其暉吉也	The Radiance Auspicious that's

Comments:
Sixer5, Centre Has Trust Auspicious, misplaced, but in Premier position No Regrets.
In Prior Completion, Truthful performance brings Radiance to whole Kingdom, Auspicious.
[Xu: 暉138光也]

上九：	**TopNiner:**
有孚于飲酒，无咎	Has Trust In Drinking Wine, No Faults
濡其首，有孚失是	Wet The Head, Has Trust Lost Correctness
象曰 *(孔子)*：	***LinerSign Says (Kongzi)*** *:*
飲酒濡首	Drinking Wine, Wetting Head
亦不知節也	Also Not Knowing Controls that's

Comments:
TopNiner enlightened top of Fire Trigram, has Trust indulgent in Wining No Faults.
Over-confident, losing controls, got drunk wetting Head, Judgement Lost Correctness that's.
Laozi says: Good-fortune indeed, where misfortune lurks. [Daodejing chapter 58]

Conclusions:
Prior Completion (Hexagram 64): Water Trigram below and Fire Trigram above.
Image: Water draining below, Fire burning above, no interaction, Prior Completion.
Symbolic: Focus Sixer5, All Liners wrong Positions, hence Prior Completion.

King Wen:
Prosperity, little fox nearing success in crossing river, wetted its tail, no easy gain in life.
Prior Completion, warns son (Wu) be vigilant till Completion, fighting King Zhou no easy gain.

Zhougong:
FirstSixer: Wetted its tail not knowing Completion has Finality, Prior Completion a Shame.
Niner2: Yang can challenge Sixer5, wheel-clamped chariots, centre stays Truthful, Auspicious.
Sixer3: weak, misplaced, not centre, (not) favor venturing big river, campaign Ominous.
Niner4: Yin positioned, 3 years fighting Devils Region, Awarded Kingdom, Truthful Auspicious.
Sixer5: Truthful Yin King Auspicious, has Trust a Beacon to Citizenry, doubly Auspicious.
TopNiner: has Trust, indulges in Wine No Faults, lost control, wetting Head Correctness Lost.
Prior Completion: all liners wrong positions, suggests new Cycle of Changes to put them right.

Kongzi:
Prosperity alluding to Zhou Dynasty, all liners not in positions but corresponding for success.
Prior Completion, Junzi examines all matters, differentiates them and knows where each stays.
(未濟：男之窮也，雜卦傳) (Prior Completion : man's ultimate that's - Misc.10th Wing)

Lessons (Prior Completion Hex.64)
Little fox wets tail at the last moment, we learn the importance of the Finality of Completion.
Little fox inexperience in the last Hex.64, also signifies a New Cycle of Changes and Learning.
Yijing: Wisdom of 4 Sages

繫辭上傳
(孔子.五翼)

Attached Text Upper Commentary
(Kongzi. 5th Wing)

天尊地卑	Heaven Honorable, Earth Lowly
乾坤定矣	Qian (Heaven) Kun (Earth) Set (status) indeed
卑高以陳	Lowliness Highness Are Displayed
貴賤位矣	Nobility Humbleness Positioned indeed
動靜有常	Action Inaction Have Regularity
剛柔斷矣	Strength (Yang) Gentleness (Yin) Clear-cut indeed
方以類聚	Forms Of a Kind Gather
物以羣分	Matters Of a Group Separate
吉凶生矣	Fortune Misfortune Arise indeed
在天成象	In Heaven Become Sign-images
在地成形	On Earth Become Solid-shapes
變化見矣	Changes Transformations Visible indeed
是故剛柔相摩	Therefore Strength Gentleness Mutually Interacting
八卦相盪	8-Kua (Trigrams) Mutually Interacting
鼓之以雷霆	Drumming-up Them With Thunder Rumbling
潤之以風雨	Moisturizing Them With Wind and Rain
日月運行	Sun Moon Cycling Moving
一寒一暑	One Cold (winter) One Hot (summer)
乾道成男	Qian (Heaven) Path Produces Male
坤道成女	Kun (Earth) Path Produces Female
乾知大始	Qian (Heaven) Knows the Great Origin
坤作成物	Kun (Earth) Labor Produces Matters
乾以易知	Qian (Heaven) With Yi Knows
坤以簡能	Kun (Earth) With Simplicity Enables
易則易知	Yi Thus Easy to Know
簡則易從	Simplicity Thus Easy to Follow
易知則有親	Yi Knows Thus Has Love
易從則有功	Yi Follows Thus Has Achievement
有親則可久	Has Love Thus Can be Long-lasting
有功則可大	Has Achievement Thus Can be Great
可久則賢人之德	Can be Long-lasting, That's Sage Person's Virtue
可大則賢人之業	Can be Great, That's Sage Person's Achievement

易簡而天下之理得矣	Yi Simplicity Thus The World's Logics Acquire that's
天下之理得	The World's Logic Acquire
而成位乎其中矣	And Successfully Position In The Midst indeed

Comments (para.1):

Sage Person builds his achievement on Yi which is easy to know, simple to follow.

Thus gaining a position between Heaven and Earth, and be a factor of the Trinity (三才).

[Xu: 易198蜥易(虫堰)蜒守宮也象形,祕書說日月爲易 ；簡95牒也；牒143札也]

第二章	***Paragraph 2***
聖人設卦觀象	Sage Persons Set-up Kua (Hexagrams) Observe Signs
繫辭焉而明吉凶	Attached Text That's To Understand Fortune Misfortune
剛柔相推而生變化	Yang Yin Mutual Interaction To Cause Changes Transformation
是故：	Therefore :
吉凶者	Fortune Misfortune Entities
得失之象也	Gain Loss Their Signs that's
悔吝者	Regrets Shame Entities
憂虞之象也	Worries Fears Their Signs that's
變化者	Changes Transformation Entities
進退之象也	Advance Retreat Their Signs that's
剛柔者	Yang Yin Entities
晝夜之象也	Day Night Their Signs that's
六爻之動	6 Liners Their Actions
三極之道也	3 Limits Their Paths that's
是故：	Therefore :
君子所居而安	Junzi (Gentleman) Wherever Stays And be Safe
易之序也	Yi Its Sequence that's
所樂而玩者	Entities For Enjoyable Appreciative-Play
爻之辭也	Liners' Texts that's (for imaginative interpretations)
是故：	Therefore :
君子	Junzi (Gentleman)
居則觀其象	Inaction Then Observe The Sign
而玩其辭	And Imaginative-Play with The Text (vary interpretations)
動則觀其變	Action Then Observe The Changes
而玩其占	And interpretative-Play with The Divination
是以：	Therefore :
自天佑之吉无不利	With Heaven Protection The Auspiciousness None Not Favorable

Comments (para.2):

Sages create Yi-Hexagrams, Junzi enjoys interpretive-Play with the written texts and learning.

第三章	*Paragraph 3*
彖者	Tuan Entity
言乎象者也	Speaks of Sign Entity that's (Hexagram)
爻者	Liner Entity
言乎變者也	Speaks Of Changes Entity that's
吉凶者	Fortune Misfortune Entities
言乎其失得也	Speak Of The Loss and Gain that's
悔吝者	Regrets Shame Entities
言乎其小疵也	Speak Of The Small Defects that's
无咎者	No Faults Entity
善補過也	Good at Mending Mistakes that's
是故：	Therefore:
列貴賤者	List the Honorable the Humble Such-things
存乎位	Registered In the Position (status)
齊小大者	Square-up Small Big Such-things
存乎卦	Registered In the Hexagrams
辨吉凶者	Assessing Fortune Misfortune Such-things
存乎辭	Registered In the Texts
憂悔吝者	Worries Regrets Shame Such-things
存乎介	Registered In the Mindfulness
震无咎者	Actions No Faults Such-things
存悔	Registered In Regrets
是故：	Therefore :
卦有小大	Hexagrams Have Small Big
辭有險易	Texts Have Dangerous types Easy kinds
辭也者，各指其所之	Texts Such-things that's, Each Pointing To Its Purpose

Comments (para.3):
This paragraph highlight the general attributes of Hexagrams (for sign), Liners (for changes).

第四章	*Paragraph 4*
易與天地準	Yi With Heaven Earth Alignment
故能彌綸天地之道	Hence Can Connect Accord with Heaven Earth Their Paths
仰以觀于天文	Look-up To Observe In Heaven, Patterns
俯以察于地理	Crouch-down To Examine On Earth, Orders
是故：	Therefore :
知幽明之故	Knows Dark Light Their Reasons
原始反終	Trace to Beginning, Return to Ending
故知死生之銳	Hence Knows Death Life Such Sharpness (contrasts)
精氣爲物	Essence of Air For Matters
遊魂爲變	Roaming Spirits For Changes

是故：	Therefore :
知鬼神之情狀	Knows Devils God-spirits Their Feelings Conditions
與天地相似	With Heaven Earth Mutually Alike
故不違	Hence Not Confronting
知周乎萬物而道濟天下	Knows Thoroughly Of All Matters And 'Dao' Ordered The World
故不過	Hence Not Excessive
旁行而不流	Side Actions And Not Flowing-along (incorruptible)
樂天知命	*Happy with Heaven Knows Destiny*
故不憂	*Hence Not Worry*
安土敦乎仁	Quiet Land, Trust With Benevolence
故能愛	Hence Able to Love
範圍天地之化	Defined Area of Heaven Earth Their Transformations
而不過	And Not Excessive
曲成萬物	Conforming Forming All Matters
而不遺	And None Left-behind
通乎晝夜之道	Connection Of Day Night Their Ways
而知	And Knows
故神无方	Hence God-spirit has No Form
而易无體	And Yi has No Body

Comments (para.4):
The Greatness of Yi is lauded, saying Junzi uses it to know and guide Destiny.

第五章	**Paragraph 5**
一陰一陽之謂道	*One Yin One Yang, This Call 'Dao' (Path, Way)*
繼之者善也	Entity Succeeding It, Goodness that's
成之者性也	Entity Forming It, Logic that's
仁者見之謂之仁	*Benevolent Person Sees It Call It Benevolence*
知者見之謂之知	*Knowledgeable Person Sees It Call It Knowledge*
百姓日用而不知	Citizens Daily Using And Not Knowing
故君子之道鮮矣	Hence Junzi's (Gentleman's) 'Dao' Rare Indeed
顯諸仁藏諸用	Manifest In Benevolence Hidden In Usage
鼓萬物而不與聖人同憂	Activate All Matters And Not With The Sage Together Worry
盛德大業至矣哉	Thriving Virtues Great Successes Achieved Indeed that's
富有	Wealth Having
之謂之大業	This Call Great Achievement
日新	Daily Renewal
之謂盛德	This Call Flourishing Virtues

生生	Creation Creation
之謂易	This Call Yi
成象	Formation of Signs
之謂乾	This Call Qian (Heaven)
效法	Conforming Methods
之謂坤	This Call Kun (Earth)
極數知來	Ultimate of Numbers Knows what's Coming
之謂占	This Call Divination
通變	Connecting Changes
之謂事	This Call Affairs
陰陽不測	Yin Yang Not Predictable
之謂神	This Call God-like

Comments (para.5):
'Dao' expression through the interactions of Yin and Yang which are also unpredictable.

第六章	*Paragraph 6*
夫易，廣矣大矣	O' Yi, Broad Indeed Big indeed
以言乎遠則不禦	With Talk About Far-distance Then No Limit (selfless)
以言乎邇則靜而正	With Talk About Neighborhood Then Quiet And Upright
以言乎天地之間則備矣	With Talk About Heaven-Earth's Space Then All-prepared indeed
夫乾	O' Qian (Heaven)
其靜也專	Its Quietude that's Focus
其動也直	Its Action that's Straight
是以，大生焉	Therefore, Great Creation indeed (quality)
夫坤	O' Kun (Earth)
其靜也翕	Its Quietude that's Close
其動也闢	Its Action that's Open
是以，廣生焉	Therefore, Broad Creation indeed (quantity)
廣大配天地	Broad and Great Match Heaven Earth
變通配四時	Changes Connection Match 4 Seasons
陰陽之義配日月	Yin Yang Their Meaning Match Sun Moon
易簡之善配至德	Yi Simplicity Their Goodness Match Absolute Virtue ('One')

Comments (para.6):
O' Yi quiet in nature, in Heaven on Earth, align with Sun Moon, changes with 4 Seasons.
[Xu: 禦9祀也，祀8祭無已，祭8祭祀也，翕75起也；闢248開也]

第七章	*Paragraph 7*
子曰：	*Teacher Says :*
易其至矣乎	Yi, Its Absolute Indeed that's
夫易	O' Yi
聖人所以崇德	Sage Person Reasons For Respecting Virtues
而廣業也	And Expanding Achievements that's
知崇禮卑	Knows Respect, Courteous to the Humble
崇效天	Respect, Emulate Heaven
卑法地	Humbleness, Emulate Earth
天地設位	Heaven Earth Establish Position (status)
而易行乎其中矣	And Yi Action In Its Midst indeed
成性存存，道義之門	Form Logic Ever-lasting, The Door to Uprightness

Comments (para.7):
Yi working in Society through the Sages, with Respect of Heaven and Humility of Earth.

第八章	*Paragraph 8*
聖人	Sage Person
有以見天下之賾	Able To See Mysteries of The World
而擬諸其形容	And Concentrate On Their Forms and Appearances
象其物宜	Signs Of Material Compatibility
是故：謂之象	Therefore : Call It Signs
聖人	Sage Person
有以見天下之動	Able To See Actions of The World
而觀其會通	And Observe Their Meeting and Connectivity
以行其典禮	To Implement The Classic Etiquette
繫辭焉以斷其吉凶	Attached Text That's To Determine The Fortune Misfortune
是故：謂之爻	Therefore : Call It Liners
言天下之至賾	Speaking of Extreme Mysteries of The World
而不可惡也	And Not Allow to Hate that's
言天下之至動	Speaking of Extreme Actions of The World
而不可亂也	And Not Allow to Confuse that's
擬之而後言	Plan It And Afterwards Speak-up
議之而後動	Discuss It And Afterwards Action
擬議以成其變化	Plan Discuss To Achieve Its Changes Transformations

鳴鶴在陰	*"Calling Crane In the Dark*
其子和之	*　The Young Harmonizes It*
我有好爵	*I Have Fine Goblet*
吾與爾靡之	*　I With You Enjoy It "*
(中孚. 第六十一卦. 九二)	(Core Trust. Hexagram 61. Niner2)
子曰：	*Teacher Says :*
君子居其室，出其言善	Junzi Stays At Home, Speaking Out Kind Words
則千里之外應之	Then Thousand Miles Away Responding to Them
況其邇者乎	Let Alone the Neighborhood People that's
居其室，出其言不善	Stays At Home, Speaking Out Unkind Words
則千里之外違之	Then Thousand Miles Away Opposing Them
況其邇者乎	Let Alone the Neighborhood People that's
言出乎身，加乎民	Words Emerge From Self, Affecting The Citizens
行發乎邇，見乎遠	Action Issue-forth From Neighborhood, Seen From Afar
言行，君子之樞機	Speech Action, Junzi's Centre of Administration
樞機之發，榮辱之主也	Centre Administration's Issuance, Master Of Shame Honor that's
言行	Speech Action
君子之所以動天地也	With Which Junzi Moves Heaven and Earth that's
可不慎乎	Possible Not be Careful that's !

同人先號咷而後笑	*"Comrades First Howling Wailing And Later Laugh"*
(同人. 第十三卦. 九五)	(Comrades. Hexagram 13. Niner5)
子曰：	*Teacher Says :*
君子之道	Junzi (Gentleman) His Way
或出或處	May Leave, May Stay
或默或語	May be Silent, May Speak
二人同心	2 Persons Same Hearts (Wills)
其利斷金	Its Sharpness Cut Metal (combined strength)
同心之言	Same Hearts' Speaking
其臭如蘭	The Smell Like Fragrance

初六藉用白茅，无咎	*"FirstSixer Use of White Thatches, No Faults"*
(大過. 第二十八卦. 初六)	(Great Excess. Hexagram 28. FirstSixer)
子曰：	*Teacher Says :*
苟錯諸地而可矣	Carelessly Spread on Floor Is Allowed indeed
藉之用茅，何咎之有	Ritual-mats Using Thatches, What Faults Is Having ?
慎之至也	Carefulness At Extreme that's
夫茅之爲物薄	O' Thatches This As Material Thin (cheap)
而用可重也	But Usage Can be Heavy that's (important)
慎斯術也以往	Careful with This Rites that's Like Before
其无所失矣	That None Whatever be Lost indeed (rites)

勞謙：　　　　　　　　　*"Accomplished Humility*

君子有终，吉　　　　　*Junzi (Gentleman) Has Finality, Auspicious"*

(謙. 第十五卦. 九三)　　(Humility. Hexagram 15. Niner3)

子曰：　　　　　　　　*Teacher Says :*

勞而不伐　　　　　　　Labor And Not Boastful

有功而不德　　　　　　Has Success And Not Virtuous (not claiming)

厚之至也　　　　　　　Solid To the Extreme that's (honesty)

語以其功，下人者也　　Speech With Claim to Credit, Kind of Lowly People that's

德言盛　　　　　　　　Virtues, Speak of Flourishing

　禮言恭　　　　　　　　Etiquette, Speak of Respect

謙也者　　　　　　　　Of Humility that's

　致恭以存其位者也　　　Person With Extreme Respect to Keep The Status that's

亢龍有悔　　　　　　　*"Stubborn Dragon Has Regrets"*

(乾. 第一卦. 上九)　　(Heaven. Hexagram 01. TopNiner)

子曰：　　　　　　　　*Teacher Says :*

貴而无位　　　　　　　Honorable But No Position (of authority)

　高而无民　　　　　　　High-ranking But No Citizens (support)

賢人在下位　　　　　　Virtuous-Talent In Lowly Position (such as)

　而无輔　　　　　　　　With No Help

是以動而有悔也　　　　Therefore Actions And Has Regrets that's

不出戶庭，无咎　　　　*"Not Stepping-out Homestead Courtyard, No Faults"*

(節. 第六十卦. 初九)　(Thrift. Hexagram 60. FirstNiner)

子曰：　　　　　　　　*Teacher Says :*

亂之所生也　　　　　　Reason for Causing Chaos that's

則言語以爲階　　　　　Thus Speech Loose-Talk Are the Steps (leading to chaos)

君子不密則失臣　　　　Junzi Not Secret-keeper Thus Lose Minister

臣不密則失身　　　　　Minister Not Secret-keeper Thus Lose Self

幾事不密則害成　　　　Planned Affairs Not Secret-safe Thus Harming Success

是以：　　　　　　　　Therefore :

君子慎密而不去出也　　Junzi Careful of Secrets And Not Venture Out that's

子曰：　　　　　　　　*Teacher Says :*

作易者　　　　　　　　Person Writing Yi

　其知盜乎　　　　　　　Does He Know Bandits ?

易曰：　　　　　　　　*Yi Says :*

負且乘致寇至　　　　　*"Loaded And Riding Thus Bandits Coming"*

(解. 第四十卦. 六三)　(Resolving. Hexagram 40. Sixer3)

負也者	This Loaded that's (riches)
小人之事也	Small Person's Affairs that's
乘也者	This Riding that's (grand)
君子之器也	Junzi's Carriage that's
小人而乘君子之器	Small Person And Riding Junzi's Carriage
盜思奪之矣	Bandits Consider Robbing It indeed
上慢下暴	Seniors Arrogant Juniors Violent
盜思伐之矣	Bandits Consider Robbing Them indeed
慢藏誨盜	Lazy to Cover-up Invites Bandits (flouting wealth)
冶容誨淫	Flirtatious Make-up Invites Licentious-conduct
易曰：	*Yi Says :*
負且乘致盜至	*"Loaded (riches) And Riding (grand) Till Bandits Come"*
盜之招也	Bandits' Attraction that's

Comments (para.8):
Kongzi elaborates on the Hexagrams texts and Liners text when disciples asked.

第九章	***Paragraph 9***
天一，地二	Heaven 1, Earth 2
天三，地四	Heaven 3, Earth 4
天五，地六	Heaven 5, Earth 6
天七，地八	Heaven 7, Earth 8
天九，地十	Heaven9, Earth 10
天數五，地數五	Heaven Numbers 5, Earth Numbers 5
五位相得而各有合	5 Positions Mutually Obtain And Each Has Combination
天數二十有五	Heaven Counts 25
地數三十	Earth Counts 30
凡天地之數五十有五	All Heaven Earth Their Counts 50 Plus 5
此所以成變化	This is What Causes Changes And Transformations
而行鬼神也	And Move Devils God-spirits that's
大衍之數五十	Great Display Its Counts 50
其用有四十九	Its Usage Has 49
分而爲二以象兩	Separate And Be 2 To Image 2 (Yin / Yang) (step 1)
掛一以象三	Hang 1 To Image 3 (step 2)
揲之以象四時	Grouping Them (by 4s) To Image 4 Seasons (step 3)
歸奇於扐以象閏	Return Odd-straw Divine To Image Leap-year (step 4)
五歲再閏	5 Years Again Intercalary-month (of lunar calendar)
故再扐而後掛	Thus Again Divine And After Hang (straws between fingers)

乾之策，二百一十有六	Qian (Heaven) Its Straw-count, 210 Plus 6 (!)
坤之策，百四十有四	Kun (Earth) Its Straw-count, 140 Plus 4 (!)
凡三百有六十，當朞之日	All 300 Plus 60, As Year's Days (number)
二篇之策	2 Sections Their Straw-counts
萬有一千五百二十	10-Thousand Plus 1 Thousand 5 Hundred and 20 (!)
當萬物之數也	As All Matters Their Numbers that's (total 11,520) (!)
是故四營而成易	Therefore 4 Admin-steps To Form Yi
十有八變而成卦	10 Plus 8 Changes To Form Hexagram (total 18)
八卦而小成	8 Trigrams Is Small Success
引而伸之	Leading And Extending It
觸類而長之	Contacting Kinds And Growing It (to 64 Hexagrams)
天下之能事畢矣	The World's Possible Affairs Complete indeed (inclusive)
顯道神德行	Manifesting 'Dao', God-spirits, Virtuous Conduct
是故：	Therefore :
可與酬酢	Possible For Discussion Consultation
可與佑神矣	Possible For Assisting God-spirits indeed (to help us)
子曰：	*Teacher Says :*
知變化之道者	Knows Changes Transformation Their "Dao", such Person
其知神之所爲乎	Who Knows God-spirits Their Whatever Doings that's

Comments (para.9):
Principled Numerical handling of 50 Straws in 4 steps and to repeat 3 rounds for each Liner.
Hence a total of 3x6=18 rounds or changes for the 6 liners of each Hexagram randomly produce.
Hexagrams are Divination tools which assist God-spirits to help us in our Consultations.
Purportedly, this is Kongzi's description of how to raise a Hexagram with Yallow-straws.
(!) It is a mystery how these numbers are arrived at and added up.
YouTube may be accessed to see how some diviners do above procedure to raise a Hexagram..

第十章	*Paragraph 10*
易有聖人之道四焉	Yi Has Sage Person's 4 Paths that's
以言者尚其辭	Regarding The Speech, Respect The Texts
以動者尚其變	Regarding The Actions, Respect The Changes
以制器者尚其象	Regarding The Making of Instruments, Respect The Signs
以卜筮者尚其占	Regarding The Divination Straws, Respect The Predictions
是以：	Therefore :
君子將有爲也	Junzi (Gentleman) Going to Have Achievement that's
將有行也	Going to Have Action that's

問焉而以言	Ask Indeed And Be Informed
其受命也如嚮	The Acceptance of Orders that's Like Directions
无有遠近幽深	Not Having Far/Near, Dark/Depth (such insights)
遂知來物	Chasing Awareness of Coming Matters (predicting)
非天下之至精	Not The World's Extreme Essence
其孰能與於此	Then Who's Able to Be Like This
參伍以變	Stars and Company For Changes
錯綜其數	Left/right Up/down The Numbers (interacting)
通其變遂成天下之文	Connecting The Changes To Form The World's Patterns
極其數遂定天下之象	Extreme Of Numbers To Fix the World's Signs
非天下之至變	Not The World's Extreme Changes
其孰能與於此？	Then Who's Able Be Like This?
易无思也	Yi, No Thought that's (selfless)
无爲也	Not Selfish that's
寂然不動	Quiet Naturally Not Moving
感而遂通天下之故	Feeling And Then Connecting The World's Facts
非天下之至神	Not The World's Extreme God-like
其孰能與于此？	Then Who's Able to Be Like This?
夫易	O' Yi
聖人之所以極深	Sage Person, Reason For Being Extremely Deep
而研幾也	With Examination of Intricacy that's
唯深也	Only Deep that's
故能通天下之志	Hence Able Connecting The World's Will
唯幾也	Only Micro-manage that's
故能成天下之務	Hence Able to Complete The World's Affairs
唯神也	Only God-like that's
故不疾而速	Hence Not Speeding Yet Fast
不行而至	No Action Yet Arrive
子曰：	*Teacher Says :*
易有聖人之道四焉者	Yi Has Sage Person's Paths 4 Indeed that's
此之謂也	Above The Description that's (of the 4 Paths)

Comments (para.10):
Kongzi elaborates how Yi assists the Sage in 4 ways, Words for Expression and Action.
Also Signs for Tools-making and Divination.

[Xu: 參141商星也，伍164相參伍也；幾84微也殆也]

第十一章	*Paragraph 11*
子曰：	*Teacher Says:*
夫易，何爲者也	O' Yi, What Its Use, that's
夫易，開物成務	O' Yi, Initiate Matters Complete Tasks
冒天下之道	Inclusive of The World's Way
如斯而已者也	Like This And Just This that's
是故：	Therefore :
聖人	Sage Person
以通天下之志	For Connecting The World's Wills
以定天下之業	For Fixing The World's Affairs
以斷天下之疑	For Breaking The World's Uncertainties
是故：	Therefore :
蓍之德圓而神	Thatch-grass's Virtue, Rounded And God-like
卦之德方以知	Hexagram's Virtue, Squared To Know
六爻之義易以貢	6 Liners' Values, Yi For Contribution
聖人以此	Sage Person With This
洗心退藏於密	Clear Heart, Retreat to Hide In Secrecy
吉凶與民同患	Fortune Misfortune With Citizens Sharing Problems
神以知來，知以藏往	God-like To Know the Coming, Knows To Hide or Venture
其孰能與於此哉	Then Who Able Be Like This indeed
古之聰明睿知	Ancients' Hearing Seeing Sharp and Knowing
神武而不殺者夫	God-like Valiant But Not Killer-like Person O'
是以：	Therefore :
明於天之道	Understanding Of Heaven's Way
而察於民之故	And Discerning Of Citizens' Needs
是興神物以前民用	Is Activating God-like Matter For Use of Ancient Citizens
聖人以此齊戒	Sage Person With These Together on Guard
以神明其德夫	With God-like Understanding The Virtues O'
是故：	Therefore :
闔戶謂之坤	Close Door, Call It Kun (Earth)
闢戶謂之乾	Open Door, Call It Qian (Heaven)
一闔一闢謂之變	1 Close 1 Open, Call It Change
往來不窮謂之通	Going Coming None Stop Call It Connectivity
見乃謂之象	Seeing Then Call It Sign
形乃謂之器	Forming Then Call It Instrument
制而用之謂之法	Make And Use It Call It Method
利用出入	Making Use of the Out/In
民咸用之謂之神	Citizens All Using It, Call It God-like
是故：	Therefore :
易有大極	Yi Has Great Limit (Ultimate Reality) (0 pattern)

是生兩儀	This Create 2 Energies (Yin and Yang) (1-liner 2 patterns)
兩儀生四象	2 Energies Create 4 Signs (2-liners 4 patterns)
四象生八卦	4 Signs Create 8 Trigrams (3-liners 8 patterns)
八卦定吉凶	8 Trigrams Fix Fortune Misfortune
吉凶生大業	Fortune Misfortune Create Great Achievements
是故：	Therefore :
法象	Emulate Signs
莫大乎天地	None Greater Than Heaven Earth
變通	Changes Connectivity
莫大乎四時	None Greater Than 4 Seasons
縣象著明	Hang-down Signs Focusing Clarity
莫大乎日月	None Greater Than Sun Moon
崇高	Respecting Highness
莫大乎富貴	None Greater Than the Wealthy the Nobility
備物致用	Stock-up Matters Ready for Use
立成器以爲天下利	Set-up Complete Instruments For Benefiting The World
莫大乎聖人	None Greater Than Sage Person
探賾索隱	Investigate Mysteries Discovering the Hidden
鉤深致遠	Examine Depth to Extreme Distance
以定天下之吉凶	For Fixing The World's Fortune Misfortune
成天下之亹亹者	Becoming The World's Tired-less Entity
莫大乎蓍龜	None Greater Than Yellow-straws and Turtle
是故：	Therefore:
天生神物	Heaven Creating God-like Matter
聖人則之	Sage Person Measure It
天地變	Heaven Earth Changes
聖人效之	Sage Person Emulate It
天垂象	Heaven Hang-down Signs
見吉凶	See Fortune Misfortune
聖人象之	Sage Person Image Them (Hexagrams)
河出圖	River Emerges Diagram (number pattern 1-10 on legendary horse)
洛出書	Luo-River Emerges Script(number pattern 1-9 on legendary turtle)
聖人則之	Sage Person Study Them
易有四象	Yi Has 4 Signs
所以示也	With-which To Show that's
繫辭焉	Attached Script Indeed
所以告也	With-which To Inform that's
定之以吉凶	Fix It With Fortune Misfortune
所以斷也	With-which To Predict that's

Comments (para.11):
The creation and usage of Yi for Divination, for promoting Fortune avoiding Misfortune.

第十二章	*Paragraph 12*
易曰：	*Yi Says :*
自天祐之	With Heaven Protecting It
吉无不利	Auspicious None Not Favorable
子曰：	*Teacher Says :*
祐者，助也	Protection Entity, Assistance that's
天之所助者	Person That Heaven Will Assists
順也	Compliant that's
人之所助者	Person That People Will Assist
信也	Honest that's
履信思乎順	Treading Honesty Thinking Of Compliance
又以尚賢也	Again For Respecting the Virtuous that's
是以：	Therefore :
自天祐之	With Heaven Protecting It
吉无不利也	Auspicious None Not Favorable that's
子曰：	*Teacher Says :*
書不盡言	Written-script, No Complete Saying
言不盡意	Saying, No Complete Will (expression)
然則聖人之意	But Then Sage Person's Will
其不可見乎	Can't It Be Seen Then ? (for the common good)
子曰：	*Teacher Says :*
聖人立象以盡意	Sage Person Set-up Signs To Complete Will (expression)
設卦以盡情偽	Stage Hexagram To Complete Feelings Falsehood (expression)
繫辭焉以盡其言	Attached Texts Indeed To Complete The Sayings
變而通之以盡利	Changes And Connecting It To Complete Benefiting
鼓之舞之以盡神	Drumming It Dancing It To Complete God-spirit (revelation)
乾坤其易之縕耶	Qian (Heaven) Kun (Earth) Their Inclusion in Yi, that's
乾坤成列	Qian Kun Complete Formation (universe)
而易立乎其中矣	And Yi is Set-up In The Midst indeed
乾坤毀	Qian Kun Destroyed (universe)
則无以見易	Then Nothing with which To See Yi
易不可見	Yi Not be Seen
則乾坤或幾乎息矣	Then Qian Kun May Almost Be Extinguished indeed

是故：	Therefore :
形而上者	Forms And Above Entities
謂之道	Call Them Dao
形而下者	Forms And Below Entities
謂之器	Call Them Instruments
化而裁之	Transform And Tailor Them
謂之變	Call Them Changes
推而行之	Push And Run Them
謂之通	Call Them Connectivity
舉而措之天下之民	Lift And Place Them on The World's Citizens
謂之事業	Call Them Affairs Achievements

是故：	Therefore :
夫象	O' Signs
聖人有以見天下之賾	Sage Person Has Means to See The World's Revelations
而擬諸其形容	And Concentrate On The Forms and Appearances
象其物宜	Image Of Matters Compatibility
是故謂之象	Therefore Call Them Signs
聖人有以見天下之動	Sage Person Has Means to See The World's Actions
而觀其會通	And Observe The Meetings Connectivities
以行其典禮	To Run The Classic Rites
繫辭焉以斷其吉凶	Attached Text Indeed To Determine The Fortune Misfortune
是故謂之爻	Therefore Call Them Yao (Liners)

極天下之賾者	That-which Exhausting World's Mysteries
存乎卦	Founded In Hexagrams
鼓天下之動者	That-which Drumming The World's Actions
存乎辭	Founded In Texts
化而裁之	Transform And Tailor Them
存乎變	Founded In Changes
推而行之	Push And Run Them
存乎通	Founded In Connectivity
神而明之	God-like And Clarify Them
存乎其人	Founded In The People
默而成之	Silence And Completing Them
不言而信	No Talk But has Trust
存乎德行	Founded In Virtuous Conduct

Comments: (para.12)
Hexagrams and Liners, their Changes and Connections are dependent on the People.
That People can be God-like, be Enlightened, are Founded on having Virtuous Conduct.

繫辭下傳 (孔子，六翼)	**Attached Text Lower Commentary** **(Kongzi, 6th Wing)**
八卦成列	8 Trigrams Formation Listed
象在其中矣	Signs In The Midst indeed
因而重之	Hence Forth Doubling It
爻在其中矣	Yao (Liners) In The Midst indeed
剛柔相推	Strong (Yang) Gentle (Yin) Mutually Interacting
變在其中矣	Changes In The Midst indeed
繫辭焉，而命之	Attached Text That's, And Ordering It
動在其中矣	Actions In The Midst indeed
吉凶悔吝者	Fortune Misfortune Regrets Shame, as Such
生乎	Life O'
動者也	Is Action that's
剛柔者	Yang Yin as Such
立本者也	Are Core Set-up that's
變通者	Changes Connectivities as Such
趣時者也	Are Interesting Timing that's
吉凶者	Fortune Misfortune as Such
貞勝者也	Are Divination Victory that's
天地之道	Heaven Earth Their Ways
貞觀者也	Are Pure Observation that's
日月之道	Sun Moon Their Way
貞明者也	Are Pure Brightness that's
天下之動	The World's Actions
貞夫一者也	Are Pure O' One that's
夫乾	O' Qian (Heaven)
確然示人易矣	Certainly Naturally Presenting to People Yi that's
夫坤	O' Kun (Earth)
隤然示人簡矣	Softly Naturally Presenting to People Simplicity that's
爻也者	Yao (Liners) that's as Entity
效此者也	Are Emulating This that's
象也者	Signs that's as Entity
像此者也	Are Imaging This that's
爻象	Yao (Liners) Signs
動乎內	Action In the Internal (at home)
吉凶	Fortune Misfortune
見乎外	Seen In the External (in society)
功業	Success Achievements
見乎變	Seen In the Changes

聖人之情	Sage Person's Love
見乎辭	Seen In the Text
天地之大德	Heaven Earth Their Great Virtues
曰生	Call-it Life
聖人之大寶	Sage Person's Big Treasure
曰位	Call-it Status
何以守位	How Else Guarding Status
曰仁	Call-it Benevolence
何必聚人	Why Necessary Gathering People
曰財	Call-it Wealth
理財正辭	Managing Wealth Correct Words
禁民爲非	Prevent Citizens Doing Evils
曰義	Call-it Justice

Comments (para.1) :
Hexagrams and Liners depicting Fortune, Misfortune, Changes and Achievements.

第二章	**Paragraph 2**
古者	Ancient Person
包犧氏之王天下也	Baoyishi As King of The World that's (legendary leader)
仰則觀象於天	Look-up To Observe Signs In Heaven
俯則觀法於地	Bend-over To Observe Regularities On Earth
觀鳥獸之文	Observe Birds Animals Their Patterns
與地之宜	With Earth's Compatibility
近取諸身	Near-by Obtain From Body
遠取諸物	Afar Obtain From Matters
於是	Therefore
始作八卦	Start Making 8 Trigrams
以通	To Connect
神明之德	God-Enlighten's Virtues
以類	To Emulate
萬物之情	All Matters' Feelings
作結繩	Working Knots of Ropes
而爲網罟	To Make Net Trap
以佃以漁	For Hunting For Fishing
蓋取諸　離	All Obtain From Fire-shine (Hexagram 30)
包犧氏沒	Baoyishi Demised (legendary leader)
神農氏作	Shennongshi Active (legendary leader)
斲木爲耜	Sharpen Wood to Make Plough-head
揉木爲耒	Shape Wood to Make Plough-handle

耒耨之利	Plough Hoe's Advantage
以教天下	To Teach The World
蓋取諸　益	All Obtain From　Benefiting (Hexagram 42)
日中爲市	Sun at Zenith Makes Market
致天下之民	Devoted to The World's Citizens
聚天下之貨	Gathering The World's Commodities
交易而退	Inter Changes Then Return-home (trading)
各得其所	Each Gets Whatever Needed
蓋取諸　噬嗑	All Obtain From　Biting-Close (Hexagram 21)
神農氏沒	Shennongshi Demised (legendary leader)
黃帝堯舜氏作	Huang Di, Yao, Shunshi Active (3 ancient kings)
通其變	Through The Changes
使民不倦	Enable Citizens Not Tired (lighten their burden)
神而化之	God-like In Transformation of It (livelihood)
使民宜之	Enable Citizens Adaptable with It (livelihood)
易窮則變	Yi　at Extreme Then Changes
變則通	Changes Then Break-through
通則久	Break-through Then Long-lasting
是以：	Therefore :
自天祐之	With Heaven Protecting Them (citizens)
吉无不利	Auspicious, None Not Favorable
黃帝堯舜	Huangdi, Yao, Shun (3 ancient kings)
垂衣裳	Let-down Blouse Skirt (relaxed)
而天下治	And The World is Managed
蓋取諸　乾坤	All Obtain From　Heaven Earth (Hexagrams 1,2)
刳木爲舟	Hollow-out Wood to Make Boats
剡木爲楫	Sharpen Wood to Make Oars
舟楫之利	Boats Oars Their Advantages
以濟不通	For Resolving No Connectivity (transport)
致遠以利天下	Reaching Far To Benefit The World
蓋取諸　渙	All Obtain From　Dispersion (Hexagram 59)
服牛乘馬	Taming Oxen Riding Horses
引重致遠	Pulling Loads Going Far
以利天下	For Benefiting The World
蓋取諸　隨	All Obtain From　Following (Hexagram 17)

重門擊柝	Double Doors Smash Broken
以待暴客	To Await Violent Guests
蓋取諸　豫	All Obtain From　Happiness (Hexagram 16)
斷木爲杵	Break Wood to Make Pestle
掘地爲臼	Dig Ground to Make Mortar
臼杵之利	Mortar Pestle's Advantage
萬民以濟	To Help All Citizens
蓋取諸　小過	All Obtain From　Small Excess (Hexagram 62)
弦木爲弧	Bend Wood to Make Bows
剡木爲矢	Sharpen Wood to Make Arrows
弧矢之利	Bows Arrows Their Advantage
以威天下	To Dominate The World
蓋取諸　睽	All Obtain From　Vision (Hexagram 38)
上古穴居	Most Ancients Cave Dwelling
而野處	In Wilderness Places
後世聖人	After Generations Sage Person
易之以宮室	Changes It For Palaces Homes
上棟下宇	Above Roof-beams Below Rooms
以待風雨	To Await Wind Rain
蓋取諸　大壯	All Obtain From　Great Strength (Hexagram 34)
古之葬者	Ancient's Burial of Person
厚衣之以薪	Thickly Clothed It With Fire-wood
葬之中野	Buried In Midst of Wilderness
不封不樹	Not Sealing No Tree-markers
喪期无數	Mourning Period No Count
後世聖人	After Generations Sage Person
易之以棺槨	Changes This To Coffin Tomb
蓋取諸　大過	All Obtain From　Great Excess (Hexagram 28)
上古結繩而治	Most Ancients Knotting Ropes For Administration
後世聖人	After Generations Sage Person
易之以書契	Changes This To Written Contracts
百官以治	Hundred Ministers For Administration
萬民以察	All Citizens For Scrutiny
蓋取諸　夬	All Obtain From　Ostracism (Hexagram 43)

Comments (para.2):
Later, Sage Persons take Hexagram Signs as guide for making instruments, improve livelihood.

第三章	**Paragraph 3**
是故：	Therefore :
易者	Yi Entity
象也	Sign that's
象也者	Sign Entity that's
像也	Image that's
彖者材也	Tuan Entity, Contents that's (Kongzi's explanation)
爻也者	Yao (Liner) Entity that's
效天下之動者也	Emulating The World's Action Things that's
是故：	Therefore :
吉凶生	Fortune Misfortune Arise
而悔吝著也	And Regrets Shame Focus that's

Comments (para.3) :
Concepts and relationships of Yi, Sign, Tuan, Fortune, Misfortune, Regrets and Shame.

第四章	**Paragraph 4**
陽卦多陰	Yang Hexagrams More Yin
陰卦多陽	Yin Hexagrams More Yang
其故何也	What are The Reason that's ?
陽卦奇	Yang Hexagram Odd (numbers)
陰多耦	Yin More Even (numbers)
其德行何也	What are The Virtuous Conducts that's ?
陽一君而二民	Yang, 1 King And 2 Citizens
君子之道也	Junzi's (Gentleman's) Way that's
陰二君而一民	Yin, 2 Kings But 1 Citizen
小人之道也	Small Person's Way that's

Comments (para.4) :
Yang, solid line like 1 King, Odd number, indivisible, strong, Junzi's (Gentleman's) Way.
Yin, split line like 2 Kings, Even number, divisible, weak, Small Person's Way.

第五章	**Paragraph 5**
易曰：	*Yi Says :*
憧憧往來	*Wavering wavering Back and Forth*
朋從爾思	*Friends Agreeing with Thy Thinking*
(咸. 第三十一卦. 九四)	(Empathy. Hexagram 31. Niner4)
子曰：	*Teacher Says :*
天下何思何慮	The World, What Thinking What Worrying !
天下同歸而殊塗	The World, Same Return (destiny), But Different Paths
一致而百慮	One Purpose But 100 Worries
天下何思何慮	The World, What Thinking What Worrying !

日往則月来　　　　Sun Gone-past Then Moon Cometh
　月往則日來　　　　　Moon Gone-past Then Sun Cometh
日月相推　　　　　Sun Moon Mutually Pushing
　而明生焉　　　　　　And Brightness Created that's
寒往則暑來　　　　Winter Gone-past Then Summer Cometh
　暑往則寒來　　　　　Summer Gone-past Then Winter Cometh
寒暑相推　　　　　Winter Summer Mutually Pushing
　而歲成焉　　　　　　And the Year is Completed that's
往者屈也　　　　　That which Gone-past Fold-in that's
　來者信　　　　　　　That which A-coming Stretch-out
屈信相感　　　　　Fold-in Stretch-out Mutually Affecting
　而利生焉　　　　　　Is Favorable for Creation that's (caterpillar in motion)

尺蠖之屈　　　　　Foot-long Worm Its Folding
　以求信也　　　　　　To Enable Stretching that's
龍蛇之蟄　　　　　Dragon Snake Their Hiding
　以存身也　　　　　　For Protection of Bodies that's
精義入神　　　　　Deeply Reasoned to Enter Godly-state
　以致用也　　　　　　To Reach Usefulness that's
利用安身　　　　　Favorable Usage for Safety in Life
　以崇德也　　　　　　By Respecting Virtues that's
過此以往　　　　　Over This To Beyond
未之或知也　　　　Not Yet Or Known that's
窮神知化　　　　　Exhausting God-spirit to Know Transformation
　德之盛也　　　　　　Virtues' Blooming that's

易曰：　　　　　　*Yi Says :*
困于石　　　　　　*Trapped Among Rocks*
　據于蒺藜　　　　　　*Stationed Among Thorns and Bushes*
入于其宮　　　　　*Entering Into The Palace*
　不見其妻，凶　　　　*Not Seeing The Wife, Ominous*
(困. 第四十七卦. 初三)　(Trapped. Hexagram 47. Sixer3)
子曰：　　　　　　*Teacher Says :*
非所困而困焉　　　Not Suppose to be Trapped And be Trapped that's
　名必辱　　　　　　　Reputation Certain be Tarnished
非所據而據焉　　　Not Suppose to be Stationed And be Stationed that's
　身必危　　　　　　　Self Certain be Endangered
既辱且危　　　　　Since Tarnished Also Endangered
　死期將至　　　　　　Time of Death Soon Arrive
　其可得見邪　　　　　This Can be Observed that's!

易曰：	*Yi Says :*
公用射隼于高墉之上	*Lord Shot Quail At High City-Wall Above*
獲之无不利	*Catching It No Disadvantage*
(解.第四十卦.上六)	*(Resolving. Hexagram 40. TopSixer)*
子曰：	Teacher Says :
隼者禽也	The Bird Flying-animal that's
弓矢者器也	Bow Arrow These are Instruments that's
射之者人也	Shooting It Is Human that's
君子藏器于身	Junzi (Gentleman) Hiding Instruments In Body
待時而動	Awaiting Right Timing Then Act
何不利有	Why Has No Advantage ?
動而不括	Action And Not Restrictive
是以出而有獲	Therefore Venture And Has Gain
語成器而動者也	This is Speaking of Readied Instruments Then Action that's
子曰：	Teacher Says :
小人不恥不仁	Small Person No Shame No Benevolence
不畏不義	No Fear No Uprightness
不見利不勸	Not Seen Gain, No Action
不威不懲	Not Fierce Not Discipline
小懲而大誡	Small Disciplined For Big Deterrence
此小人之福也	This Small Person's Fortune that's
易曰：	*Yi Says :*
屨校滅趾无咎	*Foot Shackles Destroy Toes No Faults*
(噬嗑.第二十一卦.初九)	(Biting-Close. Hexagram 21. FirstNiner)
此之謂也	This is Referenced that's (by Yi)
善不積，不足以成名	Goodness Not Accumulated, Not Enough To Be Famous
惡不積，不足以滅身	Evils Not Accumulated, Not Enough To Destroy Self
小人以小善爲无益	Small Person Considers Small Good As No Gain
而弗爲也	Thus Not Doing that's
以小惡爲无傷	Consider Small Evil As No Harm
而弗去也	Thus Not Discarding that's
故惡積	Hence Evils Accumulate
而不可掩	And Not Able to Cover-up
罪大	Crime Big
而不可解	And Not Able to Resolve
易曰：	*Yi Says :*
何校滅耳，凶	*Carrying Neck-Shackle Destroy Ears, Ominous*
(噬嗑.第二十一卦.上九)	(Biting-Close. Hexagram 21. TopNiner)

子曰：	*Teacher Says :*
危者	Person in Danger
安其位者也	Person feels Secure In Position that's (not alert to danger)
亡者	Person to Die
保其存者也	Person feels Protected In Existence that's(unaware death coming)
亂者	Person in Chaos
有其治者也	Person feels Has Good-order that's (not alert to chaotic position)
是故：	Therefore :
君子安而不忘危	Junzi (Gentleman) in Safety But Not Forgetting Danger
存而不忘亡	Living But Not Forgetting Death
治而不忘亂	Orderly But Not Forgetting Chaos
是以：	Therefore :
身安而國家可保也	Self Safe Then Kingdom Family Can be Protected that's
易曰：	*Yi Says :*
其亡其亡，繫于苞桑	*Its Death Its Death, Tethered to Luxuriant Mulberry-1tree*
（否．第十二卦．九五）	(Isolation. Hexagram 12. Niner5)
子曰：	*Teacher Says :*
德薄而位尊	Virtues Thin But Position Honorable
知小而謀大	Knows Little But Planning Big
力小而任重	Ability Little But Task Heavy
鮮不及矣	Clearly Not Efficient indeed
易曰：	*Yi Says :*
鼎折足，覆公餗	*Tripod Broke Leg, Bottom-up Lord's Food*
其形渥凶	*The Scenario is Messy and Dangerous*
（鼎．第五十卦．九四）	(Tripod. Hexagram 50. Niner4)
言不勝其任也	Says Not Over-coming The Task that's
子曰：	*Teacher Says :*
知幾，其神乎	Knows Intricacies, Its God-like, Yes !
君子	Junzi (Gentleman)
上交，不諂	Befriending Seniors, No Flattering
下交，不瀆	Befriending Juniors, Not Condescending
其知幾乎	He Knows Intricacies, Yes !
幾者	Sensitive Person
動之微	Slightest of Movement
吉之先見者也	Person First to See Auspiciousness that's
君子	Junzi (Gentleman)
見幾而作	Sees Opportunity And Act
不俟終日	Not Awaiting Whole Day

易曰：	*Yi Says :*
介于石	*Staunch As Rock*
不終日，貞吉	*Not Whole Day, Truly Auspicious*
(豫. 第十六卦. 六二)	(Happiness. Hexagram 16. Sixer2)
介如石焉	Staunch Like Rock Indeed
寧用終日	Not Needing Whole Day
斷可識矣	Certainly Able to Understand indeed
君子：	Junzi (Gentleman) :
知微，知彰	Knows the Minute, Knows the Show-off
知柔，知剛	Knows the Gentle, Knows the Strong
萬夫之望	All Individual's Aspiration
子曰：	*Teacher Says :*
顏氏之子	Yan Family's Son
其殆庶幾乎	He is Most Sensitive, Yes !
有不善	Has Not Good
未嘗不知	Never Like, Not Knowing
知之	Knowing It
未嘗復行也	Never Like, Repeating Mistake that's
易曰：	*Yi Says :*
不遠復	*Not Far-astray, Return*
无祇悔，元吉	*No Regrets, Primally Auspicious*
(復. 第二十四卦. 初九)	(Return. Hexagram 24. FirstNiner)
天地絪縕	Heaven Earth Cross Mixing
萬物化醇	All Matters Transform like Wine-undiluted
男女構精	Male Female Mixing Essence (in union as One)
萬物化生	All Matters Transform Living
易曰：	*Yi Says :*
三人行	*3 Persons Walking*
則損一人	*Then Loss 1 Person*
一人行	*1 Person Walking*
則得其友	*Then Acquire The Friend*
(損. 第四十一卦. 六三)	(Reduction. Hexagram 41. Sixer3)
言致一也	Says Devotion to One that's
子曰：	*Teacher Says :*
君子安其身，而後動	Junzi Quiet-down The Body, Then Afterwards Move
易其心，而後語	Ease The Heart, Then Afterwards Talk
定其交 ，而後求	Steady The Friendship, Then Afterwards Request

君子修此三者	Junzi (Gentleman) Cultivating These 3 Principles
故全也	Hence Totality that's (a perfect person)
危以動	Danger And Action (action in danger)
則民不與也	Then Citizens Not Receptive that's
懼以語	Fearful And Speaking (speaking with fear)
則民不應也	Then Citizens Not Responding that's
无交而求	No Friendship Then Request
則民與也	Then Citizens Not Giving that's
莫之與	None Is Helping
則傷之者至矣	Then Harmful People Are A-coming indeed (enemies)
易曰：	*Yi Says :*
莫益之或擊之	*Not Benefiting It, Or Hitting It*
立心勿恆凶	*Resolved of Heart Not Lasting, Ominous*
(益. 第四十二卦. 上九)	(Benefits. Hexagram 42. TopNiner)

Comments (para.5) :
Students ask and Kongzi elaborates on certain passages among the 64 Hexagrams.

第六章	**Paragraph 6**
子曰：	*Teacher Says :*
乾坤，其易之門邪	Qian Kun (Heaven Earth), They are Yi's Door-way that's!
乾，陽物也	Qian (Heaven), Yang Matters that's
坤，陰物也	Kun (Earth), Yin Matters that's
陰陽合德，而剛柔有體	Yin Yang Combine Virtues, Then Strength Gentleness Has Body
以體天地之撰	To Embody Heaven Earth Their Composition
以通神明之德	To Connect God-Enlighten's Virtues
其稱名也，雜而不越	The Calling of Names that's, Mix-up And Not Over-reaching
於稽其類，其衰世之意邪	In Differentiating The Kinds, The Lamenting of Society's Wishes
夫易	O' Yi
彰往而察來	Open-view of the Past And Watch the Coming-future
微顯而闡幽	Minute Exposure To Uncover the Dark
開而當名辨物	Openly And Correctly Named to Differentiate Matters
正言斷辭，則備矣	Right Speech Decisive Text, Hence Equipped indeed
其稱名也小	The Calling of Names that's Small
其取類也大	The Collection of Kinds that's Big
其旨遠	The Principles Far-sighted
其辭文	The Texts Cultured
其言曲而中	The Speech Flexible But Upright
其事肆而隱	The Affairs Wanton But Steadfast
因貳以濟民行	Because of Split To Aid Citizens Action (pros and cons)
以明失得之報	To Clarify The Report of Loss Gain

Comments (para.6) :
Through the doors of Heaven Earth, Yi's wisdom is accessible, flexible to help all humankind.

第七章	**Paragraph 7**
易之興也	Yi, Its Flourishing that's
其於中古乎	Was It At Middle Ancient time ?
作易者	Person Writing Yi
其有憂患乎	Had He Worries and Problems ?
是故：	Therefore :
履，德之基也	Treading,　Virtue's Foundation that's (Hex.10)
謙，德之柄也	Humility,　Virtue's Handle that's (Hex.15)
復，德之本也	Return,　Virtue's Basics that's (Hex.24)
恆，德之固也	Everlasting,　Virtue's Solid that's (Hex.32)
損，德之修也	Reduction,　Virtue's Repair that's (Hex.41)
益，德之裕也	Benefiting,　Virtue's Prosperity that's (Hex.42)
困，德之辨也	Trapped,　Virtue's Discernment that's (Hex.47)
井，德之地也	water-Well,　Virtue's Land that's (asset immovable) (Hex.48)
巽，德之制也	Xun (Wind),　Virtue's Regulation that's (Hex.57)
履，和而至	Treading,　Harmonious And Arrive (Hex.10)
謙，尊而光	Humility,　Respectful And Shine (Hex.15)
復，小而辨於物	Return,　Small And Discerning of Matters (Hex.24)
恆，雜而不厭	Everlasting,　Mix-in And Not Hateful (Hex.32)
損，先難而後易	Reduction, Initially Difficult And Afterwards Easy (Hex.41)
益，長裕而不設	Benefiting,　Long Prosperity And Not Flouting (Hex.42)
困，窮而通	Trapped,　Poverty Then Break-through (Hex.47)
井，居其所而遷	water-Well, Stay It Position Yet Migrate (its water) (Hex.48)
巽，稱而隱	Xun (Wind),　Praise But Invisible (accessible air) (Hex.57)
履，以和行	Treading,　To Harmonize Action (Hex.10)
謙，以制禮	Humility,　To Set-up Etiquette (Hex.15)
復，以自知	Return,　To Self Awareness (Hex.24)
恆，以一德	Everlasting, To One Virtuosity (Hex.32)
損，以遠害	Reduction,　To Distance Harm (Hex.41)
益，以興利	Benefiting,　To Raise Profit (Hex.42)
困，以寡怨	Trapped,　To Lesser Complaints (Hex.47)
井，以辨義	water-Well,　To Discern Justice (Hex.48)
巽，以行權	Xun (Wind),　To Implement Authority (Hex.57)

Comments (para.7) :
Kongzi's indepth readings of selected samples to show core teachings of Hexagrams .

第八章	**Paragraph 8**
易之爲書也	Yi, As A Book that's
不可遠	Not Allow be Distanced (keep near for consultation)
爲道也	Daoism Practice that's
屢遷	Always Migrating
變動不居	Changes Moving, Not Staying-put
周流六虛	All-over Roaming the 6 Voids (space of the Universe)
上下无常	Above Below No Regularity
剛柔相易	Yang Yin Inter Changing
不可爲典要	Not Allow Be of Classical Importance (no self-importance)
唯變所適	Only Changes to Whatever are Compatible (no fixation)
其出入，以度	Its Out-going In-coming, With Measures
外内，使知懼	Outward and Inward, Enable to Know Fear
又明于憂患與故	Also Enlighten About Worries Sadness And Problems
无有師保	***Not Having Teacher's Guidance***
如臨父母	***Like Coming-upon Father Mother***
初率其辭	Initially Following Its Text
而揆其方	Then Consider Its Methods
既有典常	Already Has Classic References
苟非其人	Careless Not The Person
道不虛行	'Dao' No Fail Actions

Comments (para.8) :
Yi the Book be kept nearby for consultation and advice, like coming upon one's parents.
Not allow be of Classical Importance; Only allow changes to whatever are compatible.

第九章	**Paragraph 9**
易之爲書也	Yi, As A Book that's
原始要終	Trace Beginning Important Ending
以爲質也	To Be Quality-content that's
六爻相雜	6 Yao (Liners) Inter Mixing
唯其時物也	Uniquely Are Timely Matters that's
其初難知	The FirstLiner Difficult to Know
其上易知	The TopLiner Easy to Know
本末也	Origin, Ending that's
初辭擬之	FirstLiner's Text Focus It (set the trend)
卒成之終	Servitude Forms The Ending (follow the trend)
若夫雜物撰德	Liken O' Mixture of Matters, Choosing the Virtuous
辨是與非	Discerning between Right And Wrong
則非其中爻不備	Then Without The Central Yao (Liners), Not Equipped

噫！	Ye!
亦要存亡吉凶	Also Need Survival Death Fortune Misfortune
則居可知矣	Then Stay and Able to Know indeed
知者觀其彖辭	Knowing Person Observe The Tuan Text (Kongzi explains)
則思過半矣	Then Thinking More than Half done indeed
二與四同功而異位	Liner2 And Liner4 Same Merits (Yin) But Different Positions
其善不同	Their Goodness Not Similar
二多譽	Liner2 (Yin position) More Honors
四多懼	Liner4 (Yin position) More Fears
近也	Proximity that's (next to position of authority Liner5)
柔之爲道	Yin (gentleness) Its Action in 'Dao'
不利遠者	Not Favorable for Distanced Person
其要无咎	Its Importance, No Faults
其用柔中也	Its Use, Gentleness and Centre (upright) that's (Liner2)
三與五同功而異位	Liner3 And Liner5 Same Merits (Yang) But Positions Differ
三多凶	Liner3 (Yang position) More Dangers (humble position)
五多功	Liner5 (Yang position) More Achievements (honor position)
貴賤之等也	Honorable or Lowly, Their Status that's
其柔危	The Gentle Dangerous (unfavorable for the Yins)
其剛勝邪	The Strong Winning to-be-sure (favorable for the Yangs)

Comments (para.9) :
Yi Book, explaining the different unique attributes of each of the 6 Liners in a Hexagram.

第十章	**Paragraph 10**
易之爲書也	Yi, As A Book that's
廣大悉備	Broad Big All Equipped (inclusive)
有天道焉	***Has Heaven's Dao that's***
有人道焉	***Has Human's Dao that's***
有地道焉	***Has Earth's Dao that's***
兼三才而兩之，故六	Together 3 Talents And Doubling Them, Hence 6
六者，非它也	These 6, None Others that's
三才之道也	3 Talents Their 'Dao' that's
道有變動，故曰爻	'Dao' Has Changes Actions, Hence Call-it Yao (Liners)
爻有等，故曰物	Yao (Liners) Has Status-level, Hence Call-it Matters
物相雜，故曰文	Matters Inter Mixing, Hence Call-it Patterns
文不當，故吉凶生焉	Patterns Not Proper, Hence Fortune Misfortune Arise that's

Comments (para.10) :
Heaven Human Earth, Talents of 3-Liners Trigram, doubling to form 6-Liners Hexagram.
Note: the 'Dao' of Yi is the 'Way' of Heaven Human and Earth, not the singular Dao of Laozi.

第十一章	**Paragraph 11**
易之興也	Yi, Its Arising that's
其當殷之末世	At About the End-period of Yin (Shang dynasty)
周之盛德邪	Zhou's (dynasty) Height of Virtues that's
文王與紂之事邪	King Wen And Zhou (King) Their Affairs Really!
是故：	Therefore :
其辭危	The Texts are of Dangers
危者使平	Person in Danger Enable Settlement
易者使傾	Person in Changes Enable Stability
其道甚大	The 'Dao' is Very Big
百物不廢	All Matters No Abandonment
懼以終始	Alert from Beginning till Ending
其要无咎	The Important-thing is No Faults
此之謂易之道也	This Is Call Yi's 'Dao' that's

Comments (para.11) :
Yi's text of dangers, reflective of the tribulation of King Wen at the hands of King Zhou.

第十二章	**Paragraph 12**
夫乾	O' Qian (Heaven)
天下之至健也	The World's Most Strong that's
德行恆易	Virtuous Conduct Everlasting Yi
以知險	To Know Danger
夫坤	O' Kun (Earth)
天下之至順也	The World's Most Docile that's
德行恆簡	Virtuous Conduct Everlasting Simplicity
以知阻	To Know Difficulties
能說諸心	Able to Speak All Heart-feeling
能研諸慮	Able to Examine All Worries
定天下之吉凶	Determine The World's Fortune Misfortune
成天下之亹亹者	Become The World's Tireless Thing
是故：	Therefore :
變化云爲	Changes Transformation Call-it Action
吉事有祥	Auspicious Affairs Have Fortune
象事知器	Signs of Affairs Knows Instruments
占事知來	Divining Affairs Knows Coming-future
天地設位	Heaven Earth Set-up Position
聖人成能	Sage Person Enable Capabilities
人謀鬼謀	People Scheming Devils Scheming
百姓與能	Citizens Given Capabilities

八卦	8 Trigrams
以象告	With Signs Inform
爻象	Yao (Liners) Tuan (Hexagram Text, Kongzi explains)
以情言	With Feelings Speak
剛柔雜居	Yang Yin Mixed Dwelling (together)
而吉凶可見矣	And Fortune Misfortune Can be Seen indeed
變動	Changes Actions
以利言	Speak Of Advantages
吉凶	Fortune Misfortune
以情遷	Transfer Of Emotions
是故：	Therefore :
愛惡相攻	Love Hate Inter Attacking
而吉凶生	Then Fortune Misfortune Arise
遠近相取	Far Near Inter Taking
而悔吝生	Then Regrets Shame Arise
情偽相感	Feelings Falsehood Inter Sensing
而利害生	Then Gain Harm Arise
凡易之情	All Yi's Feeling
近而不相得	Nearby And Not Mutual Gaining
則凶	Then Danger
或害之	Or Harming It
悔且吝	Regrets Also A-shame
將叛者，其辭慙	Person Getting Rebellious, The Speech is Ashamed
中心疑者，其辭枝	Person Doubting in the Heart, The Speech is Branching
吉人之辭，寡	Auspicious Person's Speech, Rare (little)
躁人之辭，多	Impatient Person's Speech, Plentiful
誣善之人，其辭游	Bad-mouthing Kindness such Person, The Speech Roaming
失其守者，其辭屈	Person Who Feels Lost, The Speech Dull

Comments (para.12) :
The texts of Hexagrams and Liners similarly reflect people's emotion under various conditions.

說卦傳	**Talking Trigrams Commentary**
(孔子. 八翼)	**(Kongzi. 8th Wing)**

第一章	**Chapter 1**
昔者聖人之作易也	Ancient Time Sage Person The Writing of Yi (book) that's
幽贊於神明而生著	Subtly Praise Spirit-enlighten That Created Yallow-Straws
參天兩地而倚數	Star-dome Heaven, Two-sided Earth All Based on Numbers
觀變於陰陽而立卦	Observing Changes In Yin Yang To Establish Trigrams
發揮於剛柔而生爻	Expression of Strength Gentleness Thus Creating Liners
和順於道德而理於義	Harmonise Accord With 'Dao' Virtues And Logic In Uprightness.
窮理盡性以至於命	Exhaust Logic Complete Nature To Achieve The Mission

Comments:
Ancient observation, Heaven is a Rounded 3-D Dome and Earth is a big 2-D Square.
Hence Odd-numbers for Heaven (and Yangs), Even-numbers for Earth (and Yins) in Yi.

第二章	**Chapter 2**
昔者聖人之作易也	Ancient Time Sage Person's Writing Yi (book) that's
將以順性命之理	Will Go Along the Natural Order's of Reason
是以 :	Therefore :
立天之道，曰陰與陽	Set-up Heaven's Path, Say Yin And Yang
立地之道，曰柔與剛	Set-up Earth's Path, Say Gentleness And Strength
立人之道，曰仁與義	Set-up People's Path, Say Benevolence And Justice
兼三才而兩之	Inclusive of 3 Talents And Double It
故易六畫而成卦	Hence Yi's 6 Liners To Form Hexagrams
分陰分陽，迭用剛柔	Separate Yin Separate Yang, Alternately Using Yang and Yin
故易六位而成章	Hence Yi's 6 Positions To Form Order

Comments:
Trigram's 3 liners stand for Heaven Earth and People, the 3 Talents of the Universe.
Doubling-up to form Hexagrams, alternating Yang (1,3,5) with Yin (2,4,6) positions.

第三章	**Chapter 3**
天地定	Heaven Earth Fixed Position,
山澤通氣	Mountain Wetland Connecting Atmosphere
雷風相薄	Thunder Wind Mutually Approach (work together)
水火不相射	Water Fire Not Mutually Taking-aim (not fighting)
八卦相錯	8 Trigrams Mutually Interacting
數往者順	Numbers That Go-forth, Smooth (continuing)
知來者逆	Knows What's Coming, Reverse (past numbers)
是故：易，逆數也	Therefore : Yi, Reverse Numbers that's*

Comments:
Interactions of the 8 natural elements as represented by the 8 Trigrams.
Numbers are quantitative facts, can use for planning forward smoothly.
*Yi: to predict the future, needs to study past (reverse) numbers to see the trend.

第四章	**Chapter 4**
雷以動之，風以散之	Thunder To Activate It, Wind To Scatter It
雨以潤之，日以烜之	Rain (Water) To Moisturise It, Sun (Fire) To Raise It (growth)
艮以止之，兌以說之	Kan (Mountain) To Block It, Dui (Wetland) To Enjoy It (harvest)
乾以君之，坤以藏之	Qian (Heaven) To take Charge of It, Kun (Earth) To Store It

Comments:
Relevant Attributes of the Trigrams of 8 natural elements in an ancient Farming society.

第五章	**Chapter 5**
帝出乎震	Emperor Emerges That's Zhen (Thunder)
齊乎巽	Gathering That's Xun (Wind)
相見乎離	Mutual Seeing That's Li (Fire, light)
致役乎坤	Attaining Support That's Kun (Earth)
說言乎兌	Happiness Say That's Dui (Joy)
戰乎乾	Fighting That's Qian (Heaven)
勞乎坎	Laboring That's Kan (Water)
成言乎艮	Completion Say That's Gen (Mountain)
萬物出乎震	All Matters Emerge That's Zhen (Thunder)
震，東方也	Zhen (Thunder), East Region that's
齊乎巽	Levelling That's Xun (Wind)
巽，東南也	Xun (Wind), East-South that's
齊也者，言萬物之潔齊也	Levelling Entity that's, Say All Matters' Neatly Leveled that's
離也者，明也	Li (Fire) Entity that's, Bright that's
萬物皆相見	All-Matters All Mutually Visible
南方之卦也	South Region's Trigram that's
聖人南面而聽天下	Sage Person South Facing And Listens to The World (as ruler)
嚮明而治	Aspiration Enlightenment For Management
蓋取諸此也	All Obtain From Here that's
坤也者，地也	Kun Entity that's, Earth that's
萬物皆致養焉	All-Matters All Attain Nourishment that's
故曰致役乎坤	Hence Say, Attaining Support That's Kun (Earth)
兌，正秋也	Dui (Wetland), Right Autumn that's
萬物之所說也	All-Matters Their Reasons for Joy that's
故曰說言乎兌	Hence Say, Happiness Speak That's Dui (Joy)
戰乎乾	Contention That's Qian (Heaven)
乾，西北之卦也	Qian (Heaven), West-North Its Trigram that's
言陰陽相薄也	Speaks of Yin Yang Mutually Co-operating that's

坎者，水也	Kan Entity, Water that's
正北方之卦也	Right North Region Its Trigram that's
萬物之所歸也	All-Matters' Place for Return that's
故曰勞乎坎	Hence Says, Labor That's Kan (Water)
艮，東北之卦也	Gen (Mountain), East-North Its Trigram that's
萬物之所成終	All-Matters Their Reason for Forming the Ending
而所成始也	And Reason of Forming the Beginning that's
故曰成言乎艮	Hence Says, Formation Speak That's Gen (Mountain)

Comments:
Interacting with All-Matters, more attributes, association with Directions and Seasons

第六章	**Chapter 6**
神也者	God-spirit Entity that's
妙萬物而爲言者也	Entity Enchanting All-Matters, And As Word (of Praise) that's
動萬物者莫疾乎雷	Entity Moving All-Matters, None Faster Than Thunder
撓萬物者莫疾乎風	Entity Disturbing All-Matters, None Quicker Than Wind
燥萬物者莫熯乎火	Entity Drying All-Matters, None Hotter Than Fire
說萬物者莫說乎澤	Entity Give Joy to All-Matters, None Happier Than Wetland
潤萬物者莫潤乎水	Entity Moisturising All-Matters, None More-so Than Water
終萬物始萬物者	Entity Ending All-Matters, Beginning All-Matters,
莫盛乎艮	None more Thriving Than Mountain
故水火相逮	Hence Water Fire Mutually Countering
雷風不相悖	Thunder Wind Not Mutually Opposing
山澤通氣	Mountain Wetland Free-passage of Air
然後能變化	Then Afterwards Can Change and Transform
既成萬物也	Thus Forming All-Matters that's

Comments:

Trigrams of 8 natural elements interacting, transforming with formation of All-Matters.

第七章	**Chapter 7**
乾，健也	Qian (Heaven), Strong that's
坤，順也	Kun (Earth), Compliant that's
震，動也	Zhen (Thunder), Action that's
巽，入也	Xun (Wind), Entering (invasive) that's
坎，陷也	Kan (Water), Pit-trap that's
離，麗也	Li (Fire), Bright that's
艮，止也	Gen (Mountain), Stop that's
兌，說也	Dui (Wetland), Happy that's

Comments:
Attributes of Trigrams with Actions.

第八章	**Chapter 8**
乾爲馬，坤爲牛	Qian (Heaven) as Horse, Kun (Earth) as Cow
震爲龍，巽爲雞	Zhen (Thunder) as Dragon, Xun (Wind) as Chicken
坎爲豕，離爲雉	Kan (Water) as Pig, Li (Fire) as Pheasant
艮爲狗，兌爲羊	Gen (Mountain) as Dog, Dui (Wetland) as Goat

Comments:
Association of domestic Animals with the 8 Trigrams.

第九章	**Chapter 9**
乾爲首，坤爲腹	Qian (Heaven) as Head, Kun (Earth) as Stomach
震爲足，巽爲股	Zhen (Thunder) as Legs, Xun (Wind) as Thigh
坎爲耳，離爲目	Kan (Water) as Ears, Li (Fire) as Eyes
艮爲手，兌爲口	Gen (Mountain) as Hands, Dui (Wetland) as Mouth

Comments:
Association of Body-parts with the 8 Trigrams.

第十章	**Chapter 10**
乾天也，故稱乎父	Qian (Heaven) that's, Hence Salute O' Father
坤地也，故稱乎母	Kun (Earth) that's, Hence Salute O' Mother
震一索而得男	Zhen (Thunder) First Quest And Get Son
故謂之長男	Hence Call It Elder Son (Thunder as Elder-son)
巽一索而得女	Xun (Wind) First Quest And Get Daughter
故謂之長女	Hence Call It Elder Daughter (Wind as Elder-daughter)
坎再索而得男	Kan (Water) Re-Quest And Get Son
故謂之中男	Hence Call It Middle Son (Water as Middle-son)
離再索而得女	Li (Fire) Re-Quest And Get Daughter
故謂之中女	Hence Call It Middle Daughter (Fire as Middle-daughter)
艮三索而得男	Gen (Mountain) Thrice Quest And Get Son
故謂之少男	Hence Call It Young Son (Mountain as Young-son)
兌三索而得女	Dui (Wetland) Thrice Quest And Get Daughter
故謂之少女	Hence Call It Young Daughter (Wetland Young-daughter)

Comments:
Association of Family-members with the 8 Trigrams.

第十一章	**Chapter 11**
乾	Qian (Heaven)
爲天，爲圜	as Heaven, as Ring
爲君，爲父	as King, as Father
爲玉，爲金	as Jade, as Gold
爲寒，爲冰	as Cold, as Ice
爲大赤，爲良馬	as Big Red, as Fine Horse
爲老馬，爲瘠馬	as Old Horse, as Thin Horse
爲駁馬，爲木果	as Burden Horse, as Wooden Fruit

坤　　　　　　　　　　　　***Kun (Earth)***
爲地，爲母　　　　　　　as Earth, as Mother
爲布，爲釜　　　　　　　as Cloth, as Cooking-pot
爲吝嗇，爲均　　　　　　as Miser Hoarder, as Uniformity
爲子母牛，爲大輿　　　　as Child Mother Cow, as Big Carriage
爲文，爲衆　　　　　　　as Written-sign, as Masses
爲柄　　　　　　　　　　as Handle
其於地也，爲黑　　　　　as Regard to Earth that's, as Black

震　　　　　　　　　　　***Zhen (Thunder)***
爲雷，爲龍　　　　　　　as Thunder, as Dragon
爲玄黃，爲旉　　　　　　as Black Yellow, as Covering-growth
爲大塗，爲長子　　　　　as Big Blur, as Elder Son
爲決躁，爲蒼筤竹　　　　as Quick Gallop , as Green Spring Bamboo
爲萑葦　　　　　　　　　as Reeds
其於馬也，爲善鳴　　　　as Regard Horses that's, as Strong-Neighing
爲馵足，爲作足　　　　　as White-Legged, as High-Stepping
爲的顙　　　　　　　　　as White-Forehead
其於稼也，爲反生　　　　as Regard to Grains that's, as Re-birth (transplanting)
其究，爲健　　　　　　　Its Investigation, as Health
爲蕃鮮　　　　　　　　　as Luxuriant Fresh (growth)

巽　　　　　　　　　　　***Xun (Wind)***
爲木，爲風　　　　　　　as Wood, as Wind
爲長女，爲繩直　　　　　as Elder Daughter, as Rope Straight
爲工，爲白　　　　　　　as Work, as White
爲長，爲高　　　　　　　as Length, as Height
爲進退，爲不果　　　　　as Advance Retreat, as Not Fruitful
爲臭　　　　　　　　　　as Smell
其於人也，爲寡　　　　　as Regard People that's, as Lacking Hair
爲廣顙，爲多白眼　　　　as Broad Forehead, as More White of Eye
爲近利市三倍　　　　　　as Near Favor Market 3 Folds
其究，爲躁卦　　　　　　Its Research, as Rash Trigrams

坎　　　　　　　　　　　***Kan (Water)***
爲水，爲溝瀆　　　　　　as Water, as Drainage Water
爲隱伏，爲矯輮　　　　　as Hidden Ambush, as Corrective Stopper
爲弓輪　　　　　　　　　as Bow Wheel
其於人也，爲加憂　　　　as Regard People that's, as Added Worry
爲心病，爲耳痛　　　　　as Heart Sickness, as Ear Pain

爲血卦，爲赤	as Blood Trigram, as Red
其於馬也，爲美脊	as Regard Horse that's, as Beautiful Back
爲亟心，爲下首	as Stressed Heart, as Lowered Head
爲薄蹄，爲曳	as Thin Hoof, as Drag-down (plough)
其於輿也，爲多眚	as Regard Carriage that's, as More Eye-sickness
爲通，爲月	as Connection, as Moon
爲盜	as Bandit
其於木也，爲堅多心	as Regard Wood that's, as Hard More Heart (scars)

離	***Li (Fire)***
爲火，爲日	as Fire, as Sun
爲電，爲中女	as Lightning, as Middle Daughter
爲甲冑，爲戈兵	as Full Armour, as Armed Soldier
其於人也，爲大腹	as Regard People that's, as Big Stomach
爲乾卦	as Qian (Heaven) Trigram
爲鼈，爲蟹	as Turtle, as Crab
爲蠃，爲蚌	as Snail, as Sea-shell
爲龜	as Tortoise
其於木也，爲科上槁	Its With Wood that's, as Plant Withered-Top

艮	***Gen (Mountain)***
爲山，爲徑路	as Mountain, as Trail Path
爲小石，爲門闕	as Small Stone, as Door Watcher
爲果蓏，爲閽寺	as Fruit Melon, as Hidden Temple
爲指，爲狗	as Fingers, as Dog
爲鼠，爲黔喙之屬	as Rat, as Black Mouth That Kind (wild animals)
其於木也，爲堅多節	as Regard to Wood that's, as Hard Nodular (bamboo)

兌	***Dui (Wetland)***
爲澤，爲少女	as Wetland, as Young Daughter
爲巫，爲口舌	as Wizard, as Mouth Tongue
爲毀折，爲附決	as Destroy Break, as Attachment Break
其於地也，爲剛鹵	as Regard to Earth that's, as Hard Stewed
爲妾，爲羊	as Concubine, as Goat

Comments:
Extended associations of 8 Trigrams added, bizarre with no mention in the main text !
Hence it is believed that these are wanton additions by scholars who came late after.

序卦傳	**Sequence of Hexagrams Commentary**
（孔子．九翼）	**(Kongzi. 9th Wing)**

上篇	***Upper Section***
有天地 (01, 02)	Having Heaven Earth (Hexagrams 01, 02)
然後萬物生焉.	Then Afterwards Birth of All Matters that's
盈天地之閒者唯萬物	Filling Heaven Earth In-between That Is All Matters
故受之以屯 (03)	Hence Bestow It With Sprouting (Hexagram 03)
屯者盈也	Sprouting Entity, Filling that's
屯者物之始生也	Sprouting Entity, Matters' Original Birth that's
物生必蒙	Matters' at Birth, Certainly Ignorant
故受之以蒙 (04)	Hence Bestow It With Ignorance (Hexagram 04)
蒙者蒙也.	Ignorance Entity, Ignorant that's
物之稚也	Living-things' Young-scions that's
物稚不可不養也	Living-things' Young-scions Not Allow No Nourishment that's
故受之以需 (05)	Hence Bestow It With Supplies (Hexagram 05)
需者，飲食之道也	Supplies Entity, Drink Food The Chain that's
飲食必有訟	Drink Food, Certain to Have Litigation
故受以訟 (06)	Hence Bestow With Litigation (Hexagram 06)
訟必有衆起	Litigation, Certain to Have People Rising
故受之以師 (07)	Hence Bestow It With Army (Hexagram 07)
師者衆也.	Army Entity, People that's
衆必有所比	People, Certain to Have Reasons for Closeness
故受之以比 (08)	Hence Bestow It With Neighbors (Hexagram 08)
比者比也	Neighbors Entity, Closeness that's
比必有所畜	Neighbors, Certain to Have Reasons for Constraint
故受之以小畜 (09)	Hence Bestow It With Small Constraint (Hexagram 09)
物畜然後有禮	Matters Constraint, Then Afterwards Has Etiquette
故受之以履 (10)	Hence Bestow It With Treading (Hexagram 10)
履而泰然後安	Treading And Interacting Naturally Then Afterwards at Peace
故受之以泰 (11)	Hence Bestow It With Interaction (Hexagram 11)
泰者通也	Interaction Entity, Connected that's

物不可終通
故受之以否 (12)

Matters Not Allow Forever Connected
Hence Bestow It With Isolation (Hexagram 12)

物不以終否
故受之以同人 (13)

Matters Not Be Forever in Isolation
Hence Bestow It With Comrades (Hexagram 13)

與人同者物必歸焉
故受之以大有 (14)

With Comrades Entity, Matters Certain to Home-coming that's
Hence Bestow It With Abundance (Hexagram 14)

大有者不可以盈
故受之以謙 (!5)

Abundance Entity, Not Allow Be Brim-Full
Hence Bestow It With Humility (Hexagram 15)

大有而能謙
故受之以豫 (16)

Abundance And Able be Humble
Hence Bestow It With Happiness (Hexagram 16)

豫必有隨
故受之以隨 (17)

Happiness Certainly Has Followers
Hence Bestow It With Following (Hexagram 17)

以喜隨人者必有事
故受之以蠱 (18)
蠱者，事也

Being Glad to Follow People, Person Sure Has Problems
Hence Bestow It With Belly-worms (Hexagram 18)
Belly-worms Entity, Problems that's

有事而後可大
故受之以臨 (19)
臨者，大也

Has Problems And Afterwards Able be Big
Hence Bestow It With Overseeing (Hexagram 19)
Overseeing Entity, Big that's

物大然後可觀
故受之以觀 (20)

Matters Big Then Afterwards Be Observable
Hence Bestow It With Observing (Hexagram 20)

可觀而後有所合
故受之以噬嗑 (21)
噬嗑者，合也

Being Observable Then Afterwards Has Reasons to Unite
Hence Bestow It With Biting-Close (Hexagram 21)
Biting-Close Entity, Union that's

物不可以苟合而已
故受之以賁 (22)
賁者，飾也

Matters Not Allow To Randomly Unite That Is
Hence Bestow It With Adorning (Hexagram 22)
Adorning Entity, Decor that's

致飾然後亨則盡矣
故受之以剝 (23)
剝者剝也

Absolute Decor Then Afterward Prosperity Be Ended indeed
Hence Bestow It With Stripping (Hexagram 23)
Stripping Entity, Strip that's

物不可以终盡	Matters Not Allow To End Exhausted
剝窮上反下	Stripping Impoverish Above Reverting Below
故受之以復 (24)	Hence Bestow It With Return (Hexagram 24)
復則不妄矣	Return Then Not Loss indeed
故受之以无妄 (25)	Hence Bestow It With No Delusion (Hexagram 25)
有无妄然後可畜	Has No Delusion Then Afterwards Able to Constrain
故受之以大畜 (26)	Hence Bestow It With Great Constraint (Hexagram 26)
物畜然後可養	Matters Constrain Then Afterwards Allow Nourishment
故受之以頤 (27)	Hence Bestow It With Nurturing (Hexagram 27)
頤者，養也	Nurturing Entity, Nourishment that's
不養則不可動	Not Nurture Then Not Able for Action
故受之以大過 (28)	Hence Bestow It With Great Excess (Hexagram 28)
物不可以終過	Matters Not Allow Be Ended in Excessive
故受之以坎 (29)	Hence Bestow It With Kan (Water-pit) (Hexagram 29)
坎者，陷也	Water-pit (Kan) Entity, Pitfall that's
陷必有所麗	Pitfall Certain to Have Cause for Brightness
故受之以離 (30)	Hence Bestow It With Li (Fire) (Hexagram 30)
離者，麗也	Fire (Li) Entity, Beautiful that's

下篇	***Lower Section***
有天地	Have Heaven Earth
然後有萬物	Then Afterwards Have All Matters
然後有男女	Then Afterwards Have Male Female
有男女	Have Male Female
然後有夫婦 (31)*	Then Afterwards Have Husband Wife (咸 Hexagram 31)*
然後有父子	Then Afterwards Have Father Son
有父子，然後有君臣	Have Father Son, Then Afterwards Have King Ministers
有君臣，然後有上下	Have King Ministers, Then Afterwards Have Seniors Juniors
然後禮儀有所錯	Then Afterward Etiquettes Rites Have Cause for Interaction

* (Empathy Hex.31) 咸 does not appear in the original Chinese Character text here!

夫婦之道不可以不久也	Husband-Wife's Way Not Allow Be Not Lasting that's
故受之以恆 (32)	Hence Bestow It With Everlasting (Hexagram 32)
恆者，久也	Everlasting Entity, Long-lasting that's

物不可以久居其所	Matters Not Allow Be Long Staying Its Place
故受之以遯 (33)	Hence Bestow It With Retreat (Hexagram 33)
遯者，退也	Retreat Entity, Withdraw that's
物不可以終遯	Matters Not Allow be Forever Retreating
故受之以大壯 (34)	Hence Bestow It With Great Strength (Hexagram 34)
物不可以終壯	Matters Not Allow Be Forever Strong
故受之以晉 (35)	Hence Bestow It With Advance (Hexagram 35)
晉者，進也	Advance Entity, Venture that's
進必有所傷	Advance Certainly Has Cause for Injury
故受之以明夷 (36)	Hence Bestow It With Enlighten-Hurt (Hexagram 36)
明夷者，傷也	Enlighten-Hurt Entity, Injury that's
傷於外者必反其家	Injury At Out-door, Person Certain To Return Home
故受之以家人 (37)	Hence Bestow It With Family People (Hexagram 37)
家道窮必乖	Family Condition Poor, Certain be Good
故受之以睽 (38)	Hence Bestow It With Visions (Hexagram 38)
睽者，乖也	Visions Thing, Clever that's
乖必有難	Clever, Certain Having Difficulty
故受之以蹇 (39)	Hence Bestow It With Handicap (Hexagram 39)
蹇者，難也	Handicapped Person, Difficulty that's
物不可以終難	Matters Not Allow Be Forever Difficult
故受之以解 (40)	Hence Bestow It With Resolving (Hexagram 40)
解者，緩也	Resolving Thing, Relief that's
緩必有所失	Relief, Certain Having Cause for Loss
故受之以損 (41)	Hence Bestow It With Reduction (Hexagram 41)
損而不已必益	Reduction (of desires) With No End, Certain to Benefit
故受之以益 (42)	Hence Bestow It With Benefiting (Hexagram 42)
益而不已必決	Benefiting With No End, Certain be Ostracised
故受之以夬 (43)	Hence Bestow It With Ostracism (Hexagram 43)
夬者，決也	Ostracism Thing, Ostracising that's

決必有所遇　　Ostracism, Certain Having Causes to Meet
故受之以姤 (44)　　Hence Bestow It With Encounters (Hexagram 44)
姤者，遇也　　Encounters Thing, Meeting that's

物相遇而後聚　　Matters Mutually Meeting Then Afterwards Gathered
故受之以萃 (45)　　Hence Bestow It With Grassland (Hexagram 45)
萃者，聚也　　Grassland Thing, Gathering that's

聚而上者謂之升　　Grassland Gathering And Upward That's, Call It Rising
故受之以升 (46)　　Hence Bestow It With Rising (Hexagram 46)

升而不已必困　　Rising With No End, Certain be Trapped
故受之以困 (47)　　Hence Bestow It With Trapped (Hexagram 47)

困乎上者必反下　　Trapped At Above That's Certain to Revert Below
故受之以井 (48)　　Hence Bestow It With water-Well (Hexagram 48)

井道不可不革　　water-Well's Way Not Allow No Changes
故受之以革 (49)　　Hence Bestow It With Changes (Hexagram 49)

革物者莫若鼎　　Changes of Matters That's, None Like Tripod (for cooking)
故受之以鼎 (50)　　Hence Bestow It With Tripod (Hexagram 50)

主器者莫若長子　　Master of Rite-instruments Person, None Like Elder-son
故受之以震 (51)　　Hence Bestow It With Thunder (Hexagram 51)
震者，動也　　Thunder Entity, Action that's

物不可以終動，止之　　Matter Not Allow To Forever Action, Stop It
故受之以艮 (52)　　Hence Bestow It With Kan (Mountain) (Hexagram 52)
艮者，止也　　Mountain (Kan) Entity, Stop that's

物不可以終止　　Matters Not Allow To Forever Stop
故受之以漸 (53)　　Hence Bestow It With Progress (Hexagram 53)
漸者進也　　Progress Entity, Advance that's

進必有所歸　　Advance Certain Having Cause for Homing
故受之以歸妹 (54)　　Hence Bestow It With Married Maid (Hexagram 54)

得其所歸者必大　　Person Gains The Cause for Home-coming, Certainly Big
故受之以豐 (55)　　Hence Bestow It With Expansion (Hexagram 55)
豐者，大也　　Expansion Entity, Big that's

窮大者必失其居
故受之以旅 (56)

Poor Big Person, Certain to Lose The Abode
Hence Bestow It With Traveling (Hexagram 56)

旅而無所容
故受之以巽 (57)
巽者，入也

Traveling Then Afterwards None Will Accommodate
Hence Bestow It With Xun (Wind) (Hexagram 57)
Wind (Xun) Entity, Access that's

入而後説之
故受之以兌 (58)
兌者，説也

Access Then Afterwards Enjoy It
Hence Bestow It With Dui (Wetland) (Hexagram 58)
Wetland (Dui) Entity, Joy that's

説而後散之
故受之以渙 (59)
渙者，離也

Joy Then Afterwards Disperse It
Hence Bestow It With Dispersion (Hexagram 59)
Dispersion Entity, Leaving that's

物不可以終離
故受之以節 (60)

Matters Not Allow To Forever Leaving
Hence Bestow It With Thrift (Hexagram 60)

節而信之
故受之以中孚 (61)

Thrift And Trust It
Hence Bestow It With Core Trust (Hexagram 61)

有其信者必行之
故受之以小過 (62)

Person Has The Trust, Certain To Do It
Hence Bestow It With Small Excess (Hexagram 62)

有過物者，必濟
故受之以既濟 (63)

Person Has Excess Matters, Certain to Complete
Hence Bestow It With Completion (Hexagram 63)

物不可以窮也
故受之以未濟 (64)

Matters Not Allow Be Impoverished that's
Hence Bestow It With Prior Completion (Hexagram 64)

終焉
(approx.941 characters)

End that's

雜卦傳	**Miscellaneous Hexagram Commentary**
(孔子. 十翼)	(Kongzi. 10th Wing)

乾剛　　　　　　　　Qian (Heaven) Strength
　坤柔 (1,2)　　　　　　Kun (Earth) Gentle (Hex.1,2)
比樂　　　　　　　　Neighbors Joyous
　師憂 (7,8)　　　　　　Army Worrying (Hex.7,8)
臨觀之義　　　　　　Overseeing Observing Their Meanings
　或與或求 (19,20)　　　Maybe Giving Maybe Requesting (Hex.19,20)
屯見而不失其居　　　Sprouting is Visible And Not Lost Its Position
　蒙雜而著 (3,4)　　　　Ignorance is Confused and Suffering (Hex.3,4)
震起也　　　　　　　Zhen (Thunder) is Rising that's
　艮止也 (51,52)　　　　Gen (Mountain) is Blocking that's (Hex.51,52)
損益　　　　　　　　Reduction Benefiting
　盛衰之始也 (41,42)　　Prosperity Decay Their Beginnings that's (Hex.41,42)
大畜時也　　　　　　Great Constraint is Timing that's
　无妄災也 (25,26)　　　No Delusion is Disaster that's (Hex.25,26)
萃聚　　　　　　　　Grassland Gathering
　而升不來也 (45,46)　　And Rising is Not Coming that's (Hex.45,46)
謙輕　　　　　　　　Humility is Floating-light
　而豫怠也 (15,16)　　　And Happiness is Lethargy that's (Hex.15,16)
噬嗑食也　　　　　　Biting-Close is Feeding that's
　賁无色也 (21,22)　　　Adorning is No Color that's (Hex.21,22)
兌見　　　　　　　　Dui (Joy) is Visible
　而巽伏也 (58,57)　　　And Xun (Wind) is Hidden that's (Hex.58,57)
隨无故　　　　　　　Following has No Old-friend
　而蠱則飭 (17,18)　　　And Belly-worms is Correction (Hex.17,18)
剝爛也　　　　　　　Stripping is Refining that's
　復反也 (23,24)　　　　Return is Coming-back that's (Hex.23,24)
晉晝也　　　　　　　Advance is Daylight that's
　明夷誅也 (35,36)　　　Enlighten-Hurt is Killing that's (Hex.35,36)
井通　　　　　　　　water-Well is Connectivity
　而困相遇也 (48,47)　　And Trapped is Mutual Encounter that's (Hex.48,47)
咸速　　　　　　　　Empathy is Rapid
　恆久也 (31,32)　　　　Everlasting is Forever that's (Hex.31,32)
渙離　　　　　　　　Dispersion is Leaving
　節止也 (59,60)　　　　Thrift is Limiting that's (Hex.59,60)
解緩　　　　　　　　Resolving is Relief
　蹇難也 (39,40)　　　　Limp is Difficulty that's (Hex.39,40)

睽外也	Visions are External that's
家人内也 (38,37)	Family People are Internal that's (Hex.38,37)
否泰	Isolation Interaction
反其類也 (12,11)	Opposing Their Kinds that's (Hex.12,11)
大壯則止	Great Strength Then Stop
遯則退也 (34,33)	Retreat Thus Withdraw that's (Hex.34,33)
大有衆	Abundance, the Populace
同人親也 (14,13)	Comrades are Loving that's (Hex.14,13)
革去故也	Changes is Discarding-Old that's
鼎取新也 (49,50)	Tripod is Acquiring-New that's (Hex.49,50)
小過過也	Small Excess is Mistake that's
中孚信也 (62,61)	Core Trust is Honesty that's (Hex.62,61)
豐多故也	Expansion has Many Old-friends that's
親寡旅也 (55,56)	Love Lacking, Traveler that's (Hex.55,56)
離上	Li (Fire) Up-burning
而坎下也 (30,29)	And Kan (Water) is Down-flowing that's (Hex.30,29)
小畜寡	Small Constraint is Lonely
履不處也 (9,10)	Treading is Not Staying that's (Hex.9,10)
需不進也	Supplies is Not Advancing that's
訟不親也 (5,6)	Litigation is Not Friendly that's (Hex.5,6)

大過顛也 (28)	Great Excess is Bottom-up that's (Hex.28)
姤遇也，柔遇剛也 (44)	Encounters Meeting that's, Yin meets Yang that's (Hex.44)
漸，女歸待男行也 (53)	Progress, Girl at Home Waiting Boy's Progress (Hex.53)
頤，養正也 (27)	Nurturing, Nourishment Correct that's (Hex.27)
既濟，定也 (63)	Completion, Fix-state that's (Hex.63)
歸妹，女之終也 (54)	Married Maid, Girl's Ending that's (Hex.54)
未濟，男之窮也 (64)	Prior Completion, Boy's Limit that's (Hex.64)
夬，決也，剛決柔也 (43)	Ostracism cut-off that's, Yangs Banishing Yin that's (Hex.43)
君子道長，小人道憂也	Junzi's Path Lasting, Small Person's Path is Worrying that's

Comments:
A Hexagram has 6 liners, each presenting a different aspect in the same situation.
Here Kongzi helps us focus on the primary aspect and importance of each Hexagram.

267   Summary

The contents and teachings of each of the 64 Hexagram

01 Heaven (乾) : on-high, strength, leadership, non-stop self-improvement, non-contesting.

02 Earth 坤) : lowly, gentleness, supportive, docile, thrifty, vigilant that extreme turns violent.

03 Sprouting(屯) : to expect early problems in career, marriage, but also emergence of greatness.

04 Ignorance (蒙) : to dispel with education for youngsters, with kind-correctives for adults.

05 Supplies (需) : at all time need be guarded at all levels, king to share fairly with all citizens.

06 Litigation (訟) : ominous, winning no glory, avoid with early settlement, best nip in the bud.

07 Army (師) : is poison, best elder in command, embedded compassionate citizens for defence.

08 Neighbours (比) : mutual Trust for harmony, also king hunting safely not disturbing citizens.

09 Small Constraint (小畜) : trust the Virtuous-way stay Upright, time for self-improvement.

10 Treading (履) : life-path is treacherous all the way, so take care not to step on 'tiger-tails'.

11 Interaction (泰) : of Yangs supplementing Yins' less productive actions, Auspicious.

12 Isolation (否) : Yins resort to servitude bribery to survive, Yangs alert to such Danger.

13 Comrades (同人) : Prosperity with Integrity, a contest of strength in relationships.

14 Abundance (大有) : also have people who need help, small people not contributing.

15 Humility (謙) : is Favourable for all actions, even in the use of army for defence.

16 Happiness (豫) : is having support for actions, but merry-making whole day Ominous.

17 Following (隨) : to show open-Integrity to avoid suspicion, best follow Heaven's Way.

18 Belly-worms (蠱) : study problem before and after, to fix messes with compassion, not laxity.

19 Overseeing (臨) : with frivolity, knowledge and honesty, you are also being observed.

20 Observing (觀) : Heaven, society, from afar, behind doors, close-up, also to self-observe.

21 Biting-close (噬嗑) : describe difficulty meting fair Justice, retribution for evil-doers.

22 Adorning (賁) : has small advantage, the need to adorn diminishes with rising status.

23 Stripping (剝) : is disdainful of Integrity, so to survive be a Junzi (Gentleman) always.

24 Return (復) : urges us to turn-back to the virtuous-Way when led astray at any time.

25 No Delusion (无忘) : no harvest without ploughing, but the unexpected do happen.

26 Great Constraint (大畜) : horn-guard for young oxen, good governance for citizenry.

27 Nurturing (頤) : virtuous speech for spiritual-self, to self-seeking sustenance for body.

28 Great Excess (大過) : of Yangs, oddity like marry old woman , also time for great sacrifice.

29 Water-pit (坎) : double danger, needs to keep low-profile and stay virtuous to survive.

30 Fire-shine (離) : double shine on commoners and leaders, illuminating the Upright.

31 Empathy (咸) : complex among the 6 status, best with humility accept all others.

32 Everlasting (恆) : of virtues desirable, of evils undesirable, of sexual bias unfair.

33 Retreat (遯) : tether to Uprightness and humility, is conducive to harmony and goodwill.

34 Great Strength (大壯) : do not butt our way through, else like goat horns entangled.

35 Advance (晋) : with no concern of gain / loss, not selfish, transparent in daylight.

36 Enlighten-Hurt (明夷) : talented will be envied and targeted, has humility to soften image.

37 Family People (家人) : importance of integrity, family disputes grave, frivolity painful.

38 Visions (睽) : realised, distorted by stress by suspicion, and be shared be appreciated.

39 Limp (蹇) : handicap in difficulty and danger, best turn back for support, self-improvement.

40 Resolving (解) : with humility, uprightness, authority, even with arrow shooting skill.

41 Reduction (損) : of self to help others, of sickness, of danger, of desires in self-cultivation.

42 Benefiting (益) : subordinates below raising prosperity, and subjects reciprocate.

43 Ostracism (夬) : takes no credit from subordinates, no violence, be Upright, be open.

44 Encounters (姤) : may be good or bad, and be guarded especially of the amorous kind.

45 Grassland (萃) : gathering of people, suffer trials tribulations, guard against violence.

46 Rising (升) : accord, trust, and kindness of Wen leading to ascension over evil King Zhou.

47 Trapped (困) : breakout with less complaints, resolve with upright honesty, learn anew.

48 water-Well (井) : immovable asset, but water move-out connecting locals and passers-by.

49 Changes (革) : need time to build trust, to study the past to understand the presence.

50 Tripod (鼎) : hold food for Offerings, image of authority, upturn to clean-out and be renewed.

51 Thunder-action (震) : bring rain good harvest, strike fear of retribution, to behave well.

52 Mountain-block (艮) : has great humility, not exceeding authority like naked retirement.

53 Progress(漸) : to shore, cliff, flatland, grassland, highland, to path-in-cloud, unruffled.

54 Married Maid (歸妹) : warns of elopement, the lowly concubine, infertility of old age.

55 Expansion (豐) : sun has zenith then decline, that's warning people in over-expansion.

56 Traveling (旅) : exposes no wealth, has integrity not frivolity, wealthy but not at home sad.

57 Wind-conform (巽) : everyone generally resists conformity, over-conformity Ominous.

58 Wetland-joy (澤) : harmony-Joy trust-Joy Auspicious, come-Joy lead-Joy Ominous.

59 Dispersion (渙) : of *personal interests* to help stop disintegration, unthinkable action.

60 Thrift (節) : varying degree determine if a person is thrifty or a miser, Bitter Thrift Ominous.

61 Core Trust (中孚) : between individuals in life, even bandits need trust sharing spoils.

62 Small Excess (小過) : of small people, ineffective and danger, be guarded at all time.

63 Completion (既濟) : warns of delays, ill-advice, emergency before the Finish-line.

64 Prior Completion (未濟) : individuals misplaced, to stay truthful, doubly Auspicious.

Comments:
This summarises the contents of Zhougong's "*LinerSign Says*" in the 64 Hexagrams.
Next, teachings of King Wen's "*Hexagram Text*" and Kongzi's "*HexagramSign Says*" inclusive.
They are collected in the following **Conclusion** section, "*Wisdom of 4 Sages*".

The development and connectivity sequence of all 64 Hexagrams

01 Heaven (乾) : on-high, Initiate all things need support, Earth.

02 Earth9坤) : below, nurture all things to fill the Universe, Sprouting.

03 Sprouting(屯) : is new-born is Ignorance.

04 Ignorance (蒙) : need be nurtured need sustenance, Supplies.

05 Supplies (需) : available, certain to have contesting, Litigation.

06 Litigation (訟) : ominous, best nip in the bud with a standing Army.

07 Army (師) : is poison, but needed for defence of the Neighbourhood.

08 Neighbours (比) : are independent individuals, hence has Small Constraint.

09 Small Constraint (小畜) : with Etiquette advise careful Treading.

10 Treading (履) : with care in harmony, Interaction.

11 Interaction (泰) : things cannot non-stop interacting, needs Isolation.

12 Isolation (否) : things cannot forever isolated, needs Comrades.

13 Comrades (同人) : certain to return together, creating Abundance.

14 Abundance (大有) : no good to allow self-expansion, to have Humility.

15 Humility (謙) : have abundance and humility, produce Happiness.

16 Happiness (豫) : then certain to have people Following.

17 Following (隨) : such people certain to have Belly-worms (problems) .

18 Belly-worms (蠱) : have problems that grow in dimension needs Overseeing.

19 Overseeing (臨) : and then matters develop big enough for Observing.

20 Observing (觀) : of observable dimension then have purpose for Biting-close (union).

21 Biting-close (噬嗑) : union may not be random, needs Adorning.

22 Adorning (賁) : absolute decor completed, next can only be Stripping.

23 Stripping (剝) : impoverishing above then reverting below, Return.

24 Return (復) : return and not lost, that's No Delusion.

25 No Delusion (无忘) : with no delusion then can exercise Great Constraint.

26 Great Constraint (大畜) : matters in Great constraint for Nurturing.

27 Nurturing (頤) : no nurturing for actions lead to Great Excess (redundancy).

28 Great Excess (大過) : matters ever redundant lead to Water-pit (double danger).

29 Water-pit (坎) : danger also has it bright side, hence Fire-shine (beautiful).

30 Fire-shine (離) : it is beautiful to have among people, Empathy (love).

31 Empathy (咸) : love cannot be lost among people, ought be Everlasting.

32 Everlasting (恆) : matters cannot forever stay-put at one place, hence Retreat.

33 Retreat (遯) : matters cannot forever retreat, hence develop Great Strength.

34 Great Strength (大壯) : great strength leads to Advancement.

35 Advance (晋) : venturing forward suffer injury and Enlighten-Hurt.

36 Enlighten-Hurt (明夷) : when hurt certain to return home to Family People.

37 Family People (家人) : poverty encourages good conduct and Visions.

38 Visions (睽) : good behaviour has difficulty like handicapped with Limp.

39 Limp (蹇) : matters cannot be forever difficult, and they are Resolving.

40 Resolving (解) : in the process certain to have losses and Reduction.

41 Reduction (損) : of undesirables without end lead to Benefits.

42 Benefiting (益) : without end lead to Ostracism.

43 Ostracism (夬) : ostracising certain to have meetings and Encounters.

44 Encounters (姤) : meeting lead to Grassland (Gathering)

45 Grassland-Gathering (萃) : growing upwards, that's Rising.

46 Rising (升) : with no end gets Trapped.

47 Trapped (困) : above certain to revert down below to water-Well.

48 water-Well (井) : needs upgrading and Changes.

49 Changes (革) : nothing like food in the cooking Tripod.

50 Tripod (鼎) : instrument for Offering with Thunder-action (that's Elder-son).

51 Thunder-action (震) : matters cannot forever in actions, hence Mountain-block.

52 Mountain-block (艮) : matters cannot forever be blocked, hence Progress.

53 Progress(漸) : is the gradual-path home for Married Maid.

54 Married Maid (歸妹) : homing lead to bigger family, prosperity and Expansion.

55 Expansion (豐) : to the extreme, certain to lose his abode, thus go Traveling.

56 Traveling (旅) : with no permanent abode, hence conformity like Wind-conform.

57 Wind-conform (巽) : gain access everywhere and has Wetland-Joy.

58 Wetland-joy (澤) : enjoy and depart each on his way, that's Dispersion.

59 Dispersion (渙) : matters cannot forever be leaving, hence stop it with Thrift.

60 Thrift (節) : so trust it with Core Trust.

61 Core Trust (中孚) : with Core Trust, there will be action by Small Excess.

62 Small Excess (小過) : small people certain to enable Completion.

63 Completion (既濟) : cannot forever remain, will deteriorate to Prior Completion.

64 Prior Completion (未濟) : is renewal and start of the next Cycle of Changes.

Comments:

This is a summary of Kong's 9th Wing, "*Sequence of Hexagram Commentary*".
Interestingly tracing the development and connectivity of the 64 Hexagrams in series.
Logic use for connections are hard to comprehend at times in their ancient setting.

The 8 Facets of Life

The 64 Hexagrams are truly reflective and covering the multi-facets of life.
They are organized under the 8 natural elements as follow:-

Heaven-Strength (乾, H1)

Look-up, we see Strength in the creation of all things and Observing (觀, H20).

Overseeing (臨, H19) Interaction (泰, H11) and Isolation (否, H12) in society.

The Reduction (損, H41), Benefiting (益, H42) and No Delusion (无忘, H25).

Earth-Support (坤, H2)

Bend-down, we perceive Support for growth of all things with Humility (謙, H15).

Supplies (需, H5) for Nurturing (頤, H27) and feedings Biting-Close (噬嗑, H21).

Cultivating Core Trust (中孚, H61), Thrift (節, H60) and Tripod (鼎, H50) renewal.

Thunder-Action (震, H51)

Actions for our up Rising (升, H46) and down water-Well (井, H48).

In Progress (漸, H53), Retreat (遯, H33), Following (隨, H17) and Return (復, H24).

And in Changes (革, H49).

Water-Pit (坎, 29H)

Danger warnings of Limp (蹇, H39) handicap and Belly-worms (蠱, H18) problems.

And life tribulations in the forms of sabotage (明夷, H36), Ostracism (夬, H43).

Of Trapped (困, H47) and Stripping (剝, H23) that need Resolving (解, H40).

Mountain-Block (艮, H52)

Constraint of life, Small Constraint (小畜, H9) and Great Constraint (大畜, H26).

Great Strength (大壯, H34) for Gathering (萃, H45), prevent Dispersion (渙, H59).

And blocks of Great Excess (大過, H28) Small Excess (小過, H62) to overcome.

Wind-Conform (巽, H57)

Conformity with respect for all, in harmony with Family People (家人, H37).

With Comrades (同人, H13), Neighbors (比, H8) and Married Maid (歸妹, H54).

For Encounters (姤, H44), Traveling (旅, H56) and outward Visions (睽, H38).

Fire-Shine (離, H30)

Enlightenment to guide our Sprouting (屯, H3) start and Ignorance (蒙, H4).

To guide our Litigation (訟, H6) and Army (師, H7) in dispute with others.

In Treading (履, H10) life-path Prior Completion (未濟, H64), Completion (既濟, H63).

Wetland-Joy (兌, H58)

Joy of life, there are Abundance (大有, H14) and Expansion (豐, H55).

Joy of Adorning (賁, H22) and Advance (晉, H35).

And Happiness (豫, H16) with Empathy (咸, H31) Everlasting (恆, H32).

273 Discussion

Authorships and Dating
The *Yjing* is listed among the 100 most influential books according to Seymour-Smith, 1998.
Its collective authorships include 4 ancient Sages of China, spanning a period of 1.5 millennia.

Fuxi
(伏羲 c.3000 BC legendary sovereign of ancient China)

In *Yij*ing itself, Kongzi has thus described how Fuxi has gone about creating the 8 Trigrams.
However Fuxi is only the name of a legendary figure who is said to have existed prehistorically!

古者	The Ancient
包犧氏之王天下也	Baoyishi As King of The World that's (legendary Fuxi)
仰則觀象於天	Look-up To Observe Signs In Heaven
俯則觀法於地	Bend-over To Observe Regularities On Earth
觀鳥獸之文	Observe Birds Animals Their Patterns
與地之宜	With Earth's Compatibility
近取諸身	Nearby Obtain From Body
遠取諸物	Afar Obtain From Matters
於是	Henceforth,
始作八卦	Initiated Creation of the 8 Trigrams
(繫辭下傳.第二章)	(Attached Text Lower Commentary.para.2)

The Zhou Dynasty (1,066-221 BCE), China third dynasty, written history in Small Seal script.
The Shang Dynasty (1,600-1,066 BCE), China second dynasty has history in Shell-bone script.
The Xia Dynasty (2,100-1,600 BCE), China first dynasty has no written history excavated yet!
Sima Qian's (c.145-87BCE) *Historic Records* starts with the 5 Emperors before Xia (五帝本紀)

There are no records of the 3 Leaders before them, Suiren Fuxi and Shennong(燧人,伏羲,神農).
Fuxi has been depicted as having the head of a man and the body of a snake!
Whereas Shennong has been depicted as having the body of a man and head of a ox!
(Yu Haidi, Li Na, Li Cuixiang, Li Peng, Zhou Shuiqin 2011).

So who has first drawn the 3 lines of a Trigram and has devised a beautiful set of 8 Trigrams?
This is certainly the product of development over a millennia, and not the work of one man.

Excavation from the Ruins of Shang Dynasty (殷虛) recover thousands of oracle shells bones.
Some bear burnt marks on one side and oracle Shell-bone scripts on top to record the readings.
Apparently the shells bones produce line-cracks when heat is applied to marked spots.
Oracles are probably read from the run-patterns of line-cracks in numbers, length and direction.
From these line-cracks pattern, it is not hard to imagine the emergence of 3-Liners Trigrams.

With no evidence for a better name to use, let's accept that Fuxi has initiated the 8 Trigrams.

King Wen
(文王 c.1096 BC. Zhou. father of King Wu founder-king of Zhou Dynasty)

Yijing's text of dangers, reflective of the tribulations of King Wen at the hands of King Zhou.
Evidently Kongzi is implicating King Wen's authorship of the Yi text of admonitions and such.

易之興也	Yi, Its Arising that's
其當殷之末世	At About the End-period of Yin (Shang dynasty)
周之盛德邪	Zhou's (dynasty) Height of Virtues that's
文王與紂之事邪	King Wen And Zhou (King) Their Affairs Really
是故：	Therefore :
其辭危	The Text are of Dangers
(繫辭下傳. 第十一章)	(Attached Text Lower Commentary. para.11)

Here, Sima Qian records King Wen as creator of the 64 Hexagrams during his confinement.

西伯蓋即位五十年	Duke of West On Ascension for 50 years
其囚羑里	His Confinement at Youli
蓋益易之八卦为六十四卦	Thus Expanded Yi's 8 Trigrams As 64 Hexagrams
(司馬迁, 漢.	(Sima Qian, Han.
史記. 卷四: 周本紀)	*Historic Records.* Scroll 4: Zhou Annals)

Yijing also known as *Zhouyi* because King Wen and Zhougong wrote the Original Texts.

有交易變易之義	Has Yi-Trade Yi-Change, These Meanings
其辭文王周公所擊	The Written-text, King Wen, Zhougong Who Attached
故繫之周	Hence Attached It with Zhou (name it *Zhouyi*)
(朱熹, 宋.)	(ZhuXi, Song.
周易本義. 乾卦序言)	*Zhouyi Original Meaning.* Heaven Hex.01.Preface)

And Liu directly says King Wen contributed the Hexagram-Text.

又曰卦辭，世謂	Also Call Hexagram Texts, World Says
爲文王被囚於羑里時所作	Were Written by King Wen When Confined At Youli
(劉思白, 清.	(Liu Sibai, Qing.
周易話解. 既略)	*Zhouyi Simply Explain.* Briefings)

Before overthrowing the Shang Dynasty, King Wen was Duke of West under evil King Zhou.
He was confined for 7 years at Youli, where unfazed, he has pondered and developed the Yi.
His ministers secured his release with gift-offers of precious stones, beauties and fine horses.
His benevolent Rule lay a strong foundation for his son to overthrow the Shang Dynasty later.
And King Wu the son, honored him as founder-king when the Zhou Dynasty was established.
All scholars who came after, have accepted his contribution in the creation of the *Yijing*.

Zhougong

(周公 Duke of Zhou c.1046 BC Zhou.brother of King Wu. co-author *of Zhouyi*)

I have detected no clear implication of Zhougong's authorship in Kongzi's 10 'Wings'
However Zhu Xi clearly acknowledges the Yi of Zhougong alongside with the other authors.

有天地自然之易	There's Heaven Earth Nature, Their Yi
有伏羲之易	There's Fuxi's Yi
有文王周公之易	There's King Wen's and Zhougong's Yi
有孔子易	There's Kongzi's Yi
伏羲以上	Fuxi And Before
皆无文字	Completely No Written Words
只有圖畫	Only Have Pattern and Drawing
文王以下	King Wen And Later
方有文字	Then Have Written Words
不可便以孔子之說	Not Allowable to Have Kongzi's Sayings
爲文王之說也	As King Wen's Sayings, that's (careful who has said what!)
(朱熹, 宋. 周易本義.	(Zhu Xi, Song. *Zhouyi Original Meaning.*
卦變圖九. 末言)	Hexagram-Changes Diagram 9. Appended Words)

Sima Qian's *Historic Records* makes no direct mention of Zhougong's contribution to the Yi.
But did vividly described many of Zhougong Virtuosities, like returning power to his nephew!

及七年後	Till 7 Years Later
還政成王	Return Administration-power to <u>King Cheng</u> (nephew)
北面就臣位	North Facing, Take-up Minister Position
躬躬如畏然	Humbly Humbly Like Alert Naturally
(司馬迁, 漢.	(Sima Qian, Han.
史記.:魯周公世家)	*Historic Records:* Luo Zhougong Family Annals)

And Liu directly credits Zhougong for the Liner-Texts of the 64 dHexagrams.

爻辭，世謂	Also Call Hexagram Texts, World Says
爲周公東征時所作	Were Written by Zhougong When on Eastern Campaign
(劉思白, 清.	(Liu Sibai, Qing.
周易話解. 既略)	*Zhouyi Simply Explain.* Briefings)

Zhougong, 4th son of King Wen, helped brother King Wu in establishing the Zhou Dynasty.
On Wu's death, held the Kingdom 7 years for his young nephew to grow up and be King.
His virtues are legendary, creator of etiquettes characteristic of the Zhou Dynasty (周礼).
Thus he is highly capable of expressing the high-powered sensitivities in the 384 liner-texts.
We can all certainly admire Zhougong, for he has done what he preached!

Kongzi

(孔子 551 - 479 BC Zhou.SpringAutumn. Chinese philosopher, Sage)

In the Historic Records, this is how Sima Qian describes the role of Kongzi in *Yijing*.
Kongzi's love and appreciation of the Yi is complete with writing of the 10 'Wings'.

孔子晚而喜易	Kongzi Late (in life) Do Appreciate *Yi*
序象,系	SequenceText, TuanText, AttachmentText
象,說卦,文言	SignText, TalkTrigrams, TalkText (10 'Wings')
讀易，韋編三絕	Reading *Yi*, Scrolls Binders Broken 3 times
曰：假我数年	Says: Give Me Some Years
若是，我于易則彬彬矣	If Possible, I With Yi Shall Refine yet Refine that's
(司馬迁.漢《史記》	(Sima Qian, Han. *Historic Records*.
卷四十七：孔子世家)	*Scroll 47: Kongzi Family Annals*)

But not all are written by Kongzi himself as indicated by the many "Teacher Says:"!
For these are the hallmarks of his disciples when they quote what they heard from him.

子曰：	*Teacher Says :*
君子居其室，出其言善	Junzi Stays At Home, Speaks Out Kind Words
則千里之外應之	Then Thousand Miles Away has Response to Them
況其邇者乎	Let Alone the Nearby People that's
居其室，出其言不善	Stays At Home, Speaking Out Unkind Words
則千里之外違之	Then Thousand Miles Away has Opposition to The
況其邇者乎	Let Alone the Nearby People that's
(繫辭上傳 · 第八章)	(*Attached Text (Top) Commentary, para.8*)

And the 8 Trigrams have extended associations that have no mention in the main text.
Hence it is believed that these are wanton additions by scholars who came late after !!

兌：	Dui :
爲澤，爲少女	as Wetland, as Young Daughter
爲巫，爲口舌	as Wizard, as Mouth Tongue
爲毀折，爲附決	as Destroy Break, as Attachment Break
其於地也，爲剛鹵	as Regard to Earth that's, as Hard Stewed
爲妾，爲羊	as Concubine, as Goat
(說卦傳, 第十一章)	(Talking Trigrams Commentary, para.11)

But of course there is no doubt that Kongzi is essentially the author of the 10 'Wings'.
Throughout the texts, the consistent reference to the *Junzi* is hallmark of Kongzi's writing.

天行健	Heaven moving strong (ceaseless cycles of sun, moon, stars)
君子以自强不息	*Junzi* by self-improvement never cease (to do likewise)
(第一卦 乾, 象曰 :)	(*Hexagram 01 Heaven, HexagramSign Says:*)

Kongzi (551-479 B.C.) was born of a poor scholar family in decline, in the State of Lu (魯國).
As a child he was keen to learn and displayed early, a love for knowledge, etiquette and order.
By his twenties he lost both parents, and already gained reputation as a good teacher.
In his thirties, he had come of age and been much sort after for consultation by head of states.
At forties, state affairs were bad, so he focused on writing, teaching students from far and wide.
At fifties, Lu had a good leader and he served in senior positions doing the state of Lu proud.
Jealous and fear of his successes, foes from within and without sabotaged, and Kongzi left Lu.
For 14 years he visited many other states with his disciples, living some dangerous encounters.
Aged 68 he returned to Lu to concentrate on writing and the study of *Yijing*, and died at age 73.

Teaching without bias (有教无類) he had 3 thousands students, including the 72 Multi-talented.

He has been credited with writing and restoring the 5 Classics of China (五經).

Today, his teachings influence China and beyond, with Confucianism a distinctive discipline.
(Sima Qian, Han. *Historic Records:* chapter 47 Kongzi Family Annals)

Comments:

The Rites of Zhou (周礼) has mentioned Lianshan (連山), Guizang (歸藏), two older *Yijing*s.

However they have never been seen and only the *Yijing* of Zhou (周易) survives to this day.
Fuxi is a mythology sovereign of ancient China predating The Xia Dynasty (2,100 - 1600 BCE).
The *Yijing* is initiated with Fuxi's 8 Trigrams and KingWen's development of the 64 Hexagrams.
King Wen and Duke Zhougong wrote the Divination texts, Kongzi the 10'Wings' commentaries.

Altogether the Yijing or Yi of Zhou take at least 1.5 millennia to evolve into the present form.

Concept of Yi (易)
Kongzi describes the Yi of Yijing in his Attached Text Upper Commentary (5th 'Wing'):

乾以易知	Qian (Heaven) With Yi Knows
坤以簡能	Kun (Earth) With Simplicity Enable
簡則易從	Simplicity Thus Easy to Follow
易簡而天下之理得矣	Yi Simplicity Thus The World's Logic Obtain indeed (para.1)

Through Yi, Heaven knows and Earth Simply follows, thus the logic of the World is obtained!

易與天地準	Yi With Heaven Earth Alignment
故能彌綸天地之道	Hence Can Connect Accord with Heaven Earth Their Paths
仰以觀于天文	Look-up To Observe In Heaven's Pattern
故神无方	Hence God-spirit has No Form
而易无體	And Yi has No Body (para. 4)

Yi alignment with Heaven and Earth is invisible being formless and with no body.

生生，之謂易	Creating Creating, Call This Yi
成象，之謂乾	Forming Signs, Call This Qian (Heaven)
效法，之謂坤	Conforming Methods, Call This Kun (Earth) (para.5)

Yi the creator, forming Signs of Heaven and likewise Matters of Earth.

易无思也	Yi No Thought that's (selfless)
无爲也	Not Selfish that's
寂然不動	Quiet Naturally Not Moving (para.10)

Yi not scheming, not selfish, quiet naturally and non-moving.

夫易，開物成務	O' Yi, Initiate Matters Complete Tasks
易有大極	Yi Has Great Limit (Ultimate Reality) (Zero pattern)
是生兩儀	This Create 2 Energies (Yin and Yang) (1-liner 2 patterns)
兩儀生四象	2 Energies Create 4 Signs (2-liners 4 patterns)
四象生八卦	4 Signs Create 8 Trigrams (3-liners 8 patterns) (para.11)

Yi initiates matters through Heaven Earth, the 4 Seasons and 8 Trigrams, created the myriad.

Comments:
Yijing says, Yi is creator of myriad through initiation of Heaven Earth, 4 seasons and 8 Trigrams!
"Big Bang Theory" is no better explaining the universe as the First or the Last, and we know not!
Numerically, the universe is infinite as we can always add to the existing to get a bigger number.
Likewise, dividing 1 with this new number we get a smaller number but never Zero.
Let's enjoy our exciting world now with 4G, later with 5G and ever more imaginable possibilities.
Let's not be selfish and build ever more destructive weapons that will blow us all up in the future.

We can still learn from the Yi, not scheming, not selfish, quiet naturally, evolving the myriad.

Is the *Yijing* Daoism or Confucianism ?

As a manual for divination, the *Yijing* is often regarded as a source of Daoism.
In fact it is more a source of Confucianism, with Kongzi writing more than half the text!

Lao's 'Dao' is really a hypothetical conception of the Ultimate Reality of our Universe.

有物渾成	Have matters that mixed and formed
先天地生	Created before Heaven and Earth
吾不知其名	I do not know it's name
字之曰道	Addressing it call Dao
(道德經 二十五章)	(Daodejing Chapter 25)

Whereas the 'Dao' in *Yijing* is really about the 'Ways' of Heaven, Human, Earth".

易之爲書也	Yi, As A Book that's
廣大悉備	Broad Big All Equipped (inclusive)
有天道焉	Has Heaven's Dao that's
有人道焉	Has Human's Dao that's
有地道焉	Has Earth's Dao that's
(繫辭下傳 第十章)	(Attached Text Lower Commentary.para.10)

Throughout the *Yijing*, Kongzi accords with King Wen with whatever the Junzi does!

卦辭 (文王) ：	**Hexagram Text (King Wen) :**
謙：亨	Humility: Prosperity
君子有終	Junzi Has Closure (Hex.15)
彖曰 (孔子)：	**Tuan says (Kongzi explains) :**
謙亨	Humility, Prosperity
謙尊而光	Humility, Dignify And Enlightened
卑而不可踰	Humble And Not Be Over-taken
君子之終也	Junzi Own Closure, that's (Hex.15)

Also consistently in the *Yijing*, Kongzi echoes Zhougong on how the Junzi should be!

爻辭 (周公)：	**Liner Text (Zhougong) :**
初六：	FirstSixer:
謙謙君子	Humble with Humility, Junzi
用涉大川，吉	Uses Crossing Great River, Auspicious (Hex.15)
象曰 (孔子)：	**LinerSign says (Kongzi) :**
謙謙君子	Humble with Humility, Junzi (Gentleman)
卑以自牧也	Humbleness For Self Cultivation, that's (Hex.15)

Therefore the Yijing is really a source of both Confucianism and Daoism !

Is the *Yijing* a Divination Manual ?

Indeed the *Yijing* has been used as a divination manual in China for centuries.
It has images of all 64 Hexagrams built by King Wen from stacking-up Fuxi 8 Trigrams.
King Wen has attached HexagramText (卦辭) for reading the raised Hexagram(s) as a whole.
Zhougong has attached LinerText (爻辭) for reading each of the 6 liners in a Hexagram.
Kongzi describes a procedure for raising a Hexagram in Attached Commentary Lower para.5.
Without Yellow Straws, we may use the 3- or 18-coins procedure as described in Divination.

To further illustrate, we shall do an actual Divination exercise here:-
Ask a Question: Is the *Yijing* a divination manual ?
Results:

TopSixer	— —			TopSixer	— —
Niner5	———			Niner5	———
Sixer4	— — c	changes		Niner4	———
Sixer3	— —	to		Sixer3	— —
Niner2	———			Niner2	———
FirstSixer	— —			FirstSixer	— —
(Hex. 29)	Water-Pit			(Hex. 47)	Trapped

Water-Pit: Double danger to avoid, however Danger-Barriers are also for defence.
Trapped: TopSixer says, "High no authority, trapped in entangling affairs,
               has regrets and wiser, Auspicious".

One has to read all the texts pertaining to the Hexagram(s) and decide what applies here!
Notice the *Yijing* does not give a "Yes" or "No" answer and My reading is:
Yijing can be a double Danger if superstitiously believed and used by unscrupulous people !
As rivers can be defensive barriers, *Yijing* can also be consulted for pre-emptive actions.
The associated change at Niner4 gives Hexagram 47 Trapped, and TopSixer seems to say:
Yijing on-high, with no authority, is trapped in divination affairs, regrets but wiser, Auspicious.
In short, *Yijing* though Trapped and entangled in divination has Wisdom, hence Auspicious.

仁者見之謂之仁   Benevolence Person Sees It Call It Benevolence
知者見之謂之知   Knowledgeable Person Sees It Call It Knowledge
The same divination can have very different reading depending on the diviners disposition.
Often ancient kings were still in a dilemma on a divination result with listening to his ministers.
Opposing camps offered good reasons and readings in favor for their own side of argument.
Hence unscrupulous diviners are able to capitalize on the *Yijing,* giving it a bad reputation.

The *Yijing* always give causes for failures, reasons for concerns and pragmatic predictions.
Raising an unfavorable Hexagram(s), we learn the reasons and take measures to pre-empt.
Raising a favorable Hexagram(s), we learn to be cautious and work to consolidate.

The Yijing is there and anyone can learn to use it for it wisdom without much difficulty.

Is the *Yijing* Mysticism ?

To answer this question, we can examine any of the 64 Hexagrams for evidence.
Hexagram 39 Limp (蹇) has the Trigrams Water (Kan 坎) above and Mountain (Gen 艮) below.

▬▬ ▬▬	**Water (Kan 坎)**	▬▬▬▬
▬▬▬▬		▬▬ ▬▬ **Mountain (Gen 艮)**
▬▬ ▬▬		▬▬ ▬▬

The Water Trigram looks exactly like the most ancient Chinese character written for water !
The Mountain Trigram, like a path cutting-up the land leading up the Mountain Range across.
Fuxi drawing of the 8 Trigrams is like building more such images naturally, nothing mystical.
Apparently this is how the Chinese Language is built, with more square pictograph Characters!

卦辭 *(文王)* ：	*Hexagram Text (King Wen) :*
蹇 ：	Limp::
利西南	Favors West South
不利東北	Not favoring East North
利見大人，貞吉	Favors Seeing Great Person, Integrity, Auspicious (Hex.39)

Limp, symbolic of Wen's handicap difficulty facing the tyranny of King Zhou from the East.
Limp favors West South, **Wen**'s Homeland, where he ruled with Benevolence and Integrity.
In time, the Great **Wen** is seen to rise to set the States right, Auspicious, logical prediction.
If Wen is evil like the King Zhou, has no Integrity then the Auspicious prediction is Mystical!

爻辭 *(周公)* ：	*Liner Text (Zhougong) :*
初六 ：	First Sixer:
往蹇	Forward, Limp
來譽	Come-back, Praised
往蹇來譽	Forward Difficult, Come-back be Praised
宜待也	Appropriate to Wait, that's

FirstSixer lowly, Limp forward difficult, stay back to await better timing for action, be Praised.
If **Zhougong** advises to go-forward in spite of difficulty and be Praised, that will be Mystical!

象曰 *(孔子)* ：	*HexagramSign says (Kongzi) :*
君子以反身脩德	Junzi by Turning-back Bodily, to Cultivate Virtues

Junzi meeting difficulty, halt, turn-back to self-examine and to self-cultivate Virtues.
Such good advice from Kongzi himself cannot be Mysticism, can it be!

仁者見之謂之仁	Benevolent Person Sees It Call It Benevolence
知者見之謂之知	Knowledgeable Person Sees It Call It Knowledge
(繫辭上傳 第五章)	(Attached Text Top Commentary, para.5)

In short, it will be the Mystic Person who is able to read Mysticism in the Yijing!

Is the *Yijing* Scientific ?

Science, any skill that reflects a precise application of facts or principles (Random House,1984).
For centuries, the *Yijing* is used as a divination manual by elites and commoners in China.
For this reason the *Yiing* is said to be anti-science, been blocking scientific progress in China!

Fuxi seems rather Scientific in observation and gathering of facts for the Trigrams.

古者	The Ancient
包犧氏之王天下也	Baoyishi As King of The World that's (legendary leader)
仰則觀象於天	Look-up To Observe Signs In Heaven
俯則觀法於地	Bend-over To Observe Regularities On Earth
觀鳥獸之文	Observe Birds Animals Their Patterns
與地之宜	With Earth's Compatibility
近取諸身	Near-by Obtain From Body
遠取諸物	Afar Obtain From Matters
於是	Therefore
始作八卦	Start Creation of 8 Trigrams
(繫辭下傳 第二章)	*(Attached Text Lower Commentary para.2)*

Matters then need be separated and categorised for further precision study and application.

方以類聚	Forms Of a Kind Gathered
物以羣分	Matters Of a Group Separated
(繫辭上傳)	*(Attached Text Top Commentary)*

By Kongzi's time, the Chinese has a complex numeric system describing Heaven and Earth.
With precise application, they combine the solar and lunar calendars with intercalary months.

大衍之數五十	Great Display Its Counts 50
其用有四十九	Its Usage Has 49
分而爲二以象兩	Separate And Be 2 To Image 2 (Yin & Yang) (step 1)
掛一以象三	Hang 1 To Image 3 (step 2)
揲之以象四時	Grouping Them (by 4) To Image 4 Seasons (step 3)
歸奇於扐以象閏	Return Odd-straw Of Divine To Image Intercalary-month (step 4)
五歲再閏	5 Years Again Intercalary Month (leap year, lunar calendar)
故再扐而後掛	Thus Again Divine And After Hang (straws between fingers)
(繫辭上傳 第九章)	*(Attached Text Commentary Top para.9)*

In the *Yijing* we can see precise scientific observation of facts and application.
In fact in behavioural and social system studies, it has achieved high level of sophistication.
The *Yijing* is full of wise advice with predictions on human conduct and interactions.

Yijing is certainly not anti-science as it stresses on observations, thinking and applications.

What is the Yijing To me ?

Just a divination book which I have not consulted before I made this study.
Now it seems to me a treasure trove of wisdom which I can consult directly or with divination!
So far I had made more than a hundred divinations on all sort of people, events, places ……
It is amazing that it never fail to make a focus on which I can say something interesting.
Which makes me feel that if I don't consult the *Yijing*, I cannot have a comment to make.

It seems Kongzi has said that if one does not read the *Shijing* (詩經), one has nothing to say!

I have been sensitive to little pains here and there, often worry that they are ominous signs.
Coming across the Hexagram 25 No Delusion in my study, I somehow feel relief reading:

九五：	Niner5:
无妄之疾	No Delusion Its sickness
勿藥有喜	Don't take-Medicine, Has Joy
象曰 *(孔子) :*	*LinerSign says (Kongzi) :*
无妄之藥	No Delusion Its Medicine (untried)
不可試也	Not Allow Trying, that's

Niner5, right, centre and Premier position, partner below, best of health, peak of No Delusion.
Suffers sudden unexpected sickness, don't try untried medicine, will self-resolved, has Joy.

Not able to resolve a family problem and not knowing what to do next, I made a divination.
I raise the Hexagram 37 Family People with changing liners, FirstNiner and Niner3.
Converting to the Observing (Hex. 20), and I feel guided to have patience, to wait and Observe!

Directly or raising a divination, one can consult the *Yijing* anytime when no guidance is around.
Now when I have nothing more to say on the question above, I raise a Hexagram to help:
Ask a Question: What is the *Yijing* to me ?
Results:
TopNiner   ______
Sixer5   __ __
Sixer4   __ __
Sixer3   __ __
Niner2   ______
FirstSixer   __ __
(Hex. 04)   Ignorance
Ignorance: I humbly accept my Ignorance in the first place, hence I consulted the *Yijing*.

The *Yijing* has 64 Hexagram x 64 Hexagram x 6 Liners = 24,576 situational analysis.

It seems Yijing can expose, warn, praise and advise anybody on anything, anywhere, anytime.

What is *Yijing* to the World ?

Ask a Question:	What is *Yijing* to the World ?				
Results:					
TopSixer	— — c		TopNiner	———	
Sixer5	— —		Sixer5	— —	
Niner4	———	changes	Niner4	———	
Sixer3	— — c	to	Niner3	———	
Sixer2	— —		Sixer2	— —	
FirstSixer	— —		FirstSixer	— —	
(Hex.16 豫)	Happiness		(Hex.56 旅)	Traveling	
Happiness:	The availability of the *Yijing* is Happiness to the World.				
Traveling:	Traveling the World-over, bringing consultation, solace to all people.				

Can we believe in all these goodness and is it possible that all these can happen in the future?
Yijing is recognised among the 100 most important books ever written (Seymour-smith, 1989).
Yijing is widely known in the West, but hardly appreciate and recognise for consultation.
There are sites online and offline, offering great *Yijing* divination readings to the public.
There are books written and individuals online teaching *Yijing* to the general public for free.
However most teachings are rather long-winded and often too spiritually airy to easily follow.
Thus readers and listeners are left awed, confused and not empowered to try on their own!
Here, hopefully readers will find enough improvements to encourage them to have a go DIY.
Yijing ought to come out of the dark, and be accessible to individuals who need consultation.

But warning: The use of *Yijing* can be a double edged sword cutting both ways.
To the superstitious and the unscrupulous, an apparent negative Hexagram may do more harm.
However, with correct understanding, *Yijing* never depress even with negative Hexagrams.
With a bad divination, reasons are given so that preemptive actions are taken to avoid trouble.
With a good divination, reasons are also given to be cautious to prevent careless celebration.
The *Yijing* really gives hope where there is despair and cautions where there is celebration.

All the 64 Hexagrams have good and bad situations highlighted with causes and reasons.
Therefore divination with the *Yijing* is to highlight possible failures that need our attention.
On the question "What is *Yijing* To Me?" I raised Hexagram 04 Ignorance, quite unflattering.
Thinking positive and unfazed, I humbly take note of the verdict, work harder with myself!
On above "What is *Yijing* to the World?", I get Hex.16 Happiness convert to Hex.56 Traveling.
Having difficulty writing this Discussion, *Yijing* consultation helps me to make a fine start!

Don't be afraid to consult the Yijing when you need some help, serious or non-serious!

286 Conclusions

Divination

"Red sky at night, shepherds' delight".
"Red sky in the morning, shepherds' warning".
Heaven does show signs of what is coming !

Since the dawn of time for very practical reasons, ancient people aspire to be forewarned.
Therefore ways and means are devised to consult the unknown and unseen power of nature.
Shang Dynasty capital site, the Ruins of Yin (殷虛) was excavated in China recently.
Thousands of oracle bones and shells have been recovered and partially deciphered.
The Emperor Pan Geng (盤庚) obsessed with divination has more than 10 court diviners!

Oracle bones and shells had holes drilled and burnt marks where heat had been applied.
Crack lines seemingly provide divinatory signs for readings which were etched on the front side.
Fuxi the legendary leader (cir. 3000) has been credited with drawing the 3-liners Trigrams !
Later the Xia Dynasty seems to have produced a divinatory book named *Lian Shan* (蓮山).
Reportedly Shang Dynasty that follows also has a divinatory book named *Gui Cang* (龟藏).
These 2 books are never seen, but the 3rd book *Zhou Yi* (周易) of the Zhou Dynasty survives.

King Wen of Zhou was confined by the evil King Zhou of Shang for 7 years at You Li (羑里).
Unfazed he had time to study the 8 Trigrams and created the 64 Hexagrams by combination.
And he provides the wholesome interpretation of each with a Name and Hexagram Text.
His 3rd son Zhougong is credited with fleshing-out the 6 Liner Texts for each of the Hexagram.
Kongzi loved the *Zhou Yi,* and broke the binder-string 3 times in handling the Bamboo-slips.
To explain the *Zhou Yi* he wrote commentary after commentary, now known as the 10 'Wings'.
On its own merits and on these 'Wings', the *Zhou Yi* soars to become *'first'* among the Classics.
Of the many divination traditions in the world, it is the *one* with a unique philosophical backing.

How Fuxi first drawn his line diagrams and made divination, is a mystery for our imagination.
Divination base on crack lines on bones and shells, is a technique long lost to posterity.
Fortunately for us, divination by the Hexagrams of *Zhou Yi* survives to this day!

Readings and Interpretations

Raising a Hexagram from out of 64 is a chanced event with 18 coins shaken up in a box.
I cannot therefore accept that divination as such can be accurately predictive of anything.
More logically I am incline to use the *Yijing* for consultation as Kongzi has suggested.

Reading *Yijing* is like consulting our parents when having problems with no guidance.

又明于憂患與故	Also Enlighten About Worries Sadness
无有師保	Not Having Teacher's Guidance
如臨父母	Like Coming-upon Father Mother
(繫辭下傳. 第八章)	(Attached Text Lower Commentary para.8)

Reading *Yijing* is like highly variable, and it all depend on the kind of reader you are!

仁者見之謂之仁	Benevolent Person Sees It Call It Benevolence
知者見之謂之知	Knowledgeable Person Sees It Call It Knowledge
(繫辭上傳. 第五章)	(Attached Text Upper Commentary para.5)

And interpretation of the text depends on whether you are a Small Person or a Junzi.

碩果不食	Big Fruit Not Eaten
君子得輿	Junzi (Gentleman) Gains Carriage
小人剝廬	Small Person Strips of Abode
(第二十三卦剝, 上九)	(Hex.23 Stripping, Top Niner)

童觀	Child Observe
小人无咎	Small Person, No Faults
君子吝	Junzi (Gentleman) Regrettable
(第二十卦觀, 初六)	(Hex.20 Observing, FirstSixer)

That is, when the text says it is Auspicious, it is not for you to enjoy if you are not virtuous.
And even when the text says it is Ominous, it will be alright if you are a Junzi (Gentleman).
Thus when the *Yijing* says the situation is bad, take note of the reasons given and adjust.
When the *Yijing* says the condition favorable, take note of the reasons given and do better.
In consultation, the *Yijing* Hexagram may give us a new focus, a new angle to look at matters.
Yijing never assure us of success or condemn us to failure, only encourage us to be virtuous.
That's the *Yijing* always give reasons why a situation is good or bad.

And we learn from the reasons given to change, not others but ourselves for the better!

Raising a Hexagram

The *Yijing* is used as a text-book for Divination practice in China for millennia.
Hexagrams are Divination Signs which 'god-spirits' reveal to help us in our consultations.

The Attached Text Commentary Upper para.9 describes in detail the raising of a Hexagram.
With Numerology, handling of the 50 Yellow Straws in 4 steps, produces a specific Hexagram.
The process is very laborious and not a firm believer in Divination, I don't believe I will use it.
For the consultation and divination, many simpler and quicker methods have been used.
I prefer taking 3 coins, shake them up in a container, pour them out directly on a piece of paper.
Score them as described below for the Firstliner, repeat for the Liner2 and upward till TopLiner.
Or, take 18 coins, shake them up all at once in a big container that allows their flipping around.
All at once pour out onto a piece of paper and line them up randomly in 6 rows, with 3 in a row.

Score the coins as follow:

1 reverse 2 obverses gives a *young* Yin broken-line	__ __ __ __	no change
1 obverse 2 reverses gives a *young* Yang solid-line	______ ______	no change
3 obverses gives an *old* changeable Yang solid-line	______ c __ __	changed
3 reverses gives an *old* changeable Yin broken-line	__ __ c ______	changed

One or more changed liner(s) convert an existing Hexagram to another Hexagram.
The changed liner(s) is a focus and has added importance in the interpretation.

Five fingers of a hand are numbered 1, 2, 3, 4 and 5; these are 'raw' numbers (生數).
The even-numbers 2 and 4 together make 6, hence Yin broken-liners are labeled as Sixers.
The odd-numbers 1, 3 and 5 together make 9, hence Yang solid-liners are labeled as Niners.

This is an actual performed Example

Ask a Question: How does the *Yijing* regard this new method?
Results:

3 reverses	TopSixer	__ __ c	TopNiner	______	changed
1 obverse 2 reverse	Niner5	______	Niner5	______	
3 obverses	Niner4	______ c	Sixer4	__ __	changed
1 reverse 2 obverses	Sixer3	__ __	Sixer3	__ __	
1 obverse 2 reverses	Niner2	______	Niner2	______	
1 obverse 2 reverses	FirstNiner	______	FirstNiner	______	
	(Hex. 58)	Wetland-Joy	(Hex. 61)	Core Trust	

We have Hexagram 58 of Wetland-Joy, changing to Hexagram 61 of CoreTrust.
The signs are interesting and pretty favorable to the question, the results Auspicious.
The verdict is: the new method is a Joy to use and that with it, we can Trust the consultation.
Hence the need to look further into the Hexagram text is deemed redundant.

More Consultations with the Yijing

Example 2.   Ask a Question: Who am I ?
Results:

TopNiner	——————		TopNiner	——————	
Sixer5	— —		Sixer5	— —	
Niner4	——————	changes	Niner4	——————	
Niner3	———— c	to	Sixer3	— —	
Sixer2	— — c		Niner2	——————	
FirstSixer	— —		FirstSixer	— —	
(Hex. 56)	Traveling		(Hex. 64)	Prior Completion	

Traveling: We are all Traveling on the blue planet Earth, on a journey to nowhere!
Prior Completion: Works never completed for the author, this is book 2, the next is …
                            (quite reflective of the author's thinking and working)

Example 3.   Ask a Question: On Laozi !
Results:

TopNiner	———— c		TopSixer	— —	
Sixer5	— —		Sixer5	— —	
Sixer4	— —	changes	Sixer4	— —	
Sixer3	— —	to	Sixer3	— —	
Niner2	———— c		Sixer2	— —	
FirstNiner	———— c		FirstSixer	— —	
(Hex.41)	Reduction		(Hex.02)	Earth	

Reduction: Practice Dao, daily reduction of desires (ch.48, *Dao De Jing*).
Earth: Like Earth, Laozi is supportive, has written *Daodejing* to help all mankind.
                 (accurately reflective of Laozi's work and pacific Daoism)

Example 4.   Ask a Question: On Kongzi !
Results:

TopSixer	— —c		TopNiner	——————	
Niner5	————c		Sixer5	— —	
Sixer4	— —	changes	Sixer4	— —	
Sixer3	— —c	to	Niner3	——————	
Niner2	——————		Niner2	——————	
FirstSixer	— —		FirstSixer	— —	
(Hex.29)	Water-Pit		(Hex.18)	Belly-worms	

Water-Pit: Life is a hazard, touring the kingdoms, suffered a siege with his disciples.
Belly-worms: TopNiner: " back to teaching, revision of the classics, valuable activities"
                  (pretty good at summarising Kongzi's life and Sage-hood after-life)

Example 5.   Ask a Question: On Newton !
Results:

TopNiner	———		TopNiner	———
Niner5	——— c		Sixer5	—— ——
Niner4	———	changes	Niner4	———
Sixer3	—— ——	to	Sixer3	—— ——
Sixer2	—— ——		Sixer2	—— ——
FirstSixe r	—— ——		FirstSixer	—— ——
(Hex.12)	Isolation		(Hex.35)	Advance

Opposite: Newton's 3rd Law rightly suggest no Isolation in the world of Physics.
Advance: Indeed Newton achieves great Advances in Science.
    (highlight Newton's great discovery in Physics, Advancement of Science)

Example 6.   Ask a Question: On Karl Marx !
Results:

TopSixer	—— ——
Niner5	———
Niner4	———
Sixer3	—— ——
Sixer2	—— ——
FirstSixer	—— ——
(Hex.45)	Gathering

Gathering: Father of Communism, social Gathering with all things community-own.
    (summarises the core Feature of Karl Marx's Communism)

Example 7.   Ask a Question: On The World in 2119 !
Results:

TopSixer	—— ——		TopSixer	—— ——
Sixer5	—— ——		Sixer5	—— ——
Niner4	———	changes	Niner4	———
Sixer3	—— ——	to	Sixer3	—— ——
Niner2	———		Niner2	———
FirstSixer	—— —— c		FirstNiner	———
(Hex.40)	Resolving		(Hex.54)	Married Maid

Resolving: 2 Yangs, bi-polar world when everyone has to work together resolving crises.
Married Maid: Changes to 3 Yangs, multi-polar world in 2119, together in a happy family.
(with internet instant information world-wide, we may resolve our differences more quickly)
(100 years from now, we look forward to a multi-polar world, all nations together like a family)

Comments:
It seems fairly consistent that the Yijing can be consulted for an opinion on many matters.
Yijing's coverage seems broad enough to raise interesting Hexagrams for consultation.
There are 64+64x64=4160 possible combinations of Hexagram and Conversion pairs!

Wisdom of 4 Sages

Each of the 64 Hexagrams is strewn with wisdom statements worthy of attention.
I have extracted my favourite wisdom statement from each Hexagram for sharing here.
These are very often Kongzi's appreciations as express in his "HexagramSign Says".

第一卦 乾：天行健，君子以自强不息
Hex.01 Qian : Heaven running strong eternally, likewise Junzi self-improves ceaselessly.
(to emulate the Strength of Heaven)
第二卦 坤：地勢坤，君子以厚德載物
Hex.02 Kun : Earth landscape Kun, likewise Junzi most virtuously supports all matters.
(to emulate the unbiased Supportive nature of Earth)

第三卦 屯：雲雷屯，君子以經綸
Hex.03 Sprouting : Germinating difficulty, Junzi with talents break-ground to meet sunshine.
(high-lighting inevitable Difficulty to be encountered at the beginning of any enterprise)
第四卦 蒙：童蒙吉，順以巽也 (六五)
Hex.04 Ignorance : Child innocence auspicious, obedient and docile that's (Sixer5).
(stresses importance of early Education when children are innocent and compliant)
第五卦 需：酒食貞吉，以中正也 (九五)
Hex.05 Supplies : Wine and food auspicious, King fairly correctly sharing with citizens(Niner5).
(Fairness in the distribution of wealth stabilizes nations)

第六卦 訟：君子以作事謀始
Hex.06 Litigation : Planning tasks, Junzi alert to clash of interests from the beginning.
(to nip Litigation in the bud)
第七卦 師：君子以容民畜衆
Hex.07 Army : Junzi's compassion and caring for the masses.
(to building a compassionate citizen Army for defence)
第八卦 比 ：王用三驅，失前禽，邑人不誠，吉 (九五)
Hex.08 Neighbors : King's 3-sided herding, open front allow escape, countrymen safe (Niner5).
(a wise Tactical deployment in hunting safely, that's activities, do consider safety of others)
第九卦 小畜：君子以懿文德
Hex.09 Small Constraint : Junzi uses confinement time for self-improvement.
(King Wen developed the Yi while Confined at Youli by the evil King Zhou of Shang Dynasty).

第十卦 履：君子以辯上下，定民志
Hex.10 Treading : Junzi with discerning observation of society, establishes citizens wishes.
(governing people for the People)
第十一卦 泰：上下交而其志同也 (象曰)
Hex.11 Interaction : Seniors Juniors interact, a common Will is fostered (Tuan says).
(Interaction is necessary to forge mutual understanding, a common goal and harmony)
第十二卦 否：君子以儉辟難，不可榮以祿
Hex.12 Isolation : Junzi keeps low-profile, not prosper through official position, no corruption.
(in time of Isolation and uncertainty, safer to keep low-profile and purity of character)

第十三卦 同人：于野亨，利涉大川，利君子貞 (文王卦辭)
Hex.13 Comrades : In wilderness, favors venture with integrity (Wen Hexagram Text).
(having Comrades the world-over favors great achievement, like Wen met 羌子牙 at Riverside)
第十四卦 大有：君子以遏惡揚善，順天休命
Hex.14 Abundance : Junzi stops evil, promoting kindness, in accord with Heaven and Destiny.
(helping to reduce the poverty gap between rich and poor)
第十五卦 謙：勞謙君子，有終吉 (九三)；勞而不伐，有功而不德 (子曰，繫辭上)
Hex.15 Humility : Junzi labors and not boastful, has success and not claiming credits (Niner3).
(is true Humility)

第十六卦 豫：鳴豫，志窮凶也 (初六)
Hex.16 Happiness : Tolling Happiness, incessant merriment, Wills lost, Ominous (FirstSixer).
(Over-joy is equally harmful)
第十七卦 隨：君子以嚮晦宴息
Hex.17 Following : Junzi follows the natural cycle and has a quiet rest when night falls.
(an orderly life-style according to nature is a healthy and happy life-style)
第十八卦 蠱：先甲三日，後甲三日，終則有始，天行也 (象曰)
Hex.18 Belly-worms : Study 3 days before and after the start and end of a problem (Tuan says).
(to resolve a problem, first to study the cause and effect, Heaven's way, the law of nature)

第十九卦 臨：君子以教思无窮，容保民无疆
Hex.19 Overseeing : Junzi to think ceaselessly, to do better, to protect all citizens inclusively.
(leaders' duty is to think of ceaseless improvement to better all protect subjects)
第二十卦 觀：先王以省方，觀民設教
Hex.20 Observing : Past kings traveled the land, observed citizens so as to establish teachings.
(to determine good governance, a good leader walks the ground to Observe citizens' need)
第二十一卦 噬嗑：先王以明罰勅法
Hex.21 Biting-Close : Past kings with enlightened judgement set laws to fight wrong-doings.
(Fairness in punishment is of utmost importance)

第二十二卦 賁：白賁，上得志也 (上九)
Hex.22 Adorning : White Adorning, life ambition attained, no need for color decor (TopNiner).
("no" to retired leaders' pompous life-style, supported with tax-payers money)
第二十三卦 剝：君子得輿民所載也，小人剝廬終不可用也 (上九)
Hex.23 Stripping : Junzi's carriage citizens' support, SmallOne's abode Stripped (TopNiner).
(good people ultimately survive Stripping, not evil people)
第二十四卦 復：先王以至日閉關，商旅不行
Hex.24 Return : Past kings closed city-gate on Winter-arrived Day, traders travelers all rested.
(embracing the endless cycle-of-life, action, rest and Return)

第二十五卦 无忘：无妄之疾，无妄之藥，不可試也 (九五)
Hex.25 No Delusion : Delusion illness, Delusion cure, don't try (Niner5).
(like present day health-promotion Scams with fake illnesses and fake cures, harmful don't try)
第二十六卦 大畜：君子以多識前言往行，以畜其德
Hex.26 Big Comtainment: Junzi seeks more of ancient's sayings and actions for self-enrichment.
(like this *Yijing,* is a Treasure-trove of wisdom and guidance)

第二十七卦 頤：君子以慎言語，節飲食
Hex.27 Nourishment : Junzi is careful with words and speech, thrifty in food and drink.
(improper words cut like a knife; lesser food and drink promote health and happiness)

第二十八卦 大過：君子以獨立不懼，遯世无悶
Hex.28 Great Excess : Junzi standing alone not fearful, retreat from society not unhappy.
(on ground of virtuous conduct, Junzi is not Afraid when alone, not sad when ostracized)

第二十九卦 坎：有孚，維心亨，行有尚 (文王卦辭)
Hex.29 Water-Pit : Has Trust, only with Heart's freedom and action with aspiration.
(in time of double danger, just be confident, to Free heart and mind, and act with aspiration)

第三十卦 離：大人以繼明，照于四方
Hex.30 Fire-shine : Great person endowed with enlightenment, to help lit-up the world.
(leaders endowed with enlightenment ought not be Selfish, to lit-up and not plunder the world)

第三十一卦 咸：君子以虛受人
Hex.31 Empathy : Junzi with humility accept people.
(all individuals are born free to be accepted with Equal rights)

第三十二卦 恆：君子以立不易方
Hex.32 Eternal : Junzi is for standing on the unchanging side.
(if self don't stand on the side of Eternal virtues, then who does?)

第三十三卦 遯：君子以遠小人，不惡而嚴
Hex.33 Retreat : Junzi to distance from Small people, be firm but not bullying.
(be firm but Retreat when necessary, not wise to fight evil with evil)

第三十四卦 大壯：君子以非禮弗履
Hex.34 Great Strength : Junzi does not tread where etiquette is lacking.
(though have great Strength, wise not to Court disasters)

第三十五卦 普：君子以自昭明德
Hex.35 Advance : Junzi with self-brilliance, enlightens us on what are virtues.
(be the Living-example of one's teaching)

第三十六卦 明夷：君子以莅衆，用晦而明
Hex.36 Enlighten-Hurt : Junzi facing the masses, appears dull but enlightened.
(has enlightenment also needs Humility to gain trust of citizens)

第三十七卦 家人：君子以言有物，而行有恆
Hex.37 Family People : Junzi in speech has substance, in action has sustainability.
(not be the Empty vessel, starting with Family People)

第三十八卦 睽：君以同而異
Hex.38 Visions : Junzi appreciates similarities from different view-points.
(importance of an Accommodating spirit, working towards a harmonious common goal)

第三十九卦 蹇：君子以反身脩德
Hex.39 Limp : Facing Difficulty, Junzi turns back to self-examine for self-improvement.
(better than Blaming others for all our problems)

第四十卦 解：君子以赦過宥罪
Hex.40 Resolving : Junzi pardons crimes, forgives wrongs.
(moving out of Crisis, gives people a second chance)
第四十一卦 損：君子以懲忿窒欲
Hex.41 Reduction : Junzi to suppress sadness, blocking desires.
(turning Negativities positive for self-improvement)
第四十二卦 益：君子以見善則遷，有過則改
Hex.42 Benefiting : Junzi seeing goodness then Migrate-over, has mistake then self-correct.
(truly Beneficial behaviours)

第四十三卦 夬：君子以施祿及下，居德則忌
Hex.44 Ostracize : Junzi bestows wealth to subordinates, avoid Claiming credits.
(else suffer Ostracism, as benefiting subjects is a given thing of leaders)
第四十四卦 姤：后以施命誥四方
Hex.44 Encounters : Leader of Perfection, then by executive order announces to the world.
(perfect leader with a mission for progress, like manna from heaven, a rare Encounter)
第四十五卦 萃：君子以除戎器戒不虞
Hex.45 Grassland-Gathering : Junzi removes weapons and guards against the unscrupulous.
(mindful of Crowd safety such precautions are necessary, features of present day anti-terrorism)

第四十六卦 升：君子以順德，積小以高大
Hex.46 Rising : Junzi by docile virtue, accumulates little acts of virtues becoming great sage.
(like the little acorn Rising steadily into a forest giant)
第四十七卦 困：君子以致命遂志
Hex.47 Trapped : Junzi ready to sacrifice to fulfill life mission.
(maxim: Death can be light as feather at times and heavy as Mount Tai indeed)
第四十八卦 井：君子以勞民勸相
Hex.48 water-Well : Junzi encourages the labor and productivity of Citizens.
(from water-Well to padi-fields, the life-line of the citizens is appreciated)

第四十九卦 革：君子以治歷明時
Hex.49 Changes : Junzi by government history, understand the present.
(study of past historical Changes can certainly helps us to understand the present)
第五十卦 鼎：君子以正位凝命
Hex.50 Tripod : Junzi with correct positioning, concentrates to achieve life-mission.
(Tripod symbol of authority, likewise stand firm and upright to achieve success)
第五十一卦 震：君子以恐懼脩省
Hex.51 Thunder : Junzi with alarm and fear, cultivates awareness of faults.
(Thunder can certainly evoke fear of retribution in people harboring guilt)

第五十二卦 艮：君子以思不出其位
Hex.52 Mountains : Junzi with thoughts not exceeding own position.
(Mountains solid in position, confine thoughts to area of responsibility, then boss not threaten)
第五十三卦 漸：君子以居賢德善俗
Hex.53 Progress : Junzi with dwelling among the virtuous-talents, learns good practices.
(cultural immersion is very conducive to the gradual Progress of learning)

第五十四卦 歸妹：君子以永終知敝
Hex.54 Married Maid : Junzi with established endings, knows faults.
(Elopement has long been established to have no good endings)

第五十五卦 豐：君子以折獄致刑
Hex.55 Expansion : Junzi uses to break needs of dungeons and reduces punishment.
(Expansion and prosperity reduce crimes and the need for dungeons)

第五十六卦 旅：旅瑣瑣，斯其所取災 (初六)
Hex.56 Traveling : On the road jade clinking, this is what one will get, disaster.
(exposing wealth On-the-road is asking to be robbed!)

第五十七卦 巽：君子以申命行事
Hex.57 Wind-conformity : Junzi with implementing orders takes actions.
(Junzi Obediently takes actions in fulfilling destiny for the common good)

第五十八卦 兌：說以先民，民忘其勞；說以犯難，民忘其死 (象曰)
Hex.58 Wetland-joy : First gives Joy, citizens will forget labor, forget death (Tuan Says).
(first create prosperity, then Joyful citizens forget sweat of labor, fear of death in defence)

第五十九卦 渙：先王以享于帝立廟
Hex.59 Dispersion : Past kings built temples for gathering for ancestral offerings.
(to counter Dispersion of citizens' unity with temple celebration of past pioneering spirit)

第六十卦 節：亨，苦節不可貞 (文王卦辭)
Hex.60 Thrift : Prosperity, but Bitter Thrift not be affirmed (Wen. Hexagram Text).
(even when implemented with goodwill, extreme Thrift is harmful)

第六十一卦 中孚：君子以議獄緩死
Hex.61 Core Trust : Junzi with deliberation of punishment, stays executions.
(staying execution is Core Trust, as execution is irreversible even when judgement is reversed)

第六十二卦 小過：君子以行過乎恭！喪過乎哀！用過乎儉！
Hex.62 Small Excess : Junzi, in conduct not to have excessive respect, sorrow, or thrift !
(Excessive show of respect, sorrow and thrift are not proper)

第六十三卦 既濟：君子以思患而豫防之
Hex.63 Completion : Junzi thinking of worrying possibilities, takes action pre-empting them.
(time of Completion is also time to start good maintenance for trouble-free operation)

第六十四卦 未濟：濡其尾吝，亦不知極也 (初六)
Hex.64 Incomplete : Wet its tail shamed, little fox not knowing finality of completion that's.
(warning, to persist till the Finish-line is crossed, else any task remains Incomplete)

Comments:

Fuxi's ancient wisdom is credited for creative drawing of Trigrams for the 8 natural elements.
King Wen's wisdom is construct of 64 Hexagrams with optimistic assessments, also warnings.
Zhougong's wisdom is discernment, detailing struggles among the hierarchical levels of society.
Kongzi's wisdom is about what a Junzi (gentleman) will do under the various circumstances.
Junzi's actions are self-cultivation, care for the masses and all in service of the common good.

Essentially, Yijing expounds self-cultivation of Daoism and the Confucianism of Governance.

Looking Ahead

Zhouyi is elevated to *Yijing* (or *Yi Classic*) when included for imperial exam in the Han Dynasty.
Yijing teaches the ways of a Junzi (Gentleman), ever virtuous and always respectful of authority.
Hence *Yijing* is respected as "first" among the 5 Classics by Chinese Emperors and Scholars.
And Seymour-Smith (1998) has listed it among the 100 most influential books ever written.

With the self-publication of this monograph, I hope to achieve :
A popular version of *Yijing* in English that the general public can easily access.
A fun version that the general public can use in DIY style, for consultation and fun divination.
A window to Eastern wisdom, Junzi's self-cultivation, promotes good-fortune, avoids pit-falls.

Kongzi does recommend the *Yijing* for consultation and advice, like coming upon one's parents.

又明于憂患與故	Also be Enlighten About Worries Sadness
无有師保	Not Having Teacher's Guidance
如臨父母	Like Coming-upon Father Mother

(Attached Text Lower Commentary. para.8)

Teachings in the *Yijing* are indeed conducive to the cultivation of a Junzi (Gentleman).
Junzi, unselfish virtuous-talented character, upright and caring, steadfast with trust and integrity.
Most people know of *Yijing* only as a lowly manual for divination practice by the superstitious!
The *Yijing* has been neglected as a source of wisdom by the masses, and this ought be remedied.
Teach it in school with traditions like Buddhism, Christianity, Confucianism, Islam, Taoism..

N.B.
I believe I have captured the spirit and essence of the Yijing.
I also believe that my choice of words and expressions have leave much to be desired.
I sincerely apologize for this 'brick' of a monograph.
Hopefully this thrown 'brick' can help bring out a 'jaded' version (抛磚引玉).

After Thoughts

Two major traditions today are, Christian culture in the West and Chinese culture in the East.
I often ponder the reasons for such development, and this *Yijing* study does clarify a little.
The Greek civilization (c.800BC-600AD) is considered the cradle of Western civilization.
Greek city-states populated coaster areas and islands of the Aegean Sea, Eastern Mediterranean.
Facing danger of the seas, separate from family, seafarers needed protection, hence Christianity.
Sailing far and trading with many people, they share similar languages of phonetic alphabets.
Western influence has grown to include the 2 Americas, Australia and NewZealand.

The Chinese civilization (c.3000- today) started inland on the plain of the great Yellow River.
No need to travel around, families stay together in farming communities for a stable livelihood.
They developed a complex combined solar-lunar calendar to regulate planting and harvesting.
They also develop *Yijing* to communicate with the spirit of ancestors, with Heaven and Earth.
They use a language of pictographic characters that are easy to recognise but hard to sound!
The written script is understood by all who can read it, thus uniting all Chinese as one people.
However it sound quite incomprehensible when read by people from different dialect groups!
Secure and self-sufficient, the Chinese have no need to venture beyond their borders.

Life uncertainty is real and Laozi (老子) expresses it this way (*Daodejing* ch.58):

祸兮福之所倚	Misfortune indeed, where good-fortune depends
福兮祸之所伏	Good-fortune indeed, where misfortune lurks
(景维. 2012)	(Jingwei. 2012)

Yijing or Zhouyi (Book of Changes) says, "at End-of-road, Changes to break-out".

易窮則變	Yi Impoverished Then Changes
變則通	Changes Then Break-through
通則久	Break-through Then Long-lasting
(繫辭下傳。第八章)	(Attached Text Lower Commentary. 6th Wing para.2)

Lost in the woods of Life, I am often encouraged by these beautiful phrases.

山重水复疑无路	countless mountains endless streams, suspecting no roads
柳暗花明又一村	willows shadows flowers bright, beyond spy another village
(陆游. 宋.詩人)	(Lu You. Song poet. 1125-1210CE)

Besides divination, the *Yijing* teaches how to self-cultivate to be a Junzi (Gentleman).
Everybody likes a Junzi (Gentleman), wants to be a Junzi and *Yijing* can show the way!
When everybody has a chance to be Junzi, there will be no poverty marching across borders.

So under Heaven as nations on Earth, we ought to "help thy neighbours as thyself".

299 Bibliographies

BIBLIOGRAPHY

Publications in English

Clearly, Thomas (1993). *I Ching*. Shambhala, Boston & London. ISBN 978-0-87773-661-5.
Jingwei (2012). *Laozi: Quest for the Ultimate Reality*. Self-publication. Print-on-demand, Lightning Source, UK. ISBN 978-981-07-3758-0.
New Encyclopedia Britannica (1988). 5th ed. *I Ching*. In: Vol. 6. p.209, Encyclopedia Britannica Inc. Chicago USA.
Pearson, Margaret J. (2011). *The Original I Ching*. North Clarendon, U.S.A., Tuttle Publishing. ISBN 978-0-8048-4181-8.
Stein, Jess (1984) *Random House College Dictionary*. Revised Edition. Random House, USA. ISBN 0-394-43600-8.
Seymour-Smith, Martin (1998). *The 100 most influential books ever written: the history of thoughts from ancient times to today*. Secaucus, N.J. : Carol Publ. Group. ISBN 978-0806520001.
The Bible Societies (1976). *Good News Bible*. Collins. UK. Bible Society. ISBN 0-564-00311-5.
Wikipedia (2018). *I Ching*. https://en.wikipedia.org/wiki/I_Ching.

Publications in Chinese

Liu, Sibai (Qing) (1985). *Zhou Yi Simply Explain*. Taipei, Tian Long Publishing House. Republic of China, Year 74. Taiwan Publishing Office. Record No. 2483. (劉思白 著.《周易話解》. 台北, 天龍出版社. 中華民國74年. 局版台業字第2483號).

Mao, Peiqi, Li Zefeng (1989). Edit. *Of History, Mountains and Rivers: Chinese History in Pictures*. Shanghai Ancient Books Publishing House. (毛佩琦, 李泽奉 (1989). 主编.《歲月山河: 图说中国历史》. 上海, 古籍出版社). ISBN 7-5325-0591-X /K.54.

Ren, Xiran (2013). Ed. *Zhou Yi Explain in Color*. Beijing, Overseas Chinese Publishing House. (任犀然 (2013). 主编.《彩图全解周易》. 北京市, 中国华侨出版社). ISBN 978-7-5113-3812-9.

Sima Qian (c.145-87BCE). *Historic Records*. In: Wang, Jun (2007). Compiled. *Shi Ji (Sima Qian, Han)*. Beijing Zhonghua Book Company. (王軍 (2007). 编.《史記 (司馬迁, 漢)》. 北京, 中华書局). ISBN 978-7-101-05146-9.

Xu, Shen (Han, 206BCE-220CE). *Words Explain*. Tianjin City Antiquarian Bookshop printed. 1994.(許慎 (漢).《說文解字》. 天津市古籍書店影印. 1994.)

Yu Haidi, Li Na, Li Cuixiang, Li Peng, Zhou Shuiqin (2011). Eds. *General Knowledge of National Studies that Chinese Nationals Ought to Know , the Complete Work*. Beijing, NewChinese Bookshop. (于海娣, 黎娜, 李翠香, 李鵬, 周水琴 (2011). 编委.《中國人应知國学常识大全集》. 北京, 新華書店). ISBN 978-7-5113-0809-2.

Zhang, Xiuping, Wang Xiaoming (1993). Ed. *100 Books which has affected China*. Nanning City,Guangxi People's Publishing House. (張秀平, 王晓明 (1993). 主编《影响中国的100書》. 南宁市, 广西人民出版社). ISBN 7-219-02339-1 /K.

Zhou, Bingjun (2001). Annotate. *Book of History*. Hunan Changsha City, Yuelu Bookstore. (周秉鈞 (2001). 譯注.《尚書》. 湖南長沙市, 岳麓書社). ISBN 7-80665-093-8.

Zhu Xi (1130-1200, Song). Annotated. *Zhou Yi Original Meaning*. In: Scholars (Song, 960-1279CE; Yuan, 1271-1368CE). Annotated. *The 4 Books and 5 Classics*. Tianjin City, the Ancient Shop printed, 1988. (朱熹 注.《周易本義》. In: 宋元人 (960-1278CE; 1271-1368CE). 注《四書五經》. 天津市, 古店影印, 1988).

302   Appendices

Acknowledgements

Most grateful to our 4 Sages whose works offer me this opportunity for translation and analysis. The author is greatly indebted to the authors of books listed and not listed in the Bibliographies. Particularly grateful to Zhu Xi (Song) and Liu Sibai (Qing), as their books are much consulted.

I sincerely thank the National Library Singapore for the complimentary ISBN and CIP.

I am most happy that Lightning Source UK can facilitate the print-on-demand (POD) setup. And for online distribution through Ingram International.

Due diligence has been exercised with the honest use of facts and figures in this monograph. Unreservedly, my deepest apologies for any errors and omissions that remain.

Last but not least, I wish to thank my sister Rita for her feedback on the readability of certain sections on which I have requested her help.

Upper Trigram > / Trigram Lower v	乾 Qian — Heaven	坤 Kun — Earth	震 Zhen — Thunder	坎 Kan — Water	艮 Gen — Mountain	☐ Xun — Wind	離 Li — Fire	兌 Dui — Wetland
乾 Qian — Heaven	1 乾 Heaven (lead)	11 泰 Interaction	34 大壯 Great Excess	5 需 Supplies	26 大畜 Great Constraint	9 小畜 Small Constraint	14 大有 Abundance	43 夬 Ostracism
坤 Kun — Earth	12 否 Isolation	2 坤 Earth (support)	16 豫 Happiness	8 比 Neighbors	23 剝 Stripping	20 觀 Observing	35 晉 Advance	45 萃 Grassland (Gathering)
震 Zhen — Thunder	25 无忘 No Delusion	24 復 Return	51 震 Thunder (action)	3 屯 Sprouting	27 頤 Nurturing	42 益 Benefiting	21 噬嗑 Biting-Close	17 隨 Following
坎 Kan — Water	6 訟 Litigation	7 師 Army	40 解 Resolving	29 坎 Water-pit (danger)	4 蒙 Innocence	59 渙 Dispersion	64 未濟 Prior Completion	47 困 Trapped
艮 Gen — Mountain	33 遯 Retreat	15 謙 Humility	62 小過 Small Excess	39 蹇 Limp	52 艮 Mountain (block)	53 漸 Progress	56 旅 Traveling	31 咸 Empathy
☐ Xun — Wind	44 姤 Encounters	46 升 Rising	32 恆 Everlasting	48 井 water-Well	18 蠱 Belly-worms	57 巽 Wind (conform)	50 鼎 Tripod	28 大過 Great Excess
離 Li — Fire	13 同人 Comrades	36 明夷 Enlighten Hurt	55 豐 Expansion	63 既濟 Completion	22 賁 Adorning	37 家人 Family People	30 離 Fire (shine)	49 革 Changes
兌 Dui — Wetland	10 履 Treading	19 臨 Overseeing	54 歸妹 Married Maid	60 節 Thrift	41 損 Reduction	61 中孚 Core Thrust	38 睽 Visions	58 兌 Wetland (Joy)

Imagery Chart of 64 Hexagrams for easy tracing:
Horizontally across on top are images of Trigrams (for the above or external Trigram).
Vertically down on the left are images of Trigrams (for the below or internal Trigram).
Stack the Trigrams above and below together to form the 64 unique Hexagrams.
And each is labeled with a name and its number in the listed sequence that follows.

Listing the 64 Hexagrams of *Yijing* in sequence

Part One

Hex. 01 Heaven-lead (strength)   天爲：天   (剛)
Hex. 02 Earth-support (gentle)   地爲：地   (柔)
Hex. 03 Sprouting (visibly stay-put) 水雷：屯   (見而不失其居)
Hex. 04 Ignorance (confused)   山水：蒙   (雜而著)
Hex. 05 Supplies (not advancing)   水天：需   (不進)
Hex. 06 Litigation (not friendly)   天水：訟   (不親)
Hex. 07 Army (worrying)   地水：師   (憂)
Hex. 08 Neighbors (joyous)   水地：比   (樂)
Hex. 09 Small Constraint (lonely)   天風：小畜   (寡)
Hex. 10 Treading (not staying)   天澤：履   (不處)
Hex. 11 Interaction (opposing kind) 地天：泰   (反其類)
Hex. 12 Isolation (opposing kind)   天地：否   (反其類)
Hex. 13 Comrades(loved)   天火：同人   (親)
Hex. 14 Abundance (populous)   火天：大有   (衆)
Hex. 15 Humility (floating-light)   地山：謙   (輕)
Hex. 16 Happiness (lethargic)   雷地：豫   (怠)
Hex. 17 Following (no old-friend)   澤雷：隨   (无故)
Hex. 18 Belly-worms (correction)   山風：蠱   (飭)
Hex. 19 Overseeing (giving)   地澤：臨   (或與)
Hex. 20 Observing (requesting)   風地：觀   (或求)
Hex. 21 Biting-Close (feeding)   火雷：噬嗑   (食)
Hex. 22 Adorning (no color)   山火：賁   (无色)
Hex. 23 Stripping (refining)   山地：剝   (煉)
Hex. 24 Return (come-back)   地雷：復   (反)
Hex. 25 No Delusion (disaster)   天雷：无忘   (災)
Hex. 26 Great Constraint (timing)   山天：大畜   (時也)
Hex. 27 Nurturing (nourishment)   山雷：頤   (養正)
Hex. 28 Great Excess (upsetting)   澤風：大過   (顛)
Hex. 29 Water-pit (down-flowing)   水爲：坎   (下)
Hex. 30 Fire-shine (up-burning)   火爲：離   (上)

Part Two

Hex. 31 Empathy (rapid)   澤山：咸   （速）
Hex. 32 Everlasting (long-lasting)   雷風：恆   （久）
Hex. 33 Retreat (then retreat)   天山：遯   （則退）
Hex. 34 Great Strength (then stop)   雷天：大壯   （則止）
Hex. 35 Advance (daytime)   火地：晉   （晝）
Hex. 36 Enlighten-Hurt (killing)   地火：明夷   （誅）
Hex. 37 Family People (inward)   風火：家人   （內）
Hex. 38 Visions (outward)   火澤：睽   （外）
Hex. 39 Limp (difficulty)   水山：蹇   （難）
Hex. 40 Resolving (relief)   雷水：解   （緩）
Hex. 41 Reduction (prosperity starts)   山澤：損   （盛之始）
Hex. 42 Benefits (decay begins)   風雷：益   （衰之始））
Hex. 43 Ostracism (banishing)   澤天：夬   （決也）
Hex. 44 Encounters (meeting)   天風：姤   （遇）
Hex. 45 Grassland (gathering)   澤地：萃   （聚）
Hex. 46 Rising (not coming)   地風：升   （不來）
Hex. 47 Trapped (encountering)   澤水：困   （相遇）
Hex. 48 water-Well (connecting)   水風：井   （通）
Hex. 49 Changes (discard old)   澤火：革   （去故）
Hex. 50 Tripod (get new)   火風：鼎   （取新）
Hex. 51 Thunder-action (rise)   雷爲：震   （起）
Hex. 52 Mountain-block (stop)   山爲：艮   （止）
Hex. 53 Progress (girl awaiting boy)   風山：漸   （女歸待男行也）
Hex. 54 Married Maid (girl's ending)   雷澤：歸妹   （女之終）
Hex. 55 Expansion (has old friends)   雷火：豐   （多故）
Hex. 56 Traveling (no loved ones)   火山：旅   （寡）
Hex. 57 Wind-conform (conceal)   風爲：巽   （伏）
Hex. 58 Wetland-joy (visible)   澤爲：兌   （見）
Hex. 59 Dispersion (leaving)   風水：渙   （離）
Hex. 60 Thrift (restrictive)   水澤：節   （止）
Hex. 61 Core Trust (trusting)   風澤：中孚   （信）
Hex. 62 Small Excess (mistake)   雷山：小過   （過也）
Hex. 63 Completion (set-state)   水火：既濟   （定也）
Hex. 64 Prior Completion (boy's limit)   火水：未濟   （男之窮也）

List of Important Dates   **In Chronological Order**

Old stone age (石器時代) 600,000 - 9,000 BC

New stone age (新石器時代) 8,000 - 4,000 BC

Fuxi (伏羲) c.3000 BC (legendary sovereign of ancient China)

Suiren (燧人) c.3000 BC (legendary sovereign of ancient China)

Shennong (神農) c.3000 BC (legendary sovereign of ancient China)

Emperor Yao (尭帝) c.2400 BC (legendary ruler of ancient China)

Emperor Shun (舜帝) c.2300 BC (legendary ruler of ancient China)

Emperor Yao (禹帝) c.2200 BC (legendary ruler of ancient China)

Bronze age (石器時代) 2,100 - 771 BC

Dynasties

Xia Dynasty (夏朝) 2,100 - 1,600 BC (China. 1st dynasty, with no written language)

Shang Dynasty (商朝) 1,600 - 1,066 BC (China. 2nd dynasty, writing on shells, bones)

Zhou Dynasty (西周) 1,066 - 771 BC (China. 3rd dynasty, with written history)

  Zhou Dynasty (東周) 770 - 221 BC (China. 3rd dynasty, with capital moved eastward)

  Spring Autumn (春秋) 770 -476 BC (numerous vassal states coalesced into 7 majors)

  Warring States (战國) 475 - 221 BC (7 major vassal states fighting for supremacy)

  Qin Dynasty (秦朝) 221 - 206 BC (China. 4th dynasty, unified all states and languages)

Han Dynasty (漢朝) 206 BC - 220 CE (China. 5th dynasty, consolidation, prosperity)

Song Dynasty (宋朝) 960 - 1279 CE (China. stabilized after a long period of turmoils)

Yuan Dynasty (元朝) 1271 - 1368 CE (China. under the rule of Mongolian Emperors)

Books

Yijing (易經) c.1066 BC(*Book of Changes*, Fuxi, KingWen, Zhougong, Kongzi)

Liji (礼記) c.1066 BC (*Rites of Zhou*. author Zhougong, Duke of Zhou)

Shangshu (尚書) c.500 BC (*Book of History*. records of Xia, Shang, Zhou dynasties)

Shijing (詩經) c.500 BC (*Book of Poems*. records of Xia, Shang, Zhou dynasties)

Shiji (史記) c.100 BC (*Historic Records*. author Sima Qian. Han Dynasty)

People

King Zhou (纣王) c.1105 -1046 BC (Shang. last evil king who lost the dynasty)

Jizi (箕子) c.1100 (Shang. virtuous sage, uncle of King Zhou)

Weizi (微子) c.1100 (Shang. virtuous brother of King Zhou)

King Wen (文王) c.1096 BC (Zhou. father of King Wu, co-author of *Yijing*).

King Wu (武王) c.1046 BC (Zhou. founder-king of Zhou Dynasty)

Zhougong (周公) c.1046 BC (Zhou. brother of King Wu, co-author of *Yijing*)

Laozi (老子) c.580 BC (Zhou. SpringAutumn period.Chinese philosopher, sage)

Kongzi (孔子) 551 - 479 BC (Zhou.SpringAutumn.Chinese philosopher, sage)

Sima Qian (司馬迁) 145 - 87 BC (Han. *author of Historic Records,*史記)

Xu Shen (許慎) 58 - 147 CE (Han. author of *Words Explain*, 說文解字)

Zhu Xi (朱熹) 1130 -1200 CE (Song. writer, politician,Chinese philosopher, sage)

Lu You (陆游) 1125 - 1210 CE (Song. poet)

Glossary

DIY	do-it-yourself
Dao (道)	Path, Way; *Yijing* 'Dao'of Heaven Earth People; Laozi *Daodejing*
Yi (易)	*Yijing* Concept: Creator of the Universe
Yao (爻)	Liners, of 2 types, Yin and Yang
Yin (陰)	2 short lines (__ __) symbolic of Dark Energy, things Negative
Yang (陽)	1 long line (______) symbolic of Light Energy, all things Positive
Niner (九，陽爻)	Label for Yang liner with number reflecting position in Hexagram
Sixer (六，陰爻)	Label for Yin liner with number indicating position in Hexagram
Trigrams (八卦)	3-Liner combinations of Yin Yang, thus uniquely only 8 Trigrams
Hexagrams (卦)	6-Liner combinations of Yin Yang, thus uniquely 64 Hexagrams
Hexagram Text (卦辭)	King Wen's assessment for the whole Hexagram.
Tuan Says (彖曰)	Kongzi (1st, 2nd Wings) clarify King Wen's Hexagram Text.
HexagramSignSays(象曰)	Kongzi (3rd, 4th Wings) commentaries on Hexagram as a whole.
Liner Text (爻辭)	Zhougong separate assessment of the 6 Liners in each Hexagram.
LinerSign Says (象曰)	Kongzi (3rd, 4th Wings) clarify Zhougong's Liner Text.
10 'Wings' (十翼)	Kongzi 10 commentaries on the *Yijing,* make it fly on 'Wings'
Gua (卦)	64 Hexagrams (6-liner Symbols for Divination readings)
Bagua (八卦)	8 Trigrams (3-liner Symbols, stack 2-up to form 6-liner Hexagram)
Qian (乾)	Heaven Strength, Trigram 1, symbol of Father,Head,Horse, Jade,..
Kun (坤)	Earth Support, Trigram 2, symbol of Mother, Stomach,Cow,..
Zhen (震)	Thunder Action, Trigram 3, symbol of Elder-son,Legs,Dragon,..
Kan (坎)	Water Trap, Trigram 4, symbol of Middle-son,Ears,Pig,Ambush,..
Gen (艮)	Mountain Block, Trigram 5, symbol of Young-son, Hands, Dog,...
Xun (巽)	Wind Access,Trig.6, symbol of Elder-daughter,Hens,Thigh,Wood,.
Li (離)	Fire Shine, Trig.7, symbol of Middle-daughter,Eyes,Pheasant,Sun,.
Dui (兌)	Wetland Joy, Trigram 8, symbol of Young-daughter,Mouth,Goat,.

People

Junzi (君子)	Gentleman, virtuous cultured person, king, noble, respectable
Fuxi (伏羲)	c.3000 BC (legendary sovereign of ancient China)
King Zhou (紂王)	c.1105 -1046 BC (Shang. last evil king who lost the dynasty)
Jizi (箕子)	c.1100 (Shang. virtuous sage, uncle of King Zhou)
Weizi (微子)	c.1100 (Shang. virtuous brother of King Zhou)
King Wen (文王)	c.1096 BC (Zhou. father of King Wu, co-author *of Zhouyi*)
King Wu (武王)	c.1046 BC (Zhou. founder-king of Zhou Dynasty)
Zhougong (周公)	c.1046 BC (Zhou.brother of King Wu, co-author *of Zhouyi*)
Laozi (老子)	c.580 BC (Zhou. SpringAutumn period. Chinese philosopher,Sage)
Kongzi (孔子)	551 - 479 BC(Zhou.SpringAutumn. Chinese philosopher, Sage)
Sima Qian (司馬迁)	145 - 87 BC (Han. *author of Historic Records,*史記)

Xu Shen (許慎)   58 - 147 CE (Han. author of *Words Explain,* 說文解字)
Zhu Xi (朱熹)   1130 -1200 CE (Song. writer, politician,Chinese philosopher, Sage)
Luyou (陆游)   1125 - 1210 CE (Song. poet)

Pre-historic leaders

Fuxi (伏羲)   c.3000 BC (legendary sovereign of ancient China)
Suiren (燧人)   c.3000 BC (legendary sovereign of ancient China)
Shennong (神農)   c.3000 BC (legendary sovereign of ancient China)
Emperor Yao (尧帝)   c.2400 BC (legendary ruler of ancient China)
Emperor Shun (舜帝)   c.2300 BC (legendary ruler of ancient China)
Emperor Yao (禹帝)   c.2200 BC (legendary ruler of ancient China)

Dynasties

Xia Dynasty (夏朝)   2,100 - 1,600 BC (China. 1st dynasty, with no written language)
Shang Dynasty (商朝)   1,600 - 1,066 BC (China. 2nd dynasty, writing on shells, bones)
Zhou Dynasty West (西周)   1,066 - 771 BC (China. 3rd dynasty, with written history)
Zhou Dynasty East (東周)   770 - 221 BC (China. 3rd dynasty, with written history)
Spring Autumn period (春秋)   770 -476 BC (numerous vassal states coalesced into 7majors)
Warring States period (战國)   475 - 221 BC (7 major vassal states fighting for supremacy)
Qin Dynasty (秦朝)   221 - 206 BC (China. 4th dynasty, unified all states and languages)
Han Dynasty (漢朝)   206 BC - 220 CE (China. 5th dynasty, consolidation, prosperity)
Song Dynasty (宋朝)   960 - 1279 CE (China. stabilized after a long period of turmoils)
Yuan Dynasty (元朝)   1271 - 1368 CE (China. under the rule of Mongolian Emperors)

Books

Lianshan (連山)   c.2100 - 1600 BC (Book of Divination, Xia Dynasty, never seen)
Guicang (龟藏)   c.1600 - 1066 BC (Book of Divination, ShangDynasty, never seen)
Zhouyi (周易)   c.1066 BC (Yi of Zhou, by Fuxi, King Wen and Duke of Zhou)
Yijing (易經)   c.1066 BC(*Book of Changes* by Fuxi,KingWen,Zhougong,Kongzi)
Liji (礼記)   c.1066 BC (*Rites of Zhou.* author Zhougong, Duke of Zhou)
Daodejing (道德經)   c.580 BC (*The Primal and Virtue Classic.* by Laozi, Zhou, sage)
Shangshu (尚書)   c.500 BC (*Book of History.* records of Xia, Shang, Zhou dynasties)
Shijing (詩經)   c.500 BC (*Book of Poems.* records of poems from ancient states)
Shiji (史記)   c.100 BC (*Historic Records.* author Sima Qian. Han Dynasty)

Self-Publishing

These days when one has something to say, self-publishing a book is not difficult.
Do-it-yourself all the way will cost less than SD1000/- with self-editing, self-assessment.
However as self-publisher, you have to do your own promotion of the book to readers!

My experience is as followed:
Manuscript
Have the full script between covers all completed, format digitally in a doc.file for print.

Accounting and Corporate Regulatory Authority (ACRA)
As self-publisher, I need to register an account with above authority.
First registration on site, costed SD68/- in 2012, subsequently yearly fee SD20/-.
(require a registered Office address, can be home address)

National Library Board Legal Deposit Office (online)
In Singapore these are complimentary services and takes about a week.
First apply for an International Standard Book Number (ISBN).
Then apply for Cataloguing-in-Publication (CIP) -
(require to submit title page, title page verso, copyright page, table of contents, preface and intro-
duction).

Local Printer
Have a book cover design for about SD100/-.
Print the First test copy with perfect binding for about SD30/- (paperback, 300 pages).

Nord Compo
For pre-press services exclusively for Lightning Source customers (SD$xx)

Lightning Source UK (online)
Set-up fee GBP42 (~SD84/-) for Print-on-demand (POD).
Market Distribution fee GBP7 yearly(~SD14/-) for distribution worldwide online retailers.

Optional
Kirkus Reviews (online)
For a 250-word review in 6 weeks, UDS550 (~SD850/-).
(my first book *Laozi: Quest for the Ultimate Reality*, 206 pages in 2016)

Yijing: **Wisdom of 4 Sages**
by Jingwei, February 2019

Disclaimer:
Every precaution has been taken in the preparation of this monograph.
The publisher and author apologize for any errors or omissions that may remain.
The publisher and author assume no liability whatsoever for damages suffer from its usage.

Yijing is listed among the 100 most influential book ever written (Seymour-Smith, 1998). "First" among the 5 Classics of China that scholars must study for the imperial exams since the Han Dynasty. This monograph is a new translation and analysis of the entire *Yijing* (易經). It helps the curious look into the world of *Yijing* to discover what the excitement is all about! It is also a manual for divination and consultation of the *Yijing,* DIY style.

***Yijing:* Wisdom of 4 Sages includes:**

Introduction
Presentation and Translation
The Complete Imagery of 64 Hexagrams build from the 8 Trigrams of Fuxi.
The Complete Chinese Texts of King Wen and Zhougong (Duke of Zhou),
The Complete 10 Commentaries by Kongzi (10 'Wings')
Summary
Discussion
Authorship and Dating
Concept ofYi (易)
Is the Yijing a divination manual?
Is the Yijing Mysticism?
Is the Yijing Scientific?
Is the Yijing Daoism or Confucianism?
What is the Yijing to me?
What is the Yijing to the World?
Conclusions:
Divination
Wisdom of 4 Sages
Looking Ahead
After Thoughts
Bibliographies
Appendices

Jingwei (景維) 1945-, a research-biochemist retired in 2007, first self-published in 2012. *Laozi: Quest for the Ultimate Reality* (ISBN 978-981-07-3758-0), 206 pp, nonfiction. It offers a new translation and analysis of Laozi's ancient Chinese text, the *Daodejing.* It is listed among the "Indie Books Worth Discovering", 15 May 2017 *Kirkus Reviews.* Print-on-demand (POD) by Lightning Source Inc, Amazon.com, and other online stores. Email: jjingwei11@gmail.com.